Accounting and Finance

Also available from Continuum:

Thinking Visually: Craig
Supervisory Management, 5th edn: Evans
An Introduction to Financial Products and Markets: Fell
Informative Writing, 2nd edn: Goddard
Passing Exams: Hamilton
12 Steps to Study Success: Lashley and Best
How to Get into Advertising: Neidle
Effective Crisis Management: Seymour and Moore
Self-Emplyment: Spencer and Pruss
Operations Management, 6th edn: Wild

Accounting and Finance

A Firm Foundation

Fifth Edition

ALAN PIZZEY

CONTINUUM
London and New York

To Barbara

Without whose forbearance and encouragement
this book would never have been completed.

Continuum
The Tower Building
11 York Road
London SE1 7NX
www.continuumbooks.com

370 Lexington Avenue
New York
NY 10017-6503

© 2001 Alan Pizzey

First published in 2001

British Library Cataloguing-in-Publication Data
A catalogue record for this book is available from the British Library.

ISBN   0-8264-5076-8

Designed and typeset by Ben Cracknell Studios

Printed and bound in Great Britain by TJ International Ltd, Padstow, Cornwall

Contents

Preface to the Fifth Edition

This fifth edition is written as an introductory text for first year undergraduates in accounting, but it also covers the syllabus requirements of the first level examinations of the Chartered Institute of Management Accountants (CIMA), the Chartered Association of Certified Accountants, and the Association of Accounting Technicians (AAT). The book fits comfortably into a two-semester first year course in accounting. Part 1 introduces Accounting Techniques, and Part 2 extends the technical coverage to more advanced topics as a first-semester module. The second-semester module is based on Parts 3, 4 and 5 and covers Interpretation, Finance, and a short review of Accounting Theory.

Teacher–Student contact is a luxury these days, so the book is written to allow students to work at their own pace, with many explanations in the step-by-step format. Small tasks are built into the text, to give the student an opportunity to pause, and think about the subject. There are discussion topics and practice questions at the end of each chapter, with solutions at the end of the book. Two Appendices have been introduced to provide yet more opportunities for practice. Appendix A is an exercise to adjust a trial balance with journal entries and draft a set of accounts. Appendix B is a mock examination paper, with solutions, in order to give that all-important examination practice, and to enable students to monitor their progress.

The aim of this book is to help students to master the introductory techniques of accounting, and to understand the principles on which those techniques are based. A *firm foundation* of understanding helps the student to proceed to more advanced studies, and generates in a future accountant the ability to apply principles in a rapidly changing economic environment. Technique is important, but so is comprehension, which enables the accountant to interpret financial statements for others. Above all a critical approach to methods and theory will encourage the young accountant to question established ideas which may become outdated as economic conditions change.

Alan Pizzey
November 2000

List of Abbreviations

AAT   Association of Accounting Technicians
APB   Auditing Practices Board
ASB   Accounting Standards Board
CIMA   Chartered Institute of Management Accountants
CFS   Cash Flow Statement
FIFO   First In First Out
FRC   Financial Reporting Council
FRED   Financial Reporting Exposure Draft
FRRP   Financial Reporting Review Panel
FRS   Financial Reporting Standard
GAAP   Generally Accepted Accounting Principle
IAS   International Accounting Standards
IASC   International Accounting Standards Committee
ICQ   Internal Control Questionnaire
IPR   Independent Professional Review
LIFO   Last in First Out
LLP   Limited Liability Partnership
MBO   Management Buy-out
OFR   Operating and Financial Review
ROCE   Return on Capital Employed
ROI   Return on Investment
SORP   Statement of Recommended Practice
SSAP   Statement of Standard Accounting Practice
STRGL   Statement of Total Recognized Gains and Losses
UITF   Urgent Issues Task Force

Complacency is the enemy of study.
Mao Tse Tung

They should have . . . a supercilious knowledge of accounts.
Mrs Malaprop, in *The Rivals*

Receive before thou wryte, and wryte before thou paye;
Thus wilst thou well assured be, thy counte will never decay.
From the Tomb of an Old Burgher in Chester Cathedral

PART ONE

Basic Principles and Techniques

CHAPTER 1

Accounting Introduced

THE AIMS OF THIS CHAPTER

To enable students to

- Understand the range of activities covered by the term 'accounting'
- Appreciate the stakeholder groups who have an interest in financial information
- Learn the basic elements of a corporate report

WHAT IS ACCOUNTING?

Accounting consists of identifying, measuring and communicating business information to facilitate judgements and decision-making.

Accounting is difficult to define since it comprises diverse activities, and affects many different entities or organizations. Note that accounting does not only concern business entities, but is also applied in organizations which do not function to make a profit even though they may record transactions and attempt to control costs, e.g. hospitals, charities, local authorities. Accountants undertake a very wide range of tasks in business enterprises and those other organizations. A definition of accounting which is capable of satisfying all accountants has not yet been drafted, but an analysis of the accounting process may help to explain the scope of the subject. In this sense accounting is concerned with:

1. **Identification and recording of transactions.** A transaction is an economic event which will affect the financial situation of the entity, such as the sale of a product, the purchase of raw materials or a machine, the payment of wages, or the negotiation of a loan. The accounting system must be organized so that *all* transactions are recognized when they occur and are then recorded. This is part of the book-keeping aspect of accounting and concerns the maintenance of accurate records of what has taken place.

2. **Classification and measurement of transactions** once they are recorded. Economic events may create assets (items which the business owns), or liabilities (what is owed), or revenues (income from sales), or costs (amounts incurred to make products or operate the business), so correct classification is important. Once transactions are classified into appropriate accounting headings, measurement must be undertaken to ensure that each classified transaction is processed in the accounting system at a proper value. It is at this stage that book-keeping gives way to accounting, and judgement is required to measure each transaction properly, e.g. how much of the costs concern this year's transactions and how much should be carried forward to next year. Two accountants may exercise judgement in different ways over the same item, say the valuation of a doubtful debt, so what is considered to be correct may depend on estimate and opinion.

3. **Summarization** of what has been recorded, to show the performance of the entity during a period (a month or a year) and its financial position at the beginning and end of the period. Financial statements, such as the profit and loss account and the balance sheet are summaries of economic events, and the cash flow statement gives yet another view of how transactions have affected the cash and liquid funds held by the entity.

4. **Communication, analysis and interpretation.** Financial statements report to a wide range of users and must therefore be drafted with care to enable the recipient to understand the message which they contain. If necessary the accountant will analyse and interpret that message to enhance the value of the information provided. Corporate Reporting is the term used when a company reports on its profit and financial position to shareholders and others. Accounting is a costly activity and the benefits it brings to users of the information must exceed that cost.

THE PURPOSE OF ACCOUNTING

As conditions change, so accounting must develop and assume new functions and roles. Traditionally, accountants have acted to record in monetary terms the relationship of the business enterprise or other entity with its environment. The entity meets that environment in its transactions with customers (debtors), suppliers (creditors), employees, owners and lenders. A record of these transactions enables the organization to communicate with its transaction partners in the commercial environment. In this respect accounting is the language of business, e.g. 'Our records show that you owe us £10,000 for the purchase of components and payment is due on . . .' Once transactions have been recorded and summarized into financial statements, the accountant can use this information to inform shareholders, managers and other interested parties.

Stewardship

A traditional purpose of accounting has been that of 'stewardship', which implies that a financial statement is drafted to report events, performance or position. In medieval times a steward would report to his overlord, informing him of what the steward had accomplished with the overlord's possessions which had been left in his care. Translated to a modern context, stewardship means that when the board of directors of a company issue their 'corporate report', the annual accounts of the company, they are reporting on their stewardship of the business to the shareholders, who are the legal owners. Stewardship implies that managers are responsible for maintaining resources invested in a business and using them efficiently. A corporate report gives a measure of control to owners, who can dismiss management if they do not approve of its activities. The right of shareholders to receive such information is enshrined in company law. The Companies Act 1985 sets out in detail the statutory minimum of information which must be disclosed and the form which such disclosures must take. Stewardship also discloses the profit which has been made and the amount which can, therefore, be paid to the owners as a dividend.

There are, of course, many other stakeholders who have a claim to be informed of past performance and present position, so the stewardship relationship is not confined to directors and shareholders. It can extend to management committees, and the like, in 'not for profit' organizations such as charities. Accountability is a term implying the duty to report to interested parties, sometimes termed 'stakeholders' in the business.

Decision-Usefulness

A further purpose of accounting concerns the decision-usefulness function of financial statements. This idea holds that a purpose of accounting is to provide information which will enable those who use it to make decisions about their future interest in the entity. A shareholder wishes to know whether to sell shares, hold them or increase the investment; just as a donor needs information when deciding whether to give more to a charity or to donate elsewhere. The difficulty in achieving this purpose is that, while stewardship reports on past transactions, decision-making requires information about the future which the cautious accountant is loath to make public because of the uncertainty associated with forecasting future events. Investors need to assess the ability of a business to generate cash flow and to adapt to a changing business environment.

Confirmation

A pragmatic purpose of the corporate report is to confirm or deny 'market information'. Comments about a business made by financial journalists, stockbrokers and the public relations department of the business itself may influence the price at which shares are bought and sold. Some of this information may be rumour, guesswork or subject to bias, which can only be validated when compared with periodic, audited financial statements.

Management Accounting

The purposes explained above have dealt with reporting to interested parties outside the business, but management accounting concerns the ways in which accounting skills can be used to help managers within the business. The tasks of managers can be analysed as planning, deciding, communicating, organizing and controlling, so financial information will be of great assistance in successful management. The Chartered Institute of Management Accountants defines accounting as being, among other things, 'the projection in monetary terms of future activities arising from alternative planned courses of action'. The management accountant sees the functional relationship of accounting as covering

(a) **financial accounting,** the recording and classification of transactions;

(b) **cost accounting,** the analysis and classification of costs to products and cost centres;

(c) **budgeting,** the planning and coordination of future activities in financial terms to fit them into the corporate plan or strategy of the organization;

(d) **control,** the comparison of actual performance with that set out in the budget or plan, to formulate action to remedy any departures from the plan;

(e) **treasurership,** the funding of the organization and the provision of adequate finance to support managerial operations;

(f) **audit,** the attest function to protect assets and prove the effectiveness of the recording/reporting system.

We can now see that the task of the accountant is to record, analyse and report as a steward, and also to look into the future and assist management with decision-making and control. Both aspects of this task require figures to be assembled in statements that are easily assimilated, interpreted and used in the evaluation of performance by both accountants and non-accountants. Regulation, through the Companies Act 1985, and Financial Reporting Standards, brings order to the system of providing financial information. There is an increasing awareness that accounting is a social science, with a recognition that groups other than shareholders and managers are rightly interested in financial information, and that accountants have a responsibility to provide meaningful information for such groups. If business uses the resources of society, in terms of wealth, people and the environment, then appropriate reporting should ensue. A proper management of resources will benefit all members of society and not only the legal owners of the business.

ACCOUNTANTS IN PRACTICE

Some accountants set up in business as sole practitioners, or in partnership, to provide accounting services to a number of clients. These services take the form of accounting, auditing, taxation work, acting as liquidator to failed businesses and giving general financial advice.

1. Many businesses are too small to employ an accountant of their own, so they record transactions as best they can and then ask a practising accountant to complete the work of drafting the financial statements. Such 'incomplete records'

work is important in practice, involving the production of accounts for small firms where proper books of account have not been maintained and the basic records may be difficult to assemble.

2.   The auditing task involves checking that the accounts of a business which have been prepared by accountants within the business show a true and fair view. Although the term 'true and fair' has been enshrined in company law since 1948, it has never been defined. The Companies Act 1989 states that the need to provide a true and fair view in accounts is of paramount importance, and if the strict application of rules in the Act inhibits the production of a true and fair view such rules may be 'overridden'. The auditor must ensure

   (a) that the accounts have been properly drawn up according to best accounting practice as expressed in financial reporting standards approved by the Financial Reporting Council;
   (b) that legal requirements concerning limited companies have been complied with; and
   (c) that the system of accounting operated by the business is such that fraud is discouraged.

   Once the accounts are audited, the shareholders, lenders and other interested parties are assured that they are correct and can be relied upon.

3.   A further task often undertaken by the accountant in practice is to prepare a taxation computation to translate the accounting profit into a taxable profit by applying the rules embodied in the tax laws. Some companies are large enough to employ a permanent tax specialist, but in most cases the practising accountant with special taxation expertise will undertake this work. The practitioner may be involved with tax planning, advising clients, both companies and individuals, about how best to reduce the burden of taxation.

4.   When a company goes 'bust' or ceases trading for reasons of inadequate finance, a practising accountant will act as liquidator to sell off the assets of the business and use the funds released to repay creditors and shareholders so far as is possible.

5.   Many small businesses receive advice as to how to finance their operations from the practitioner who undertakes their accounting, auditing and tax work. This accountant may draft a statement of future cash flows for the business and then help to negotiate overdraft or loan facilities with the client's bank. Some practising accountants have joined together to form large worldwide practices. It is now a common feature of such practices to operate a financial consultancy division as a limited company advising on managerial problems, the raising of capital and the provision of insurance and financial services. A current problem found in practice is that of 'low balling', when a firm of practising accountants may cut the tender price for an audit, hoping to recoup the amount by selling consultancy services to the client after the audit contract has been awarded. The profession is concerned at this practice, in case such price cuts might reduce the thoroughness with which the audit is conducted.

ACCOUNTANTS IN ORGANIZATIONS

These accountants work for companies or some other organization such as a local authority, hospital board or charity. Their work can be subdivided into financial accounting and management accounting. With financial accounting the main task is to record transactions and to maintain accurate records of assets and liabilities. Financial accountants are concerned with the system of book-keeping used to record sales and purchases, wages paid, the payment and the receipt of cash, and keeping an account of stocks, debts and fixed or long-term assets of the company. Thus financial accountants act as stewards, showing the financial effect of the actions of the managers to the owners of the business. The financial accountant drafts the published accounts, which are later checked by the auditor. Such accounts provided for shareholders and available to the public are produced within the strict disclosure rules of the Companies Act, and financial reporting standards. Other duties of a financial accountant may be company secretarial work, dealing with insurance, pension funds, share transfers and statutory meetings, or general management of office procedures, business systems and computerized methods of recording transactions. Some companies have an internal audit section which liaises with the external auditors, checks systems and protects the assets of the business.

The management accountant applies accounting expertise to help the managers of the company in the administration of the organization and the formulation of policy, budgets and decisions. Management accountants prepare financial reports and statements which give information about the subject of a decision or compare what has happened in the recent past with the budget or plan. In this way managers are made more aware of the financial effects of transactions which have taken place so that they can act quickly to control a situation where, for example, losses are being incurred, and they are better able to plan the future operations of the business and allocate scarce resources between alternatives. Cost analysis and budgetary control are important tools for the management accountant.

THE MAIN FINANCIAL STATEMENTS

The corporate report published by a company comprises a number of documents, specified by the Companies Act 1985 and Financial Reporting Standards agreed among accountants. They are

(a)   the balance sheet;

(b)   the profit and loss account;

(c)   the cash flow statement;

(d)   the statement of accounting policies – the accounting rules used;

(e)   the director's report – information required by law;

(f)   the notes to the accounts – explaining some of the figures;

(g)   the auditor's certificate – providing quality assurance.

These items are usually published in the corporate report together with other unaudited information which is not specified by law or accounting standard. Usually there is a measure of public relations material in the corporate report of the business, e.g. the chairman's statement and a five- or ten-year summary of accounting figures. It is important to realize that this is unaudited information, which may be carefully phrased to show the company's progress in an optimistic light.

Items (a), (b) and (c) above are the three main financial statements commonly used by accountants to produce an extract from the figures in the books so that others may use this for their own purposes.

1. **The balance sheet** shows the financial position of the business at a particular moment in time and sets the assets of the business against the liabilities or sources from which funds have been raised to finance those assets. If the amount of liabilities owed to lenders is subtracted from the total of the assets, this will disclose the extent of the shareholders' or owners' investment in the business.

2. **The profit and loss account** is a summary of transactions for a stated period, e.g. a year. This sets the cost of the period against the revenue earned during the period, thus showing the profit or loss made for that period, which can in turn be analysed as the amount to be paid in taxation, the amount to be paid to shareholders as a dividend, and the amount to be reinvested in the business. The profit and loss account is linked to the balance sheet because any profit not paid out as a dividend or in taxation belongs to the shareholders and is thus added to capital on the balance sheet. A financial reporting standard requires that the company's turnover (sales), profit and capital employed should be analysed to the various segments of the business so that users of the financial statements can see the profitability of the various activities undertaken in a complex group of companies.

3. **The cash flow statement** analyses the sources from which cash has flowed into the business and the ways in which that cash has been spent and therefore flowed out. A company with a positive cash flow of inflows over outflows is financially strong because it will probably be able to meet its future obligations to repay and have enough spare funds to be flexible in its choice of future activities. The relationship between profit and cash flow, and between cash flow and solvency give significant information about financial performance.

4. **The Budget** of the business sets out in detailed financial terms a plan for the future operation of that business. Since future plans are confidential to managers, the budget does not form part of the corporate report. All aspects of the business are covered by the budget, e.g. sales, purchases and expenses, so that it is possible to forecast what the balance sheet and profit and loss account might be at a future stated date. The budget is a managerial statement drafted to suit the circumstances of a particular business. As it is not part of the corporate report the budget is not subject to the constraints of statutes or accounting standards, which prescribe the format of the other financial statements.

THE USERS OF ACCOUNTING INFORMATION

Many different groups use accounting information and see themselves as stakeholders in the business with a right to information about its position and progress. Each group needs to access information for its own purposes from the basic financial data produced by the accountant. There is also a wide difference in financial understanding across the range of users. The accountant must, therefore, design reports in such a way that the appropriate information is visible and understandable. The major groups of users are as follows:

1. **Management** are perhaps the most important users of accounting information. An analysis of past and expected future revenues and expenses will provide information which is useful when plans are formulated, performance is evaluated and decisions are made. Once the budget for a business is complete, the accountant can produce figures for what actually happens as the budget period unfolds, so that they can be compared with the budget to measure achievement. Management will need to know, in great detail, and soon after the event, the cost consequences of a particular course of action, so that steps can be taken to control the situation if things go wrong. Speed and ability to communicate and interpret are needed here. Management accounting will use confidential information which the business may not wish to publicize , since it may prove useful to competitors. Managers are vitally interested in the progress of the company since their own career prospects may depend upon its success, and they will use published accounts to gain an overview if management accounting information provided to them concerns only a small section of the business which they manage.

2. **Shareholders and potential shareholders** are another important group of users of financial statements. This group includes the investing public at large. Shareholders should be informed of the manner in which management has used their funds which have been invested in the business. They are interested in the profitability and safety of their investment, to help them to appraise the efficiency of the management. This is simply a matter of reporting on past events. However, both shareholders and potential shareholders are also interested in the future performance of the business, and use past figures as a guide to the future if they have to vote on takeover proposals or decide whether to disinvest.

   A specialist group of potential shareholders are takeover bidders. This group comprises the managers of other rival companies who plan to buy the shares of a company in order to control its operations and add it to their group. These users are more sophisticated in their appreciation of financial statements than the normal shareholder, and are interested in the detailed notes which accompany the financial statement. However, this class of users would also expect to obtain market information about the company which they propose to take over, from sources other than the published accounts.

   The accountant has an obligation to all those in this category to provide information on which they can depend when making their decisions, but the fact that some members of the group are more financially sophisticated than others causes difficulties, since the volume of information required by a sophisticated takeover bidder may confuse the ordinary shareholder.

3. **Employees and their trade union representatives** also use accounting information to assess the potential of the business. This information is relevant to the employee, who wishes to discover whether the company can offer safe employment and promotion through growth over a period of years, and to the trade-unionist, who uses past profits in the calculation of claims for higher wages or better conditions. The viability of different divisions of a company are of interest to this group. Employees have invested their careers and efforts in the business, and thus have a right to accounting information. Good industrial relations are fostered if there is disclosure of such information, so that employees can participate in decisions, and negotiate profit-sharing arrangements. This fact is recognized by many companies which produce an 'employee report' based on the accounts, but highlighting certain items such as training expenditure and statistics (sales per employee, profit per employee) of interest to employees.

4. **Lenders.** This group of users of published accounts comprises long-term and short-term lenders. The long-term loans will be in the form of debentures or loan stock, where lenders have entered into a contract to allow the business to use their money for a long period, e.g. 3–15 years , in return for a fixed rate of interest. These lenders check that profits are sufficient to cover the interest which they are to receive. Some long-term lenders have their investment secured either against certain specific fixed assets, or as a floating security over the general assets of the business. Therefore they are also interested to use the published accounts to check that the value of the security is sufficient to cover them in the event of a liquidation.

   Short-term lenders comprise trade creditors; suppliers, who may have lent money to the business for the matter of a few months or weeks; the bank, which may have provided overdraft facilities renewable after a period of months; and perhaps the Inland Revenue, who are awaiting payment of taxes due on a certain date. These users of the published accounts will be concerned to check via the balance sheet that there is ample working capital in the business, and that current assets to be turned into cash during the forthcoming months will be more than adequate to repay the current liabilities. This is a matter of future cash flow, but the published accounts do not provide this information. It is left to the users to draw their own conclusions as to future circumstances from the financial statements which report on past transactions.

Task1.1

As a supplier who is being asked to sell bricks to a building contractor in the sum of £250,000, for payment in three months' time, what would you seek to learn from the published financial statements of the builder.

Solution

1. How much cash is in the balance sheet and how plentiful is the future cash flow expected to be?

2. Is the builder overdrawn at the bank?

3. How many other short-term creditors are owed money to be repaid from cash flow in the near future?

5. **Government agencies** are interested users of financial accounting statements for two main reasons. First, the accounting profit forms the basis on which tax adjustments are made in order to determine the taxable profit of the business. Clearly, a tax computation which begins at the point of audited accounts is based on a firm foundation. The revenue authorities are also interested to check on capital expenditure and other items in the accounts which are adjusted on the tax computation. Central government is also interested in published financial accounts from the point of view of statistics concerning economic activity.

6. **Customers and competitors.** Customers are interested users of the financial statements of a business in order to ensure that they are buying from a reputable business which is likely to have ample resources to complete the contract. If a company purchases, say, a large piece of switchgear from an electrical manufacturing business, it would be wise to review the financial position of its supplier before placing the order, to ascertain that it is getting into a contractual relationship with a company whose financial position is such that it will be able to complete the contract. Competitors are also interested in the published financial statements of a business to compare the profitability and financial status of their rivals with themselves. Some trades or industries organize inter-firm comparison schemes which compute accounting ratios as an average for all the companies participating in the scheme, and set the ratios of each individual company against the averages in a report to that company. Competitors are particularly interested to discover an analysis of turnover from a company's published accounts to compute the market share of their rivals. For this reason directors may be unwilling to disclose too much information in the published accounts and are allowed by the Companies Act to treat certain disclosures as confidential, since to make the information public would harm the company concerned

7. **Financial analysts and commentators.** Stockbrokers analyse accounts as part of the background information supplied to their clients. Analysis is also provided to the investing public by the financial correspondents of most newspapers. This class of users is the most sophisticated group which reviews financial statements.

8. **The public at large.** As explained above, a business is using community resources and may affect the physical and commercial environment within its locality. Thus the public may be interested to use the financial statements of a business.

Task 1.2

As a director of a manufacturing business, what information would you try *not* to release in the corporate report, in case competitors could use it to their advantage?

Solution

1. Market share – sales made in various products and areas. The profitability of segments of the business.

2. Plans for future expansion, including the purchase of other companies and entry into new markets.

3. The relationship of the company with its bankers (overdraft limit) and other short-term creditors.

CONCLUSION

This chapter has introduced accounting as a practical discipline which includes many business activities undertaken by practising and organizational accountants. Financial statements have a wide range of users, with an equally wide range of financial ability to assimilate the information which they contain. The corporate report, with its contents carefully prescribed by statute and accounting standards, attempts to satisfy the diverse needs of these users of financial information.

Discussion Topics

Thirty-minute essay questions:

1. Define accounting with reference to the various activities undertaken by accountants.

2. Classify the users of accounting information. Discuss their different requirements and the problems encountered by accountants in attempting to reconcile these requirements.

3. Name three major accounting statements found in the corporate report and explain the purpose of each one.

CHAPTER 2

Fundamental Principles Explained

THE AIMS OF THIS CHAPTER

To enable students to

- Understand the major characteristics which make financial statements useful

- Appreciate the lesser characteristics which contribute to each major characteristic

- Explain the four major accounting conventions which underpin the balance sheet and profit and loss account

WHAT CHARACTERISTICS MAKE FINANCIAL STATEMENTS USEFUL?

Useful financial information should be

1. **Relevant.** This means information which will help users to focus on the judgements and decisions which they have to make. Such information must be provided in good time if it is to influence the decision. Decisions concern the future, so users need to judge how far past events are relevant for future results. To this end unusual or infrequent gains or losses should be identified so that users can understand the recurring and non-recurring nature of events. Good information about past events enables users to check on previous assessments and confirm how correct were their past decisions. Basic to the relevance of information is that it should concern an entity which is a 'going concern', i.e. one that will continue to operate in the foreseeable future.

2. **Reliable.** Information can be relied upon by users if it is

    (a) **Showing the real situation.** This means that the economic substance of a transaction must be properly disclosed even though the legal form of the transaction has been arranged to imply a different commercial effect.

Task 2.1

Can you think of a transaction where the substance is different from the legal form?

Solution

A company may sell raw material stock to a bank just before its year end to improve the amount of cash disclosed in its balance sheet, with a condition of the sale that the company must buy back the stock soon after the year end. The economic substance of this transaction is really that the bank has loaned cash to the company for a few days either side of the balance sheet date. The difference between the selling and rebuying price is in reality interest on the short-term loan.

(b) **Neutral.** Financial information must be unbiased in that its presentation should not seek to influence judgement in one way or another.

(c) **Complete.** Financial statements must disclose all significant information, since if major items are omitted the statement may be false, misleading and unreliable.

(d) **Correct.** Information which is free from material error is of course reliable, and the addition of an auditor's certificate means that the auditor reinforces that reliability.

(e) **Prudent.** Many items in financial statements are uncertain as to value, or future situation. Accordingly a degree of caution must be exercised when judgement is used to estimate such items to ensure that profits or asset values are not overstated, and losses and liabilities are not understated. A note to the accounts should also explain the nature of the uncertainty in such cases.

3. **Comparable.** It is advantageous to be able to compare one business with another, or one business with itself at a different time period. Trend information is very useful.

    (a) **Consistent.** This means that accounting methods and accounting policies should be used consistently from year to year. It is wrong to change the method of say stock valuation at one point in time, with the purpose of improving the profit for that year. Conversely this does not mean that accounting methods can never be changed as a new method may lead to an improvement in the true and fair view given by the accounts.

    (b) **Disclosure of Accounting Policies.** Differences between the financial performance or position of two businesses can only be properly investigated if any difference in accounting method between the companies can be identified by a note to the accounts which states the methods used.

4. **Understandable.** The ability of users to understand financial statements is improved if information is clearly presented, with explanatory notes to cover items which

are disclosed in group classifications. Many users complain that some large items in the financial statements are not explained by notes to the accounts, but other users are confused by the technicality and volume of some information.

5. **Material.** In all businesses there is a size threshold below which amounts cease to be relevant for a proper understanding of the financial statements. This amount varies with the size of the company, so that what is considered to be material for a small business may be less important or influential for the accounts of a larger business. Too much detail including immaterial items can often impair the understandability of the statement. A material item is one which might influence the decision of users, and which must therefore be stated or noted in financial statements rather than aggregated with other items so that it becomes less visible to users.

Task 2.2

Explain how a conflict between relevance and reliability can arise over the timeliness of information?

Solution

Delay to a financial report can soon make it outdated and thus less relevant, but the early publication of accounts, including transactions whose outcomes are as yet uncertain, means that figures are less reliable. The exclusion of items from a statement, because they cannot yet be reliably quantified, reduces the completeness required of the statement but estimates of some values reduces reliability. Judgement is necessary in this situation.

Task 2.3

Explain the tension which can develop between neutrality and prudence when a financial statement is drafted?

Solution

Prudence seeks to ensure that where uncertainty exists profits and assets are not overstated, and losses and liabilities are not understated. A cautious bias in this situation may run counter to the need for neutrality, which excludes deliberate or systematic bias in accounts.

CONCEPTS, STANDARDS AND THE LAW

Part of the theoretical framework of accounting is considered so important that it has been included in a Standard Accounting Practice, and in the Companies Act 1985. Statement of Standard Accounting Practice (SSAP) 2 is concerned with the disclosure of accounting policies. This standard attempts to improve the comparability of financial accounting statements by ensuring that the principles applied when the statement was drafted are clearly understood by those using the statement. If different rules are applied in subsequent statements, this fact must be clearly disclosed with information as to the effect of the change of accounting policy on the financial statements. The rule is that it can be assumed that four basic concepts have been followed in drafting a published financial statement and that a note to the accounts must state clearly the fact if any of these four fundamental accounting concepts have not been used. The concepts mentioned by the standard are the going-concern concept, the accruals concept, the consistency concept and the prudence concept. The Companies Act 1985 underlines the importance of these basic ideas. Schedule 4 to the Act states that amounts included in the accounts for publication must be determined in accordance with certain accounting principles, which are:

1. The company shall be presumed to be a going concern.

2. Accounting policies must be applied consistently.

3. The amount of any item shall be determined on a prudent basis – only realized profits may be included in the profit and loss account.

4. The accruals concept must be followed.

The law states that a note to the accounts must disclose particulars of any departure from these basic principles, with the reasons for the departure and the effect of the departure on the accounting statement. In this case the law and the standard practice are in accord, but they appear to be out of step with international practice.

International Accounting Standard 1 (IAS 1) 'Disclosure of Accounting Policies'

This world standard holds that fundamental accounting assumptions are the going-concern, consistency and accruals rules. Also that disclosure of such assumptions is not required in a financial statement unless they have not been followed, in which case facts and reasons should be disclosed. IAS 1 goes on to state that accounting policies should be selected and applied according to the ideas of prudence, substance over form, and materiality. Thus the international accounting fraternity seem to use slightly different basic principles from accountants in the UK.

THE MAJOR PRINCIPLES EXPLAINED

Going Concern

Unless there is evidence to the contrary, it is assumed when accounting statements are compiled that the business which is the subject of those statements is going to continue in operation for an indefinite period. Without this principle, year-end accounts would have to be worked out on a 'winding-up' basis, that is, on what the business is likely to be worth if sold piecemeal at the accounting date. This value is often different from its value if the present owners intend to carry on the business. Fixed assets, for example, are shown at cost less depreciation to date, rather than at their current value in the second-hand market, because they are held by the firm not for immediate resale, but to be used by the business until their working life is over. This is clearly an assumption on which the balance sheet is based.

Before the accounts are certified as showing a true and fair view, the auditor must be satisfied that the company is a going concern and that it will continue to function successfully in the future.

Thus the profit measurement calculation is insulated from fluctuations in the value of fixed assets, and the spread of the capital cost of an asset over the years of its useful life, by depreciation, is supported by this principle.

Task 2.4

What factors would you consider to determine whether a business was a going concern?

Solution

1. **The market.** Is there a steady demand for the company's product which has a reasonable chance of being sustained in the future?

2. **Finance.** Does the company possess sufficient liquid (cash) resources to meet all known liabilities in the future? A profitable business may be brought to a halt if its creditors no longer give it financial support and it is unable to pay its way.

3. **Sound capital structure.** Are there sufficient long-term funds in the business to give enough strength to overcome inflation, high interest rates, a credit squeeze, increases in taxation or any other hazard of the business world?

4. **What is the company's competitive condition?** Here one must consider the efficiency of the company compared with that of its rivals, and its ability to acquire sufficient raw materials and labour, and to replace worn-out plant and equipment.

Matching

This is sometimes called the accruals principle. Its purpose is to match effort to accomplishment by setting the cost of resources used up by a certain activity against the revenue or benefits received from that activity. When a profit statement is compiled, the cost of the goods sold should be set against the revenue from the sale of those goods, even though cash has not yet been received. Expense and revenue must be matched up so that they concern the same goods and time period, if a true profit is to be computed. Costs concerning a future period must be carried forward as a *prepayment* and charged in that period, and not charged in the current profit and loss account. Expenses of the current period not yet entered in the books must be estimated and inserted as *accruals*.

There has been much argument among accountants about whether overhead expenses should be charged against the period in which they are incurred or carried forward to the period in which the goods made when these costs were incurred are eventually sold. According to SSAP 2, the need for prudence prevails over matching in cases where they conflict, e.g. it may be wiser to write off the cost of certain outdated stock at once rather than carry it forward to match with revenue which may not be received in the future.

Conservatism or Prudence

Business transactions are characterized by uncertainty, which exists until the deal is complete. The accountant responds to this uncertainty by a prudent or conservative approach to the valuation of assets such as stock; or by not accepting that a profit has been made until a situation is certain.

Prudence can be summarized by the phrase 'anticipate no profit and provide for all possible losses', and stems from the accountants' fear that if they approach the compilation of accounting statements with too much optimism they may overstate profits and cause dividends to be paid out of capital. If an unrealized profit is distributed to shareholders as dividend, the danger exists that the funds will be paid out, yet the profit may never be realized. In the absence of certainty it is best to be prudent and understate profit where doubt arises, since mistakes in this direction can be corrected later when the situation is clarified. Gains should be recognized only when they can be reliably measured.

Prudence can be misused by accountants, for it is biased to deliberately undervalue assets and understate earnings. To understate is as bad as to overstate, and accountants must not lose sight of the need for figures which are reliably measured.

Consistency

With many accounting transactions there is more than one method which can be adopted to deal with the item in the accounts. Accountants must use their judgement to select the most appropriate method, but once that choice is made the same method must be used with consistency in forthcoming periods. Such consistency enables users to make a useful comparison of results over time. Thus investors can see the extent of profit or loss, comparing this year with last year, and make their investment decisions accordingly.

The methods used should only be changed if the new method selected improves the true and fair view given by the accounting statements. A note of the change of accounting policy must be appended to the statement concerned, since the calculation of profit may be radically affected during the period of the change. Every set of accounts has a full note concerning the accounting policies which have been used, and details of the change, the reason for the change and the effect of the change must be disclosed in this note.

Example

Suppose a company calculated depreciation at 15 per cent per annum, and applied this rate to all new plant for the year in which it was purchased. An annual investment of £600,000 in new plant would mean a charge of £90,000 to the profit and loss account for this machinery. Suppose also that the investment is made in the last quarter of the year, and the company decides to change its system and to calculate depreciation at 15 per cent, *but pro rata to time*, in the first year. This means that only a quarter of £90,000 will be charged to the profit and loss account, so profits in that year will be improved by £67,500 at a stroke.

It would be quite unfair to use whatever procedure gave the best profit each year, since the accounts would then show the best possible position rather than the true and fair position, and comparison of one year with another would be impossible.

Consistency may give a comparison over time for the same company, but it cannot offer a comparison between companies unless the same basis is consistently used in each of them. Unfortunately the idea of consistency is used as a weapon to resist change, since any new method suffers from the disadvantage that it is inconsistent with what has gone before. The answer to this dilemma is to change bases as little as possible, but when a change is made, to inform users of accounts, by means of a note to the statement, of exactly what the change is, why it has been made and the impact it has had on the profit and loss account and balance sheet.

OTHER CONVENTIONS CONCERNING THE MEASUREMENT PROCESS IN ACCOUNTING

Monetary Measurement

Accounting statements are expressed in monetary terms, since money acts as a common denominator to express the many different facets of an organization, e.g. costs, sales, the value of stocks, machinery, debts and investments. If all the items covered by an accounting statement are stated as an amount of money, then the relative cost or value of these items can be seen and their aggregate cost or value determined. The disadvantage of monetary measurement is, of course, that the value of money may not remain stable, especially in a period of inflation. Not only does this hinder comparison of statements computed at different times, but it also creates difficulties when the costs of assets bought at different times are added together in the same statement.

Example

Suppose a company bought a machine two years ago for £5,000 and another exactly the same last week for £8,000. Would it be correct to add these two amounts together to express the two machines in a balance sheet? Certainly £13,000 has been invested in the assets, financed by funds entrusted to the business by investors, who will expect to be repaid £13,000 if the business is terminated. However, the managers of the business are able to use two machines which would currently cost £16,000 to replace, when they apply investors' funds to profit-earning activities.

Liabilities are payable, according to the law, as an agreed amount of money, so it seems correct to record them in money terms. If the purpose of a financial statement is to disclose the legal obligation of the business to repay lenders and shareholders, then monetary measurement is a useful convention, but for purposes of performance-evaluation, monetary measurement should perhaps be adjusted to reflect changing price levels.

Accountants are now beginning to realize, however, that some elements of a business, such as morale of employees and competitive advantage, cannot be measured in money terms, even though they must be regarded as assets since profit derives from them. A good labour relations record in a company means that there will be little disruption of production through strikes, and thus profits will increase, but it is hard to calculate exactly the profit that would have been made had labour relations in the business been less harmonious, and impossible to compute an accurate value for such an 'asset' which could be disclosed in a balance sheet. Other assets which are difficult to quantify are 'know-how', the possession of a good management team, and goodwill. This last intangible asset often appears in balance sheets of companies, though its existence and valuation may not be agreed upon by all accountants. Fixed assets can be quantified in money terms, but the figure shown makes no comment about their state of repair, or their suitability for the tasks which they undertake. The fact that a competitor has developed a new rival product and is poised to take a considerable share of a company's market does not appear on the balance sheet as a liability.

Realization

This postulate is significant in the calculation of sales revenue and profit, since it determines the point at which the accountant feels that a transaction is certain enough to be completed for the profit made on it to be calculated and taken to the profit and loss account, and if necessary distributed as a dividend to the shareholders. Realization is when a sale is made to a customer, and stock at cost becomes cash or a debt measured at selling price. The basic rule is that revenue is created at the moment a sale is made, and not when the price is later paid in cash. Profit can be taken to the profit and loss account on sales made, even though the money has not been collected. The firm has acquired a debt, and provision must be made in the profit statement for debts not likely to be collected, termed bad debts. The sale is deemed to be made when the goods are delivered, and thus profit cannot be taken to the profit and loss account on orders received and not yet filled. Goods manufactured but not yet delivered are not deemed sold, so no element of profit can enter into the value of stocks of such goods at the accounting date. There are some exceptions to this basic rule, e.g. long-term contracts, which involve payments on account before completion of the work.

Realization implies that no increase in the value of an asset can be recognized as a profit unless it is realized. Assets are recorded at the historical cost at which they were purchased (the objectively determined amount which was paid out for them), and it is often considered prudent to keep them in the books at this amount even if there is reliable information that they are worth more. It is a matter of certainty. The prudent accountant will prefer to use the lower figure until the profit is realized, in case the value increase is only temporary. Others would not agree with this prudent approach, preferring to recognize a value increase when it can reliably be measured, so that shareholders can be informed when assets such as property increase in value.

Objectivity

This concept holds that an accounting statement should not be influenced by personal bias on the part of the accountant who compiles it. Of course, there are times when an accountant has to use judgement when drawing up a set of accounts. For example, a change in value of an asset should be recognized when it can be measured in objective terms. Estimates sometimes have to be made in accounting and are permissible if they are made with care and within reasonable tolerances and accuracy, e.g. provision for doubtful debts. Another example of an objective figure is the amount actually paid out by the company when it acquires an asset. This figure is real and can be proved by documentation recording the transaction. Unfortunately, such a figure for an asset purchased many years ago is not indicative of current value.

Figures built into accounting statements should rely as little as possible on estimates or subjective decisions. Historical cost represents an amount actually paid out for an asset, which can be proved by means of a voucher and certified as the market cost of the asset at its date of purchase. This amount, it is argued, is to be preferred to a current subjective valuation of an asset based on estimates of its future profitability, but after a period of inflation, historical cost becomes misleading. Perhaps, however, a balance sheet containing some assets at historical cost and others at revalued amounts is worse still.

Cost

Fixed assets are often shown in the accounts at the price paid to acquire them, i.e. their historical cost, less depreciation written off to date. They are acquired by a company to be used, and it is argued that their historical cost should be spread as an expense to the income statement over the years of their useful life. However, inflation or obsolescence may change the value of a long-lived asset. The concepts of consistency, objectivity and conservatism are used to support the use of historical cost in accounting for such assets. The opponents of the historical cost principle use the concepts of disclosure and materiality to support their arguments that current cost amounts are more useful to readers of accounting statements.

To account for an asset at an amount in excess of its cost is to assume that a profit has been made by holding the asset. Such a profit is a matter of estimate and uncertainty which is only realized when the asset is sold for its current value. The convention of prudence argues against recognition of an unrealized profit because the value of the asset may subsequently fall before the asset is sold.

Conversely, users of the financial statements should be informed of the current value of assets, if decisions or judgements are to be made in the light of the most recent information, and if such values can be reliably measured.

Accounting Bases and Accounting Policies

Accounting bases are the methods which have been developed by accountants to apply the fundamental concepts. Business activity is complex, and many different types of transaction need to be accounted for, so there may be more than one basis which can be applied to the accounting treatment of a particular item. The standard further states that accounting policies are the specific accounting bases selected by a business as being more appropriate for application to its own transactions. Accounting policies should be consistently followed and disclosed as a note to the accounts so that all users of the financial statements will be aware of the rules used in their drafting.

The accountant must exercise judgement when deciding how to apply the concepts, bases and policies mentioned in this standard. It is a matter of estimate as to whether a cost incurred in one year should be written off against profit in that year or carried forward to a future accounting period to be matched against revenue earned in that period. Examples of this type of decision are

(a) the valuation of year-end stocks,

(b) the depreciation rate and method to be applied to fixed assets, and

(c) the amount of development expenditure to be written off or carried forward.

It must be emphasized that accounting bases should be used to assist such decisions. An accounting policy is not a substitute for commercial judgement, but provides a limit to the judgemental area in which the accountant must operate. Once the rules to be applied to the drafting of a set of accounts are explained, and consistently applied, they will provide an orderly framework for the company's annual accounts.

CONCLUSION

In this chapter the characteristics which make financial statements useful have been reviewed to demonstrate the fundamental principles of accounting. Some of these principles are expressed in company law, and all of them underpin the accounting methods promoted by financial reporting standards and international accounting standards. Accounting principles draw their strength from their acceptance by accountants as best practice, and will thus change as accounting itself changes to fit the business environment. At present the prudence convention is becoming less important, and there is still much discussion as to whether assets should be stated at historical cost or revalued amounts.

Discussion Topics

Thirty-minute essay questions:

1. The idea of substance over form leads accounting figures away from reality. Discuss.

2. Explain the limitations of monetary measurement as a principle on which to base accounting statements.

3. Prudence when applied to items in financial statements introduces bias rather than caution to accounting, but 'reliable measurement' substituted for prudence can also introduce estimates stemming from the bias of the valuers. Discuss.

CHAPTER 3

Financial Position

THE AIMS OF THIS CHAPTER

To enable students to

- Appreciate the function of the balance sheet as a statement of financial position

- Understand the real meaning of assets, liabilities and ownership interest

- Draft a simple balance sheet

- Use the accounting equation to explain the relationship of the balance sheet to the profit and loss account

THE BALANCE SHEET

This accounting statement shows the financial position of a business 'as at' a certain moment. The balance sheet shows the items owned by the business, which are termed assets, and sets against them a list of claims on those assets by those who have provided the funds with which the assets have been purchased; these are termed liabilities, or what the business owes. Thus when shareholders put money into a business or when a lender makes funds available to a business, a claim for the return of the funds is acquired. The funds are then invested by the business in assets which it buys and uses in its chosen trade. Thus everything owned by a business must have been financed and the finance must have been provided by those who have claims on the business, so liabilities or claims must equal assets.

Some authorities see the balance sheet as a list of the sources of funds used in the business set against a list of the ways in which the funds have been applied by the management. The term 'balance sheet' may give an erroneous view of this statement since it implies that it is correct if it is able to balance assets against liabilities. In practice the statement is made up as a list of balances taken from ledger accounts in the books of the business The balance of asset against liability is derived from the principle of double entry, under which every transaction has a double effect on the accounts of the business. An American term which is now being used in the UK is 'position statement', since it implies that the balance sheet should correctly reflect the position of a business rather than merely summarize the balances in its books. A strong financial position is achieved when assets are seen to be sufficient to repay lenders, and those assets are in sufficiently liquid form to provide cash for repayment.

The balance sheet is like a photograph in that it shows the position of a business at one point in time but does not show how that position was arrived at. It also suffers from the disadvantages of the monetary measurement principle in that assets which cannot be measured objectively in money terms may be left out of the statement, and assets included at historical cost are shown as an unrepresentative amount after inflation.

What is an Asset?

An item belonging to a business is considered to be an asset of the business so long as it conforms to three conditions. These are

(a) that the asset has a value,

(b) that the value can be objectively measured, and

(c) that the ownership of the asset can be proved.

An auditor will consider these conditions when verifying the situation of assets included on the balance sheet. The market value of an asset is the amount which a user is prepared to pay to control and use that asset at one point in time. Value is therefore derived from expectations of what an asset can earn, and an asset is an item from which future economic benefits will flow, the right to which belongs to the business.

An asset can therefore be considered as a probable future benefit controlled and accruing to a particular company as a result of past transactions or events. When plant is shown in the balance sheet it is not perhaps the physical item which is disclosed, so much as the value of the economic benefits to be derived from that physical item by working the plant in future periods. Control over an asset implies the ability to obtain the future benefits or to restrict the access of other parties to those benefits. If economic benefit establishes the existence of an asset, control is the critical event which decides the appropriate accounting treatment of the asset. A company which has spent its advertising budget on the promotion of its product would argue that the expenditure is not a cost but the creation of an asset, a brand name, which will increase sales and profits in the future.

Task 3.1

What assets might be excluded from a balance sheet because it is difficult to obtain a value for them?

Solution

- The possession of skilled management and a labour force with high morale will earn extra profits for a business. It is difficult to quantify this amount, and key employees may also leave, perhaps even to work for a rival business.

- A company with an established trade connection or reputation will earn extra profits from repeat orders. Reputation, however, can easily be lost.

- The control of 'brand names' for which consumers express a market preference is a further source of profit which is difficult to quantify.

These items are often shown on the balance sheet as part of an intangible asset – goodwill.

Traditionally accountants record assets at their historical cost and not their estimated current market value, in order to conform to the principles of objectivity, realization and prudence. It is considered imprudent to rely on a valuation for an asset which cannot be tested by a cross-market transaction, and which may subsequently be reduced by market forces and thus not realized. In some cases, however, the historical cost of an asset gets out of line with the current value of the asset, and a professional valuer is asked to revalue the asset so that the balance sheet can reflect current conditions with greater accuracy.

The value of some assets cannot be assessed with accuracy. For example, a patent or trademark owned by a business, or the funds invested by a business in developing a new product, will both earn extra profits for the business in the future but the amount of those extra profits is difficult to determine. Accordingly 'intangible' assets of this type are recognized as assets but carried in the balance sheet at cost rather than value. An economist might wish to value an asset by determining the current value of the future stream of income to be derived from the asset. Such a value is the subject of great uncertainty, and for this reason the prudent accountant prefers to use the idea of cost rather than value when stating assets in the balance sheet.

Assets can be classified as fixed assets, current assets and intangible assets.

Fixed Assets

The fixed assets of the business are not held for resale but are intended as investments of the company's funds in significant items which will be used over a long period, certainly exceeding the accounting year. Such items are termed long-lived assets and it is said that capital has been 'sunk' in them. Normally a significant proportion of the assets of a manufacturing business will be held in the form of factory buildings, plant and machinery, vehicles and perhaps office fixtures and fittings. Most of these items are concerned with making the goods which are sold for a profit. Consequently accountants take the view that profit stems from, or is earned by, the fixed assets of the business. Another type of fixed asset is the long-term investment which takes the form of a share stake in another company owned by a business for purposes of strategy or control. An item considered to be a fixed asset for one company may be a current asset for another. For example, a car is a tangible fixed asset if it is to be driven by a salesman for the next two years, but it is a current asset if it is held as stock for sale by a car sales company.

The going-concern principle assumes that the business will continue. Accordingly the historical cost of fixed assets less any depreciation charged against them to date is used to state such assets in the balance sheet rather than the lower and more conservative scrap value of a fixed asset if it were sold immediately in the second-hand market. By tradition the assets on a balance sheet are always shown in reverse order of liquidity, i.e. the least liquid, land and buildings held more or less permanently, come at the top.

The development of services businesses such as architectural practices requires little in the way of fixed assets. The existence of dot.com internet companies is a further example of businesses which do not require much investment in fixed assets.

Intangible Assets

This category of fixed assets is usually shown on the balance sheet above the tangible fixed assets and long-term investments. Intangible assets are items which, although they are not visible and cannot be physically touched, nevertheless make a contribution to the profits of the business. As shown above, the possession of a patent or trademark can earn extra profits for a business, and if such an asset has been purchased, its cost can be objectively valued and recorded in the balance sheet as one of the items which the business owns. Other forms of intangible asset are the goodwill of the business, or the possession of a 'brand' name for the product which will increase sales and profits.

Current Assets

The current assets of a business are held for a short period, traditionally less than the accounting year. This means that such assets held at the balance sheet date are expected to be turned back into cash within the passage of 12 months. These assets are said to 'oil the wheels' of the business so that the fixed assets can make a profit more easily. It is difficult to use factory buildings and plant to manufacture goods without the current asset of raw material stock to back you up, and difficult to sell your product without working capital available to provide trade credit to your customers (debtors). The current assets of a business are also listed in reverse order of liquidity, as stock (inventory), debts, short-term investments and cash.

1. **Stocks** may be in the form of raw materials, work in progress (semi-finished items in the factory) or finished goods awaiting sale. These are always shown at cost or net realizable value, whichever is the lower, to adhere to the concept of conservatism. This ensures that no element of profit is taken before stocks are sold, but that any loss made because stocks held are currently worth less than their cost is taken into account at once.

2. **Debts** are sums owed to the business, usually by customers who have bought goods on credit terms. It is expected that these debts will be turned back into cash in the near future when the debts are paid.

3. **Short-term investments** are held to provide a safe repository for idle funds, so that they can earn some return while at the same time they can be quickly liquidated if funds are required for use elsewhere in the business.

4. **Cash** covers the money in the bank account and also money held at other points in the business, such as the tills of the shops or the petty-cash box in the office safe.

LIABILITIES AND CAPITAL

A liability is an amount owed by a business to any person or business who has provided funds to finance the assets controlled by the business. Such persons are lenders who have provided funds for the short or long term. The shareholders (the owners) have also invested funds in the business, but share capital is more permanent than other liabilities. All have a right to be repaid the funds they have invested if the business is wound up.

1. **Share capital** represents the original amount invested in the business by the owners, plus any share issued by the company since that time. As they are the last to be repaid in the event of the business being discontinued, shareholders are deemed to take the greatest risk. Share capital is sometimes for this reason called venture capital.

2. **The reserves** of the business also belong to the owners or shareholders, but represent profits made by the business in the past and not distributed as a dividend. When a profit is made it is appropriated or divided up, some being paid to the Inland Revenue as taxation, some being paid to the shareholders in the form of a dividend, and the remainder being retained in the business as a source of finance. Thus reserves or profits 'ploughed back' into the business represent a further investment by the shareholders made out of past profits.

   When added together, share capital and reserves total the owner's interest in the business, being the funds provided initially and out of past profits by the legal owners of the business. Sometimes this amount is termed the 'equity interest', since all ordinary shareholders have an equal right to participate pro rata to their holding of shares, if these funds are repaid. Some reserves are not available for distribution as dividend for legal reasons. These are known as capital reserves and they are disclosed on the balance sheet below share capital but above general reserves.

   The remaining liabilities of the business are divided according to the period for which they are lent. A theoretical definition of a liability is that it is a present obligation of a company, which entails a probable future sacrifice when the business transfers assets, or provides a service to another business. The term 'present obligation' has a wider scope than a mere 'legal liability' which can be proved at law.

3. **Long-term liabilities** include loans made for periods of more than one year and often for such long periods as to be viewed as part of the long-term capital employed in the business. These loans are sometimes termed mortgages or debentures and are often secured on the assets of the business. This means that if

the company fails to pay the annual interest on a loan, or goes into liquidation before the period of the loan is ended, the lender may take possession of some assets of the business and sell them in order to recoup the funds lent to the business.

4. **Current liabilities** are amounts lent to the business for a period of less than one year. They include

   (a) trade creditors who have supplied goods and services and are awaiting payment;
   (b) short-term loans from the bank, usually in the form of an overdraft;
   (c) the Inland Revenue awaiting payment of tax on the due date; and
   (d) the shareholders themselves awaiting payments of a dividend from the previous year's profit.

5. **Contingent liabilities** are amounts which might become liabilities of the firm depending upon circumstances which may arise after the balance sheet date, e.g. damages in a court action where judgement is pending at the balance sheet date. These items are shown as a note under the balance sheet and do not form part of the liabilities.

THE FORM OF THE BALANCE SHEET

The vertical form of balance sheet is now stipulated for companies by the Companies Act 1985. This statement sets out the fixed assets and then the current assets. The amount of current liabilities is deducted from current assets to disclose the *working capital*, which, when added to fixed assets, gives the long-term funds employed in the business. The term 'net current assets' is sometimes used instead of 'working capital', implying that the current liabilities are netted off against the current assets. Amounts lent to the business over a long period (long-term liabilities) are then deducted to disclose the net assets.

A second part to the statement analyses the equity interest between the amount originally invested by the shareholders or owners (share capital), and reserves which usually represent profits reinvested over the years since the business began to trade. Capital reserves which, by law or for reasons of financial prudence, are not available for distribution to shareholders are also shown in this part of the balance sheet. The Companies Act does not favour the use of the term 'current liabilities' but prefers 'creditors: amounts falling due within one year'. By the same token the term 'creditors: amounts falling due after more than one year' is preferred to the term 'long-term liabilities'.

On the balance sheet of XYZ plc shown (*opposite*), the capital reserve takes the form of a *share premium account*. This means that when the 5 million £1 ordinary shares of the company were issued to the public, the issue price was £1.40 per share. Thus investors were so keen to buy shares in XYZ plc that they were willing to pay a premium for the shares. The premium means that for each share certificate with a nominal value of £1 the shareholder was willing to pay £1.40 i.e. 5 million £1 ordinary shares issued at £1.40 raised £7 million in cash as the investment by the shareholders

Balance Sheet of XYZ plc* as at 31 December 2000

		£	£	£	£
Fixed assets					
Intangible assets – goodwill			*Less*		40 000
		Cost	*Depreciation*	*Net*	
Tangible assets –	Land and buildings	8 272 000	612 000	7 660 000	
	Plant	4 447 000	1 723 000	2 724 000	
	Vehicles	120 412	66 208	54 204	
		12 839 412	2 401 208	10 438 204	
					10 438 204
Investments					660 000
					11 138 204
Current assets					
Stock				1 658 640	
Debtors				1 435 325	
Investments				20 000	
Cash				12 411	
				3 126 376	
Less					
Creditors: amounts falling due within one year					
Trade creditors				1 186 310	
Bank overdraft				559 618	
Taxation				24 134	
Dividend payable				100 000	
				1 870 062	
Net current assets (working capital)					1 256 314
Total assets less current liabilities					12 394 518
Long-term liabilities – amounts falling due after more than one year					
long-term loan at 10% interest					(2 000 000)
Net assets					10 394 518
Financed by:					
Capital and reserves					
Share capital					5 000 000
Capital reserve – share premium account					2 000 000
General reserve – retained earnings					3 394 518
Equity interest					£10 394 518

*The letters 'plc' in the title of the company indicate that it is a public limited company and that its shares are listed for trading on a stock exchange. A company not listed on the stock exchange would use the letters 'Ltd'.

in XYZ plc when it began to trade. By law the share premium account must be shown as a capital reserve since it is part of the permanent capital of the business and cannot be repaid to shareholders under normal circumstances. The capital reserve thus differs from the general reserve, which represents past profits retained in the business and reinvested by the directors on behalf of the shareholders and which are still legally available to be paid out as a dividend if necessary.

THE ACCOUNTING EQUATION

The balance sheet and its relationship to the profit and loss account can be expressed as a simple formula:

Assets – Liabilities = Capital; (A – L = C)

Capital refers to share capital plus reserves – the ownership interest in the business. Since all assets have been financed by funds invested by shareholders or lent to the business by creditors, assets equal claims. If the claims of creditors (liabilities both long and short term) are deducted from assets, all that remains belongs to the shareholders as the legal owners of the business. This represents the shareholders as the risk-takers, since they own the residual amount after all other claims have been met. Figures from the balance sheet above show

Fixed Assets £11,138,204 + Current Assets £3,126,376 – Liabilities £1,870,062 and £2,000,000 = Equity Interest £10,394,518

When a profit is made part is paid out as tax and part paid to shareholders as a dividend, but any amount left after these payments increases the general reserve in the balance sheet as part of 'retained earnings' or ploughed-back profits.

Task 3.2

Can you demonstrate the connection between the balance sheet and the profit and loss account by using the accounting equation?

Solution

Assets = Current Liabilities + Long-term Liabilities + Share Capital + Retained Earnings

Assets = Current Liabilities + Long-term Liabilities + Share Capital + Retained Earnings at the beginning of the year + Retained Earnings transferred from the profit and loss account for that year.

Retained Earnings from that year = Sales – Costs – Tax – Dividend

CONCLUSION

The balance sheet is a major accounting statement which shows the position of the business at one point in time. This position comprises the assets owned by the business and the funds used to finance those assets. The accounting equation differentiates between borrowings and the owners' investment to focus on the residual nature of the shareholders' equity in the business, when liabilities are deducted from assets. The net assets equal the ownership interest in a business.

Assets are rights to future economic benefits controlled by a business which can be analysed as fixed assets or current assets. Liabilities are the obligations of a business to transfer economic benefits to others at a future time, e.g. to repay a long-term loan or an overdraft, or pay a supplier for materials purchased on credit terms.

Discussion Topics

Thirty-minute essay questions:

1. Are there any assets of a business which do not appear on the balance sheet? If so, why are they excluded and how can it be said that the assets which *are* shown equal the claims on the business by those who have financed the assets?

2. Define an asset for balance sheet purposes. Differentiate between current assets and fixed assets.

3. How, if at all, would you record the following events in the books of a business?
   (a) Oil is discovered under the company's car park.
   (b) The sales director leaves to work for a rival company.
   (c) Political changes cause the company to be expelled from a country in which it owns mineral rights.
   (d) A fire destroys the accounting department's building and all the records stored in it.
   (e) The company suffers its first strike in ten years.

SEMINAR EXERCISES

3.1. Prepare a position statement from the following information presented to you on 31 December. Your answer should be in good form.

Company A	£
Creditors	43 614
Cash in hand	1 270
Bank balance	8 186
Stock	29 941
Freehold land	60 000
Long-term loan owed by the firm	20 000
Wages payable	1 102
Nottingham Corporation Bonds	8 000
Debtors	19 487
Buildings	35 000
Expenses paid in advance	904
Share capital	50 000
Vehicles	8 000
Plant at cost	25 000
Depreciation on plant	6 000
Shares of company X	7 000
Taxation owed	13 000
Depreciation on buildings	10 000

3.2. Show how each of the following transactions changes the balance sheet which you produced in answer to Question 3.1.

(a) Shareholders invest a further £20,000 in the company.
(b) The wages payable are paid.
(c) The company buys raw material for cash. £1,200.
(d) The company buys raw material for credit. £4,000.
(e) The company sells its property at book value.
(f) The company pays £5,000 to its creditors.
(g) The Nottingham Bonds are realized for cash. £8,000.
(h) £10,000 is paid to the Inland Revenue as taxation.

3.3. Company B has been in business for a number of years. Recently there has been a fire at the head office in which the accounting records of the business have been destroyed. The company's accountant has left and the directors have asked you to reconstruct the records, as far as possible. You take stock, visit the bank, inform customers and investigate the ownership of buildings, machinery and other assets. You discover the following information:

	Balance or Market Value £
Cash in safe	8 000
Bank balance	36 000
Stock of raw material and finished goods	74 000
Debtors	52 000
Shares of other companies	18 000
Land and buildings	156 000
Machinery and vehicles	64 000

After a check of invoices received from creditors and statements of account received, you compute that £80,000 is owed to such creditors and a further £40,000 is owed to the Inland Revenue. The land and buildings are mortgaged in the sum of £70,000. The share register is at the office of the company's solicitor, and shows that 100,000 ordinary shares of £1 each have been issued.

(a) Draw up a balance sheet for Company B.
(b) How has the accounting equation helped you to find an answer?

CHAPTER 4

The Measurement of Income

THE AIMS OF THIS CHAPTER

To enable students to

- Understand the matching principle and its influence on the measurement of income
- Comprehend the components of the income statement
- Calculate accruals and prepayments
- Learn the form of a profit and loss account

THE PROFIT AND LOSS ACCOUNT

Income is measured by the accountant, using the matching or accruals principle. The revenue earned in a period (sales or turnover are other words used) is calculated and the accountant then charges the cost of earning that revenue against the revenue, to reveal a surplus or a deficit. Thus income is measured by matching effort to accomplishment. The difficulty is to ascertain what costs and revenues should be recognized in a particular accounting period if a true and fair profit or loss is to be disclosed. The accountant must use judgement when profit is measured; for example,

1. Will all sales revenue be received in cash, or should a provision for doubtful debts to be set against profit?

2. Have the fixed assets lost value because they have been used to earn profit – should a provision for depreciation be charged against profit?

3. Have all costs incurred been recorded or is an accrual necessary?

4. Are all recorded costs properly chargeable to this accounting period or have expenses been paid in advance?

The income statement is designed to measure the results of transactions which have taken place between two balance sheet dates. Since it shows the result of operations for a period of time it is not a statement 'as at' but a statement 'for the year ended'. It is a summary of all trading transactions which have taken place during a period, not a statement to show the position at one moment in time.

Sometimes it is called the revenue account and sometimes the income statement, but in the UK the term 'profit and loss account' is usually used. This term, however, is a misnomer, since the income statement is often divided into four parts, one of which itself is called the profit and loss account.

COMPONENTS OF THE INCOME STATEMENT

1. **The manufacturing account.** This reveals the cost of production and in some cases a factory profit. This part is produced only for a manufacturing company and is sometimes called the work-in-progress account.

2. **The trading account,** in which the cost of goods sold is set against sales revenue to show a gross profit.

3. **The profit and loss account,** in which the general expenses of the business are set against gross profit to reduce it to net profit.

4. **The appropriation account,** which shows how the net profit is divided up according to the various ways in which it is used; e.g. some is set aside for taxation, some is used to cover dividends paid to shareholders, and the remainder is retained in the business as part of its reserves.

The manufacturing and trading accounts are produced for internal management purposes, while under the Companies Act the shareholders and investors at large are entitled to see only certain figures on the profit and loss account and the appropriation account. Companies treat the income statement as a confidential document, since a rival business might gain a significant advantage if the full details were disclosed. Examples of the various accounts are shown below:

Dr		Manufacturing Account	Cr
	£		£
Materials used	14 708	Cost of completed production	
Direct labour	12 653	transferred to stores	37 207
Prime cost	27 361		
Factory overheads	9 846		
	£37 207		£37 207

Factory overhead is the indirect cost of running the factory and includes such items pertinent to the factory operation as rent, light, heat, power, maintenance, depreciation and managerial salaries

Dr	Finished Goods Stores Account		Cr
	£		£
Opening stock	6 425	Cost of goods sold transferred	39 448
Costs of goods transferred		to trading account	
from factory	37 207	Balance, closing stock c/f	4 184
	£43 632		£43 632
Opening stock bid	4,184		

Dr	Trading Account		Cr
	£		£
Cost of goods sold	39 448	Sales	62 871
Gross profit carried to			
profit and loss account	23 423		
	£62 871		£62 871

Note: The calculation of opening stock plus purchases less closing stock to show the cost of goods sold is sometimes undertaken in the trading account. In other systems the finished goods stores account stands between the manufacturing account and the trading account.

Dr	Profit and Loss Account		Cr
	£		£
Administration expenses	5 786	Gross profit brought down	
Selling expenses	8 612	from trading account	23 423
Distribution expenses	4 904	Miscellaneous income	1 530
Financial expenses	2 107		
Net profit transferred			
to appropriation account	3 544		
	£24 953		£24 953

Note: The profit measured is usually appropriated for three purposes:

(a) for taxation;

(b) to pay a dividend to shareholders;

(c) to retain in the business to finance future operations.

Dr	Appropriation Account		Cr
	£		£
Provision for taxation	1 200	Net profit brought down from	
Transferred to general reserve	1 000	profit and loss account	3 544
Dividend to shareholders	850		
Unappropriated profit carried forward	494		
	£3 544		£3 544
		Balance brought down	494

This balance (£494) appears in the balance sheet as retained profits, and is part of the owners' interest in the business. Transfers from the profit and loss account each year will be added to the amount of the reserve shown in the balance sheet. The provision for taxation is a balance sheet liability because it is waiting to be paid.

In a business which is not formed as a company, e.g. a partnership or a sole trader, the proprietor withdraws part of the profit instead of receiving a dividend. The term 'drawings' appears in the appropriation account instead of a dividend.

Note that in the profit and loss section the expenses have been grouped under certain convenient headings. The statements could also be presented in columnar form.

A disadvantage of the balance sheet is that it shows the position at one moment in time only, but this is to some extent remedied by the income statement, which shows in part how that position has been attained. The result in the statement, the profit or loss figure, can be set against the capital employed in the business, as revealed by the balance sheet, to show as a percentage the profitability of the operation and the return earned by the management on the funds entrusted to them by the owners. This return is satisfactory only if it is sufficient to compensate for the risk taken by the owners when investing their capital in the enterprise.

THE ACCRUALS PRINCIPLE

The accruals, or matching, principle, is the device adopted by the accountant to isolate the transactions of any one accounting period from those of the next period. If a true profit is to be computed, sales revenue for the period must be set against the cost of goods sold during that period. This means that the cost of the products sold this year must be charged in the revenue account this year, even though those products were made last year. It also means that there is a difference between expense and expenditure, since money may be paid out for costs incurred in one accounting period, but those costs cannot be charged against sales as an expense until the next accounting period, when the goods are sold (See Figure 4.1)

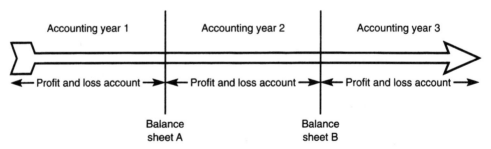

Figure 4.1

A cost is the amount paid out for a service or benefit received, or a sacrifice made in order to achieve a stated end. The cost is entered in the books of account when it is paid for, or when a liability for such a payment is recognized, i.e. a bill is received. At this point the cost has been incurred to acquire an asset, say materials purchased and received into the stores, and this asset, material stock, is charged to the profit and loss account as a cost when it is consumed or used up. At this point the asset has turned into an expense, and is no longer a balance sheet item because it must be charged to the profit and loss account as a cost for the period. The date on which the bill is paid (expenditure) is not relevant in deciding whether the cost has been incurred. The raw material purchased may be paid for in cash when the goods are received, or payment may be made weeks or months after the material has been used up if the supplier is willing to allow the purchaser a period of credit.

A cost incurred in one period to make products can be carried forward at the end of the year as a balance sheet asset if the goods made have not been sold at that point in time. These costs represented by the unsold stock of finished products will be charged against the profit and loss account in the next period when they are sold, so that the revenue from the sale is correctly matched with the cost incurred to make the goods which have been sold. Cost properly chargeable to the income statement in a particular year includes the production cost of products sold that year (materials, labour and factory overhead expenses) even though the products were made in a previous year and the costs were paid for in that year. The stock of finished goods made in year 1 but not sold by the end of that year appears in the balance sheet as an asset at an amount equal to the costs incurred in year 1 to make the goods. This cost is not set against sales of year 1 in the profit computation but is carried forward as a balance sheet asset at the beginning of year 2 so that it can be set against revenue from the sales of these goods in the profit computation of the second year.

Five separate cases emerge:

Matching cost to revenue

1. **A cost this year which is paid for this year**. An example of such a cost is the payment of wages for labour used to make products which have been sold during this year.

2. **A cost this year which was paid for last year**. This means that an asset acquired last year, and shown in the balance sheet at the end of that year, becomes a cost in the profit and loss account this year. For example, raw materials purchased last year and kept in stock are charged to the income statement this year, when they are consumed in the production process.

3. **The cost of a future period which is paid for this year**. For example, raw materials bought during the year but not used, which appear in the closing balance sheet as an asset, stock. The calculation – opening stock £5,000 plus purchases £60,000 less closing stock £3,000 – computes the cost of materials used up during the period at £62,000.

   Likewise an insurance premium paid for a year from 1 July 2001 up to 30 June 2002 in the sum of, say, £1,000, should be apportioned, half the cost being charged to the profit and loss account of 2001 for the six months to 31 December covered by the premium in that year. The other half should be carried forward as a balance sheet asset in the balance sheet dated 31 December 2001, and then charged as a cost in the profit and loss account for 2002, since the premium concerns the first six months of that accounting year. This is a prepayment.

4. **The cost of this year which will be paid for in a future period.** For example, raw materials delivered and used up during the year for which a bill has not been received and payment has not yet been made. This is an accrual.

5. **Part of the cost of buying a machine several years ago which has manufactured goods this year.** This cost is allocated to each year of the life of the machine as a provision for depreciation.

ACCRUALS

An accrued expense is a cost for the current year which has been incurred but not yet paid for or even invoiced. As such it does not appear in the ledgers of the business. In this case the accountant must use expertise to estimate what the expense is likely to be when the bill is eventually presented, and to charge this amount in the income statement so that a true profit is shown. According to the principal of duality, if a cost is entered on the debit side of the ledger a liability to meet the cost must be shown on the other side.

The cost of electricity provides a good example of an accrued expense. Electricity will have been used by the office and factory right up to the accounting date, but the most recent bill for electricity will show only the cost up to the date on which the meter was read, which could be a month or more before the year end. The accountant must estimate the liability for electricity for the period between the meter reading and the year end and charge it in the income statement. The balance sheet will show a liability for this amount, and when the electricity bill is presented at some date in the next year, that part of it which concerns this year will already have been charged to the profit and loss account and thus will not distort next year's costs.

Electricity consumed but no bill received – an accrual

Dr		Electricity Account		Cr
	£			£
Year 1: 10 April electricity bill	514	Profit and loss account		
14 July electricity bill	632	charge for the year		2 326
9 October electricity bill	580			
31 December accrued				
balance carried forward	600			
	£2 326			£2 326
Year 2: 20 Jan electricity bill	612	1 Jan balance brought down		600

The accountant has estimated the missing bill for the electricity consumed in the last three months of the year as £600. This has been charged to the profit and loss account of year 1 within the figure £2,326. The amount of £600 is carried forward as a credit balance on the balance sheet at the end of year 1 because the accountant believes the electricity company is owed £600 by the business at that time. This should therefore be recorded in the balance sheet as a creditor. When the bill for £612 is received on 20 January in year 2, there is a credit balance of £600 waiting in the account to offset it. Thus a year 1 expense is not allowed to interfere with profit measurement in year 2 except in so far as the accountant has incorrectly estimated the amount of the bill, by £12.

Task 4.1

A publisher pays royalties to its authors in arrears, after the end of the accounting year in which the books are sold. Author A is owed £5,000 for books sold to 31 December in year 1. How should this item be treated in the financial statements of the publishing business for that year?

Solution

No entry appears in the publishing company's ledgers at 31 December. The amount of £5,000 is estimated, and charged in the profit and loss account as a cost. At the same time the balance sheet must disclose that £5,000 as a current liability, which is to be paid to the author within a few months of the balance sheet date.

PREPAYMENTS

The amounts recorded in the books of the business have to be adjusted for the five cases shown above, so that the true cost is entered in the income statement. A prepayment, or payment in advance, is such an adjustment. Suppose that rent is paid on business premises for a year in advance on 30 June. If the accounting year of the business runs from 1 January until 31 December, at the end of the year half of the rent paid on 30 June will be a cost properly chargeable for the year to 31 December, and the other half will represent the cost of the next accounting period, paid in advance. This prepayment is an asset at 31 December, since the business possesses the right to use the premises for the next six months. Technically the landlord owes the business six months' rent, or six months' use, at 31December, and this is shown in the balance sheet as a debtor. In the next accounting period this asset will be converted to a cost and charged to the income statement. Other expenses which can be paid in advance include insurance premiums, usually paid annually, rates for a half year, rentals on leased plant and vehicles, and the annual road fund license for a vehicle. An example of prepayments for a business whose accounting year ends on 31 December is shown below.

Rent paid in advance

Dr		Rent Account		Cr
	£			£
Year 1: 30 June cash paid	1 200	31 December		
		charge to profit and loss		600
		31 December		
		balance carried forward		600
	£1 200			£1 200
Year 2: 1 January balance		31 December		
brought down	600	charge to profit and loss		1300
30 June cash paid	1 400	31 December		
		balance carried forward		700
	£2 000			£2 000
Year 3: 1 January balance				
brought down	700			

(Note that the rent has increased in the second year. It is paid annually in advance in June. The charge for the second year is £600 + £700, as rent is increased halfway through the year)

Task 4. 2

If business rates for the local government year from 1 April year 2002 to 31 March year 2003 cost £40,000 and are paid in two instalments on 1 April and 1 September year 2002 how much would be paid in advance on 31 December year 2002 if that were the end of the accounting year for a business?

Solution

The second payment covers the period September year 2002 to March year 2003. Only three of the six months concern the accounting period to 31 December 2002, so $3/6 \times £20,000 = £10,000$ should be charged on the profit and loss account, and the remaining £10,000 carried forward on the balance sheet at 31 December as an asset, a debtor, to be charged against profit in 2003.

OTHER PREPAYMENTS

1. **Fixed assets** of a business are acquired for use in more than one accounting period. Thus the cost of a machine with a 10-year life should be charged out to the ten accounting periods covered by that life. The term used for spreading the cost of a fixed asset over several accounting periods is depreciation (see Chapter 6). A charge for depreciation is made in the income statement each year, and gradually the asset is turned into an expense and written off against sales revenue in the

years in which it makes a contribution to those sales. A machine costing £5,000 might be charged at £1,000 per annum to the profit and loss account if it has a 5-year working life.

2. **Deferred revenue expenditure** is a term applied to costs which provide a benefit in more than one accounting period and which are spread across those periods for this reason. An advertising campaign to establish a new product may give benefit by generating sales over the next two or even three years. Accordingly it may be considered fair to charge out this cost to the accounting periods which benefit from it, so that at the end of the first year the cost of advertising not yet charged out will appear in the balance sheet as an asset.

3. **Development expenditure** on a product or project yet to be marketed is sometimes carried forward as an asset until such time as there is sales revenue from that product against which the development cost can be written off (matched). An accountant , however, will defer such revenue expenditure only if it is certain that sales will follow, since it is contrary to the principle of prudence to carry forward the cost if there is a chance that revenue will not ensue.

4. The matching principle also applies to **revenue from sales**. Cash received is not synonymous with sales. Goods may be sold on credit, and even though the payment has not been received the sales can be counted in the income computation. Once again the principle of prudence ensures that a provision for doubtful debts is made in this case. Cash received in one year may not concern sales of that year, since it may represent payments made by debtors for sales made in a previous period. In this case one asset, a debt, has been exchanged for another, cash, with no impact on the income statement.

A simple rule of thumb is: for accruals increase the recorded cost charged to the profit computation and show the accrual as a creditor in the balance sheet; for payments in advance decrease the recorded cost charged against profit and show the amount as a debtor in the balance sheet.

RESERVES AND PROVISIONS

A provision is an amount charged against profit for depreciation, or to provide for any known cost the exact amount of which cannot be accurately determined, such as bad debts. An accrual is a provision, since it is the charge made against profits for a cost which has been incurred but cannot be determined accurately at the accounting date. Thus provisions are charges against the profit figure in the profit and loss account.

A reserve is an amount set aside out of profit for other purposes. It is an appropriation of profit and represents that part of the year's profit which is to be retained in the business for various reasons. On the balance sheet the reserves show the total of past profits retained in the business. Although these 'ploughed back' profits represent a further investment in the business by the shareholders, the legal position is that reserves are available for distribution as dividend unless it is stated on the balance sheet that they are not available for distribution. Certain reserves cannot by law be distributed as a dividend and are known as 'statutory reserves', e.g. share premium.

Format of a profit and loss account in vertical form

		£	£
Sales			500 000
Less cost of sales			300 000
Gross profit			200 000
Less expenses	Administration costs	80 000	
	Selling and distribution costs	50 000	
	Financial charges	20 000	
			150 000
Net profit before taxation			50 000
Taxation			20 000
Net profit after taxation			30 000
Dividends			15 000
Retained profit for the year			£15 000

CONCLUSION

The measurement of income depends on a correct recognition of those costs which have been incurred to produce the goods or services sold during a period. The calculation – opening stock plus purchases less closing stock – shows the cost of goods sold, or the cost of materials used in a factory situation. Accruals and prepayments also help to identify the cost figure which should be set against sales revenue if a true profit is to be measured.

Discussion Topics

Thirty-minute essay questions:

1. Differentiate between payments made in an accounting period and costs incurred in that period. Why is this difference important?

2. What effect will profit have on the amount of the owner's interest in the business? Are dividends an expense of the business?

3. Differentiate between a reserve and a provision. What do the reserves represent in the balance sheet and how are they linked to the income statement?

SEMINAR EXERCISES

4.1.

(a) Indicate the extent to which each of the following items is an expense of the year ended 31 December and show the total expenses for the year:

   (i) goods received and paid for during the year, £37,712, of which items costing a total of £2,430 were still in stock at the year end;
   (ii) goods received during the year but not yet paid for, £3,840, of which items costing a total of £360 were still in stock at the year end;
   (iii) goods in stock at the beginning of the year, £800, and all sold during the year;
   (iv) payments during the year (additional to the above) to suppliers for goods received last year, £937;
   (v) wages paid during the year and all earned during the year £230;
   (vi) insurance policy taken out on 30 June, one year's premium of £360 being paid in advance;
   (vii) other expenses relating to the year and all paid for in that year, £1,790;
   (viii) equipment purchased in earlier years, having a value at the beginning of the year of £4,000 and expected to be used for a further three years;
   (ix) you estimate electricity used but not paid-for at 31 December to be £380.

(b) Complete the following calculation of profit (or loss) for the year:

	£
Revenue for the year from sales	45 000
Less total expenses as in (a) above	?
Profit (or loss) for the year	?

(c) Complete the balance sheet as it would have appeared at the *beginning* of the year:

	£		£
Owners' capital	?	Equipment	?
Trade creditors	?	Stock	?
		Debtors	2 100
		Cash	450
	£ ?		£ ?

(d)   Write up the summary of the cash book to compute the balance at the end of the year:

Cash Book

	£		£
Balance at beginning	?	Payments for	
Receipts for sale of goods		Goods	?
(all goods sold were		Wages	?
paid for during the year)	?	Insurance	?
Debtors	?	Expenses	?
		Balance at end*	
	_____		_____
	£		£

(e)   Draw up the balance sheet as it would appear at the *end* of the year:

	£		£
Owners' capital		Equipment	
Balance at 1 January		Stock	
Add profit or deduct loss		Debtors	
Creditors		Cash	
Accruals		Payments in advance	
	_____		_____
	£		£

(f)   What assumptions have you made in producing these figures?

4.2. **M. A. Tellow** started to trade as an agent for the sale of canal cruisers on 1 January. During his first month of trading he sold boats for £53,000 comprising £10,800 for cash and the remainder on credit terms. He introduced £20,000 of his own money into the business at its inception, and an aunt lent him a further £10,000. He rented premises on 1 January and paid £500 as two months' rent in advance on that day. The costs of running his premises, including the wages of an assistant, were paid in cash on the last day of the month in the sum of £980. He was unable to pay his electricity bill as the meter had not been read, but estimated the cost for the month as £50. An insurance premium for a year's cover was paid on 1 January. It cost £1,200. During the month boats were purchased for £47,000 and so far £7,000 has been paid to the suppliers. Boats remaining unsold on 31 January had cost £15,000

Required:

(a)   Compute the bank balance of M. A. Tellow as at 31 January.

(b)   Calculate the profit he made during January.

CHAPTER 5

The System of Recording Transactions

THE AIMS OF THIS CHAPTER

To enable students to

- Understand the double entry system using the quadrant

- Write up ledger accounts, balance them and extract a trial balance

- Comprehend the system of source documents from which accounting information is derived

- Follow through a chart of accounts relating source documents to the profit and loss account and balance sheet

DOUBLE ENTRY

Every transaction has a double effect on the business, and therefore should be recorded twice to reveal this effect.

For example

   (a) **Shares are issued for cash**. Share capital increases and cash increases – a claim and an asset.

   (b) **Machinery is purchased for cash**. Machinery increases and cash is reduced – one asset is exchanged for another.

   (c) **Material is purchased on credit**. Purchases increase, and creditors increase – an asset and a liability.

(d) **Sales are made for cash.** Sales increase and cash increases – a revenue and an asset.

(e) **Sales are made on credit terms.** Sales increase and debtors increase – a revenue and an asset.

The terms 'debit' and 'credit' have been in use since the Middle Ages with the amounts recorded for assets and costs as debits, and liabilities, capital and revenue as credits. Since assets equal liabilities and capital, the debits must be equal to the credits. These terms have been developed over time so that we now 'debit' or 'credit' an account. Debiting an asset account is to increase the account, and conversely decreasing an asset account is to credit that account. Crediting a liability account is to increase that account but reducing a liability is a debit entry.

For example

(a) A company issues a share capital of £10,000 which shareholders pay for by cash. The asset cash is a debit entry and the share capital is a credit entry.

(b) A machine is bought for £8,000, paid for by cash. The asset account machinery is increased (a debit entry) and the asset cash is decreased (a credit entry)

(c) Materials are purchased on credit terms for £5,000. Purchases increase (a debit entry) and liabilities (trade creditors) increase (a credit entry).

These transactions can be written up as ledger accounts as follows, with debits traditionally on the left hand side of the ledger and credits on the right.

Debit		Capital Account		Credit
				£
		Shares issued for cash		10 000

Debit		Cash Account		Credit
	£			£
Shares issued for cash	10 000	Cash paid for a machine		8 000

Debit		Machinery Account		Credit
	£			
Machine purchased for cash	8 000			

Debit		Purchases Account		Credit
	£			
Material purchased on credit terms	5 000			

Debit		Trade Creditors Account		Credit
				£
		Material purchased on credit terms		5 000

The terms debit and credit are usually abbreviated to Dr and Cr. In the cash account above the amount of £10,000 has been reduced by £8,000 so the balance remaining in cash is £2,000 on the debit side.

The basic rules of double entry book-keeping

1. Each transaction is recorded twice, once on each side of separate accounts in the ledgers. Every debit must have a corresponding credit and every credit must have a debit.

2. In the ledger the assets and costs are debit balances and the liabilities and sales revenue are credit balances. The purchase of every asset by a business is financed by funds invested in or lent to the business by owners or creditors (lenders), who then have a claim against the company for the return of their funds. Thus claims equal assets in the balance sheet. In the income statement if sales revenue (credit) exceeds costs (debit) and a profit is made, this profit is a credit balance and is added in the balance sheet to capital, as retained profit, part of the claims on the credit side, to balance the increase in assets represented by the profit.

3. When an asset or cost account is to be increased the entry is on the debit side and when a liability or sales revenue account is to be increased the account is credited. When, however an account is to be decreased, the amount is not deducted from the side on which the balance is shown, but is instead posted to the opposite side, so that the balance is reduced in this way. For example, an asset or cost account is decreased by crediting the account and a liability or sales revenue account is decreased by debiting the account. If a loan is repaid, the appropriate entries would be debit loan account to decrease its credit balance, and credit cash or bank account (an asset) to decrease its debit balance.

4. The 'giving' account is credited while the 'receiving' account is debited. For example, when wages are paid, the wages account receives and is debited, while cash is given out so this account is credited, and when a debtor pays what is owed, the cash account receives and is debited, while the debtor gives and that account is credited (thus reducing the debit balance). This is a rather rough and ready rule which does not have a logical application in all cases.

THE QUADRANT

The quadrant is a diagram with four boxes which helps to explain the double entry required for each transaction, and the effect of transactions on the profit and loss account and balance sheet. Figure 5.1 shows the constituents of the balance sheet (assets, capital and liabilities) in the upper boxes, while costs and revenue, which form the profit and loss account, are in the lower boxes. Note that assets and costs appear on the debit side while capital, liabilities and revenue are credit balances.

DEBIT BALANCES	CREDIT BALANCES	
Assets Premises Plant Vehicles Stock Debtors Cash Prepayments	**Capital** Shareholders'/Owners' funds **Liabilities** Trade creditors Accruals Taxation owed Bank loan and overdraft Long-term loans	Balance sheet
Costs Material Labour Factory overheads Selling costs Administration expenses	**Revenue** Sales Investment income	Profit and loss account

Figure 5.1 The quadrant. Debit balances must equal credit balances in a trial balance. Assets = capital + liabilities on the balance sheet. If revenue exceeds cost, there is a profit which belongs to the shareholders. If cost exceeds revenue, there is a loss which reduces the shareholders' funds.

Task 5.1

Consider the dual impact of each of the following transactions on the business and enter them on a quadrant in order to demonstrate the dual effect of each one and the total balance between debits and credits.

Remember

- to increase debit items (assets and costs), debit the account
- to decrease debit items (assets and costs), credit the account
- to increase credit items (capital and liabilities and revenue), credit the account
- to decrease credit items (capital and liabilities and revenue), debit the account

Follow the double entries for each transaction on the quadrant shown below using the letter codes (a) to (n).

(a) Share capital subscribed, £20,000: a liability (capital) is recorded as a credit item and a receipt of cash as a debit item.

(b) Plant purchased for cash, £10,000: assets have increased on the debit side but the payment in the cash book is a credit side entry to reduce the debit balance of cash.

(c) Material purchased on credit terms, £5,000: assets have increased again but are balanced by an increased liability as a credit item.

(d) Part of the material is paid for, £4,000: the payment of cash is recorded as a credit (CR) and is balanced by a decrease of the liability, a debit entry (DR).

(e) Some of the material is used in production, £3,000: an asset has decreased (CR) but it is balanced by an increase in cost (DR), also on the debit side. If accounting statements were prepared at this moment, part of the stock would be charged as a cost and the remainder carried forward as an asset in the balance sheet.

(f) Wages paid, £2,000: costs have increased on the debit side and are balanced by a payment of cash as a CR entry.

(g) Payment of insurance premium, £600: an increase in cost (DR) balanced by a payment of cash (CR).

(h) Part of the insurance premium concerns the next accounting period and is thus a prepayment in the sum of £200: costs must be decreased (CR) and balanced by an increase in assets (DR) when the provision for payment in advance is made and recorded in the balance sheet as a debtor.

(i) Plant depreciated by £1,000: costs have increased (DR) and are balanced by a decrease in assets (CR). Depreciation is deducted from the cost of plant shown on the balance sheet.

(j) An accrual is made for electricity costs, £100: costs have increased on the debit side and are balanced by an increased liability when the estimated amount is recorded as a creditor in the balance sheet.

(k) Goods are sold on credit terms, £12,000: the sales revenue is recorded as a credit item and is balanced by the creation of an asset, debtors, on the debit side.

(l) Some debtors pay, £6,000: the decrease in the asset (CR) is balanced by the receipt of cash (DR).

The accounts in the quadrant can now be balanced at the end of the year.

(m) The board decide to pay a dividend of 10 per cent: thus £2,000 is to be appropriated out of the profit and paid to the shareholders. This will increase the debit items costs (though a dividend is not really a cost) and, since the dividend is not yet paid, it must appear in the balance sheet as a liability. Alternatively, the provision of a dividend can be seen as a reduction in the owner's interest, since profits retained are reduced.

(n) **Closing**: in the cash book any surplus of receipts (DR) over payments (CR) will be recorded as an asset, cash, in the balance sheet. The income statement can then be completed so that the surplus of sales (CR) over costs (DR) can be added to the owners' interest on the liabilities side of the balance sheet. The other balances outstanding in the accounts in the ledger are recorded in the balance sheet, which must therefore balance.

BALANCING ACCOUNTS

Each ledger account resembles a set of scales. If the debits are greater than the credits for that account, the balance is said to be on the debit side, and vice versa. The cash transactions recorded in the quadrant on page 53 could be written up and balanced as a cash ledger account as follows:

Debit Receipts side		Cash Account	Payments side	Credit
Received from:	£	Paid to:		£
(a) Capital	20 000	(b) Plant		10 000
(i) Debtors	6 000	(d) Creditors		4 000
		(f) Wages		2 000
		(g) Insurance		600
		Balance carried forward c/f		9 400
	£26 000			£26 000
Balance brought down b/d	9 400			

The debit side is greater than the credit side when they are added up, and a balancing figure of £9,400 must be inserted on the credit side to bring the total to £26,000. This balancing figure is then carried forward and brought down on the debit side. Abbreviations c/f and b/d are used for 'carried forward' and 'brought down'.

Solution to task 5.1

Tick each debit to its corresponding credit.

DEBIT ITEMS			CREDIT ITEMS		
	DR	CR		DR	CR
Assets	*Increase*	*Decrease*	**Capital**	*Decrease*	*Increase*
Cash (a)	20 000		Share capital (a)		20 000
Cash (b)		10 000			
Cash (d)		4 000			
Cash (f)		2 000	**Liabilities**		
Cash (g)		600	Trade Creditors (c)		5 000
Cash (l)	6 000		Trade Creditors (d)	4 000	
Insurance (h)	200		Electricity (j)		100
Debtors (k)	12 000		Cumulative depreciation (i)		1 000
Debtors (l)		6 000	Dividend owed (m)		2 000
Plant (b)	10 000		(n)	£4 000	28 100
Materials (c)	5 000		(n)		4 000
Materials (e)		3 000	Net increase (n)		£24 100
(n)	53 200	25 600			
(n)	25 600				
Net increase (n)	£27 600				
	DR	CR		DR	CR
Costs	*Increase*	*Decrease*	**Revenue**	*Decrease*	*Increase*
Materials (e)	3 000		Sales (k)		12 000
Wages (f)	2 000				
Insurance (g)	600				
Insurance (h)		200			
Depreciation (i)	1 000				
Electricity (j)	100				
Appropriation					
Dividend (m)	2 000				
(n)	8 700	200			
(n)	200				
Net increase	£8 500		Net increase		£12 000

Assets	27 600		Capital and liabilities	24 100
Costs	8 500		Revenue	12 000
Debit balances	£36 100		Credit balances	£36 100

Task 5.2.

Write up ledger accounts for the other items in the quadrant from Task 5.1 above.

Solution

Use the alphabetical notation for transactions to relate debits to credits

Share Capital Account

£		£
	(a) Cash	20 000

Plant Account

	£		£
(b) Cash	10 000		

Materials Stock Account

	£		£
(c) Creditors	5 000	(e) Used	3 000
		Balance c/f	2 000
	£5 000		£5 000
Balance b/d	2 000		

Creditors Account

	£		£
(d) Cash	4 000	(c) Materials	5 000
		(j) Electricity	100
Balance c/f	1 100		
	£5 100		£5100
		Balance b/d	1100

Materials Used Account

	£		£
(e) Stock account	3 000		

Wages Account

	£		£
(f) Cash	2 000		

Insurance Account

	£		£
(g) Cash	600	(h) Cost for the year c/f	400
		Balance c/f	200
	£600		£600
(h) Balance b/d	200		
Profit and loss	400		

Annual Depreciation Account				Cumulative Depreciation Account			
	£		£		£		£
(i) Provision	1 000					(i) Provision	1000

Electricity Account				Sales Account			
	£		£		£		£
(j) Electricity cost owed	100					(k) Debtors	12 000

Debtors Account				Dividend Account			
	£		£		£		£
(k) Sales	12 000	(l) Cash	6 000	(n) Dividend provided from income	2 000		
		Balance c/f	6 000				
	£12 000		£12 000				
Balance b/d	6 000						

Dividend Owed Account		
		£
	(n) dividend owed to shareholders	2000

The transactions have been entered on both sides in the ledger, and a set of ledger accounts, such as those above, produced. A trial balance could be extracted after the book-keeping is complete.

THE TRIAL BALANCE

At the end of an accounting period, the total of debit entries in the ledger should equal the total of credit entries if the double-entry system has been properly applied. Each account must be balanced by adding up each side and finding whether a debit or credit balance is brought down. The accounts in the ledger are then listed on a separate sheet with the balance of the account shown in a debit or a credit column. If the total of debit balances equals the total of credit balances then *prima facie* each transaction has been recorded as a debit and a credit. This is a valuable check on the accuracy of the book-keeping, but it does not reveal the situation where an item had been debited to the wrong account, omitted entirely, or analysed incorrectly, or where compensating errors have been made. The trial balance is a summary of the balances recorded in the ledger accounts, and can thus be used as a basis from which the profit and loss account and balance sheet can be computed. The transactions recorded in the ledgers have to be adjusted for accruals and prepayments by extending the trial balance to include these items.

A trial balance extracted from the quadrant example

	Debits £	Credits £	Financial statements
Capital		20 000	BS
Cash	9 400		BS
Plant	10 000		BS
Materials stock	2 000		BS
Creditors		1 100	BS
Materials used	3 000		PL
Wages	2 000		PL
Insurance – cost	400		PL
– paid in advance	200		BS
Annual depreciation cost	1 000		PL
Cumulative depreciation to date		1 000	BS
Electricity cost	100		PL
Sales		12 000	PL
Debtors	6 000		BS
Dividend proposed	2 000		PL
Dividend owed to shareholders		2 000	BS
	£36 100	£36 100	

Relate this trial balance to the figures in the quadrant for task 5.1. Note that the balances would be recorded in the appropriate financial statement – balance sheet (BS) and profit and loss account (PL). The profit and loss account is really a year end summary, whose balance is added to shareholders' funds, so items carried to the profit and loss account are removed from the ledger. This leaves only the balances which appear on the balance sheet. The insurance account needs adjustment to reflect transaction (h), whereby the cost of £600 is allocated as £400 to be charged against this year's income and £200 to be carried forward in the balance sheet, so that it can be charged next year.

The balance of £100 on the electricity account would be transferred as a cost to the profit and loss account – credit electricity and debit profit and loss.

Financial statements drafted from the trial balance

As a T account the profit and loss account would then show:

Profit and Loss Account

Materials	3 000	Sales	12 000
Wages	2 000		
Depreciation	1 000		
Electricity	100		
Insurance	400		
Total Costs	6 500		
Profit c/f	5 500		
	£12 000		£12 000

Dividend to be paid out of profit	2 000	Profit b/d	5 500
Balance of retained profit c/f	3 500		
	£5 500		£5 500
		Retained profit b/d	£3 500

The balance sheet can be drafted as follows from the balances remaining in the books.

	£	£	Dr/Cr
Fixed assets:			
Plant at cost		10 000	Dr
Less deprecation to date		(1 000)	Cr
		9 000	
Current assets:			
Stock of materials	2 000		Dr
Debtors	6 000		Dr
Insurance paid in advance	200		Dr
Cash	9 400		Dr
	17 600		
Less current liabilities:			
Creditors	(1 100)		Cr
Dividend payable	(2 000)		Cr
Net current assets		14 500	
Net assets (Assets – liabilities)		£23 500	
Share capital		20 000	Cr
Retained profits		3 500	Cr
Owners interest in the business		£23 500	

A–L = C

RECORDING TRANSACTIONS: THE SOURCES OF INFORMATION

Before entries can be made in the ledger accounts, transactions must be recorded and evidenced on working documents.

Some of these 'prime documents' are listed below:

(a) **Invoices** or bills to evidence the cost, date and exact description of items purchased or expenses incurred, and the supplier who must be paid.

(b) **Credit notes**, which are used when an invoice is cancelled or when the amount of a bill is reduced for some reason, e.g. goods returned.

(c) **Cheque book stubs** to record money paid out. These documents are often supported by a remittance advice which lists the items paid for by the cheque.

(d) **Petty cash vouchers** to show what has been bought for cash.

(e) **The paying-in book** to record cash and cheques received from sales, debtors, etc. and which have been paid into the bank.

(f) **Clock cards and wages sheets** to analyse the amount paid out for labour.

(g) **Sales invoices** to record sales made, whether for cash or credit, and the customer who received the goods.

(h) **Goods received notes** (GRNs) to evidence the receipt of goods from a supplier, for which an invoice can be expected in the near future. The invoice should only be passed for entry into the ledgers and eventual payment if it agrees with the order for the goods and the GRN.

(i) **Journal vouchers** for internal transactions and transfers between accounts.

BOOKS OF PRIME ENTRY

When there is a large volume of transactions the prime documents have to be summarized and analysed before they are posted into the books of account. Originally the daybook for sales or purchases was the device used for this purpose. It used to be written up daily with a total column and sub-columns for analysis. At the end of the month the daybook would be closed, and the columns cast. The analysis column totals were cross-cast to reconcile with the total of the major column. The analysis column totals were then entered into the appropriate ledger accounts and the individual items posted to the personal account of the customer or supplier. Daybooks were maintained for purchases, sales, internal transactions and transfers (the journal), and cash. Some systems had a daybook for returns inwards (goods sold sent back by the customer) and for returns outwards (purchases returned to suppliers). The cash book acted both as a book of prime entry, from which items were posted to other accounts, and also as a ledger account, to record the balance of the asset cash. In the case of the purchases daybook the analysis column totals would be debited to the various expense accounts to show the costs incurred, while the individual amounts in the total column would be credited to the personal accounts of suppliers in the creditors ledger. The sales daybook analysed sales to product or area (a credit entry) and allowed each sale in the major column to be debited to the customer's (debtor's) personal account.

As business became more sophisticated and the number of transactions to be accounted for increased, so the old handwritten system of keeping the books became inadequate to deal with the new volume of work. The daybook was replaced by a machine list or computer list of transactions, and analysis is now undertaken by mechanical or computer systems which sort and total entries. The ledgers produced by book-keeping machines show additions and deductions in the form of black and red entries in one total column. In some cases the account itself is little more than a set of positive and negative pulses on a computer tape which can be printed out on demand. Some systems of ledgerless book-keeping avoid the maintenance of personal ledgers by filing all invoices owed to one supplier or by one customer in the same filing pocket, adding new invoices as they arrive and extracting invoices when they are paid. Basically, however, prime documents are still summarized and analysed, and recorded as both a debit and a credit in the ledger accounts of the business no matter what form those accounts take.

THE JOURNAL

In some systems the journal for recording internal transactions and alterations is normally the only book still entered by hand. If by mistake the wrong account has been debited with an expense or an asset acquired, the mistake must be put right by crediting the account entered in error and debiting the correct amount. A journal entry will record the appropriate account to be debited and credited with a 'narration' explaining the reason for the alteration. In some systems even this book has been replaced by a file of journal vouchers which evidence and authorize the debit and credit entries made in the mechanized or computer system. Some internal transactions, however, are extremely important and must be evidenced by an extract from the minutes of the board meeting at which the decision concerning the transaction was made. The payment of dividends, transfers to reserve accounts, and changes in the share capital of the business are all examples of the type of transaction which enters the books of account through the journal.

The form of the journal is that it is ruled in four columns, with the second column wider than the others.

Date	Narration	Debit £	Credit £
1 April	Mr J. Bloggs	500	
	Mr R. Goodfellow		500
	Being goods purchased		
	by Bloggs, charged to		
	Goodfellow in error		

The narration column names the accounts to be debited or credited, and gives a short description of the reason for the entry. In the example above Bloggs's account is debited, since he owes £500 for goods not yet paid for, and Goodfellow's account is credited to nullify the debit of £500 entered in his account in error.

THE LEDGER ACCOUNTS

Transactions recorded in the daybooks would next be entered in the ledger accounts. There is usually a general ledger for costs and revenues, and personal ledgers for debtors (sales) and creditors (purchases). The books are divided into accounts or pages in the ledger, an account being opened not for each transaction but to summarize transactions of a similar nature on the same page, e.g. a page for repair costs, another for factory wages, another for sales revenue and another for rent. If there are many transactions of one type, then a separate book or ledger will be opened, e.g. the cash book to record the cash part of transactions, payments or receipts, and a debtors ledger to maintain a detailed record of amounts owed to the business by customers who have bought goods on credit. In this case each debtor will have an account or page of their own in the debtors ledger. Alternatively the data can be recorded on computer tape and printed out as a statement, or shown on a visual display unit. The two-sided form may not be used but the principle of debit and credit (plus and minus) still holds true.

Each page acts as a T-account, having two sides, one for debits (Dr) and one for credits (Cr). The debits are always on the left hand side, and the credits on the right hand side. When the two sides of an account are added up (the old term 'cast' is sometimes used), if the entries on the debit side are greater than those on the credit side then the account is said to have a debit balance, and vice versa.

Task 5.3

Follow the transactions through the chart of accounts for a manufacturing company which is shown in Figure 5.2. Note that debit entries are on the left hand side of each account and credit entries on the right. The source documents are shown on the arrows which indicate the debit and credit entries. There is an arrow at the end of each connecting line to show that every debit has a credit. (B) denotes a balance remaining at the end of the year after the income measurement entries have been extracted. These balances will appear on the balance sheet.

GP = Gross Profit   NP = Net Profit

Starting at the top, purchase invoices cause a debit to material purchases and a credit to creditor suppliers. Requisitions from managers cause materials to be issued to the factory as part of the manufacturing cost (debit the cost and credit materials), thus reducing the balance of materials left in stock.

CONCLUSION

Double entry book-keeping shows in the ledger accounts the dual effect on the business of each transaction. It reinforces the accounting equation to provide revenue and costs for the profit and loss account, and assets, liabilities and capital for the balance sheet. The trial balance acts as a check on the book-keeping entries. Before any entries can be made in the ledgers, a system of source documents must be organized to provide the raw data which is then analysed and posted to the ledger accounts.

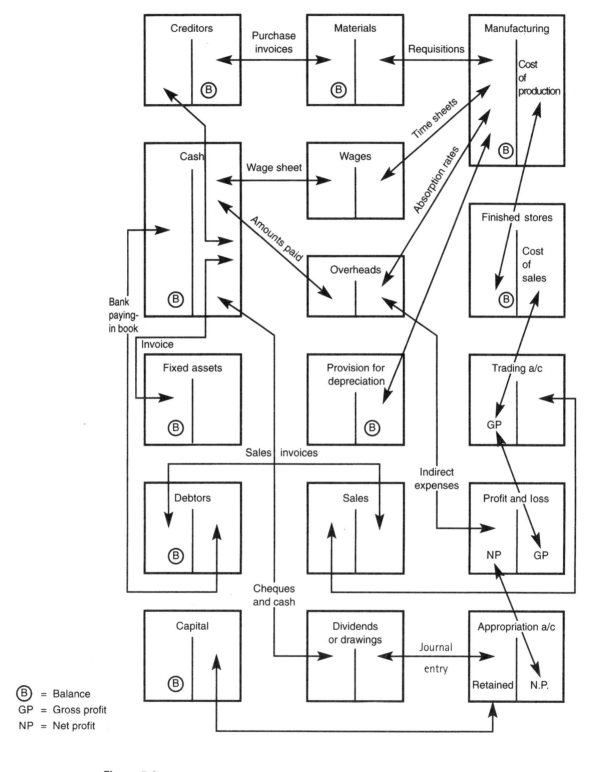

Figure 5.2

SEMINAR EXERCISES

5.1. On 1 January Albert started a business factoring a variety of goods for the growing leisure market. The following events took place in the first few days of January:

4 January **Albert** opened a business account at the Church Street branch of the bank, paying in a cheque for £20,000 drawn on his private account. After a long discussion with the branch manager, an overdraft facility for up to £10,000 was agreed, Albert depositing the deeds of his private residence with the bank as security for the overdraft.

5 January A small building was purchased for £25,000 and paid for by cheque.

6 January Office equipment was purchased for £4,000 (paid by cheque).

7 January Stock was purchased for resale at an agreed price of £10,000 to be paid not later than 28 February.

10 January Stock was sold to two customers. The first paid £1,000 in cash, and the second agreed to pay £4,500 in one month's time.

11 January Albert visited two prospective customers. Both expressed interest in his products and he was delighted to receive a firm order for the balance of his stock (which had cost him £5,000) at a price of £6,000, to be delivered on 31 March. Cash was to be paid on delivery of the goods.

Required:

Give the accounting representation of these transactions using the quadrant.

5.2. **Brian Grange** starts to trade as a wholesale dealer on 1 September at a warehouse which he owns himself and which is valued at £24,000. Grange has provided fixtures and fittings which cost £17,000, and has brought into the business his car, worth £2,800, and a van valued at £900. He opens a business bank account by paying £8,500 into it. He has already bought goods on credit from the following firms, and these goods comprise his opening stock: Collie and Co., £471; Lot and Mee, £360; and Edmunds, £615. Grange's capital is the amount of his investment in the business, whether injected in the form of cash or assets.

Required:

(a) Calculate Grange's capital and enter the balances shown in the appropriate ledger accounts. These opening entries could be made direct to T-accounts or through an opening journal entry (A - L = C).

(b) Record the undermentioned transactions in ledger accounts and the cash book. Prove your work by extracting a trial balance.

1 September Bought on credit terms from Apple Ltd two typewriters at £180 each.
Bought office stationery, £174 paid by cheque.
Drew £250 from bank to cover petty cash expenses.

2 September   Sold goods to T. Veron for £627 and K. Jones for £460.
Paid cheque for cartons, £61, and cleaning materials, £16.
3 September   Cash sales to date, £165, banked.
4 September   Paid wages in cash, £83.
5 September   Bought goods from J. Lewin, £190, less 10% trade discount (not yet paid for).
Paid cheques as follows: Collie and Co. £300 on account; Edmunds Ltd £600.in full settlement after deducting £15 as a cash discount.
6 September   Goods returned from T. Veron, £127.
7 September   Paid rent on premises, cheque for £181.
Exchanged van at book value at Car Sales Ltd for a new van, costing £2,800, and accepted liability for the balance.
Returned goods costing £20 to J. Lewin.
Sold goods on credit terms to H. Same Ltd, £430.
8 September   Withdrew goods from stock for own use, £53.
Paid wages in cash, £76.
Banked cash sales, £431.
Paid office expenses in cash, £18.
9 September   Paid insurance premium by cheque, £160.
Bought goods on credit terms from Edmunds Ltd, £280.
Received cheque from T. Veron in settlement of his account net of 5% cash discount.
10 September   Paid Lot and Mee £200 on account by cheque.
Sold goods on credit terms to H. Same Ltd, £165.
Drew £5 from cash to pay for Grange's lunch.
11 September   Paid carriage charge, £29, and telephone bill, £23, by cheque.
Banked all office petty cash except a float of £50.

CHAPTER 6

Tangible Fixed Assets

Their Measurement, Valuation and Depreciation

THE AIMS OF THIS CHAPTER

To enable students to

- Recognize capital expenditure and appreciate its significance for the measurement of a true profit

- Understand the basis on which tangible fixed assets are valued

- Discuss the rationale of depreciation, and its methodology

- Draft ledger accounts for entries concerning depreciation

- Apply the main accounting rules for depreciation

Accounting for tangible fixed assets is regulated by Financial Reporting Standard (FRS) 15. The rules explained in this chapter reflect this standard accounting practice.

MEASURING CAPITAL EXPENDITURE

Tangible fixed assets are items such as machinery, vehicles, buildings and fittings. They are separated from intangible fixed assets such as goodwill or brand names.

Business funds invested in tangible fixed assets which will contribute to profit for more than one accounting year should be capitalized. This means they are treated as an asset, and not as a cost to be written off to the profit and loss in the year of expenditure. Depreciation spreads the capital investment over the useful life of the asset so that a fair profit can be computed for each year that the asset works for the business. The recognition of capital expenditure is thus significant for profit measurement. Funds used to purchase or add to the value of fixed assets, to extend or improve the work which they can do and thus increase their earning capacity, can be classed as capital expenditure. Whether purchased or constructed by the business, tangible fixed assets should be measured at cost, to include only costs that are *directly attributable* to bring the asset into working condition. Such costs comprise

(a)   the purchase price net of any trade discounts, but including stamp duty and import taxes;

(b)   the cost of site preparation, installation and delivery;

(c)   the labour cost of company employees involved in construction of the asset;

(d)   professional fees to solicitors, architects, engineers, etc; and

(e)   the estimated cost of dismantling the asset at the end of its life.

Abnormal costs derived from design errors and operating losses during construction of the asset are not considered to be directly attributable costs. Some businesses however capitalize the cost of interest on the money invested during the construction period before the plant starts to contribute to profit, as part of the capital cost of the asset. The cost of a start-up or commissioning period to run and test machinery is only considered attributable if such a period is needed to attain normal levels of capacity. If the final cost of an asset exceeds what it is considered to be worth, the asset should be written down to that recoverable amount.

Subsequent expenditure on an asset during its life, in order to maintain its performance should be charged against profit for the year in which it is incurred. Such a subsequent expenditure may be capitalized and added to the cost of the asset if it

(a)   increases the profitability of the asset by increasing the range of tasks it can perform or reducing the running costs; or

(b)   replaces a component of the asset which should be treated separately from the asset itself, e.g. a new roof on a building; or

(c)   relates to a major inspection or overhaul of the asset.

Task 6.1

The foundry of a copper wire factory is to be equipped with a new furnace. The following costs have been incurred. Make a reasoned judgement to allocate the costs as capital or revenue items.

(a) The price charged for the furnace delivered to the factory.

(b) Adapting existing foundry machinery to the new furnace.

(c) Dismantling the old furnace.

(d) Training staff to operate the new machinery.

(e) Servicing existing foundry machinery.

(f) Salary of an engineer diverted from normal work to advise on the installation.

(g) New components to extend the range of existing machinery in the foundry.

(h) Cleaning up and redecorating the foundry.

(i) Loss of profit in the first week of operation due to a design error.

(j) Loss of profit in the first week of operation while testing the furnace.

Solution

Judgement must be applied to consider the cost of acquiring, extending or improving the assets. Only items (e) and (h) would be revenue expenditure, but (j) might be if the machine is not capable of operating at normal levels without such a test.

VALUATION

Fixed assets are normally accounted for at cost throughout their useful economic lives, but over time values may change and shareholders should be informed of such value changes. Accordingly businesses have the option of revaluing fixed assets, especially property, but if they do adopt a revaluation policy it must be operated on a consistent basis. 'Cherry picking' is the term applied when managers report value increases for some assets, but ignore value changes in others which might be less favourable. When revaluation occurs the 'carrying amount' of the asset (its value shown in the financial statements) should be its current value at the balance sheet date. This is derived from a *full* valuation every five years with an interim valuation in year 3. For tangible fixed assets other than property when there is an active second-hand market, the directors can make an annual revaluation. A *full* valuation should be conducted by a qualified valuer. The business must disclose the name and qualifications of the valuer, the bases of the valuation, the date of the valuation and the difference between the value and depreciated historical cost.

Task 6.2

What items should be checked to find a value for an office building?

Solution

(a) Physical condition, wear and tear and additions to the premises.

(b) Changes to the locality which will affect property values.

(c) Local planning authorities to discover projected developments.

(d) Recent market transactions in the area to establish price trends.

The Basis of Valuation

The value to a business of a tangible fixed asset will be the lower of its replacement cost or its recoverable amount. If an asset can be replaced for £100,000, and it will earn (recover) more than £100,000 for the business it will be replaced. It is worth its replacement cost. Conversely, if the replacement cost of an asset is £100,000 but its net realizable value is less than this, the business would not pay more to replace the asset than it is currently worth on the market, unless future earnings are greater than NRV. If future profits from the asset (value in use) are greater than its net realizable value, the asset will be put to work. If however cash from an immediate sale is greater than future earnings the asset will be sold. This is the recoverable amount. If a market value is not available for an asset, depreciated replacement cost can be used. This logic can be demonstrated by the diagram in Figure 6.1.

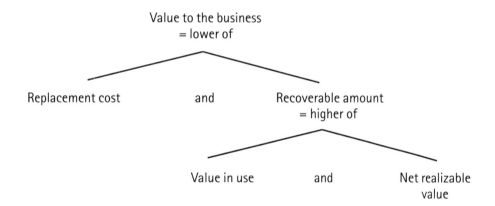

Figure 6.1

Example

An asset can be replaced for £150,000, but its future earnings are £200,000, and its net realizable value from immediate sale is £180,000. The recoverable amount is £200,000 as the asset will be used rather than sold. The value to the business is £150,000 because it will be replaced at that amount to earn £200,000.

For properties various valuation bases are recommended:

(a) Non-specialized property can be valued on the basis of its existing use. This means what a normal user would pay to control and use the property.

(b) Specialized properties which have a limited use such as refineries, docks, etc., should be valued at depreciated replacement cost. This means if a new unit currently costs £1,000,000 and the unit to be valued is halfway through a 30-year life, it is valued at £500,000.

(c) Properties surplus to requirements should be valued at open market value, less selling costs.

Disclosure

Revaluation gains must be disclosed in the profit and loss account, but in a special section separate from normal business income – this is the 'statement of total realized gains and losses'.

Revaluation losses caused by the consumption of the economic benefits stemming from the asset are recognized in the profit and loss account. Profits and losses on the disposal of tangible fixed assets also appear in the profit and loss account. A subsequent increase in value which reverses a previous fall in value which was charged to profit and loss account, can also be recognized in that account.

DEPRECIATION

Company law stipulates that depreciation must be charged on assets with finite useful lives. Fixed assets have a useful economic life of more than one year, and earn profit for a business throughout that life. Accordingly, fixed assets are gradually used up over the period of their life. Under the matching concept, part of the original cost of the asset should be charged against the revenue earned in successive periods to measure a true and fair profit. Thus the asset is gradually turned into an expense. The charge made each year to represent the amount of fixed asset used up during that year is depreciation. Judgement is required to calculate how much of the cost is to be charged in a particular accounting period. Under the prudence concept a fall in value of a fixed asset should be recognized in the profit computation when it takes place, to ensure that the disclosed value is not overstated. For this reason depreciation appears as a cost in the income statement, while in the balance sheet when fixed assets are disclosed at cost and the cumulative depreciation to date is subtracted the unexpired portion of the original capital cost is revealed. Note that depreciation is not a cash cost, in that no payment is made when depreciation is provided. Cash leaves the business when the fixed asset is purchased.

Depreciation based on historical cost does not disclose the cost of using up the asset at current prices, nor does it reveal in the balance sheet the current value of that part of the asset not yet used up. For this reason companies may adopt a revaluation policy.

Depreciation can be defined as the measure of the cost or revalued amount of the economic benefits of the tangible fixed asset that has been consumed during an accounting period. Factors underlying diminution in value of a fixed asset are

(a) physical wear and tear through use or the passage of time;

(b) obsolescence arising from changes in the demand for the product of the machine, or the development of new machines that are cheaper to operate, or which can produce an improved product: for example, starched collars are rarely worn nowadays, so a collar starching machine is worthless to a laundry, even though it can work as efficiently as on the day it was originally purchased;

(c) legal or other limits on the value of the asset: for example, a lease will be granted for a period of years, and its value falls as those years are used up.

Thus the fundamental objective of depreciation is to allocate the cost of an asset less its scrap value, over the useful economic life of the asset. This will reflect the cost of using the asset in terms of economic benefits consumed, when the profit is measured each year. Depreciation should therefore be a systematic charge, using a method selected by the managers to reflect the manner in which those economic benefits are consumed.

CAPITAL MAINTENANCE

Profit measurement is one objective of depreciation, but the maintenance of capital is another. Depreciation means that a charge is being made to the income statement to set aside out of revenue something to make up for that part of a past investment which has been used up during the accounting period. If this is not done then capital depletion will occur. A business which fails to take depreciation into account finds, at the end of the life of a particular asset, that it has used up the asset over a period of years without setting aside, out of the profits of those years, amounts with which to replace the capital of the company which was invested in the asset many years previously. A provision for depreciation reduces profit by an amount which might otherwise have been seen as available for distribution as a dividend. Without depreciation the fixed asset is used up, profits are overstated since no charge for the use of the asset has been made, and if those profits are all distributed in the form of a dividend, the funds invested in the business will have been run down during the life of the asset. When this asset is worthless, the store of assets representing the shareholders' funds invested in the business will have been depleted, unless the annual provision for depreciation (reinvested in the business and not distributed) maintains the general stock of assets, and thus the amount of shareholders' capital employed.

The concept of capital maintenance is crucial to the correct measurement of business income. If profit is a surplus, the true profit can only be measured after making sure that the business is as well off at the end of the accounting year as it was at the beginning. The provision for depreciation which is made to avoid capital depletion ensures that the original capital invested in the business will be maintained.

DEPRECIATION AND REPLACEMENT

Many students make a connection between depreciation and replacement saying that the amount calculated for depreciation is set aside to provide a fund with which to

replace the asset. However, this is not so. The amounts set aside for depreciation reduce the profit available for distribution and are reinvested in the business. At the end of the life of the asset these amounts are tied up in the general assets of the business and can be released by the sale of those assets to provide liquid funds (cash). These funds can be used to buy another similar asset, but need not be so used. They are available to be used in whatever way the directors of the company wish. They can be withdrawn from the business, they can be used to finance a new venture, they can be used to buy more machinery, or they can stay where they are as finance supporting the general assets of the business. It is unlikely that they will be used to buy exactly the same type of machine, since as technology is improved more sophisticated machines replace the old ones which are being retired. Depreciation is not a saving scheme to provide funds for replacement, unless of course it is linked to a 'sinking fund' whereby cash is set aside and invested outside the company to mature at the end of the life of the asset. The annual investment of an amount of cash, equal to the provision for depreciation, outside the business is a separate operation, and is not part of accounting for depreciation as such. Very few managers now use this sinking fund technique, since they take the view that the best use of the depreciation amount is to reinvest it in their own company and avoid an outflow of cash.

Example

Jack Spratt starts up in the demolition business and uses all his funds to buy a bulldozer for £50,000. He expects the machine to last for four years before it is worn out. Each year he receives £80,000 for work he has done and pays out £60,000 for the cost of the work. Thus his cash book will show a balance of £20,000 at the end of his first year trading.

An accountant advises him that he has not made a profit of £20,000, and warns him that he must spread the cost of the bulldozer over the years of its useful life by charging £12,500 against profit as depreciation each year. His real profit is £7,500 and this is the amount he can draw out of the business that year. The depreciation is calculated as £50,000 ÷ 4 years of work, with no scrap value at the end.

Opening Balance Sheet of Jack Spratt		Profit and Loss Account	
	£		£
Assets - Cash	50 000	Sales	80 000
Capital	50 000	Costs	60 000
		Cash surplus	20 000
Balance Sheet of Jack Spratt at end of Year 1		Depreciation	12 500
		Profit	£7 500
	£		
Assets – Bulldozer at cost	50 000		
less depreciation	12 500		
	37 500		
Cash (20 000 – 7 500)	12 500		
	£50 000		
Capital	£50 000		

At the end of four years his balance sheet would appear as follows:

Balance Sheet of Jack Spratt

	£
Assets – Bulldozer	50 000
less depreciation	50 000
	Nil
Cash (12 500 × 4)	50 000
	£50 000
Capital	£50 000

Thus Jack Spratt is back in the same position as at the start of the life of the asset, with a capital of £50,000 represented by cash. The bulldozer is shown at no value, and this is a true statement of the situation. If he had failed to provide for depreciation he would have shown a profit of £20,000 each year, and if he had drawn that amount each year capital would have been depleted, and would have been completely consumed by the end of year 4. As it is, he now has funds in liquid form again, and it is for him to decide what he wishes to do with them. He may wish to buy another bulldozer, he may retire and buy a country cottage, or he may decide to invest his funds in Stock Exchange securities and live off the income from them. Unfortunately, in a period of inflation, depreciation puts back out of profits only the money amount of the original investment used up, and this may not be sufficient to buy the same amount of goods and services as the original funds could buy. In a more sophisticated example the £50,000 of cash in the balance sheet of year 4 would instead be held in the form of general assets such as stock or debtors.

DEPRECIATION: A JUDGEMENTAL APPROACH

Depreciation is a matter of estimate and the accountant must use judgement when calculating the useful economic life of an asset, the residual value and indeed the true cost of the asset. It may be necessary to consult specialists such as engineers who can advise on the working life of a machine, or economists who review the market and estimate the likely effect of obsolescence on the useful economic life of the machine. Estimates are often wrong, so it is essential to review the remaining working life of an asset and its likely scrap value at frequent intervals in order to adjust the depreciation charge to a realistic amount.

THE METHODS USED

The methods used to account for depreciation are arbitrary and reflect the uncertainty in the estimates made by accountants and their colleagues. The economic life of a machine and its eventual scrap value are by no means certain when the machine is purchased. FRS 15 does not recommend any one method as being better than others. It is the responsibility of the directors to select a method which is most appropriate to the asset concerned, and which allocates depreciation as fairly as possible to the periods which benefit from its use. In practice managers select a depreciation policy for groups of similar assets and this is applied by using the same method for all assets in that group.

The Straight Line Method

The cost of an asset less its scrap value is divided by the years of its useful life to compute the charge per annum. Thus this method gives an equal charge per annum over the assumed life of the asset. It is simple to compute, and spreads the cost in a fair way over the years of the life of the asset. The obsolescence factor can be built into the estimate of the useful life in the formula.

The formula for this method is:

$$\frac{\text{Cost} - \text{Scrap}}{\text{Forecast economic life}} = \text{charge for the year}$$

However, this method does not take into account use, since the same charge is made to the profit and loss account each year although the asset may not work as hard in one year as in another. Some accountants argue that even though a machine does not work it is still losing value, and that this loss is the cost of holding the asset for the year even though it is not used. Others take the view that if there is no revenue for the use of an asset during the year then the cost of holding the asset has not been matched with the revenue produced by the asset, and that it is wrong to have the same charge each year, since it is unlikely that the asset will depreciate evenly over the years of its life. They further argue that the cost of repairs for a machine is likely to be heavier in the later years of its life, while its performance will be least effective at this time, and therefore a lighter depreciation charge is needed to compensate for this situation.

In spite of this argument the straight line method remains the most widely used method of depreciation in the UK.

As a matter of policy, depreciation may be charged pro rata to time in the year when an asset is acquired, i.e. six months' use merits half the annual charge. It is usual not to charge depreciation in the year of disposal for plant sold before the end of its expected working life.

In the circumstances of the example below, a machine costing £20,000 with a scrap value of £5,240 and an estimated working life of six years would be depreciated at £2,460 per year.

$$\frac{£20,000 - £5,240}{6} = £2,460$$

The Reducing Balance Method

This method writes off a constant proportion of a continually reducing balance each year and has the merit of making a high charge in the early years of the asset's life and a low one later, when repair bills may be heavy. It is argued in favour of this method that this will provide a uniform expense throughout the life of the asset. Also, if the obsolescence factor of the asset is high then more is written off in the early years, so that a smaller amount is left in the later years to form a sudden loss if the asset should prove worthless before the end of its estimated life. Some accountants, however, argue that it is not right to charge a different amount of depreciation for the use of the same machine in successive years, and that the fact that repair bills are high in the later years only reflects the facts which should influence what appears in the accounting statements.

This method is nevertheless widely used, but the percentage to be written off the reducing balance each year is often decided arbitrarily as a matter of accounting policy. Those who wish to be more scientific of the rate can use the formula.

$$R = \left(1 - \sqrt[N]{\frac{S}{C}}\right) \times 100\%$$

where R = the rate, S = the scrap value, C = the cost, and N = the number of years. This formula cannot be applied if there is no known scrap value, since a residual amount is required. It also works only for individual assets, but usually a predetermined rate is applied to all fixed assets in a set category.

Example

A machine costing £20,000 is deemed to have a six-year life and a scrap value of £5,240 at the end of its working life. By application of the formula a rate is found which can be applied to the reducing balance:

$$R = \left(1 - \sqrt[N]{\frac{S}{C}}\right) \times 100\% = \left(1 - \sqrt[6]{\frac{5240}{20000}}\right) \times 100\%$$

$$= \left(1 - \sqrt[6]{0.262}\right) \times 100\%$$

$$= (1 - 0.8) \times 100\%$$

$$= 20\%$$

The depreciation computation is as follows:

Cost	20 000
Depreciation year 1 (20% × £20 000)	4 000
Written down value	16 000
Depreciation year 2 (20% × £16 000)	3 200
Written down value	12 800
Depreciation year 3 (20% × £12 800)	2 560
Written down value	10 240
Depreciation year 4 (20% × £10 240)	2 048
Written down value	8 192
Depreciation year 5 (20% × £8 192)	1 638
Written down value	6 554
Depreciation year 6 (20% × £6 554)	1 310
Written down value when sold	£5 244

The difference of £4 is due to rounding in the calculation.

If the machine makes 4,000 articles each year, is it fair to charge for depreciation £1 to the cost of each article made by the machine in year 1, and only 33 pence to each of 4,000 articles made in year 6? The difference represents no cost saving or efficiency, but is a result of the method of depreciation selected. Unless the situation is suitable to this method, the calculation may give a rate which distorts the cost and profit shown. For example, a machine costing £20,000, with a four-year life and a scrap value of £512, produces a rate of 60 per cent, which, when applied, writes off £12,000 as depreciation in the first year.

The Revaluation Method

This method takes the view that the charge for depreciation, or the cost of holding the asset during the year, is the amount by which the asset has fallen in value during the year. Thus the asset is revalued at the end of each year and the amount of depreciation is computed. This method is advantageous where the amount of deterioration of the asset is uncertain, because objective valuation can be used to provide the amount. Items such as contractors' plant, loose tools, livestock, etc. are all examples of assets which can be depreciated in this way. However, much depends upon the efficiency of the valuer, since bias can intrude into the valuation process. If this method is to be used correctly the same valuer should be employed each year. Arguments against this method are that valuation takes time, is expensive, and is after all only an estimate. It is also difficult to separate the increase in the value of an asset caused by inflation from the decrease in the value of an asset caused by wear and tear. In certain cases special conditions could result in a negative charge for depreciation. This is the only method in which depreciation noted by the economist equals the amount provided by the accountant.

The Production Unit Method

This method attempts to relate depreciation to the use of the asset. The cost of the asset net of the scrap value is divided by the number of units the asset is expected to produce during its useful life. Thus a rate is computed which can be applied each year to the number of units actually produced to calculate the depreciation charge. The production unit method can be operated successfully if all units produced by the asset are the same and have the same work value. It is sometimes used to depreciate the cost of excavating a mine where one can forecast the amount of ore to be produced before the mine is worked out, or a press which should perform a certain number of operations before it is worn out. However, the depreciation charge is made only when the machine is used, so obsolescence during an idle period cannot be accounted for. Attempts are sometimes made to build an obsolescence factor into the calculation of the units in the life of the asset, but this amount is often an estimate of doubtful validity. The formula for this method is:

$$\frac{\text{Cost} - \text{Scrap}}{\text{Expected units}} = \text{Unit rate}$$

e.g. $$\frac{£20,000 - £5,240}{60,000 \text{ units}} = £0.246 \text{ per unit}$$

If production equals 10,000 units in a year, the provision for depreciation will be £2,460.

The Production Hour Method

This is a variation of the production unit method; it provides a rate per hour for depreciation rather than a rate per unit produced. To compute the rate to be used, the cost of the asset less the scrap value is divided by the working hours in the life of the asset. The advantage of this method is that it can be applied to a machine which produces different items and takes different amounts of time to produce them. A machine such as a lathe can be employed on many different operations, and since time is the common denominator, depreciation can be linked directly to the product cost. Once again depreciation is related to use, and there is the disadvantage that no charge is made if the asset is not used. The formula is

$$\frac{\text{Cost} - \text{Scrap}}{\text{Total Hours in the working life of the machines}} = \text{Rate}$$

e.g. $$\frac{£20,000 - £5,240}{30,000 \text{ hours}} = £0.492 \text{ per hour}$$

If the machine works for 5,000 hours in a certain year, the provision for depreciation that year will be £2,460.

THE ACCOUNTING ENTRIES

The accounting entries to record depreciation have a dual purpose. They show the charge to be made in the profit and loss account for the use of the asset during the year. In the balance sheet they show the cost of the asset less the cumulative amount of depreciation which has been provided against the original investment in the asset so far.

The method of depreciation must be disclosed as an accounting policy and the accounts must state the amount of depreciation provided that year and any additional charges for renewal. Provision for replacement of fixed assets other than by depreciation charge, or the reason why no provision has been made, must be noted.

An interesting position arises when assets are used after they have been fully depreciated. This means that their actual life is longer than estimated when they were first purchased, and therefore the depreciation charge in past profit and loss accounts has been too high, so profit has been understated. Accordingly a regular review of the future life of an asset should be undertaken.

A machine may be revalued part way through its life. Best accounting practice is to revalue the machine, debiting the asset and crediting a capital reserve account with the increase, and then to write off the new asset value over what is considered to be the remaining life of the asset. It is of course preferable to discover that the depreciation charge is too high well before the end of the life of the asset, so that the annual charge for the remaining years can be revised. Capital expenditure on an asset during its life, e.g. the cost of an extra fitment to extend the range of a machine, should be written off over the remaining life of that machine, unless the fitment can be transferred to another machine and thus has a finite working life of its own.

Premature Retirement: The Disposal Account

Where assets are retired prematurely, i.e. their actual life is shorter than estimated, there may be a loss, since they may not be written down to the realizable value at the time of their retirement. In this case past depreciation has been too small and thus past profits have been overstated. For these reasons some accountants argue that the loss on disposal should be written off at once, although they can see that it is unfair to charge any of this loss to a particular product or department of the business. In this situation, however, the accountant often meets pressure from management to spread the burden of the sudden loss over more than one accounting period. Such pressure must be resisted, and can be avoided by a frequent review of the remaining life of the asset.

Example: Depreciation in the ledger accounts

A company acquires a machine for £2,100 and decides to depreciate it over a five-year life. The company assumes that the scrap value at the end of five years will be £100.

$$\frac{\text{Cost} - \text{Scrap}}{\text{Life}} = \frac{£2\,100 - £100}{5} = £400 \text{ p.a. as depreciation}$$

The machine is sold half way through its fourth year of life for £300 cash.

Dr	Machine Account		Cr
	£		£
Year 1: Cash paid for asset	2 100	Year 4: Transfer to disposal account	2 100

Dr	Cash Book		Cr
	£		£
		Year 1: Asset bought	2100
Year 4: Asset sold	300		

Dr	Profit and Loss Account		Cr
	£		
Year 1: Depreciation	400		
Year 2: Depreciation	400		
Year 3: Depreciation	400		
Year 4: Loss on Disposal	600		

Dr	Depreciation Provision Account		Cr
	£		£
		Year 1: Charge to profit and loss account	400
		Year 2: Charge to profit and loss account	400
Year 4: Transfer to disposal account	£1 200	Year 3: Charge to profit and loss account	400
	£1 200		£1 200

Dr	Disposal Account		Cr
	£		£
Year 4: Cost of machine	2 100	Year 4: Depreciation to date	1 200
		Cash from sale of asset	300
		Loss to profit and loss account	600
	£2 100		£2 100

Steps in the accounting procedure are (follow them through the ledger accounts):

1. Record the acquisition of an asset, a machine, for cash, as the reduction of another asset.

2. Record the depreciation as a cost in the income statement each year and show the year end position, i.e. cost less depreciation to date gives the unexpired capital cost at the end of year 3 before the sale. (£2,100 − £1,200)

3. Record the disposal of the asset for cash at the end of year 4 and the transfer of any profit or loss on the deal to the income statement for that year. Use a disposal account for these entries.

Note: Under the principle of duality every debit must have a credit.

Excerpt from the balance sheet as at end of year 3 before sale of the machine:

Fixed assets	Cost	Depreciation	Net
	£	£	£
Plant and machinery	2 100	1 200	900

In the last example the balance sheet at the end of year 3 showed as a net figure the written-down value at that time. When the asset was sold the balances for this asset in the machinery account and the depreciation account were transferred to the disposal account, thus ensuring that they no longer appeared in the balances of those two accounts shown in the balance sheet after the sale of the machine. The term used for these entries is 'writing off' to the disposal account. The cash received from the sale of the asset was set against the written-down value of the asset in the disposal account, to reveal whether a profit or a loss had been made on the sale. A loss at this point means that depreciation to date set off against profits in previous years has not been sufficient to keep pace with the declining value of the asset, and as such shows that past profit has been overstated. The loss is transferred at once to the debit side of the profit and loss account so that it is set off against profits in the year of its discovery. If the price received for the asset had exceeded the written-down value, then a profit on the sale would have been made. This profit would have appeared as a debit balance in the disposal account, and would have been credited to the profit and loss account.

FRS 15 states that where the cost of an asset is not likely to be recouped from revenue generated by that asset, the book value of the asset must be reduced accordingly as soon as possible.

Extension of Useful Life: The Revaluation Account

Suppose that the machine in the example above had instead worked on until the end of its expected life, and had then been found to have several more years of useful working life left in it. The management at that time estimate the extra life to be three years, and the value of the machine at the beginning of those three years to be £700. The eventual scrap value is still £100. The accounting entries to record these circumstances are as follows:

1. The balances of the machinery account and the depreciation account are closed off to a revaluation account. This means that the original cost and depreciation to date are summarized in this account as the written-down value of £100 (£2,100 − £2,000).

2. The increase in the value of the asset, as disclosed by the valuer, is debited to the revaluation account and credited to a revaluation reserve account.

3. The revaluation account is closed off by a credit entry of £700, which is reflected as a debit to the machinery account – the new value of the asset.

4. Thus the new value of the machine is disclosed as £700 by this account, and depreciation can go ahead normally in the forthcoming years, at £200 p.a. ((£700 − £100) ÷ 3).

The ledger entries are:

Dr	Machinery Account		Cr
	£		£
Year 1: Purchase at original cost	2 100	Year 5: Transfer to revaluation account	2 100
Year 5: Revaluation of machine	700		

Dr	Depreciation Provision Account		Cr
	£		£
Year 5: Transfer balance to		Year 5: Accumulated depreciation	2 000
revaluation account	2 000	Year 6: Profit and loss account	200

Dr	Revaluation Account		Cr
	£		£
Year 5: Original cost	2 100	Year 5: Depreciation to date	2 000
Increase in value transferred		New value recorded in	
to reserve	600	machine account	700
	£2 700		£2 700

Dr	Revaluation Reserve Account		Cr
	£		£
		Year 6: Revaluation of machine	600

Generally Accepted Accounting Practice for Depreciation

The major rules are as follows:

(a) A range of depreciation methods is available to the accountant, who must select the method which is most appropriate to the assets used in the business. The selected method should also allocate depreciation as fairly as possible to periods expected to benefit from the use of the asset, and reflect the pattern in which the asset's economic benefits are consumed.

(b) There is no validity in the argument that if the current market value of an asset is greater than its net book value it is incorrect to charge depreciation. In such cases the asset should be revalued and the new value less residual amount allocated to the remaining years of the asset's life.

(c) The depreciation charge in the profit and loss account should be based on the carrying value of the asset in the balance sheet, whether historical cost accounting or revaluation accounting is used. It is wrong to charge historical-cost-based depreciation against profit and to show the asset at a revalued amount in the balance sheet.

(d) The whole of the depreciation charge should be passed through the profit and loss account; it is wrong to set any part of the depreciation charge against a reserve account.

(e) Identical asset lives should be used for the calculation on an historical cost basis and on a current cost basis. It is wrong to depreciate an asset over, say, a four-year life for historical cost purposes, and to use a different life period when accounting on a different basis. The useful economic life of the asset is the same whichever accounting base is used.

(f) It is permissible to change from one method of depreciation to another only if the new method will give a fairer presentation of the results and of the financial position. The standard states that such a situation is not considered to be a change of accounting policy, but the effect of the change, if material, should be disclosed in the year of change together with the reason for the change. The book value of the asset at the date of the change of method should be written off over the remaining useful economic life under the new method.

(g) When an asset is revalued, the depreciation charge should be based on the revalued amount less residual value and the remaining useful economic life at the date of the revaluation. In the year of revaluation a note should disclose the effect of the revaluation on the depreciation charge, plus the basis on which the revaluation has been calculated.

(h) If it is considered that there has been a permanent diminution in the value of an asset the net book value should be written down immediately through the profit and loss account. The new value should be systematically depreciated over the remaining useful economic life. If later the reasons for making such a provision cease to apply, the provision should be written back if it is no longer needed.

(i) The useful economic life of a tangible fixed asset should be reviewed at the end of each accounting period. If the residual value is a material amount, it too should be reviewed each year. The carrying value of the asset, net of the residual amount, should be depreciated over the remaining economic life.

(j) Capital expenditure spent on an asset part way through its life should be depreciated over the remaining years of that life. Some tangible fixed assets comprise several component parts with different lives, and these parts should be depreciated separately.

(k) Freehold land is not normally depreciated unless it suffers a fall in value, e.g. as a result of planning blight or the extraction of minerals. Buildings, however, are considered to be no different from other fixed assets and should be depreciated over their useful economic lives, even though that life may be in excess of 100 years.

(l) When a tangible fixed asset is revalued, the revaluation surplus is transferred to a revaluation reserve. If subsequently the asset is sold for less than its net book value, the consequent loss can be set against the revaluation surplus. Any excess of loss over that surplus is written off to the profit and loss account.

Task 6.3

Apply the rules of best accounting practice to calculate the depreciation to be charged each year for the tangible fixed asset whose life is chronicled below:

A company purchased a complex item of plant on 1 January 2002. The plant was expected to have a life of eight years. It cost £850,000, and the managers expected to sell it on 31 December 2009 for £50,000. The following events have been arranged to take place every two years in the life of this asset.

(a) On 1 January 2004 an extension to the machine was purchased for £90,000. The life and residual value of the machine was not affected by this purchase.

(b) On 1 January 2006 the life of the machine was reviewed and it was expected to continue to operate until 31 December 2013, but with no scrap value.

(c) On 1 January 2008 the machine underwent a major overhaul costing £30,000. Life expectancy of the machine remained the same with no scrap value but the machine was revalued at £450,000.

(d) On 1 January 2010 the machine was considered to be obsolete and was sold for £200,000.

Solution

			£	
1 January 2002	Cost		850 000	
Depreciation P/L	2002	–	100 000	(850 – 50 ÷ 8 years = 100)
			750 000	
Depreciation P/L	2003	–	100 000	
			650 000	
1 January 2004	Purchase	+	90 000	(Capitalize expenditure)
			740 000	
Depreciation P/L	2004	–	115 000	(740 – 50 ÷ 6 years = 115)
			625 000	
Depreciation P/L	2005	–	115 000	
			510 000	
Depreciation P/L	2006	–	63 750	(510 – Nil ÷ 8 years = 63.75)
			446 250	
Depreciation P/L	2007	–	63 750	
			382 500	
1 January 2008 Revaluation reserve *		+	67 500	(Value increase to reserve)
1 January 2008 New Value			450 000	
Depreciation P/L	2008	–	75 000	(450 – Nil ÷ 6 years = 7.5)
			375 000	
Depreciation P/L	2009	–	75 000	
Written down value at point of sale			300 000	
1 January Sold for cash		–	200 000	
Deficit			100 000	
Transfer from reserves *			67 500	
Loss to P/L	2010	–	£32 500	

Note that the overhaul in 2008 is treated as a maintenance cost charged to profit and loss. It is not capital expenditure.

DEPRECIATION AND TAXATION

If depreciation was a tax-allowable expense it might be possible to affect the amount of tax payable by a judicious choice of depreciation method. For this reason, and to bring consistency to the tax computation, depreciation is added back to profit for purposes of taxation, and 'capital allowances' are deducted. Capital allowances are the tax allowances permitted by the tax authorities to account for the use of fixed assets during the tax year. They are calculated in a manner similar to the reducing balance method, using 25 per cent as the annual rate, for most plant and vehicles. Buildings are normally written down at 4 per cent and some favoured classes of asset can be written off to tax at 100 per cent in the first year of their life.

Example

A company purchases a machine for £80,000 in year 1. Corporation tax is calculated at 31 per cent of taxable profit, so for every £100 of allowance the tax paid will be reduced by £31. Corporation tax is normally paid nine months after the end of the accounting year. The machine is sold for £20,000 during the fourth year of its life.

The computation would be as follows:

	£		£
Cost	80 000		
Tax allowance year 1 – (25%)	20 000	× 0.31 = tax saved	6 200
Tax written down value	60 000		
Tax allowance year 2 – (25%)	15 000	× 0.31 = tax saved	4 650
Tax written down value	45 000		
Tax allowance year 3 – (25%)	11 250	× 0.31 = tax saved	3 487
Tax written down value	33 750		
Machine sold during year 4	20 000		
Balancing allowance	13 750	× 0.31 = tax saved	4 262

If the machine was sold in year 4 for more than its written-down value, say £38,000, a balancing charge of (£38,000 – £33,750) £4,250 would increase corporation tax paid by £1,317 on profit of year 4.

CONCLUSION

Tangible fixed assets earn the profits of the business in the long run. It therefore follows that their measurement is important to determine how much to capitalize. Their valuation is important to inform shareholders of the current value tied up in those assets and to charge an appropriate amount against profit each year as depreciation to represent the amount of that value which has been used up. Depreciation also sets aside out of profits an amount to replace the funds tied up in fixed assets which have been used up during an accounting period.

Depreciation is a matter of estimate to ascertain the life and residual value of the asset. Several depreciation methods are available, but it is the task of the accountant to select an accounting policy which reflects the pattern in which economic benefits of the asset are consumed.

Discussion Topics

Thirty-minute essay questions:

1. 'Depreciation writes down the plant to its true value' – managing director.
   'Depreciation allocates the cost of plant to the years in which it is used' – accountant.
   'Depreciation maintains the capital of the business' – economist.
   Who is right?

2. Albert Jones is in business as a builder. He started business with equipment which cost £55,800 and which he thinks will last five years before it is worn out. He has consulted an accountant, who suggests that he should depreciate his plant. What will be the result if he ignores this advice?

3. Value to the business is the lower of replacement cost and recoverable amount. Recoverable amount is the higher of value in use and net realizable value. Explain.

SEMINAR EXERCISES

6.1. Your new client is a **Miss Ira Maiden** who runs Heavy Metal Limited, a business producing ball bearings and window frames. She says: 'My last accountant kept on trying to tell me that we must charge depreciation in our accounts. I don't really understand what depreciation is for and what items it applies to. If my company buys a machine for £20,000 and pays for it immediately, with money we've saved up, why on earth don't we show that in the profit and loss account rather than fiddling about over the next five years? Is this something to do with putting money aside to buy a new machine?

'As the boss I don't really need to know all the possible methods of calculating depreciation in detail, but I would like to know what is so magic about depreciating over five years and also what sort of details have to be disclosed in the annual financial statements.'

Required:

In preparation for a meeting with Miss Ira Maiden, to be held next week, you are required to draft brief notes which answer the questions raised by the above statement.

6.2. Write up ledger accounts to record the transactions in Task 6.3 above.

CHAPTER 7

The Accounting Treatment of Current Assets

THE AIMS OF THIS CHAPTER

To enable students to

- Understand the importance of stock valuation for the measurement of income

- Calculate the cost and net realizable value of stock

- Differentiate between alternative methods of stock valuation

- Account for bad and doubtful debts

The rules for the accounting treatment of stock covered in this chapter reflect the terms of SSAP 9: Stocks and Work in Progress.

THE IMPORTANCE OF CURRENT ASSETS

The current assets which usually appear in a balance sheet are stocks, debtors, short-term investments and cash. They are disclosed in reverse order of liquidity, that is with stocks first because they are the most difficult to turn into cash, and cash itself last. All current assets are liquid assets because within the term of an accounting year they will be exchanged for cash as the working capital cycle takes its course. Cash is spent to buy stocks of raw material, which after storage may be used to make products, which when sold become debtors, and return to cash when the customers pay. Without stocks to draw on, the manufacturing process would be impaired, and without trade credit to offer to debtors, the selling activity would be handicapped. Short-term investments disclose the amount of uncommitted liquid funds at the disposal of the business which have been invested to earn some form of income until they are required in the business.

STOCKS

Task 7.1

How many different forms of stock can you identify?

Solution

(a) Raw materials and components waiting to be used in production;

(b) work in progress – products and services at an intermediate stage of completion, e.g. semi-finished items in the factory;

(c) finished goods waiting to be sold;

(d) consumable stores – items to be used up in the manufacturing process but not built into a product, e.g. fuel oil;

(e) retail stock – goods purchased by a shop and not yet sold to customers.

These categories of stock are covered by SSAP 9.

The accounting treatment accorded to stocks is significant, since it will affect both income measurement and the position statement. Opening stock plus purchases less closing stock equals the cost of goods sold, and this figure, when subtracted from sales, discloses the gross profit. Thus the basis used to find the cost of stocks will affect both the profit and the stock figure in the balance sheet.

The measurement of income implies that costs will be matched with related revenues, and that stocks of unused items will be carried forward to a later period when their sale produces revenue to offset their consumption. The principle of matching, however, must be subordinated to the concept of conservatism in so far as that, if there is no reasonable expectation that revenue in the future will be sufficient to cover the costs incurred and a loss is likely to be made, it is prudent to provide for that loss as soon as possible. For this reason stocks and work in progress are shown in the accounting statements as at the lower of cost or net realizable value. If they are now worth less than their original cost the loss is recognized, but if they are worth more than their cost no element of profit is taken until it is realized when a sale is made. This is the basic rule of stock valuation.

The standard states that the comparison of cost and net realizable value should be made for each item of stock, or at least for groups of similar items. If the total net realizable value is set against the total cost, a situation could arise where foreseeable losses are set off against unrealized profits.

What is Cost?

The definition of 'cost' for stock purposes covers all expenditure incurred in the normal course of business to bring the product or service to its present location and condition. This includes

(a)   the purchase price,

(b)   any import duties payable, and

(c)   transport and handling costs,

(d)   less trade discounts negotiated with a supplier.

The cost attributed to work in progress is, however, a less straightforward matter. It is accepted that the cost of work-in-progress stocks should include the prime cost (direct labour and material) expended on them to date. However, not all accountants agree with SSAP 9, which stipulates that a share of normal production overhead expenses should be added to prime cost when the value of stocks of work in progress or of finished goods is computed, as forming part of the cost of converting materials to their present condition. Overhead costs such as rent, salaries, depreciation and storage are considered by some accountants to accrue over time, i.e. they are incurred on an annual basis, and as such should be matched with the revenue of the year rather than carried forward in the cost of stock to be matched with the revenue arising when the stock is eventually sold. SSAP 9 excludes abnormal conversion costs and the costs of unused production capacity from the calculation, since they should be written off against profit in the year when they are incurred. Selling and administrative overheads are not normally included in the cost of stock, but the costs of design, marketing and selling can be included if a firm sales contract has been signed. Companies which fail to follow the rules of SSAP 9 run the risk of their auditors qualifying the accounts.

What is Net Realizable Value?

Net realizable value is defined as the actual or estimated selling price of the stock net of any trade discount, from which is deducted any cost which must be incurred to put the stock into a saleable condition, and all costs to be incurred in marketing, selling and distribution of the stock. Those who argue that it is not prudent to carry forward overhead expenses from one year to another are answered by the point that an element of prudence can best be injected into the situation through the calculation of net realizable value.

Events occurring between the balance sheet date and the date of finalization of the accounts must be considered when the net realizable value is determined. If prices fall after the year end, then current stocks may not be sold at more than their cost in the future. In a famous case concerning a publishing company, the stocks of unsold magazines were carried forward at cost over a period of several years, until reporting accountants decided that a net realizable value based on their sale as scrap paper was more appropriate, and the subsequent stock write-down had a devastating impact on profits that year. Net realizable value is likely to fall below cost when

(a) selling prices fall,

(b) stocks deteriorate physically,

(c) products requiring those stocks become obsolete,

(d) a product is sold as a 'loss leader', or

(e) mistakes in production or purchasing have been made.

The length of time that stocks spend in the store before being used or sold is called the stock turnover period. A long turnover period creates an increased risk of obsolescence, deterioration or adverse price movements, and must therefore be considered when assessing the net realizable value.

   The rule that stock should be valued at the lower of cost or net realizable value has been criticized by some accountants on the grounds of inconsistency. A conservative approach to profit measurement can, it is argued, lead to an understatement of profit in one year, and an overstatement in the next year. If you recognize a decrease in value which occurs before sale, but ignore an increase in value before sale, then the full amount of the increase is taken as profit in the year of realization. Academic accountants ask why, if net realizable value is better than cost when it is *less than* cost, it is not preferred for the same reasons of objectivity, certainty, verifiability, etc. when it *exceeds* cost. No academic answer has been made to this question, but accountants continue to use the lower of cost or net realizable value rule because they consider that the practical advantages of conservatism outweigh the disadvantages. The same argument applies to the provision for doubtful debts.

How the Stock Valuation Rule is Applied

Chiltern Chairs plc is a furniture company, importing timber from Brazil to manufacture a range of dining room chairs. For Model A there are 300 completed chairs in stock at the year end. Cost information discloses that 3 kilos of timber are used in each chair, which is purchased from a foreign supplier for £7 per kilo. Six thousand kilos have been purchased and used this year, incurring transport costs of £2,300, port dues of £1,200, and import duties of £1,000. Direct manufacturing costs are two and a half hours of labour time at £8 per hour, and one and a half hours of machine time at £6 per hour.

   For Model A overhead costs for the year are:

	£
Production	16 800
Design	3 000
Transport	4 000
Selling	18 000
Administration	9 000

Production overheads includes an abnormal cost of spoilt raw material of £1,800. Model A chairs sell at £120 each, with a trade discount of 20 per cent to retailers. Packaging costs are £5 each unit.

Task 7.2

Calculate the amount at which the stock of Model A chairs should be included in the year-end accounts of Chiltern Chairs plc.

Solution

6,000 kilos of timber is purchased and used. At 3 kilos per chair this means production of 2,000 Model A chairs.

	£
Cost per chair	
Materials, 3 kilos at £7 per kilo	21.00
Transport, port and import charges	
[(£2,300 + £1,200 + £1,000) ÷ 6,000 kilos = £0.75 per kilo]	
3 kilos at £0.75 per kilo	2.25
	23.25
Labour $2^{1}/_{2}$ hours × £8 per hour	20.00
Machine time $1^{1}/_{2}$ hours × £6 per hour	9.00
Direct cost of manufacture	52.25
Production overhead	
[(£16,800 − £1,800 abnormal cost) ÷ 2,000 chairs produced	7.50
	£59.75
Net realizable value per chair	
Selling price	120.00
Less discount at 20 per cent	24.00
	96.00
Less packaging costs	5.00
	91.00
Indirect overhead-design/selling/transport/admin.	
(£3,000 + £18,000 + £4,000 + £9,000) ÷ 2,000 chairs	17.00
	£74.00

Cost is lower than NRV, so the amount used in the accounts would be
300 × £59.75 = £17,925

Note:

(a) If market forces are likely to force a price cut on the company, the figure of £120 which starts the NRV calculation may need to be reduced, and NRV could fall below cost. It is at this stage that an element of prudence affects the calculation.

(b) Stocks of 300 chairs on production of 2,000 per annum show a ratio of stock to production of

$$\frac{300}{2,000} \times \frac{50 \text{ weeks}}{1} = 7^{1}/_{2} \text{ weeks production}$$

This is based on a working year of 52 weeks less 2 weeks' holiday when the factory is closed down.

THE FLOW OF COSTS

The activities of a trader are to buy, store and sell, whereas a manufacturer buys raw materials, combines them with machinery and labour and converts them into manufactured goods which are then sold. Therefore costs flowing through a trading organization will follow a different pattern from the costs flowing through a manufacturing business. The flow of costs can be seen from the interrelationship of the ledger accounts used to record, accumulate and summarize the figures. Assumptions made about the flow of costs will have an impact on the profit figure eventually computed.

There is some argument as to whether factory overheads should be charged in full to the accounting period in which they are incurred, or whether part of them should be allocated to the stock of work in progress and carried forward in the cost of that stock to the next accounting period, when the work in progress is completed and perhaps sold. Some accountants see factory overheads as period costs and wish to relate them to time, since they concern such items as rent, insurance and factory managers' salary all for the year. Other accountants prefer to match the full cost of goods sold with the revenue from their sale. They argue that the overhead expenses of one period must be carried forward in the cost of work in progress to set the full cost of these items against the revenue from their eventual sale, if a true profit is to be shown. They believe that overhead costs are incurred to bring the work-in-progress stock to its present condition and location.

This argument has never been settled, and different firms adopt different practices. In a leading case some years ago the Inland Revenue authorities took the Duple Motor Body Company Ltd to the House of Lords in an attempt to define whether overhead expenses should be written off or carried forward. The answer they got was that either system is acceptable so long as it is followed consistently. Thus the cost flow assumption as to the treatment of factory overhead expenses can have an impact on the profit calculation.

STOCK VALUATION METHODS: PROFIT AND POSITION

The four main methods of valuing stocks of raw materials for inclusion in the balance sheet and profit and loss account are:

(a)   the first in first out method (FIFO);

(b)   the last in first out method (LIFO);

(c)   the weighted average method (AVCO);

(d)   the standard cost method.

The assumption as to the flow of raw materials through the stores will have an effect on the amounts charged from the stores into the manufacturing account for materials used, and also on the balance sheet, since it affects the cost of closing stocks. An assumption must be made as to the sequence in which stocks are used up, because batches of material or components purchased at different prices cannot normally be segregated in the stores, e.g. sand bought at £10 a tonne is mixed with sand bought at £15 a tonne and the two batches cannot easily be identified when transferred to the production process. Liquids mixed in a tank cannot be segregated into different delivery batches bought at different prices.

The bases on which raw materials are valued, both for charging to the manu-facturing account and for inclusion in the balance sheet, may vary. Different methods will suit firms in different industries and situations, but it must be stressed that, once a firm has chosen to use one method, then it should act consistently and not change from one method to another without very good reason. Different methods of stock valuation can, as we shall see, cause a very different profit to be disclosed, and it is often tempting for a company with disappointing results to suggest a change of stock valuation method in order to show a better profit.

First in First Out

Some firms will assume a first in first out (FIFO) pattern, i.e. the first batches of raw materials to be bought and stored are the first to be transferred to the manufacturing processes and used up. It follows that those raw materials remaining at the end of the period under this assumption are from the most recently purchased batches. Materials used will be charged to production at cost and closing stocks will also be shown in the balance sheet at cost. If the price of raw materials fluctuates during the year so that early batches are bought at one price and later batches bought at a higher price, this assumption will ensure that the manufacturing account is charged with the lower-priced materials while the higher-priced batches are shown in the balance sheets as stocks. Thus the cost flow assumption will influence the profit figure and the balance sheet.

During a period of inflation the FIFO cost flow assumption shows stocks in the balance sheet at an accurate current cost, while charging raw materials to the manufacturing process at an outdated cost. Therefore it can be said that under this assumption if material prices rise profits are overstated, since the replacement cost of the raw materials used is not charged in measuring the profit.

Last In First Out

An alternative to FIFO is last in first out (LIFO), which assumes that the most recent batches bought and stored are the first to be used up. Thus, using LIFO, in a period of inflation the manufacturing process will be charged with materials at the later higher price, while the balance sheet will show stocks at a lower or historical cost.

The LIFO cost flow assumption will charge current cost to the manufacturing process and thus compute a truer profit, while the balance sheet figure for closing stocks will be shown at an outdated cost. If the volume of stock falls during a period under LIFO it might seem that these old stocks are used up, and outdated costs will be set against current revenues when profit is measured. There has been some pressure from accountants in the UK to persuade the Inland Revenue to accept accounts produced on a LIFO basis, since under the FIFO system, which is approved by the Inland Revenue, profits are overstated, and it can be argued that taxation is levied on a book profit caused by inflation rather than a manufacturing profit from transactions.

It is of course impossible to substantiate, with many raw materials, that those which have been in stock longest will be used first. If, for example, there is a large bin containing 10,000 bolts, or a pile of sand, or a vat of paint, there is no way of telling from which delivery batch the units used up in production have been drawn.

Weighted Average Cost

The AVCO valuation method calculates a weighted average based on the price of all deliveries received during the year, and values the closing stock on the basis of this weighted average. Materials charged to production on the basis of a weighted average will measure a profit figure between the extremes of FIFO and LIFO, and the balance sheet stock figure based on AVCO will similarly produce a compromise amount. The method suffers from two disadvantages. First, the weighted average must be recalculated for every fresh delivery, and second, the average produced by the calculation may not correspond with a price actually paid for materials during the year. A simple average calculated by totalling the unit price paid for all deliveries and then dividing by the number of deliveries received during the period is not used, because it fails to bring into the calculation the fact that one delivery may be for a large quantity and another delivery for only a small quantity. The weights used in the AVCO calculation are the quantities delivered at each price.

Other Methods

The base stock method of stock valuation assumes that the same quantity and value of stock is in store or process at the end of the year as at the beginning. Thus the cost of all material movements is written off to the manufacturing account each year. This method is now rarely used, since it requires conditions in which similar volumes are in process at the beginning and end of the year. This method is rejected by SSAP 9.

Standard costing values opening and closing stocks at a standard cost per unit computed in advance of the accounting period. Any difference between actual cost and standard is written off to the profit and loss account as a 'variance' from standard.

THE STANDARD, THE LAW AND THE TAXATION AUTHORITIES

SSAP 9 does not approve of LIFO, since it states that LIFO does not bear a reasonable relationship to actual cost, but it does not substantiate this view. However, an international accounting standard states that both the LIFO and base stock methods may be used, even though they are specifically rejected by SSAP 9. This international standard is otherwise in broad agreement with the UK standard. The situation has, however, been complicated by the Companies Act 1985 in the UK, which permits the use of FIFO, LIFO, AVCO or any other similar method and requires the directors to choose a method appropriate to the business.

The LIFO method is not acceptable to the taxation authorities in the UK, but it is widely used in the USA and accepted there for taxation purposes.

FIFO, LIFO AND AVCO compared

This example demonstrates the impact on profit of the various stock valuation bases. A trading company buys the following quantity of raw materials during the first six months of the year:

	Tonnes	Price (£)	Cost (£)
3 January	40	228	9 120
15 February	60	240	14 400
21 March	50	210	10 500
19 April	80	252	20 160
15 May	30	258	7 740
25 June	20	264	5 280
Total tonnes	280	Total Cost	£67 200

On 28 June the company sold 200 tonnes of material at £260 per tonne.
Under the FIFO assumption the 80 tonnes of stock remaining will comprise the most recent purchases:

			£
Purchased	25 June	20 tonnes at £264	5 280
	15 May	30 tonnes at £258	7 740
	19 April	30 tonnes at £252	7 560
		80	£20 580

Under the LIFO assumption the 80 tonnes of stock remaining will comprise the earliest purchases made in the period:

			£
Purchased	3 January	40 tonnes at £228	9 120
	15 February	40 tonnes at £240	9 600
		80	£18 720

In the trading account opening stock plus purchases less closing stock determines the cost of sales, which in its turn influences the profit. Under FIFO the closing stock will be £1,860 more than under LIFO (£20,580 – £18,720), so the cost of sales will be correspondingly less and the profit correspondingly more.

If stock had been carried forward at the beginning of the period in January it would have been assumed to form part of the closing stock in June under LIFO. In this way a batch of material can form part of the stock for several years under this system, and the balance sheet figure can become very outdated. If the stock level eventually falls below the amount brought forward at the beginning of the year, this outdated (cheap) stock appears to have been used up in the factory, and will measure a greatly overstated profit when the products are sold at current post-inflation prices. By the AVCO (average cost) method the 280 tonnes purchased are divided into the cost of £67,200 to give a weighted average of £240, and this figure is applied to the closing stock to calculate an amount of £19,200. The average calculation must be weighted for quantities purchased at different prices. In formula terms that is

$$\frac{\text{Aggregate of price} \times \text{weight}}{\text{Total weight (tonnes)}} = \frac{£67,200}{280} = £240$$

The profit on the transaction is measured at different amounts according to the method used:

	FIFO £	LIFO £	AVCO £
Purchases	67 200	67 200	67 200
Less closing stock	20 580	18 720	19 200
Cost of sales	46 620	48 480	48 000
Sales	52 000	52 000	52 000
Profit	£5 380	£3 520	£4 000

Note that FIFO shows the largest profit, which is more likely to be overstated during an inflationary period when historical costs lag behind current prices. The AVCO result is a compromise between the other two methods, and while it is true to say in criticism that the average used, £240, was the real price paid for only one batch and is thus not a realistic figure to use in accounts, the fact remains that this method, unlike LIFO, is acceptable to the Inland Revenue in the UK.

The Maximum/Minimum Reordering System

It is essential that a factory should not run out of material if disruption to production is to be avoided.

Accounting for movements of stock in stores, both receipts and issues, needs care and a measure of internal control. Many companies operate a bin card system whereby when stock is withdrawn from a bin the card (or computer record) is entered and a new running total calculated to show the quantity which remains in the bin. When the reorder point is reached, the buyers are automatically warned to order more stock. The reorder point is calculated with reference to the 'lead time'. The buying department will order materials and there may be a lead time of, say, three weeks before they are delivered, during which period the factory will still be using materials. There will also be a safety margin below which as a matter of policy stocks are not allowed to fall. The amount of the safety margin plus the quantity which will be used during the lead time sets the reorder point. The management accountant, together with the buyers, will have computed the economic order quantity as the optimum amount to be purchased so that the advantages and disadvantages of buying and holding large quantities are finely balanced. The economic order quantity plus the amount in store at the safety margin will determine the maximum amount of storage space required for each material or component stored.

Safety margin + lead time quantity = reorder point

Safety margin + economic order quantity = maximum stock

The operation of a 'just in time' system will reduce safety margins and lead times, but depends for success on trustworthy suppliers.

Example

A company uses 300 kilos of raw material per week, when working at normal capacity, but the usage can rise to 500 kilos in certain weeks when production is increased. The lead time between placing an order and taking delivery of the material is usually four weeks, but can be as long as six weeks. The management require a safety margin, in that stock should never fall below one week's usage.

Using the most conservative figures:

Safety stock = 500 kilos	500 kg
Lead time (6 weeks × 500 kg)	3 000 kg
Reorder point (ROP)	3 500 kg
When stocks fall to 3,500 kilos, a new order must be placed	
Assume economic order quantity is 10,000 kilos	
ROP	3 500 kg
Less minimum usage in lead time *	1 200 kg
Maximum likely stock level on delivery day	2 300 kg
Delivery of EOQ	10 000 kg
Maximum stock space required	12 300 kg

* Four weeks at 300 kilos per week

Stock Record Cards

A stock record card will be maintained for each material to record receipts and issues to production. The cost at which materials are issued to the factory will depend on whether a FIFO, LIFO or AVCO system is in operation.

In many businesses the stock records are maintained on computer. This means that at the touch of a button the present stocks can be shown on a visual display unit or by a printout. The computer program is written to use the FIFO, LIFO or AVCO system and will make the same calculations as shown below in the stock record example. The computer suffers from the same difficulty as handwritten records in that mistakes can occur in reading receipts and issues of stock so that the balance shown on the stock record may not be correct. An audit check made from time to time will disclose such discrepancies.

Example

Material XD 131 has the following receipts and issues:

Date	Invoice	Receipts	Requisition	Issues
1 January	800	1,000 at 50p		
2 January			B481	500
20 January	962	800 at 60p		
25 January			B508	500
1 February			B512	500
4 February	980	700 at 80p		
20 February			B521	500

Write up a stock record card for FIFO, LIFO and AVCO for January and February:

FIFO Stock Record Card, Material XD 131

Date	Receipts		£	Issues		£	Balance	£
	Invoice			Requisition				
1 January	800	1 000 at 50p	500				1 000 at 50p	500
2 January				B481	500 at 50p	250	500 at 50p	250
20 January	962	800 at 60p	480				500 at 50p ⎫	
25 January							800 at 60p ⎭	730
				B508	500 at 50p	250	800 at 60p	480
1 February				B512	500 at 60p	300	300 at 60p	180
							300 at 60p ⎫	
4 February	980	700 at 80p	560				700 at 80p ⎭	740
20 February				B521	300 at 60p	180		
					200 at 80p	160	500 at 80p	400
				Charge to		_____		Closing
				production		£1 140		stock

Lines across the issues and receipts columns help to show when each batch is used up.

LIFO Stock Record Card, Material XD 131

Date	Receipts Invoice		£	Issues Requisition		£	Balance	£
1 January	800	1 000 at 50p	500				1000 at 50p	500
2 January				B481	500 at 50p	250	500 at 50p	250
20 January	962	800 at 60p	480				500 at 50p ⎫ 800 at 60p ⎭	730
				B508	500 at 60p	300	500 at 50p ⎫ 300 at 60p ⎭	430
1 February				B512	300 at 60p	180		
					200 at 50p	100	300 at 50p	150
4 February	980	700 at 80p	560				300 at 50p ⎫ 700 at 80p ⎭	710
20 February				B521	500 at 80p	400	300 at 50p ⎫ 200 at 80p ⎭	310
				Charge to production		£1 230		Closing stock

Note the greater charge to production than under FIFO and that some material in stock on 1 January is assumed to be still there on 28 February.

AVCO Stock Record Card, Material XD 131

Date	Receipts Invoice		£	Issues Requisition		£	Balance	£
1 January	800	1 000 at 50p	500				1 000 at 50p	500
2 January				B481	500 at 50p	250	500 at 50p	250
20 January	962	800 at 60p	480				1 300 at 56p	728
25 January				B508	500 at 56p	280	800 at 56p	448
1 February				B512	500 at 56p	280	300 at 56p	168
4 February	980	700 at 80p	560				1 000 at 73p	730
20 February				B521	500 at 73p	365	500 at 73p	365
				Charge to production		£1 175		Closing stock

Note that a fresh weighted average is calculated after each receipt. Alternative methods of calculation may be used.

Workings

	£		£
500 at 50p	250	300 at 56p	168
800 at 60p	480	700 at 80p	560
1 300	730	1 000	728

$$\frac{£730}{1\,300} = \text{say } 56p \qquad \frac{£728}{1\,000} = \text{say } 73p$$

DEBTORS

The accounting treatment of debtors ensures that all balances owed to the company are recorded, and cancelled when payment is received. Difficulties arise if payment is not made and a bad debt occurs. In this case the debt must be written off to the profit and loss account as a cost via the bad debts account. The procedure is to credit the debtors' personal account and debit the bad debts account when the debt goes bad, and to credit the bad debts account and debit the profit and loss account with the total at the end of the year. The significance of a bad debt is shown by the following example.

A company sells goods to Mr A for £100. The mark-up on the goods is 25 per cent on cost, so the profit made is £20 (£80 × $^{25}/_{100}$). If Mr A fails to pay for the goods then four times the volume of goods sold to him must be sold to make a profit equal to the cost of the goods he has received. Thus it is important to ensure that goods are sold on credit terms only to customers who are likely to pay for them.

A further difficulty with bad debts concerns the matching principle. If debts go bad during the year when the goods are sold they are written off against profit in that year, but if a debt carried forward at the year end in the balance sheet is subsequently found to be bad, it will be written off against profit in the year after the sale was made. This distortion overstates profit in the first year, understates profit in the second year, and overvalues the asset debtors in the balance sheet between those two years. At the end of an accounting year the debtor balances must be carefully reviewed to identify 'doubtful' debts which may go bad in a subsequent period, so that a provision can be made out of profits for the first year, thus matching cost with revenue and calculating profit on a comprehensive basis. The provision will appear in the books as a credit balance (debit profit and loss account) and in the next year if any of the previous years debts are not collected they can be debited against it, and thus have no impact on profit measurement in the second year. Some companies adopt a routine policy for the calculation of the provision for doubtful debts, but it must be stressed that such provision requires the accountant to exercise judgement to recognize the loss as soon as it arises, and before it has been confirmed.

Those companies which use a formula for doubtful debt provision are not exercising judgement unless the percentage applied to debts or to credit sales is based on past experience and reviewed at frequent intervals. An accountant or credit controller should scrutinize all debtor balances, taking into account their age and what is known about the creditworthiness of the customer, when the provision is computed.

Examples

The accounting entries are as follows:

(A) Bad debt written off to the profit and loss account. In this example only one bad debt is experienced. In reality the bad debts account acts as a collecting point for bad debts before they are charged as one figure to the profit and loss account.
Kester Jon owes Jos Ltd £500, but is unable to pay. In the books of Jos Ltd:

Dr	Kester Jon		Cr		Dr	Bad Debts		Cr
	£		£			£		£
Sales	500	Balance written off to bad debts (a)	500		Kester Jon (a)	500	Bad debts for the year written off to profit and loss (b)	500
	500		500			500		500

Dr	Profit and Loss	Cr
	£	£
Bad debts (b)	500	

The ledger entries are:

(a) Write off the balance from Kester Jon's personal account in the debtors ledger, by transferring the amount to the bad debts account.

(b) At the year end charge the total of bad debts as a cost in the profit and loss account.

(B) Provision for doubtful debts which later go bad. Kester Jon owes Jos Ltd £500 at the year end, 31 December, and is unable to pay on 30 June of the next year. Jos Ltd provides for the bad debt at 31 December.

Dr	Kester Jon		Cr		Dr	Provision for Doubtful Debts		Cr
	£		£			£		£
31 Dec Sales	500	31 Dec Balance c/f	500		31 Dec Balance c/f	500	31 Dec Charge to profit and loss (a)	500
	500		500			500		500
1 Jan Balance b/d	500	30 June Bad debt written off to provision (b)	500		30 June Kester Jon (b)	500	1 Jan Balance b/d	500
	500		500			500		500

Note that the bad debt has not affected profit measurement in the second year, but the provision reduces profit in the first year.

The ledger entries are:

(a) Jos Ltd doubts whether Kester Jon can pay, so a provision is made (debit profit and loss, credit provision for doubtful debts).

(b) In the second year, when the debt is confirmed as bad, it is written off against the provision and not against the profit of year 2.

(C) Bad debt written off is later collected and must be written back. Suppose Kester Jon pays the £500 he owes on 31 March of the third year:

Dr	Cash		Cr	Dr	Kester Jon		Cr
	£		£		£		£
31 March				31 March			
Kester Jon (a)	500			Bad debt written		31 March	
				back (b)	500	Cash (a)	500

Dr	Bad Debts		Cr
	£		£
31 Dec		31 March	
Other bad debts	2 500	Kester Jon (b)	500
		31 Dec	
		Balance to profit	
		and loss	2 000
	2 500		2 500

The ledger entries are:

(a) Cash is received, and is credited to Kester Jon's personal account in the debtors ledger.

(b) The debt is reinstated, thereby reducing the effect on profits of other bad debts experienced in year 3.

(D) Overestimate of provision for doubtful debts. Jos Ltd provided £1,000 for doubtful debts last year, but only £500 of bad debts occur this year.

Dr	Provision for Doubtful Debts		Cr	Dr	Bad Debts Account		Cr
	£		£		£		£
31 Dec		1 Jan		31 Dec		31 Dec	
Bad debts		Opening		Bad debts of the		Bad debts	
written off (b)	500	balance (a)	1 000	year from personal		written off	
				accounts	500	to provision (b)	500
Balance to profit							
and loss							
account (c)	500						
	1 000		1 000				

Dr	Profit and Loss	Cr
£		£
	31 Dec	
	Doubtful debts	
	overprovided in	
	a previous year (c)	<u>500</u>

The ledger entries are:

(a) The opening balance on the provision account.

(b) Bad debts are written off against the provision, which is more than adequate to cover them.

(c) Part of the provision which is not required is credited to the profit and loss account.

The underutilized balance on the provision account is written back to the profit and loss account as soon as it is decided that it is not required. Profit last year was understated as the result of an excess of caution, but this is no reason why the position should not be corrected as soon as objective information is available. In practice the underutilized balance reduces the charge to the income statement for the provision next year.

Note that in these four examples every debit has a credit, and vice versa.

Debtors are shown in the balance sheet under current assets as the total of debtor balances in the personal ledger. The provision for doubtful debts is shown as a deduction from the debtors figure.

INVESTMENTS

Investments made by a company can be treated as either long-term or short-term investments. The purchase of shares in another company is often undertaken for strategic purposes, e.g. some commercial advantage gained by the possession of a share stake in a supplier of raw materials or chain of retail outlets. Investments of this nature are shown separately in the balance sheet, as part of the fixed assets, above the current assets. This indicates that the investment has been made for a long-term reason, and is not for resale or to act as a temporary repository of idle funds which cannot be gainfully employed in the business in the near future. Short-term investments such as deposits with local authorities or commercial banks, as well as investments in shares intended for resale within a year, are current assets.

The basic rule for accounting for long-term investments is to show them in the balance sheet at cost. Long-term investments can be revalued from time to time, but this is wise only if the change in value is permanent and not a short-term fluctuation. It is considered prudent to recognize a rise in the value of an investment only when it is realized. Although investments are shown at historical cost, their correct worth ought to be communicated to shareholders and others. For this reason the Companies Act 1985 requires that investments listed on a recognized stock exchange must be the subject of a note to the accounts disclosing the market value of the quoted investments. Short-term investments are subject to the lower of cost or net realizable value rule.

CONCLUSION

Current assets are the short-term assets which are soon to be turned into cash. The amount at which stock is recorded will affect the accuracy of the profit measured, and the assets disclosed in the balance sheet. Stocks are valued at the lower of cost or net realizable value, and there are close definitions of what should be included in these items.

The flow of costs through the business introduces the additional complication of a FIFO, LIFO or AVCO valuation, with the amount of profit dependent on the valuation basis used. This difficulty is compounded by the refusal of the Inland Revenue authorities to accept LIFO based accounts for the purpose of taxation, even though the LIFO system is recognized by the Companies Act 1985, and widely used in other countries.

Accounting for debtors mainly concerns the difficulty of providing for doubtful debts which may go bad in the future, and matching up their cost with the appropriate accounting period.

Discussion Topics

Thirty-minute essay questions:

1. Discuss the impact of the matching and conservatism concepts on the accounting treatment of stocks.

2. What is the significance of a FIFO or LIFO assumption concerning stock valuation for income measurement and the position statement?

3. What costs should be included when the amount of work in progress and finished goods stock for a manufacturing company is computed? What difficulties exist in measuring these costs?

4. Why should an enterprise provide for doubtful debts?

SEMINAR EXERCISES

7.1. **Marmalade Ltd** uses ginger in a manufacturing process and presents the following information concerning its purchases, requisitions and balances for the year ending 30 October 2002. Each unit is a small keg of ginger.

Date	Received (units)	Quantities issued to production (units)	Balance (units)	Unit price of purchases (£)
2001				
1 November	–	–	200	150
24 November	600	–	800	156
8 December	–	160	640	–
2002				
16 January	–	280	360	–
11 April	300	–	660	160
18 June	–	260	400	–
6 July	–	220	180	–
15 August	300	–	480	170
29 October	–	280	200	–

Required:

Calculate the cost of the closing inventory and the cost of material used under

- (a) first in first out method,
- (b) last in first out method,
- (c) weighted average method (to three decimal places).

7.2. **Mr Spice** is in business as a general import and export merchant. In December 2002 he decided to enter the pepper market. Purchases of pepper were made by Mr Spice as follows:

	Tonnes	Price (per tonne)
3 January 2003	20	114
18 February 2003	30	120
11 March 2003	25	105
20 April 2003	40	126
12 May 2003	15	129
20 June 2003	10	132

On 27 June 2003 Mr Spice sold 100 tonnes of pepper at £130 a tonne; he received payment on 8 July 2003.

Required:

- (a) Compute the value of stock on hand on 30 June 2003 by each of the following stock pricing systems:
  - (i) first in first out (FIFO),
  - (ii) last in, first out (LIFO),
  - (iii) weighted average cost.

(b) Show the effect of each system in (a) on Mr Spice's pepper trading profits for the six months ended on 30 June 2003.

(c) Explain briefly why stock is always accounted for at the lower of cost or net realizable value.

7.3. **Simoco Limited** sells used cars, which the company acquires through contacts in the motor trade or from customers who have part exchanged them for newer models. The company has a service department, which often has to repair cars bought to bring them up to 'retail' condition. This department charges the sales department the cost of materials and labour plus 50 per cent of cost to cover the service department's profit. The company's year end is 31 August and the stock of used vehicles at that date includes the following:

Car	A	B	C	D
Cost	2 750	1 500	4 800	3 450
Service department charges (Cost + 50 per cent) work done	450	270	120	150
Work needed to bring car to good retail condition (Cost + 50 per cent)	60	–	90	120
'Black Book'* retail market values:				
When bought	4 000	1 800	5 500	3 800
At 31 August	3 750	1 650	5 400	3 500
Sales manager's estimated sale price if sold in September	3 600	1 600	5 700	3 850

*The *Black Book* is a national publication available to the motor trade which estimates the retail sale value of used cars in good condition. The cars detailed above are deemed to be in good condition.

Required:

(a) Explain the major principle of stock valuation used by accountants, with reference to fundamental accounting concepts.

(b) Calculate the value at which each car should be included in the company's stock as at 31 August. Relate your answer to (a) above.

(c) By using different stock valuation methods a company can influence its annual reported profit and therefore its share price. Discuss the effect on profit of the FIFO, LIFO and AVCO methods.

The Production of Accounting Statements From a Trial Balance

THE AIMS OF THIS CHAPTER

To enable students to

- Convert a list of balances to a trial balance

- Make adjustments to the recorded figures at the year end

- Demonstrate the double entry effect of accruals and prepayments

- Draft a trading account, profit and loss account and balance sheet in columnar form

- Draft a manufacturing account
  This chapter is written as a practical example so that the reader can proceed from step to step to produce a set of accounts. Some of the adjustments are presented in the form of tasks which the reader can use to underpin the knowledge of techniques introduced in previous chapters.

Kohlslau Kitchens Ltd is a company which operates three health food shops. The shop premises and a small warehouse are owned by the company, but the administrative office is in rented premises. Food for sale to customers is bought in from a number of suppliers, and sales are normally for cash although there are some customers who are allowed to buy on credit terms.

Kohlslau Kitchens Ltd

List of balances extracted from the ledger accounts on 31 December this year.

	£
Advertising	18 500
Cash	30 700
Consumable supplies	26 500
Trade creditors	245 000
Debtors	26 200
Directors' salaries	84 000
Fixtures and fittings at cost	142 000
Provision for depreciation on fixtures up to 31 December last year	18 400
Freehold land and buildings	940 000
Provision for depreciation on buildings up to 31 December last year	25 000
Heat, light and power	55 600
Loan at 8% repayable in ten years time	200 000
Interest on the loan	12 000
Motor expenses	20 200
Vehicles at cost	48 000
Provision for depreciation on vehicles up to 31 December last year	12 000
Office expenses	19 200
Purchases of food	2 476 800
Rent	18 000
Retained profits	175 000
Share capital – ordinary shares of £1 each	400 000
Shop expenses	52 200
Sales	3 230 000
Stock at 31 December last year	46 300
Telephone	9 500
Wages	279 700

Task 8.1

Convert this list of balances to a trial balance by allocating the Debit items to a left hand column and the Credit items to a right hand column. The total of Debits should equal the total of Credits.

Solution

Kohlslau Kitchens Ltd – Trial Balance at 31 December this year

	Debits £	Credits £
Advertising	18 500	
Cash	30 700	
Consumable supplies	26 500	
Trade creditors		245 000
Debtors	26 200	
Directors salaries	84 000	
Fixtures and fittings at cost	142 000	
Fixtures and fittings provision for depreciation to 31 December last year		18 400
Freehold land and buildings	940 000	
Freehold land and buildings provision for depreciation on buildings to 31 December last year		25 000
Heat, light and power	55 600	
Loan at 12% repayable in ten years' time		200 000
Interest on the loan	12 000	
Motor expenses	20 200	
Vehicles at cost	48 000	
Vehicles Provision for depreciation to 31 December last year		12 000
Office expenses	19 200	
Purchases of food	2 476 800	
Rent	18 000	
Retained profits		175 000
Share capital – ordinary shares of £1 each		400 000
Shop expenses	52 200	
Sales		3 230 000
Stock at 31 December last year	46 300	
Telephone	9 500	
Wages	279 700	
	4 305 400	4 305 400

Once a trial balance has proved that the double entry bookkeeping is correct the accounting can begin by adjusting the book figures to reflect the transactions for the year

Adjusting the Trial Balance

The following information is relevant to the preparation of accounts for the year ended 31 December this year.

1. The company provides depreciation on fixed assets at the following rates using the straight line method:

Buildings   2% on cost
Fixtures and fittings   10% on cost
Vehicles   25% on cost
The land part of freehold land and buildings is deemed to be £600,000.

2. The closing stock at 31 December this year was £68,200.

3. Bonuses of £6,400 are to be paid to staff in February next year in respect of this year's sales.

4. Late invoices not yet entered in the books are as follows:

Purchases of food   £4,500   Electricity   £3,200
Motor repairs   £2,000   Consumable supplies   £840

5. The rent for the year to 31 March next year, which amounts to £16,000, has been paid in full.

6. Included in office expenses is insurance, for which premiums are paid annually in advance on 1 July each year amounting to £10,000.

7. Normally credit is allowed only to highly regarded customers, but recently the directors have become concerned about the solvency of a credit customer, a restaurant which owes £12,000. The directors wish to provide for 50% of this doubtful debt.

8. A provision of £75,000 for corporation tax payable should be made.

9. The directors wish to provide for a dividend of 10 pence per share to be paid next year out of this year's profits.

10. What is missing?

Task 8.2

Think out the effect of each of the ten items above on the recorded figures in the trial balance, and show how the adjustments would affect ledger accounts.

Solution

1. **Depreciation** (No depreciation on land)

- Buildings £940,000 − £600,000 = £340,000 × 2% = £6,800
  Debit depreciation (a cost), credit provision for depreciation
- Fixtures £142,000 × 10% = £14,200
  Debit depreciation (a cost), credit provision for depreciation
- Vehicles £48,000 × 25% = £12,000
  Debit depreciation , credit provision for depreciation

The ledger accounts would reveal:

Provision for Depreciation – Buildings

		£
	Balance b/d	25 000
	Profit and loss this year	6 800
	Balance in balance sheet	31 800

Provision for Depreciation – Fixtures

		£
	Balance b/d	18 400
	Profit and loss this year	14 200
	Balance in balance sheet	32 600

Provision for Depreciation – Vehicles

		£
	Balance b/d	12000
	Profit and loss this year	12 000
	Balance in balance sheet	24 000

Depreciation

	£		£
Buildings	6 800	Charged to profit	
Fittings	14 200	and loss a/c	33 000
Vehicles	12 000		
	33 000		33 000

2. Stock Adjustment

The calculation opening stock plus purchases less closing stock shows the cost of food sold.

£46,300 + £2,476,800 – £68,200 = £2,454,900

Stock Account

	£		£
Stock at 31 December last year	46 300	Charged to trading account	46 300
Stock at 31 December this year			
credited to trading account	68 200		

3 & 4. Accruals

The bonus is a cost of this year but it has not yet been paid, nor recorded in the books. As with all accruals the adjustment is: Increase the cost by a debit and balance this with a credit to reflect the amount which is owed.

Wages

	£		£
Balance b/d	279 700	Charged to Profit and Loss a/c	286 100
Accrual c/f	6 400		
	286 100		286 100
		Balance b/d	6 400

The other adjustments in note 4 can be effected on the trial balance by increasing

Purchases	£4 500 – debit
Motor repairs	£2 000 – debit
Heat, light and power	£3 200 – debit
Consumable supplies	£840 – debit
Accrued trade creditors	£10 540 – credit

Every debit has a credit. The accrued amounts could be entered in the ledger cost accounts, as with the bonus above.

5 & 6. Payments in Advance

Rent has been paid for three months of next year. This amount must not be a cost of this year, but must be reflected in the balance sheet as the business is owed three months' rent – £16,000 x $^3/_{12}$ = £4,000.

Rent

	£		£
Balance b/d	18 000	Prepayment c/f	4 000
		Remainder charged to profit and loss	14 000
	18 000		18 000
Balance b/d	4 000		

The debit balance of £4,000 will now correctly be a cost of next year.
Insurance paid in advance is £10,000 × $^6/_{12}$ = £5,000 in office expenses.

Office Expenses

	£		£
Balance b/d	19 200	Prepayment c/f	5 000
		Charge to profit and loss	14 200
	19 200		19 200
Balance b/d	5 000		

7. Doubtful Debts

A customer owes £12 000 but is estimated to pay only £6 000. The loss must be charged to the Profit and Loss Account but since the result is not yet certain, the debt is still shown as £12 000 but with a provision of £6 000 for the doubtful proportion.

Doubtful Debts

	£		£
Provision carried forward	6 000	Provision for doubtful debt charged to profit and loss a/c	6 000
	6 000		6 000
		Provision b/d	6 000

8 & 9.   Provisions

The amount of tax to be paid on the profit for the year is not certain on 31 December. It must be negotiated with the taxation authorities, so an estimated amount is provided out of profit. This amount also appears in the balance sheet as a current liability since it will be paid during the next year.

Provision for Taxation

	£		£
Amount owed to taxation authorities c/f	75 000	Estimatimate fo tax for the year charged to profit and loss a/c	75 000
	75 000		75 000
		Balance b/d	75 000

A dividend of 10 pence per share is 400,000 £1 shares $\times$ £0.1 = £40,000.
This will not be paid until well after 31 December so it must be provided out of profit and shown as a current liability.

Dividend Payable

	£		£
Amount owed to shareholders c/f	40 000	Dividend provided in the profit and loss a/c	40 000
	40 000		40 000
		Liability b/d	40 000

10. The Missing Item is interest on the long-term loan. £200,000 at 12% is £24,000 but the trial balance shows only £12,000 has been paid. The remaining £12,000 (the second instalment if interest is paid half yearly) is owed and must be treated as an accrual. Increase the cost and show the liability in the balance sheet.

Interest

	£		£
Balance b/d	12 000	Charge to profit and loss a/c	24 000
Half year interest accrued c/f	12 000		
	24 000		24 000
		Interest owed b/d	12 000

The Extended Trial Balance

When these adjustments are entered on the trial balance, if every debit has a credit, the balance between debit and credit will be maintained. The adjusted trial balance will then contain the 'real' figures instead of only those recorded in the books, and these figures can be entered into the framework of the trading account, profit and loss account and balance sheet.

The device of an extended trial balance is used in practice to ensure a balance and to calculate the amounts correctly. An extended trial balance for Kohlslau Kitchens Ltd is shown in Table 8.1 (overleaf).

The next step is to draft the financial statements. Tick off the amounts from the extended trial balance. (See pages 114–115)

Comment on the Kohlslau accounts

Note that in this explanatory set of accounts (pages 114–115), the expenses have been set down in the order in which they appeared on the trial balance. An accountant might try to arrange them in groups of similar costs such as shop costs, administration costs, finance costs, to present them in a more meaningful way to the managers.

In the balance sheet it is interesting to note that the working capital (current assets less current liabilities) is a negative figure (£260,840). This is not usually the case in most companies, but Kohlslau Kitchens have relatively small stocks and debtors but large trade creditors, as you would expect with a food retail business. The trade creditors appear to be willing to help finance this business with short-term credit amounting to £245,000.

The business makes a good profit on its trading activities. The gross profit rate is calculated as:-

$$\frac{\text{Gross Profit}}{\text{Sales}} \times \frac{100}{1} = \frac{£770,600}{£3,230,000} \times \frac{100}{1} = 23.8\%$$

For every £1 of sales a gross profit of 23.8 pence is earned. However this profit is consumed by the expenses of the business. The net profit rate is

$$\frac{\text{Net Profit}}{\text{Sales}} \times \frac{100}{1} = \frac{£120,760}{£3,230,000} \times \frac{100}{1} = 3.7\%$$

Expenses account for 21.1 pence (23.8 − 3.7) of each £1 of sales. Managers should examine these costs with a view to making some economies.

Table 8.1 Kohlslau Kitchens Ltd Extended Trial Balance

Ledger Account	Original trial balance			Adjustments	
	Debit	Credit	+ / −	Debit	Credit
Advertising	18 500	−		−	−
Cash	30 700	−		−	−
Consumable supplies	26 500	−		*840	−
Creditors	−	245 000		−	−
Accruals Note 4	−	−		−	10 540* ⎫
Accruals bonus	−	−		−	6 400¢ ⎭
Debtors	26 200	−		6 000	6 000
Prepayments insurance	−	−		¢5 000 ⎫	−
Prepayments rent				4 000 ⎭	
Directors salaries	84 000	−		−	−
Fixtures and fittings	142 000	−		−	−
Fixtures and fittings depreciation	−	18 400		14 200	14 200
Land and buildings	940 000	−		−	−
Land and buildings depreciation	−	25 000		6 800	6 800
Heat, light and power	55 600	−		*3 200	−
Long term loan	−	200 000		−	−
Interest	12 000	−		12 000	12 000
Motor expenses	20 200	−		*2 000	−
Vehicles	48 000	−		−	−
Vehicles depreciation	−	12 000		12 000	12 000
Office expenses	19 200	−		−	5 000¢
Purchases	2 476 800	−		*4 500	−
Rent	18 000	−		−	4 000
Retained profit	−	175 000		−	−
Retained profit for the year	−	−		−	−
Share capital	−	400 000		−	−
Shop expenses	52 200	−		−	−
Sales	−	3 230 000		−	−
Stock	46 300	−		68 200	68 200
Telephone	9 500	−		−	−
Wages	279 700	−		¢6 400	−
Tax	−	−		75 000	75 000
Dividend	−	−		40 000	40 000
	4 305 400	4 305 400		260 140	260 140

Trial balance figure plus or minus the adjustment equals Profit and Loss or Balance Sheet figure.

*Accruals credit adjustment 10,540 balances against 840, 3,200, 2,000 and 4,500 on the debit side.

	Trading and profit and loss accounts			Balance sheet	
=	Debit	Credit	or	Debit	Credit
	18 500	—		—	—
	—	—		30 700	—
	27 340	—		—	—
	—	—		—	245 000
	—	—		—	16 940
	6 000	—		26 200	6 000
	—	—		9 000	—
	84 000	—		—	—
	—	—		142 000	—
	14 200	—		—	32 600
	—	—		940 000	—
	6 800	—		—	31 800
	58 800	—		—	—
	—	—		—	200 000
	24 000	—		—	12 000
	22 200	—		—	—
	—	—		48 000	—
	12 000	—		—	24 000
	14 200	—		—	—
	2 481 300	—		—	—
	14 000	—		—	—
	—	—		—	175 000
	—	—		—	5 760*
	—	—		—	400 000
	52 200	—		—	—
	—	3230000		—	—
	—	21900		68 200	—
	9 500	—		—	—
	286 100	—		—	—
	75 000	—		—	75 000
	40 000	—		—	40 000
	3246 140	3 251 900		1 264 100	1 264 100
		3 246 140			
Retained profit		*5760			

Kohlslau Kitchens Ltd Trading and Profit and Loss Account

		£	£
Sales			3 230 000
Opening stock		46 300	
Purchases		2 481 300	
		2 527 600	
Less closing stock		68 200	
Cost of goods sold			2 459 400
Gross profit			770 600
Expenses	Advertising	18 500	
	Consumable supplies	27 340	
	Doubtful debts	6 000	
	Directors salaries	84 000	
	Depreciation	33 000	
	Heat, light and power	58 800	
	Interest	24 000	
	Motor expenses	22 200	
	Office expenses	14 200	
	Rent	14 000	
	Shop expenses	52 200	
	Telephone	9 500	
	Wages	286 100	
			649 840
Net profit before tax			120 760
Tax			75 000
Net profit after tax			45 760
Dividend			40 000
Retained profit			£5 760

Kohlslau Kitchens Ltd Balance Sheet as at 31 December

	£ Cost	£ Depreciation	£
Fixed assets			
Land and Buildings	940 000	31 800	908 200
Fixtures and Fittings	142 000	32 600	109 400
Vehicles	48 000	24 000	24 000
	1 130 000	88 400	1 041 600
Current assets			
Stock		68 200	
Debtors (26,200 – 6,000)		20 200	
Prepayments (5,000 + 4,000)		9 000	
Cash		30 700	
		128 100	
Current liabilities			
Creditors	245 000		
Accruals (10,540+6,400)	16 940		
Interest	12 000		
Tax owed	75 000		
Dividend payable	40 000		
		388 940	
Working capital			(260 840)
			780 760
Long-term loan at 12% interest			200 000
Net assets			£580 760
Share capital			400 000
Retained profit			180 760
			£580 760

The Manufacturing Account

In the example above, Kohlslau Kitchens Ltd buys in all the food which it sells. If however it manufactured this food, then a manufacturing account would be needed to disclose these costs. This account is sometimes called a work in progress account because it shows the costs of activity in progress through the factory. These costs are materials, labour and factory overheads incurred to operate the manufacturing process. Work in progress is the term given to work that is not complete at the end of an accounting period.

The manufacturing account features stocks of raw material and stocks of work in progress, and a stock adjustment is required for both. The completed production is transferred from the factory into the finished goods stores, to await sale. Goods sold to customers are withdrawn from the stores, so a finished goods stock adjustment is needed in the trading account. In the case of Kohlslau Kitchens Ltd above, the purchases of £2,481,300 would instead be the cost of finished goods transferred from the factory to the stores. The manufacturing account would then disclose this amount using figures introduced to the example for that purpose.

Kohlslau Kitchens Ltd Manufacturing Account for year ended 31 December

		£
Opening stock of raw materials		74 900
Purchases of raw materials		1 100 350
Less closing stock of raw materials		(86 100)
Cost of materials used		1 089 150
Factory labour (directly employed on production)		590 250
Prime cost		1 679 400
Factory overheads		780 200
Factory cost		2 459 600
Add opening stock of work in progress	83 400	
Less closing stock of work in progress	(617 00)	21700
Cost of finished goods transferred to the stores		£2 481 300

The brackets show negative figures in this vertical form account – credit manufacturing account with the closing stocks and show the corresponding debit in the balance sheet as a current asset. The size of the stocks of material, work in progress and finished goods would depend on how perishable these food items are.

The accounting system would need to be extended to provide ledger accounts for raw materials, factory labour and the many cost headings covered by factory overheads, e.g. power, indirect labour, rent, rates, light, heat, depreciation, insurance, etc. These items would be the subject of accruals and prepayments in the normal way. The depreciation of plant and factory buildings is a cost of manufacturing, while depreciation of office furniture and vehicles would appear as an administration expense in the profit and loss account. Some costs such as rent, insurance, light and heat, etc. are sometimes apportioned to the manufacturing account and the profit and loss account on a basis determined by the management.

CONCLUSION

This chapter marks the transformation from recording transactions to measuring them, and presenting results in the form of a statement which can be used to interpret the performance and position of the business. The system of accruals, prepayments and provisions enables the accountant to adjust what has been recorded so that it reflects what has actually taken place. The manufacturing account, trading account and analysed expenses in the profit and loss account focus attention on separate aspects of the activity of the business.

SEMINAR EXERCISES

8.1. **Sally and Denise (Hair Styles) Ltd** runs a small chain of hairdressing salons. Its books of account show the following balances at 30 April this year (in £000).

Sally and Denise (Hair Styles) Ltd

	Debit £	Credit £
Cash in bank	435	
Cash in hand	25	
Cleaning expenses	160	
Creditors		590
Debtors	250	
Directors' salaries	40	
Equipment and machines at cost	1 500	
Equipment and machines, provision for depreciation		300
Freehold premises at cost	860	
Freehold premises, provision for depreciation		80
Hairdressing materials, shampoos, etc.	400	
Heat, light and power	480	
Receipts		4 510
Rent	490	
Reserves		540
Salon expenses	920	
Salon furnishings at cost	1 460	
Salon furnishings, provision for depreciation		430
Share capital, ordinary shares of £1		2 000
Stock of materials, 1 May last year	140	
Telephone and office expenses	210	
Wages	1 080	
	£8 450	£8450

The following information is also relevant:

(a) Depreciation is charged on fixed assets on a straight line basis at the following rates: buildings (but not land), 2% p.a.; equipment and machines, 20% p.a.; salon furnishings, 10% p.a. Freehold premises is made up of land, £360,000, and buildings, £500,000.

(b) Included in rent are half a year's rent for the main salon for the period April–September this year, £84,000, and a quarter's rent for some other rented properties for April–June this year, £60,000.

(c) Closing stock at cost is £160,000.

(d) Wages outstanding amounted to £40,000.

(e) Some of the customers who owe the company money are proving difficult to trace, and the company wishes to provide for doubtful debts of £12,000.

(f) Some of the closing stock has deteriorated in store, and an £8,000 write-down is required.

(g) Corporation tax of £90,000 is to be provided, and a dividend of 6p per ordinary share is proposed.

You are required to:

(a) Prepare a profit and loss account for the company for the year ended 30 April this year and a balance sheet as at that date.

(b) Comment on the company's dividend policy

8.2. The trial balance (*opposite*) has been extracted from the books of **Grumbleweed Ltd.** The following adjustments are required.

(a) Depreciation is to be provided on the fixed assets as follows:

Plant and machinery	15 per cent on cost
Office equipment	10 per cent on cost
Motor vehicles	25 per cent written-down value

(b) Prepayment of rent, £6,000.
Prepayment of insurance, £500.

(c) Amount owing for light and heat, £1,000.

(d) Rent, light and heat and insurance to be apportioned $5/6$ to the factory and $1/6$ to office expenses.

(e) The bad debt provision is to be 1 per cent of the debtors.

(f) The share capital is:
400,000 ordinary shares of 50p
A dividend of 10p per share is to be provided on the ordinary shares.

(g) Directors' salaries include the production director at £15,000.

(h) Corporation tax of £100,000 is to be provided.

(i) Stocks at cost at 31 December were as follows:

	£
Raw materials	28 000 at cost
Work in progress	47 000 at cost
Finished goods	100 000 at cost

Required:

Prepare from the trial balance below, for the directors of the company only, a manufacturing, trading and profit and loss account for the year ended 31 December 2000 and a balance sheet as at that date, having first adjusted for points (a) to (i) above.

Trial Balance as at 31 December

	Debit £	Credit £
Ordinary shares		200 000
Profit and loss account, 1 January	121 000	
Plant and machinery: cost	300 000	
Office equipment: cost	205 000	
Motor vehicles: cost	100 000	
Accumulated depreciation at 1 January		
Plant and machinery		80 000
Office equipment		44 500
Motor vehicles		40 000
Debtors/creditors	250 000	178 000
General provision for bad debts at 1 January		500
Manufacturing wages	250 000	
Stocks at 1 January: raw materials	35 000	
work in progress	63 000	
finished goods	125 000	
Purchases of raw materials	260 000	
Sales		1 300 000
Bank balance		30 000
Carriage outwards	25 000	
Directors' salaries	80 000	
Rent	60 000	
Advertising	95 000	
Insurance	5 900	
Office salaries	83 000	
Light and heat	8 000	
Factory power	10 000	
Bank interest	8 500	
General administration expenses	30 600	
	£1 994 000	£1 994 000

PART TWO

Developing Accounting Skills

CHAPTER 9

Accounting for Partnerships

THE AIMS OF THIS CHAPTER

To enable students to

- Understand the complexities of the relationship between partners and the significance of the partnership agreement and the Partnership Act of 1890

- Draft an appropriation account for a partnership

- Appreciate the significance of goodwill to partners

- Account for changes to a partnership such as when an existing partner leaves, or a new partner joins or when a partnership is dissolved or sold to a company

PARTNERSHIP – A LEGAL RELATIONSHIP

Partnership has been defined as 'the relationship which exists between persons carrying on a business in common with a view to profit'. Three essentials must exist before partnership can be established.

(a) carrying on a business,

(b) working in common, and

(c) having a view to profit.

It is important to ascertain whether a partnership exists, since if the business ceases with a deficit of funds, there is no limited liability to protect the private assets of the partners. If creditors can establish that somebody is a partner they can use the private assets of that person to make good the debts of the partnership. Alternatively, if a person can establish a claim to partnership, that person can claim a share of the profits and a share of the assets of the business when it ceases trading.

Partnership means that there is a mutual agency in existence between the partners. Each partner can act as an agent for the other, and also as a principal for the business. Thus a partner, when acting on behalf of the business, can bind the other partners in law. A partnership in the UK is governed by the Partnership Act of 1890 and by the Limited Partnership Act of 1907. The Act of 1890 lays down that partnership shall be limited to a maximum of 20 partners, unless the partnership is a banking partnership, in which case the limit is 10 partners. Partnerships in banking can apply to the Department of Trade and Industry to extend the partnership to 20. Under the Companies Act of 1985, firms of solicitors or accountants qualified to audit public companies may have any number of partners.

Because the action of a partner, whether careless, inefficient or dishonest, can affect other partners, the relationship between partners is one *uberrimae fidei*. This means that the utmost good faith must exist between partners, and that one partner can rely on information given by other partners when entering the partnership and during the trading. If such information is found to be false, a claim for damages can be sustained in the courts. Partnerships can be established for a limited period by agreement, or 'at will', which means they can be wound up by the partners at any point in time, subject to reasonable notice being given.

A partnership is a relationship, and a legal agreement will be needed to govern this relationship. The Partnership Act lays down the rules to be applied in a partnership in the absence of an agreement, but wherever there is a partnership agreement, the rules in the Act are subordinated to the terms of the agreement.

PARTNERSHIP: A COMMERCIAL RELATIONSHIP

The success of the business of a sole trader may be limited by the ability of the proprietor and by the amount of capital a single person can invest These limitations are overcome by the amalgamation of two or more sole traders into a partnership. The business can expand if more principals join it and bring capital with them, while each partner will bring a measure of expertise to the business. Decisions in a partnership are no longer the responsibility of an individual, but are usually the outcome of discussion among the partners. Partners must have absolute trust in one another, and therefore it is important to select one's partner with care. One partner can bind the whole of the partnership by his actions, and the debts of the business can be recovered by the creditors from the private resources of all the partners. The Limited Partnership Act 1907 allowed a certain class of partners, who provided capital but took no part in the management of the business, to have their liability for its debts limited to their investment. Large international firms of accountants are formed as complicated partnerships. As a mistake by one partner could result in millions of pounds of damages payable by the partnership, these large firms have persuaded the government to enact a new limited partnerships act which would limit the liability of the partnership in such cases. Partners of a firm who are remote from that part of the business whose negligence has caused the damages would thus be able to protect their private fortunes against claims caused by the mistakes of others.

PARTNERSHIP VERSUS COMPANY AS A FORM OF BUSINESS ORGANIZATION

The major differences between the company form of business organization and the partnership may be summarized as follows:

1. A company is a legal person in its own right, whereas a partnership is not a separate legal entity from its members. This gives a shareholder in a company the right to sell a share in the company without the termination of the business. This is known as perpetual succession. A partnership ceases when the partners change.

2. Shareholders in a company are protected by limited liability, whereas in a partnership each partner may be made liable for the debts of the firm to the full extent of his private fortune.

3. A limit of 20 is usually put upon the number of partners who can engage in a partnership business, but in a public company the only limit to the number of shareholders is the number of shares authorized. This means that a public company can recruit capital from a much wider market than can a partnership or a private limited company.

4. In a partnership all partners have a right to join in the management of the business and have access to the books and vouchers, but in the company form of business organization management is delegated by shareholders to the board, and once that delegation has taken place the shareholders have only a statutory right to the information specified in the Companies Act 1985.

5. Since a company is incorporated by registering under the Companies Act, it must file certain information about its accounts etc. with the Registrar. A partnership, however, does not have to disclose information about itself to the public.

6. The Partnership Act 1890 lays down the rules within which a partnership is administered, unless there is an agreement among the partners which can override the Act. The Companies Act 1985 lays down rules by which companies must abide, even though in some cases they might wish to vary those rules.

7. The capital of a company is authorized by the terms and conditions laid down in its 'memorandum'. It is an administrative matter to increase the capital, but to reduce capital may be a matter for the court. In a partnership, however, capital is fixed only by agreement and can be changed if the partners so wish.

8. Under the Companies Act, a company must appoint an auditor and must maintain certain books. There is no such requirement for the audit of a partnership, and nowhere in the Partnership Act is a list of statutory books laid down.

9. The profit of a partnership business is divided among the partners according to their agreed profit-sharing ratio, and can be withdrawn by them if they so wish. The profit of a company is distributed as a dividend pro rata to shareholding at a rate determined by the company in a general meeting. The board decides how much of the profit is to be paid out in dividend and recommends its decision to be adopted by the shareholders.

THE LIMITED LIABILITY PARTNERSHIP (LLP)

The LLP act of July 2000 has created a new form of legal entity, which provides partners with limited liability but does not require the administrative work connected with a limited company. Partnership flexibility and the individual tax status of partners are maintained by the LLP. Limited liability for partners stems from the fact that the LLP is a legal person separate from its members, which can be sued by aggrieved third parties. Unlimited liability for partners has caused problems for partners because

(a)   the incidence of litigation for claims for professional negligence, and the size of claims, have increased;

(b)   the size and extent of partnership businesses has increased so that in some cases partners are not all known to one another;

(c)   partners tend to specialize, with members of different professions working together (lawyers and accountants);

(d)   partners risk their own assets when a large claim caused by another partner affects the firm.

Large global firms of accountants are expected to use this form of business even though they will need to publish audited accounts, and file an annual return. Two 'designated partners' will act as a director and a company secretary. LLPs will not have a share capital, nor will they need to hold an AGM. Partnerships need only register at Companies House. A negligent partner's assets will still be at risk because a professional person owes a duty of care to a client.

THE PARTNERSHIP AGREEMENT

Task 9.1

A partnership relationship is a complex matter, and as such the agreed terms of the relationship should be clearly expressed in a partnership agreement. If you were in partnership, what financial items would you expect to be covered by your agreement with your partners?

Solution

Capital. Is capital per partner to be a fixed amount settled at the beginning of the partnership or is it to vary from year to year?

The division of profits. The profit-sharing ratio which exists between the partners states what proportion of the business profit each partner is to receive.

Current accounts. These are maintained to record the remuneration of partners by means of salary, interest and share of profits, and to set against this remuneration the amount of drawings made by each partner. It is usual in a partnership agreement to decide that capitals will be of a fixed amount, and that the shares of profit etc. and drawings shall be passed through a current account. How much capital is withdrawn is a matter of mutual agreement.

Interest on capital or drawings. The agreement should specify whether partners are to be paid interest on capital, and the rate concerned. Where partners have contributed different amounts of capital, interest is seen as a method of compensating the partner who has contributed most. Alternatively, it may be agreed among the partners that they should pay interest on their drawings, so that any partner who draws out part of their profit share before it is earned and is thus overdrawn will pay for this.

Interest on current accounts. If partners leave their share of business profits in a current account, this is equivalent to the profits ploughed back into the reserves of a limited company. A partner should be paid interest on his current account balance, which is an extension of his fixed capital amount.

A limit to drawings. The partners may wish to limit the amount by which partners can overdraw current account profits.

The remuneration of partners. Some partners may work harder for the business than others, and thus the profits are attributable to their efforts. The senior partner may have contributed more in capital to the partnership, but the junior partner with a much smaller capital may work harder. If interest is paid on capital, then salaries should be paid to those partners who contribute most in terms of effort. Such partnership salaries are an appropriation of profit, and not a charge thereto. Both interest on capital, and partners' salaries, must be deducted from profit before the figure to be divided in the profit-sharing ratio is computed.

The preparation of accounts. Financial statements should be produced at least once per annum, and these accounts should be binding on the partners once they are agreed *inter se*.

Goodwill. Goodwill arises in partnerships when a new partner joins the original team or when one of the original partners leaves. In order to ensure that a new partner pays a fair price for a share of the partnership assets, or that a retiring partner takes with them the appropriate amount, goodwill is valued on these occasions. There are many different ways of making such a valuation, and the method to be used for the partnership should be contained in the agreement.

Retirement. The agreement should state how the amount to be paid to a partner on retirement shall be determined, and what steps shall be taken to pay this amount. If a retiring partner does not withdraw capital, the amount is transferred to a loan account.

THE PARTNERSHIP ACT

The terms of the Act of 1890 are subordinated to those in the partnership agreement, but where there is no agreement or where the agreement is silent on any point, then the terms of the Act apply. Section 24 of the Act lays out the terms which are to apply in partnership accounts.

1. Partners have an equal share of capital on cessation of business and share equally any business profits or losses.

2. The partnership indemnifies a partner for payments made on behalf of the partnership business. If a partner pays a partnership expense out of a private bank account, he may draw that money from the partnership bank account, although usually such an adjustment is made through the current account. This indemnity extends to contracts made by partners on behalf of the firm in the ordinary course of business or in order to preserve the business. Thus if a partner buys raw material for the business the other partners cannot refuse to accept what has been purchased in the normal course of the business. Payments made to preserve the business are more difficult to define, but if a partner sees vacant shop premises near those already occupied by the partnership business and decides to lease them on behalf of the partnership, this action could be construed as an act to preserve the business, since the partner could claim that this action denied the premises to a rival and allowed the partnership business to expand. Although there was no consultation with other partners prior to this action they would have to ratify what has been done.

3. Interest is paid on loans made to the business by partners at a rate of 5 per cent. A loan in this context is defined as an advance beyond the amount of a partner's agreed capital.

4. Interest on capital is not payable.

5. All partners are allowed to play an equal part in managing the business.

6. Partners are not to be paid salaries.

7. Before a new partner can be admitted to the business all existing partners must consent to the change. One dissenting voice will be sufficient to keep out the joining partner.

8. In all decisions of the partnership the majority is seen to rule. However, in any decision which changes the nature of the business all partners must agree before that change can take place.

9. The books of account of the partnership must be maintained at the partnership office, and all partners must be able to view them on request.

THE APPROPRIATION ACCOUNT

The profit and loss account of a partnership is the same as for a company or sole trader down to the net profit before tax. The appropriation account is used in partnerships to make adjustments for the rights of partners *inter se*, so that the accounting profit is reduced by interest payable on the capital of the partners, and salaries before the profit to be divided among the partners in their profit-sharing ratio is determined. These amounts are debited to the appropriation account, and credited to the current account of each partner. Drawings are set against them (a debit) and the balance of undrawn profit is carried forward and shown on the balance sheet. A current account in columnar form will be easy to assimilate, and can also be used to show up adjustments between the partners, such as where partner A guarantees partner B a certain minimum income. In such a case, if partner B's income does not reach the guaranteed minimum, he will be credited with the appropriate amount and partner A will be debited.

Partners pay tax as individuals, declaring their partnership income separately to the taxation authorities. The partnership as such is not taxed, so no tax entry appears in the profit and loss account.

Example: an appropriation account

There are three partners, Frank, Fearless and Bold, who agree to share profits in the ratio 3:2:1. Their partnership agreement stipulates that partners will receive interest on their capital at 10 per cent per annum, that Bold is entitled to a salary of £10,000, and that 10 per cent interest is to be charged on drawings and overdrawn balances. Frank has guaranteed Fearless a minimum income of £46,000 per annum as profit and interest on capital. The last agreed capitals of the partners were: Frank £150,000; Fearless £110,000; and Bold £115,000. The opening balances on their current accounts stood at £13,000 for Frank, £2,000 for Bold and £6,000 *overdrawn* for Fearless. The net profit as disclosed by the accounts was £145 100 for the year. Partners' drawings during the year to date were : Frank £15,000, Fearless £13,000 and Bold £13,000. The accounts to record these circumstances would appear as follows.

In the balance sheet partners' capitals are usually shown separately from partners' current account balances.

Frank, Fearless and Bold, Appropriation Account

	Year Ending	
	£	£
Net profit per accounts		145 100
Add interest on drawings:		
Frank	1 500	
Fearless (13 000 + 6 000 × 0.1)	1 900	
Bold	1 300	4 700
		149 800
Deduct salary, Bold		10 000
		139 800
Deduct interest on capital:		
Frank	15 000	
Fearless	11 000	
Bold	11 500	37 500
		102 300
Deduct share of profits:		
Frank ($^3/_6$)	51 150	
Fearless ($^2/_6$)	34 100	
Bold ($^1/_6$)	17 050	
		102 300

				£
Calculation of income of Fearless:				
Profit share				34 100
Interest on capital				11 000
				45 100
From Frank				900*
Minimum guaranteed				46 000

Frank, Fearless and Bold, Current Accounts

	Frank £	Fearless £	Bold £		Frank £	Fearless £	Bold £
Opening				Opening			
balance b/d	—	6 000	—	balance b/d	13 000	—	2 000
Transfer to				Salary			10 000
Fearless	900*			Interest on			
				capital	15 000	11 000	11 500
				Share of			
Drawings	15 000	13 000	13 000	profit	51 150	34 100	17 050
Interest on				Transfer			
drawings	1 500	1 900	1 300	from Frank			
Balance c/f	61 750	25 100	26 250	per agreement		900*	
	79 150	46 000	40 550		79 150	46 000	40 550
				Balance	61 750	25 100	26 250

CHANGE OF PARTNERS

Partnerships change by the addition of one or more new partners or by the retirement or death of an existing partner. Often the retirement of one partner is accompanied by the addition of a new partner. All the remaining partners must agree about the person, and the terms on which the new partner joins the group. The legal position is that the partnership ends when a partner leaves or joins and a new partnership is then created

The incoming partner usually introduces capital into the firm, in the form of cash or assets such as cars or plant, but occasionally in the form of goodwill. The accounting entry here is to debit the appropriate asset account and credit the capital account of the new partner with the agreed value of the items introduced. It is important to revalue assets whenever there is a change of partner, since if the real value of the assets is more or less than their book value, the true value must be used in transactions between the partners at this point. An incoming partner will be entitled to a share of the assets and, if there is a surplus of real value over book value, the new partner will receive a share of this surplus without paying for it, unless the surplus is recognized when he joins the firm.

A retiring partner will wish to ensure that the assets are properly valued on the date of retirement, so that the share of partnership capital due to him is accurately computed and adequate compensation is paid for the items which are left behind by those who are going to continue the business after the retirement. Goodwill is a significant item in such a valuation. Sometimes a business is worth more as a whole than the aggregate value of all its assets less liabilities. The surplus is called goodwill, and arises from a number of factors.

Goodwill

Goodwill is generated because

(a) a business is a going concern with a good reputation and established customers;

(b) its owners have know-how and experience, which earns more profit than is expected from the assets involved; or

(c) harmonious labour relations ensure trouble-free working which leads to extra profits.

Goodwill is the price an investor would pay for these extra profits. The revaluation of assets and the creation of goodwill should feature in the accounts of a partnership when there is a change of partners.

Accounting Entries for a Joining Partner

The most common method is to recognize the true value of the assets and the existence of goodwill, and to apportion the surplus or capital profit to the existing partners in their profit-sharing ratio before a new partner joins the firm. This involves the creation of a *revaluation account*, to which the debit balances of the asset accounts are written off, while the newly agreed values of the assets are credited to the revaluation account and debited in turn to the asset accounts. A credit balance on the revaluation account means that there is a surplus on revaluation which is divided among the partners in their profit-sharing ratio and credited to their capital accounts.

Next value the goodwill and debit the *goodwill account*. Divide the amount of goodwill in the *old* profit-sharing ratio, crediting it to partners' capital accounts. Then divide the goodwill in the *new* profit-sharing ratio to be used after the new partner has joined the firm and debit it to partners' capital accounts. The corresponding credit is to goodwill account, so that the goodwill balance does not appear in the balance sheet.

Example: An Incoming Partner

Albert and Brian are in partnership, sharing profits in the ratio 2:1. Albert has capital of £470,000 invested in the business, while Brian's capital is £270,000. This means that the net assets of the business have a book value of £740,000. The partners agree that Clare shall join them as a partner, and that in return for introducing capital of £300,000 in cash and £20,000 in the form of machinery, she is to receive a fifth share of future profits. The net assets are revalued at £890,000 at this point, and a goodwill account of £66,000 is also to be created.

Step 1
A balance sheet before revaluation of the assets would show

	£	£
Capital:		
Albert	470 000	
Brian	270 000	£740 000
Represented by net assets		£740 000

The new profit-sharing ratio is computed as follows. At present, A (Albert) and B (Brian) share 2:1, and C (Clare) is in future to get one-fifth. Thus four-fifths will be left for A and B to share in the ratio 2:1 ($3 \times 5 = 15$). In future, A gets $^8/_{15}$, B gets $^4/_{15}$ and C gets $^3/_{15}$.

Step 2
The journal entries to record the transactions are as follows:

Journal Entries

	Dr	Cr
	£	£
Asset accounts	150 000	
Revaluation account		150 000
Being surplus on revaluation of assets		
Revaluation account	150 000	
Capital account		
Albert		100 000
Brian		50 000
Being apportionment of surplus on revaluation to partners' capital accounts in the ratio 2:1		
Goodwill	66 000	
Capital account		
Albert		44 000
Brian		22 000
Being creation of a goodwill account and its apportionment between the partners in their profit-sharing ratio 2:1		
Cash	300 000	
Assets	20 000	
Capital account Clare		320 000
Bring capital introduced by Clare		

Task 9.2

Enter these journal entries into ledger accounts and draft a balance sheet.

Solution

The balance sheet would show

	£	£
Capital:		
Albert (470 000 + 100 000 + 44 000)	614 000	
Brian (270 000 + 50 000 + 22 000)	342 000	
Clare	320 000	£1 276 000
Represented by:		
Goodwill		66 000
Net assets (740 000 + 150 000 + 20 000)		910 000
Cash		300 000
		£1 276 000

Step 3

Write the goodwill out of the books (credit goodwill) to the partners' capital accounts in the new profit-sharing ratio (debit capital in ratio 8:4:3).

The journal entries would be as follows:

	Dr	Cr
	£	£
Capital account:		
Albert (8)	35 200	
Brian (4)	17 600	
Clare (3)	13 200	
Goodwill		66 000
Being goodwill written back to partners' capital accounts		

A balance sheet would now show:

	£	£
Capital:		
Albert (614 000 − 35 200)		578 800
Brian (342 000 − 17 600)		324 400
Clare (320 000 − 13 200)		306 800
		£1 210 000
Represented by:		
Net assets		910 000
Cash		300 000
		£1 210 000

Example – A Retiring Partner

When a partner dies or retires, the assets, including goodwill, are revalued to compute accurately his or her share of the business. The surplus on revaluation is credited to capital accounts in profit-sharing ratio. It is usual to pay out the retiring partner in cash, but the balance on the capital account of the retiring partner may be transferred to a loan account.

Suppose, in the partnership above, Brian decides to retire and goodwill is now valued at £75,000. His share will amount to $^4/_{15}$ of the new value placed on the goodwill (£75,000 × $^4/_{15}$ = £20,000) Albert and Clare agree to share profits in the ratio 9:3 after Brian's retirement. If the remaining partners do not wish to leave goodwill in the accounts at this stage the entries would be:

	Dr £	Cr £
Goodwill	75 000	
Capital account:		
Albert (8)		40 000
Brian (4)		20 000
Clare (3)		15 000
Being goodwill written into the books on the retirement of Brian		
Capital account:		
Albert (9)	56 250	
Clare (3)	18 750	
Goodwill		75 000
Being goodwill written out of the books after Brian has retired		

Brian would receive £344,400 (324,400 + 20,000) on his retirement. Until he is paid, the balance sheet would show

	£
Capital:	
Albert (578,800 + 40,000 − 56,250)	562 550
Clare (306,800 + 15,000 − 18,750)	303 050
	£865 600
Represented by:	
Net assets	910 000
Cash	300 000
	1 210 000
Less loan account: Brian	344 400
	£865 600

DISSOLUTION OF A PARTNERSHIP

Technically a partnership is dissolved whenever there is a change of partners, but often the business carries on and a new partnership comes into existence. If there is bankruptcy or all partners retire, the business will cease and the partnership will be dissolved. The assets are sold for cash (and/or shares if they are sold to a company), the debts are collected, the liabilities are paid and any funds remaining are repaid to the partners. Profit on the sale of the assets shown as the credit balance on a *realization account* is apportioned in the profit-sharing ratio and posted to the credit of the capital accounts.

Section 44 of the Partnership Act 1890 lays down rules for the disbursement of partnership funds on a dissolution. The assets of the firm are to be applied first to repay the debts and liabilities of the firm to persons who are not partners, second to repay partners' loans to the firm, third to repay partners' capital balances and last to pay out any surplus on dissolution to the partners in their profit-sharing ratio. If the assets are insufficient to meet the liabilities of the firm the deficiency shall be met out of profits and, if they are insufficient, out of capital, and if that is still not enough then the partners must contribute to the remaining deficiency in their profit-sharing ratio. If at this stage one partner is bankrupt and is unable to contribute a share of the deficiency, under the rule in *Garner* v. *Murray,* a case decided in 1904, the solvent partners must make up the share of the deficiency of an insolvent partner, in the ratio of the *capital* accounts before the dissolution commenced.

Example

Alan, Ben and Chris decide to dissolve their partnership. They share profits equally*. Their balance sheet is as follows, after selling the assets for £21,000 less than their book value:

Balance Sheet of Alan, Ben and Chris as at 31 December

	£	£
Capital:		
Alan	50 000	
Ben	20 000	
Chris	5 000	
		75 000
Current accounts:		
Alan	10 000	
Ben	10 000	
Chris	(16 000)	
		4 000
Loan Account: Alan		20 000
		£99 000
Represented by:		
Assets:		
Cash		78 000
Losses on realization		21 000*
		£99 000

*The loss will be divided equally between the partners, but Chris, who is overdrawn, is found to be bankrupt and cannot contribute his share of the loss. The cash would be apportioned among the partners as follows: first Alan would be repaid his loan of £20,000, leaving cash available of £58,000. The cash would be distributed as follows:

Capital and Current Accounts

	Alan £	Ben £	Chris £
Opening balances – capital	50 000	20 000	5 000
– current	10 000	10 000	(16 000)
Share of loss (£21,000)*	(7 000)	(7 000)	(7 000)
	53 000	23 000	(18 000)
Chris deficit apportioned in			
Opening capital ratio 5:2	(12 860)	(5 140)	18 000
Cash paid out	£40 140	£17 860	Nil

These amounts equal the cash of £58,000.

SALE OF PARTNERSHIP TO A LIMITED COMPANY

When a partnership is sold to a company and the partners either retire or carry on in business as directors of the company, a *realization account* is used to sort out the transactions.

Step 1

The fixed assets are closed off to the realization account, i.e. credit fixed assets and debit the realization account. Sometimes retiring partners will take certain assets in lieu of cash, and if they take such assets at a price in excess of their book value, this constitutes a sale at a profit. The appropriate entries are: credit the asset with the agreed price, debit the partner's capital account, and transfer the balance on the asset account to the realization account (as a credit if it is a profit and a debit if it is a loss).

Step 2

Compute the price or consideration to be paid by the company. This may be in cash or in the form of shares, or a mixture of cash and shares. The amount should be debited to the purchaser's account and credited to the realization account. When the price is paid, the purchaser should be credited and accounts for either shares or cash should be debited.

Step 3

The debtors and investments should be realized for cash. A profit on the sale of investments should be posted from the debit side of the investment account to the credit side of the realization account. If debtors do not realize the book amount (some bad debts are encountered or discounts allowed for early payment), then the difference is a loss and should be debited to the realization account. Pay the creditors (credit cash and debit creditors). Any discount received will go to the credit side of the realization account. The costs of realization will be credited to cash and debited to the realization account. A credit balance on the realization account means that the consideration is greater than the book value of assets sold, and a profit on realization has been made.

Step 4

The profit is apportioned in the profit-sharing ratio and posted to the credit of the partners' capital accounts. The balance on the capital account is then settled in cash or shares, or both, and at this point all accounts will be closed – debit capital and credit shares or cash.

Example

William and Samantha are in business as partners sharing profits in the ratio of 3:1. A summarized balance sheet for their business as at 31 December is as follows:

	£	£
Capital accounts:		
William	300 000	
Samantha	100 000	
		£400 000
Represented by :		
Fixed assets		184 000
Investments		48 000
Current assets :		
Stock	90 000	
Debtors	168 000	
Cash	25 200	
	283 200	
Less trade creditors	115 200	
		168 000
		£400 000

Included in the fixed assets were two motor cars at book values of £18,000 and £13,400 respectively, i.e. a total of £31,400.

The partners have decided to cease trading as a partnership and have sold their stock and fixed assets to Stockholders Ltd for a price of £440,000, to be satisfied by a payment in cash of £160,000 and the issue to the partners of 280,000 ordinary shares of £1 each in Stockholders Ltd. The two vehicles mentioned above were excluded from the sale, since William had agreed to take over the first car at a valuation of £22,000, and Samantha had agreed to take over the other car at £12,800.

On final realization £166,000 was received from the debtors, the investments were sold for £52,000, and creditors settled for £114,000. The costs of dissolving the firm were paid in cash for £2,400.

The partners agreed that the ordinary shares were to be allocated in proportion to the capitals shown in the balance sheet above (3:1) with any final balance to be settled by cash.

Required:

Record the above transactions to close the books of the partnership.

Dr   **Realization Account**   **Cr**

	£	£		£	£
Fixed assets			Stockholders Ltd		
£(184,000 – 31,400, the cars)		152 600	Purchase consideration:		
Stock		90 000	Shares	280 000	
Dissolution costs		2 400	Cash	168 000	440 000
Bad debts (168,000–166,000)		2 000	Profit on sale of		
Loss on Samantha's vehicle (13,400–12,800)		600	investments (52,000 – 48,000)		4 000
Profit on realization			Profit on William's vehicle (22,000 – 18,000)		4 000
William (³/₄)	151 200		Creditors (115,200 – 114,000)		
Samantha (¹/₄)	50 400		discount received		1 200
		201 600			
		£449 200			£449 200

Dr	Fixed Asset Account		Cr
	£		£
Balance	184 000	Vehicle A – disposal account	18 000
		Vehicle B – disposal account	13 400
		Realization account	152 600
	£184 000		£184 000

Dr	Vehicle A Disposal Account		Cr
	£		£
Fixed assets – book value	18 000	William capital account	22 000
Profit on disposal to realization	4 000		
	£22 000		£22 000

Dr	Vehicle B Disposal Account		Cr
	£		£
Fixed assets – book value	13 400	Samantha capital account	12 800
		Loss on disposal to realization	600
	£13 400		£13 400

Note: The profit of William's vehicle arises since he has agreed to take it over at a valuation in excess of its book value. Samantha takes over her car at a value which is less than its book value, so a loss is made. The investments were sold for more than their book value. The accounting entries are:

Dr	Investment Account		Cr
	£		£
Balance	48 000	Cash	52 000
Profit to realization account	4 000		
	£52 000		£52 000

Dr	Cash Book		Cr
	£		£
Balance b/d	25 200	Creditors	114 000
Stockholders Ltd	160 000	Dissolution costs	2 400
Sale of investments	52 000	William's capital account	219 200
Debtors	166 000	Samantha's capital account	67 600
	£403 200		£403 200

Dr	Stockholders Ltd		Cr
	£		£
Purchase consideration	440 000	Cash	160 000
		Shares in Stockholders	280 000
	£440 000		£440 000

Dr	Shares in Stockholders Ltd		Cr
	£		£
Stockholders Ltd	280 000	William capital account	210 000
		Samantha capital account	70 000
	£280 000		£280 000

The shares are apportioned between the partners according to their capital ratio, i.e. 3:1.

Partners' Capital Account

	William	Samantha		William	Samantha
	£	£		£	£
Motor cars	22 000	12 800	Balances b/d	300 000	100 000
Shares	210 000	70 000	Profit on		
			realization	151 200	50 400
Cash (Balance)	219 200	67 600			
	£451 200	£150 400		£451 200	£150 400

The capital account tells a simple story : how much each partner had before realization, what each share of profit was on realization, and how capital was withdrawn – shares, cash and goods.

The partnership assets will now be recorded in the books of Stockholders Ltd. If the consideration paid for them exceeds their value, the amount of the excess will appear as an extra asset, goodwill.

CONVERSION OF A PARTNERSHIP TO A LIMITED COMPANY

Partners may decide to change the form of their business to a limited company. The entries for this change are similar to those for the sale of a partnership to the company. The fixed and current assets and current liabilities are transferred to a company, and shares are issued to the partners in place of their capital accounts. Often the partnership books are used for the company's accounts, and in some cases the conversion entries are not made until after the event. If the conversion takes place during an accounting year it is necessary to apportion the profit for the year to a partnership period, when it will be divided in profit-sharing ratio, and a company period, when it will be divided pro rata to shareholdings. If a partner retires on the conversion date he will not be a shareholder and cannot receive a share of post-conversion profits, but if his capital was not repaid to him on the conversion date it will appear as a loan in the company's accounts and interest thereon would normally be provided.

Partnership assets are usually revalued at the conversion date. The consideration for net assets in the partnership is the amount of shares issued to the partners. It seems logical to allocate shares on the basis of partners' capital accounts, but if this is done profits in the company may be shared on a different basis from that ruling in the partnership. Agreement can be reached if partners become directors and draw salaries or fees which will compensate for any loss of income.

Example

Frank, Victor and Jon are in partnership, sharing profits in the ratio of 2:2:1. Jon decided to retire from the partnership on 30 June taking with him stock, which cost £50,000, at a valuation of £65,000.

Balance Sheet of Frank, Victor and Jon as at 30 June

	£	£
Fixed assets (net of depreciation)		
Premises		420 000
Plant		280 000
Vehicles		40 000
		740 000
Current assets		
Stock	225 000	
Debtors	270 000	
Cash	16 000	
	511 000	
Less creditors	180 000	
Working capital		331 000
Net assets		£1 071 000
Capital:		
Frank		460 000
Victor		273 000
Jon		338 000
		£1 071 000

Frank and Victor decided to convert their business to a limited company on the day Jon retired. Premises were revalued at £510,000, and some surplus plant with a book value of £50,000 was sold for £40,000. The company was to be called Fravic Ltd. It would take over the assets and liabilities of the partnership, and would issue 1,200,000 £1 ordinary shares to Frank and Victor, in consideration for their partnership capitals. Jon was to receive all the cash, in the partnership bank account, and the remainder of his investment would be left with Fravic Ltd as a long-term loan.

The steps to account for these transactions would be:

1. Revalue the premises and divide the surplus equally between the partners in a **revaluation** account.

2. Some assets have been sold to Fravic Ltd, some to Jon, and some for cash; therefore a **realization** account is required to calculate the surplus and divide it between the partners.

3. An account must be opened for Fravic Ltd, which has bought most of the assets of the business and assumed the liabilities. The consideration (the price) will be settled by the issue of shares to the partners and a loan from Jon.

4. These transactions must be reflected in the capital accounts of the partners.

5. A retiring partners' account should show Jon's share of the business and how he will be paid out.

6. Last, a balance sheet for Fravic Ltd at 30 June can be drafted.

Step 1

Dr		Revaluation Account		Cr
		£		£
Premises at old valuation		420 000	Premises at new valuation	510 000
Surplus on revaluation to				
capital accounts				
Frank (2)	36 000			
Victor (2)	36 000			
Jon (1)	18 000			
		90 000		
		£510 000		£510 000

Step 2

Dr		Realization Account		Cr
		£		£
Premises		510 000	Creditors	180 000
Plant		280 000	Retiring partner – stock	65 000
Vehicles		40 000	Cash – sale of plant	40 000
Stock		225 000	Fravic Ltd	1 200 000
Debtors		270 000		
Profit on realization				
To partners' capital account				
Frank (2)	64 000			
Victor (2)	64 000			
Jon (1)	32 000			
		160 000		
		£1 485 000		£1 485 000

Step 3

Dr		Fravic Ltd		Cr
	£			£
Price for net assets	1 200 000	Settled by		
		* Shares:		
		Frank's capital		560 000
		Victor's capital		373 000
		Loan:		
		Retiring partner		267 000
	£1 200 000			£1 200 000

*Shares issued are the balancing figure on the capital accounts of Frank and Victor.

Step 4

Dr				Partnership Capital Accounts				Cr
	Frank	Victor	Jon		Frank	Victor	Jon	
	£	£	£		£	£	£	
Retiring partner	—	—	388 000	Opening balance	460 000	273 000	338 000	
Shares in Fravic Ltd	560 000	373 000	—	Surplus on revaluation	36 000	36 000	18 000	
				Profit on realization	64 000	64 000	32 000	
	£560 000	£373 000	£388 000		£560 000	£373 000	£388 000	

Step 5

Dr		Retiring Partner's Account – Jon		Cr
	£			£
Stock	65 000	Balance of capital		388 000
Cash £(16,000 + 40,000)	56 000			
Fravic Ltd loan	267 000			
	£388 000			£388 000

The cash balance was £16,000, but this is increased by £40,000 when some items of plant are sold.

Step 6

Fravic Ltd has purchased certain net assets for £1,200,000. If the fair value of the assets is less than the price paid, the difference is accounted for by the creation of an intangible asset – goodwill in the accounts of Fravic Ltd.

The computation is:

	£
Fixed assets £(510,000 + 280,000 + 40,000 − 50,000 sold for cash)	780 000
Current assets £(225,000 + 270,000 − 50,000 sold to Jon)	445 000
Less liabilities assumed	(180 000)
Net assets acquired at 'fair value'	1 045 000
Price	1 200 000
Goodwill (surplus of price over fair value)	£155 000

Fravic Ltd Balance Sheet at 1 July

	£	£
Intangible asset – goodwill		155 000
Fixed assets:		
Premises		510 000
Plant £(280,000 − 50,000)		230 000
Vehicles		40 000
		935 000
Current assets:		
Stock £(225,000 − 50,000)	175 000	
Debtors	270 000	
	445 000	
Less current liabilities	180 000	
Working capital		265 000
Total assets less current liabilities		1 200 000
Loan account (retiring partner – Jon)		267 000
Net assets		£933 000
Share capital £(560,000 + 373,000)		£933 000

CONCLUSION

Accounting for partnerships is concerned with appropriating profit according to the agreement made between the partners, or the law if there is no agreement on a certain point. When partners leave or join the firm it is important to ensure that the full value of their share of the partnership assets is determined. This implies the valuation of goodwill and its treatment in the accounts. The entries for partners' capital and current accounts are significant for both appropriation of profit and change of partners.

Discussion Topics

Thirty-minute essay questions:

1. Explain the significance of accounting items you might expect to find in a partnership agreement

2. What is goodwill? What factors generate the extra profits in a partnership on which goodwill is based?

SEMINAR EXERCISES

9.1 **Alan, Bill and Chris** are in partnership and have traded together successfully for many years, making and selling identification equipment for the export packaging trade. Bill perceived a new business opportunity which he intended to develop on his own and advised his partners that he would leave the partnership on 31 December. Alan and Chris considered the situation and agreed to convert the business to a limited company on that date. The new company was to be incorporated as Alchris Ltd.

The balance sheet of the partnership as at 31 December was as follows:

	£	£		£	£
Partners' capital			Fixed assets		
Alan	300 000		Freehold property	600 000	
Bill	300 000		Plant	255 272	
Chirs	150 000		Vehicles	42 613	
		750 000	Fixtures and		
			fittings	32 505	
Current accounts					930 390
Alan	41 118		Current assets:		
Bill	94 260		Stock	328 422	
Chris	36 209		Debtors	181 875	
		171 587	Cash	15 624	
Loan account					525 921
Alan	210 000				
Current liabilities					
Trade creditors		324 724			
		£1 456 311			£1 456 311

During December the partners met to agree the terms of the changes outlined above. They agreed that:

(a) Part of the premises was not required by the new company and was to be sold for £112,500. Bill was to be allowed to retain his car at a valuation of £6,000, and he would also take out of the business some stock valued for balance sheet purposes at £30,000.

(b) The remaining assets and current liabilities of the partnership, except cash, were to be purchased by Alchris Ltd for a consideration of £1,050,000. Legal and valuation expenses related to these changes were £751 and were to be borne by the partnership, and paid immediately.

(c) The consideration was to be paid by Alchris Ltd partly by the issue of a 14 per cent loan to Alan in lieu of his loan account, and to Bill to cover his remaining investment in the partnership after he had been paid all the cash in the partnership bank account. The balance of the consideration would be settled by the issue of ordinary shares of £1 to Alan and Chris.

Required:

Draft the closing entries for the partnership books

9.2 **Eric, Fred and Geoff** are in partnership, sharing profits and losses in the ratio 3:2:1. The balance sheet for the partnership as at 30 June is as follows:

	£	£		£	£
Capital			Fixed assets		
Eric		92 500	Premises		88 000
Fred		67 500	Plant		39 000
Geoff		25 000	Vehicles		14 000
		185 000	Fixtures		3 000
					144 000
Current accounts			Current assets		
Eric	4 714		Stock	63 479	
Fred	(2 009)		Debtors	33 880	
Geoff	4 178	6 883	Cash	560	97 919
Loan – Geoff		27 000			
Current liabilities					
Creditors		23 036			
		£241 919			£241 919

Geoff decides to retire from the business on 30 June and Hal is admitted as a partner on that date. The following matters are agreed:

(a) Certain assets were revalued:

	£
Premises	118 000
Plant	37 000
Stock	54 279

(b) Provision is to be made for doubtful debts in the sum of £2,000.
(c) Goodwill is to be recorded in the books on the date Geoff retires in the sum of £21,000. The partners in the new firm do not wish to maintain a goodwill account, so that amount is to be written back against the new partners' capital accounts.
(d) Eric and Fred are to share profits in the same ratio as before, and Hal is to have the same share of profits as Fred.
(e) Geoff is to take his car at its book value of £2,900 in part payment, and the balance of all he is owed by the firm in cash, except £30,000, which he is willing to leave as a loan account.

(f) Hal is to contribute £79,000 in cash as his capital. Eric is to transfer £10,000 from current account to capital account.

You are required to:
(a) Account for the above transactions, including goodwill and retiring partners' accounts.
(b) Draft a balance sheet for the partnership of Eric, Fred and Hal as at 30 June.

9.3 **Garner, Murray and Wilkins** are trading in partnership together, sharing profits and losses equally. The balance sheet of the business as at 31 December is as shown on page 148.

The partnership business has made losses in recent years and the bank and trade creditors are pressing for repayment of funds advanced to the business. Garner and Murray consider the suggestion that they should inject more capital into the business, but decide against the plan. Wilkins is now bankrupt and so cannot advance more funds, but his wife is owed £200,000 by the business. The partners decide to sell the business as at 31 December to Scott plc, a company in the same trade.

The terms of the sale are as follows:

(a) Scott plc agrees to purchase the land and buildings, plant, two of the vehicles and the stock, all for £1,002,000.
(b) The third vehicle, a car, which has a book value of £12,000, is to be taken by Murray as part of his capital repayment. The price agreed for the car is £8,000 but Murray also agrees to settle personally the hire purchase debt owing on the car.
(c) The partners collect the debts of their business but, because of their haste, £8,000 bad debts are incurred and £4,000 of cash discounts are allowed.
(d) The consideration is to be partly settled by Scott plc by the payment of £737,200 in cash and the assumption of the trade creditors (all except a personal contact of Garner, who is owed £20,000 and is paid separately by the partnership). The balance of the consideration is to be settled by the issue of £1 ordinary shares in Scott plc at par to the partners.

Required:

Draft ledger accounts to close the books of the partnership, and account for Wilkins deficit.

Garner Murray and Wilkins Balance Sheet as at 31 December 2003

	£	£
Capital:		
Garner		140 000
Murray		70 000
Wilkins		<u>42 000</u>
		252 000
Current accounts:		
Garner	10 000	
Murray	16 000	
Wilkins	(6 000)	20 000
Loan account:		
Mrs Wilkins		<u>200 000</u>
Net capital employed		£472 000
Represented by:		
Fixed assets, at book value		
Land and buildings		901 640
Plant		154 230
Vehicles		<u>36 130</u>
		1 092 000
Current assets:		
Stock	74 000	
Debtors	<u>102 000</u>	
	176 000	
Less current liabilities:		
Trade creditors	(182 800)	
Hire purchase on car	(6 000)	
Overdraft	<u>(607 200)</u>	
		<u>(620 000)</u>
		£472 000

CHAPTER 10

Accounting from Incomplete Records

THE AIMS OF THIS CHAPTER

To enable students to

- Understand that an accountant must use the information available to estimate missing amounts when records are incomplete

- Use figures to calculate an opening statement of affairs, sales and purchases for the year, and cash and petty cash accounts

- Draft a receipts and payments account and an income and expenditure account

- Draft accounts for a club or 'not for profit' organization

WHAT ARE INCOMPLETE RECORDS?

Some businesses do not maintain a complete double entry accounting system. The reason for this situation is neglect, the absence of good systems analysis at the design stage, or the piecemeal growth of the accounting system over a number of years. Sometimes the lack of a complete set of records, or indeed of any records at all, is caused by their loss, for example in a fire or a burglary. The accountant must use expertise to work with whatever information is to hand to complete the accounting statements.

Some systems will be more complete than others, and the procedure adopted by an accountant to produce sensible statements will depend on the records and documents discovered when the job is commenced. Perhaps there will be a single entry system, where one side of each transaction has been recorded, in the cash book for example, so that all that is needed to complete the system is to post the single entries to the appropriate accounts in order to produce a set of double entry records. The bank statement is a very useful document in this respect, since all movements in and out of the bank account of the firm will be shown here, even though some items on the bank statement are not shown in the cash book. In more primitive systems the accountant will have to build up the figures by drawing conclusions from the answers to enquiries and by deduction from other scraps of information gleaned from the business.

THE OPENING STATEMENT OF AFFAIRS

The starting point is the computation of an opening statement of affairs. This is a list of assets and liabilities, so that when liabilities are deducted from assets the capital invested in the business at the beginning of the period will be calculated. A - L = C.

It is difficult to value assets as they stood at the beginning of the accounting period, and some accountants use the original cost less an amount for accumulated depreciation up to the opening date of the accounting period. The figures for stock, debts and liabilities have to be estimated, but the bank balance can be determined from the bank statement. Cash not yet banked or held as a float is an asset in this calculation. If an account is opened for each of the fixed and current assets and the liabilities and capital amount, then the foundation of the double entry system has been laid.

ANALYSIS

The next task is to analyse the bank statement, for the receipts and payments of cash. Receipts are generated by cash takings paid into the bank and money received from debtors (these make up the figures for sales). Other receipts include

(a) miscellaneous income (discounts or dividends on investments)

(b) amounts of fresh capital introduced into the business, and

(c) liquid funds generated by the sale of assets.

The payments shown on the bank statement can be analysed into separate columns for

(a) expenses paid in cash,

(b) amounts paid to creditors for purchases,

(c) wages paid,

(d) petty cash expenses paid,

(e) cash drawn out by the proprietor or expenses paid for the proprietor through the business bank account, and

(f) assets purchased.

Capital expenditure items must be identified and treated accordingly. The bank statement may not show a complete picture of all monies received, since some amounts received from cash takings may not have been paid into the bank because they were used to pay in cash the running expenses of the business, or because they were used by the proprietor for personal expenditure (drawings). Enquiries reveal such amounts so that sales, and costs or drawings, can be increased by the appropriate amount. Further enquiries should determine the amounts of stock drawn from the business for the personal use of the proprietor (debit drawings and credit (reduce) the cost of goods sold). The opening cash float is included in the statement of affairs, and if this float increases this will be part of the cash takings figure.

The totals of the analysis columns can be posted to the relevant accounts, and a set of double entry accounts emerges. Journal entries will introduce into the system the amounts of takings used to pay cash expenses or withdrawn by the proprietors. Estimates of amounts prepaid, and accrued expenses must be made in the normal way.

COMPUTING PURCHASES AND SALES

It is possible to calculate the sales and purchases figures by deduction. Purchases can be computed from the creditors figures by taking the amount paid to creditors during the year, subtracting the amount owed to creditors at the beginning of the year, and adding on the amount owed to creditors at the end of the year. One disadvantage of this technique is that it produces a figure for credit purchases only, so the amount of cash purchases must also be added on if the correct total is to be obtained.

Sales can be calculated from debtors by taking the amount paid by debtors during the period, subtracting from it the amount owed by debtors at the start of the period, and adding on the amount owed by debtors at the end of the period. This formula only provides a figure for credit sales and any cash sales must be added to this amount to find the correct total. Cash sales are not always the same as cash takings banked, since this amount must be increased to cover those cash takings which have been spent in cash to pay the running expenses of the business, or taken as drawings.

Sometimes the use of the mark-up or gross profit percentage is helpful as a check on the accuracy of figures. The application of the mark-up to the cost of goods sold will show a figure for sales, and likewise if the gross profit percentage is applied to sales, an amount for costs can be worked out. For example, if the cost of goods sold is £1,000 and the mark-up on cost is 20 per cent, then the figure for sales must equal £1,200. A gross profit of £200 on sales of £1,200 is a rate of 16.67 per cent. Thus sales minus a gross profit margin of 16.67 per cent will show the cost figure, so £1,200 minus 16.67 per cent of £1,200 proves £1,000, the cost of goods sold.

Note: A mark-up of one-fifth on cost means that one-sixth must be subtracted from the sales figure to get back to the cost figure. Five-fifths plus one-fifth equal six-fifths, and this figure must be divided by six to get back to one-fifth of cost.

Example to calculate purchases

The incomplete records technique is similar to using a child's building bricks to compute the figure needed from the evidence available.

	£
Cash paid to creditors during period	5 000
Less opening creditors	2 000
	3 000
Plus closing creditors	1 000
Purchases on credit terms	£4 000

Add cash purchases, if any, to find total purchases. Ensure that all cash paid to creditors is for revenue rather than capital items. By a simple rearrangement you can deduce the missing cash figure if the purchases and opening and closing creditors are known.

	£
Opening creditors	2 000
Plus purchases	4 000
	6 000
Less closing creditors	1 000
Cash paid	£5 000

Example to calculate sales

The same logic can find the credit sales figure by using the cash received and the opening and closing debtors. The computation of the overall sales figure does, however, require more information concerning the takings from cash sales and the way in which cash not yet banked has been spent.

		£
Cheques received from debtors		14 000
Less opening debtors		4 000
		10 000
Plus closing debtors		5 000
Credit sales		15 000
Plus cash takings banked	8 000	
Cash takings spent on expenses	3 000	
Increase in cash float	500	
Cash drawn from till by proprietor	1 000	
Cash sales		12 500
Total sales		£27 500

Any debts written off during the year must be added back to show the true sales figure. Goods withdrawn by the proprietor for his own use will be debited to drawings and credited to sales if they are at selling price, or alternatively credited to purchases if they are at cost price.

The gross profit percentage or mark-up can often be used to compute the sales figure. If the cost of goods sold can be found, then by applying the gross profit percentage, the figure can be 'grossed up' to sales. The sales figure can also be used to work back to cost of sales.

Sales of £440,000 at a mark-up **on cost** of 10 per cent means a deduction of $^{10}/_{110}$ or $^1/_{11}$ from sales to get back to cost, £400,000. Once the cost of sales is determined, the opening and closing stocks can be used to compute the purchases figure using 'opening stock plus purchases less closing stock equals cost of sales'. If the opening and closing creditors are known, the cash paid to creditors can be found, or, if cash paid and opening creditors are known, the closing creditors figure can be computed.

Example of drafting accounts from incomplete records

Peter Bean commenced business on 1 January as a wholesaler of frozen vegetables. The accounting system used in the business is rudimentary, and you have been asked to produce accounts for the year ended 31 December.

The following is a summary of the bank statements for the year:

Receipts. Cash introduced as capital on 1 January £122,000; banked from cash received from customers £234,300.

Payments. Motor van £14,000; freezer equipment £30,000; office furniture £15,000; factory rent £7,500; wages £27,088; commission to sales manager £14,800; goods purchased for resale £139,600; electricity £1,800; repairs £1,250; insurance £1,220; van expenses £1,746; drawings by cheque £10,000.

Note: The following cash payments were made before banking the balance of the takings: motor expenses £1,516; wages £3,593; sundry expenses £1,100; drawings by Peter Bean £254 *per week*.

The following information is also relevant:

1. Discounts allowed to customers during the year were £2,490, while discounts received totalled £1,200. Goods sold to Rooster during the year amounted to £1,800, but he has now disappeared without paying for them. Peter Bean has taken goods for his own use which could have been sold for £2,500. Discounts allowed are a cost, discounts received are a revenue, Rooster is a bad debt and Bean has drawn goods as well as cash during the year.

2. On 31 December £8,000 was owed to suppliers and £16,200 was owed by customers. The prepayment of insurance was £320. Stock at cost amounted to £14,820. The factory had been occupied since 1 January at an annual rent of £10,000 – if not paid this should be accrued.

3. Peter Bean tells you that in his view the van will have a useful life of four years, and the office and freezer equipment will last ten years. Do not forget that depreciation should be provided on the van at 25 per cent of cost, and on the freezer and office equipment at 10 per cent of cost. In the absence of a scrap value it is best to act conservatively and assume that the assets will be worthless when worn out.

4. On 31 December there was £100 in the petty cash box.

The steps to take are:

Step 1
Write up the petty cash account to determine as the balancing figure the amount of sales receipts used to pay expenses. Do not forget the £100 closing balance, especially in the balance sheet.

Dr		Petty Cash Account		Cr
	£			£
Sales receipts	19 517	Motor expenses		1 516
(*balancing figure* – to debtors account)		Wages		3 593
		Sundries		1 100
		Drawings (£254 × 52)		13 208
		Balance c/f (Petty cash box)		100
	£19 517			£19 517
Balance b/d	100			

Step 2
Write up the cash book to find the closing bank balance. If, instead, the bank balance is found from the bank statement, the figure for cash received from customers can be computed as the balancing figure on the account, e.g. if as below £92,296* is known then £234,300* can be found by deduction. If cash received from customers is also known, another balancing figure might be drawings.

Dr		Cash Book		Cr
	£			£
Capital	122 000	Motor van		14 000
Received from customers	*234 300	Freezer equipment		30 000
		Office furniture		15 000
		Rent		7 500
		Wages		27 088
		Sales commission		14 800
		Purchases paid for		139 600
		Electricity		1 800
		Repairs		1 250
		Insurance		1 220
		Van expenses		1 746
		Drawings		10 000
		Balance c/f		*92 296
	£356 300			£356 300
Balance b/d	92 296			

It would be possible to start a set of double entry accounts by recording the other side of these cash transactions. There is, however, a difference between cash recorded and the profit and loss account items. Some cash items will need to be capitalized, and accruals and prepayments must be introduced.

Step 3
Write up accounts for creditors and debtors, to find the amounts needed for the trading account – purchases and sales. There are no opening balances because the business only commenced on 1 January. This step merely formalizes into T-account form the computations shown on the previous page.

Dr		Creditors Account		Cr
	£			£
Bank, payments	139 600	Trading account – purchases		148 800
Discounts received	1 200	(*balancing figure*)		
Creditors on 31 December c/f	8 000			
	£148 800			£148 800
		Balance of creditors b/d		8 000

Dr		Debtors Account		Cr
	£			£
Trading account – sales	276 807	Petty cash		19 517
(*balancing figure*)		Bank		234 300
		Drawings in kind		2 500
		Discounts allowed		2 490
		Bad debts, Rooster		1 800
		Debtors on 31 December c/f		16 200
	£276 807			£276 807
Balance of debtors b/f	16 200			

Step 4
Prepare the trading and profit and loss accounts, together with a balance sheet.

Trading and Profit and Loss Account for the Year Ended 31 December

	£	£
Sales		276 807
Purchases	148 800	
Less closing stock	14 820	133 980
Gross profit		142 827
Add discounts received		1 200
		144 027

	£	£
Expenses		
Wages £(27,088 + 3,593)	30 681	
Rent £(7,500 cash + 2,500 accrued)	10 000	
Electricity	1 800	
Insurance £(1,220 cash - 320 prepaid)	900	
Sales commission	14 800	
Motor expenses £(1,746 + 1,516)	3 262	
Bad debt, Rooster	1 800	
Discounts allowed	2 490	
Repairs	1 250	
Sundries	1 100	
Depreciation		
Van £(14,000 ÷ 4)	3 500	
Freezer equipment £(30,000 ÷ 10)	3 000	
Office furniture £(15,000 ÷10)	1 500	76 083
Net profit		£67 944

Peter Bean, Balance Sheet as at 31 December

	£ Cost	£ Depreciation	£
Fixed assets:			
Freezer equipment	30 000	3 000	27 000
Office equipment	15 000	1 500	13 500
Vehicle	14 000	3 500	10 500
	59 000	8 000	51 000
Current assets:			
Stock		14 820	
Debtors (including prepayments of £320)		16 520	
Bank		92 296	
Cash		100	
		123 736	
Less current liabilities:			
Trade creditors	8 000		
Accruals – rent	2 500	10 500	
Working capital			113 236
Net assets			£164 236
Financed by			
Peter Bean capital			122 000
Add net profit		67 944	
Less drawings £(13,208 + 2,500 + 10,000)		25 708	42 236
Net capital employed			£164 236

INCOMPLETE RECORDS – EXTENDING THE TECHNIQUE

In the situation where an amount of disorganized information is supplied to the accountant, the task is to assimilate the data, understand the transactions and construct a set of ledger accounts. Accruals and prepayments follow, and accounts for the business can be produced. In this situation the identification of cash and bank movements enables the accountant to write up a cash book which acts as the cornerstone to the system of ledger accounts. A question illustrating this variation of incomplete records techniques is to be found among the seminar exercises at the end of this chapter (Question 10.2)

A further example of incomplete records concerns the theft of cash or stock through fraud or burglary, or the loss of stock during a fire. The task in this situation is to calculate how much stock should have been in the warehouse, or how much cash should have been banked, which when compared with stock counted or money banked will disclose the amount of the loss. The use of mark-up and gross profit ratios, and the application of the building bricks discussed above, will help to solve the problem.

Example: Calculating amounts stolen

There was a burglary at the warehouse of **Neptune Ltd** in the early hours of 1 December, and items of stock were stolen. The company does not keep continuous stock records, and stock was last counted (by internal staff) on 30 September, for the quarterly accounts. In addition, the company's cash box was stolen.

You ascertain the following:

(a) Stock according to the internal stocktake amounted to £74,380 in September. However, closer inspection reveals two major errors: (i) one stock sheet totalled £11,360, but this had been carried forward into the total as £13,160; (ii) 200 items costing £28 each had been costed at £2.80.

(b) Sales recorded in October and November amounted to £54,280, but of this total £9,600 of goods had been despatched by 30 September.

(c) Sales are made on credit at a mark-up of $33^1/_3$ per cent on cost.

(d) Purchases in October and November amounted to £37,320. Of November purchases, £3,200 did not arrive in the warehouse until 4 December.

(e) Sales returns amounted to £1,240 (sales value) in October and November; there were no purchase returns in that period. The returned goods were perfect, but not as ordered by the customer.

(f) Items which had been valued at cost £1,175 at 30 September were written down to £600 net realizable value in October.

(g) Stock at 1 December amounted to £56,740, after the burglary.

(h) The value of cash on hand on 30 September was £251.

(i) An analysis of the bank statement shows that bankings in October and November amounted to £55,120.

(j) Debtors at 30 September amounted to £48,740 and at 1 December to £44, 980.

(k) Cash disbursements for sundry small expense items during October and November are estimated to have been £1,470.

Required:

Compute the value of stock and of cash lost in the theft.

Neptune Ltd: A solution for stock

The relevant note in the question is shown in brackets. *First*, correct the stock sheet for 30 September.

	£
Stock 30 September as per stocktake	74 380 (a)
Less transposition error (£13,160 − £11,360)	1 800 (a)
	72 580
Add pricing error (200 × (£28 − £2.8))	5 040 (a)
True stock on 30 September	77 620

Next find the amount of stock purchased in October and November.

	£	
October and November purchases	37 320 (d)	
Less December deliveries (after the burglary)	3 200 (d)	34 120
		111 740

Next, deduct the cost of sales taken out of stores in October and November.

	£	
Sales	54 280 (b)	
Less September despatches	9 600 (b)	
Sales despatched October and November	44 680	
Less returns	1 240 (e)	
	43 440	
Less mark-up ($^{33}/_{133}$ to reduce to cost)	10 860 (c)	32 580
		79 160
Less write-down of stock from cost £(1,175 − 600)		575 (f)
Stock 1 Dec should be		78 585
Stock value at 1 Dec according to stock count		56 740 (g)
Stock loss		£21 845

Neptune Ltd: A solution for cash

	£	£	£
Balance as at 30 September			251 (h)
Receipts from customers			
Opening debtors		48 740 (j)	
Sales	54 280 (b)		
Less returns	1 240 (e)	53 040	
		101 780	
Less closing debtors		44 980 (j)	
Cash and cheques received from customers			56 800
			57 051
Less sundry expenses paid in cash before banking			1 470 (k)
			55 581
Less bankings October and November			55 120 (i)
Cash balance stolen on 1 December			461

RECEIPTS AND PAYMENTS ACCOUNTS, AND INCOME AND EXPENDITURE ACCOUNTS

The double entry system is often not used for a club or a non-trading organization, so the production of accounting statements is an incomplete records problem.

Bills are received and paid through the bank account operated by the organization or from its cash resources, and monies are received by the organization for various reasons. The majority of transactions are therefore on a cash basis and thus it is very possible to prepare from the vouchers of the organization a *receipts and payments account* provided all vouchers are retained by the treasurer. This account shows on one side the monies received and on the other side the payments made by the organization. It is a summary of the cash book and combines movements through the bank account and cash transactions. The account commences with a debit balance which represents the cash and bank account of the organization on the first day of the accounting period. It is debited with funds received, and credited with payments made so that its closing balance represents the cash and bank account on the last day of the accounting period. The receipts and payments account is merely a cash account; there is no attempt to distinguish capital transactions from revenue ones, or to bring into the account accruals or prepayments, so any balance shown cannot be described as a surplus or profit revealed by the account.

The *income and expenditure account* represents the profit and loss account of a club or non-trading organization. In this account the expenses of a period are set against the revenue so that a profit, or excess of revenue over expense, can be revealed. This surplus is added to the accumulated fund, which is the term used for the capital account in the balance sheet of clubs and societies, etc.

The major differences between these two accounts are that while the receipts and payments account

(a)   deals only with cash transactions,
(b)   includes capital items as well as revenue ones, and

(c)   shows as its balance the total of funds held in cash or in the bank account of the organization,

the income and expenditure account

(a)   includes accruals and prepayments or depreciation,

(b)   excludes capital transactions, and

(c)   shows as its balance the surplus or deficit (profit or loss) made by the organization during the period.

Preparing the Accounts of a Club

An accountant will prepare an income and expenditure account from a receipts and payments account. **The first step** is to analyse the receipts and payments account so that the costs of various club activities are grouped together, and receipts from such activities are identified, and then to post the items to the income and expenditure account. This account will be credited with such items as subscriptions, fees, grants received and other items of miscellaneous income, all of which have appeared on the debit side of the receipts and payments account. The costs of the organization shown on the credit or payments side of the receipts and payments account are debited to the income and expenditure account.

The next step is to adjust the income and expenditure account for accruals, prepayments and depreciation. Once expenditure shows the true expense the account can be analysed to show separately the effect on income of the separate activities undertaken by the organization. Transactions of a capital nature shown in the receipts and payments account should be posted to asset or liability accounts in the general ledger and thus appear in the balance sheet. Any surplus of assets over liabilities at the beginning of the accounting period will be balanced in the general ledger by the amount in the accumulated fund account. This is like the capital of the club. Any surplus or profit made during the period is added to this account.

The third step is to account for peculiarities of each entity. In some cases the accumulated fund is not the only capital account of the organization; there may also be an account for life members' subscriptions or for a building fund. Some clubs and societies may hold part of their accumulated capital in separate funds since they have been raised separately from the main capital of the society for a distinct purpose.

The accounting treatment of the subscriptions of *life members* is as follows. A life member makes a large single payment instead of paying a subscription each year and is a member of a club or society until his or her death. Thus a life fund can be built up from these subscriptions which is represented, as is the accumulated fund, by the general assets of the club. As new life subscriptions are made they should *not* be taken to the credit of the income and expenditure account, but should be added to the balance on the life members' fund, and when a life member dies that part of the life fund represented by his payment should be transferred to the credit of the accumulated fund.

A similar difficulty concerns *entrance fees* to a club where these are separate from the annual subscription. There is some confusion about whether these are of an income or of a capital nature, the only principle to guide the accountant being that their treatment should be consistent from year to year. If entrance fees are written off to the income and expenditure account, the profit of the club or society could be distorted in a year when many new members join.

Subscriptions in arrears are technically debtors of the club, but in many cases they are not likely to be paid. A realistic review of the probability that arrears will be received will determine whether they are an asset. It is wrong to credit the income and expenditure account with subscriptions which are not likely to be received, but the profit of a subsequent period could be distorted if many arrears are paid in that year and counted as income of that period.

Example of the accounts of a club

This example combines the incomplete records technique with the production of the accounts of a non trading organization. The following balances were taken from the books of **Paddington Green Golf Club**, as at 1 January, the start of the club's accounting year.

	£	£
Course at cost		80 000
Clubhouse at cost		20 000
Creditors for bar supplies		350
Life membership fund		5 000
Bar stock		4 850
Clubhouse equipment at cost		3 400
Cash in hand (Treasurer's float)	100	
Cash in bank	950	1 050

An analysis of the bank account operated by the club showed the following summary of receipts and payments during the year ended 31 December

		£
Receipts	Subscriptions	26 000
	Life members (2 persons)	2 000
	Sale of instruction manuals	800
	Green fees paid by visitors	200
	Sale of old carpet from clubhouse	22
	Bar takings banked	28 600
		57 622
Payments	Upkeep of course	17 150
	General clubhouse expenses	7 950
	Bar staff wages	4 200
	Petty cash, expenses	1 550
	Bar supplies paid for	23 150
	Purchase of instruction manuals	350
	Piano purchased	700
	Replacement carpet for clubhouse	1 250
		£56 300

The following information is relevant to the preparation of the club accounts.

(a) The club maintains a capital fund and life membership fund. The capital fund and life membership fund are represented by the general assets of the club.

(b) There were five life members at the beginning of the year, one of whom has since died. Two other life members have joined the club, paying £1,000 each.

(c) There is no depreciation on the course or clubhouse. Renewals of clubhouse furnishings are to be treated as revenue expenditure.

(d) Outstanding at 31 December were:

	£
Creditors for bar supplies	1 600
Subscriptions in advance (next year)	900
Subscriptions in arrears (this year)	300

(e) Bar stocks at 31 December were valued at £4,350.

(f) It is a rule of the club that a cash float of £100 should be maintained in the treasurer's hands.

(g) An insurance premium of £480 has been paid by cheque during this year for the year to 31 March next year.

Draft an income and expenditure account for the year ended 31 December, and a balance sheet as that date.

The best method of approaching this problem is to compute as 'workings' some significant figures, using the process of deduction already described, and then build them into the accounting statements.

1. **The opening accumulated fund.** This is the recorded amount of the net assets of the club at the start of the accounting period.

	£	£
Course and clubhouse at cost		100 000
Bar stock		4 850
Equipment		3 400
Cash (at bank and in hand)		1 050
		109 300
Less: Creditors	350	
Life fund	5 000	5 350
Capital Fund		£103 950

2. **Subscriptions**

	£
Amounts paid in cash	26 000
Plus closing subscriptions in arrears	300
	26 300
Less closing subscriptions in advance	900
Subscriptions for the year	£25 400

3. **Renewals**

	£
Cost of new carpet	1250
Less scrap value of old	22
	1228

4. Bar trading account

	£
Paid to creditors	23 150
Less owed at start	350
	22 800
Plus owed at end	1 600
Purchases*	£24 400

	£
Opening stock	4 850
Plus purchases	24 400*
	29 250
Less closing stock	4 350
Cost of sales	24 900
Wages	4 200
	29 100
Bar takings	28 600
Loss	£500

5. General expenses

	£
Payments	7 950
Petty cash	1 550
Less prepayment ($^3/_{12} \times 480$)	(120) insurance
	£9 380

6. **Instruction Manuals.** Sales £800 − Costs £350 = Profit £450. Note: no closing stocks of manuals are accounted for.

7. **Life fund.** Opening balance, £5,000, minus one deceased plus two new members, £6,000. (Life membership £1,000.)

8. Bank Account

	£
Opening balance	950
Add total of receipts	57 622
Less total of payments	(56 300)
Closing balance	£2 272

Note: A petty cash float of £100 appears on the balance sheet. Once these 'workings' are completed, the accounts can be produced as follows:

Paddington Green Golf Club

Dr	Income and Expenditure Account Year Ended 31 December		Cr

	£	£		£
Course upkeep		17 150	Subscriptions	25 400
General expenses		9 380	Green fees	200
Renewals (net)		1 228	Profit on manuals	450
Bar loss:			Deficit for year	2 208
Cost of sales	24 900			
Wages	4 200			
	29 100			
Takings	28 600			
		500		
		£28 258		£28 258

Paddington Green Golf Club Balance Sheet as at 31 December

	£	£	£
Capital fund as at 1 January			103 950
Transfer from life membership fund			1 000
			104 950
Less deficit for the year			2208
			102 742
Life members' fund as at 1 January		5 000	
Less transfer to capital fund		(1 000)	
Add new life members		2 000	6 000
Funds employed			£108 742
Represented by:			
Fixed assets			
Course at cost			80 000
Clubhouse at cost			20 000
Clubhouse equipment at cost		3 400	
Additions : piano		700	
			4 100
Current assets			
Bar stocks		4 350	
Subscriptions in arrears		300	
Prepayments – insurance		120	
Bank		2 272	
Cash in hand		100	
		7 142	
Less current liabilities			
Subscriptions in advance	900		
Creditors for bar supplies- accrual	1 600		
		2 500	
			4 642
Net assets			£108 742

Task 10.1

What advice would you give to the committee of the Paddington Green Golf Club.

Solution

Apart from the need to collect subscriptions in arrears, and avoid a bar loss in future years, there is no depreciation on the clubhouse or clubhouse equipment. Accordingly the loss *may* be understated and some assets *may* be shown in the balance sheet at amounts in excess of their real value.

CONCLUSION

Drafting accounting statements from incomplete records requires the accountant to use investigative skills, and to demonstrate a knowledge of the relationship of one accounting item to another. It is possible to find missing amounts by building up available figures in a simple computation. It is of course necessary to appreciate the difference between a receipts and payments account and an income and expenditure account.

SEMINAR EXERCISES

10.1 **Mr Feckless** holds the view that a system of stock record cards is an expensive luxury for a business such as his. He says, 'When quarterly accounts are compiled, all that is needed for accuracy is a physical stocktake and the extension of the physical totals at cost to provide the figure for closing stock.' Stock was taken on 30 November, the end of the quarter, but Mr Feckless has lost his briefcase containing the stock sheets.

The quarterly accounts are needed urgently. It is now 15 December, so stocktaking carried out now would not necessarily reflect the position at 30 November, and in any case would take time and effort to undertake.

Your enquiries uncover the following facts:

(a) Sales invoiced to customers during the months September, October and November amounted to £85,627, but this figure includes £7,346 which relates to goods despatched in August.

(b) Goods despatched in November but not yet invoiced total £7,912 at selling price.

(c) Stocks at 31 August were £53,278.

(d) An examination of the stock sheets for 31 August reveals the following errors. The total of page 3 was £24,690, but it had been carried forward on to page 4 as £26,490. Four hundred items which had cost £17 each had been extended at £1.70 each. Page 5 had been overcast by £81.

(e) The mark-up on stock sold is $33\frac{1}{3}$ per cent.

(f) Items in stock at £725 on 31 August had been scrapped in October.

(g) Purchase invoices entered in the bought daybook during September, October and November totalled £64,539, but included goods received in August totalling £2643. Goods received in November but not yet entered in the daybook totalled £3129.

(h) Sales returns during the quarter recorded in the sales daybook were £796 and purchase returns in the bought daybook were £958.

Required:

Compute the stock figure as at 30 November for inclusion in the accounts and make a brief comment on stock levels in the firm.

10.2

Dear Mrs Jones,   31 December 20 . . .

I am very pleased that you have agreed to help me draft out the accounts of my second-hand trading business, which as you know commenced on 1 January last. Such records as I have kept are, unfortunately, to be found on tattered scraps of paper kept in an old cardboard box. I expect you will want to examine these records for yourself, but I thought it might help you if I were to summarize my business dealings up to 31 December 20 . . . as I recall them.

I was lucky enough to win £10,000 on the football pools, and with this and £2,000 lent to me by an aunt (I agreed, incidentally, to pay her 10 per cent per year interest) I started my business. I put £11,000 into the bank immediately, in a separate business account. I needed a van to enable me to collect and deliver the second-hand goods, and I am pleased to say I made a profit of £920 here; a dealer was asking £2,600 for a second-hand lorry, but I beat him down to £1,680. I have paid by cheque only £400 of this so far, but as I will finish paying the full £1,680 in three years, it will be mine before it falls to pieces in another five years from now.

I rent an old shed with a yard, and I pay only £700 a year. I've paid by cheque this year's rent and also £100 in respect of next year.

My first deal was to buy a job lot of 4,000 dresses for £12,000. I've paid a cheque for £8,000 so far and my supplier is pressing me for the rest. To date I've sold 3,000 dresses and received £11,600, which I promptly banked as it was all in cheques. I reckon I'm still owed £1,000, most of which I should be able to collect.

I bought 2,000 ties for £2,400 out of my bank account. I've sold 1,500 of these for cash (£3,000 in all) but as the remainder have been damaged I'd be lucky if I got £100 for them all. I managed to get some cigarette lighters cheaply – 100 of them cost me only £800. I'm rather pleased I haven't paid for them yet, as I think there is something wrong with them. My supplier has indicated that he will in fact accept £400 for them and I intend to take up his offer, as I reckon I can repair them for £2 each and then sell them at £16 a time – a good profit.

I haven't paid my cash into the bank at all, as the cash I got for the ties and my initial cash float enabled me to pay for my diesel, £800, and odd expenses, £500. Also it enabled me to draw £40 a week for myself. As I've done well I also took my wife on holiday. It made a bit of a hole in the bank account but it was worth all £1,200 of it.

Perhaps from what I have told you you can work out what profit I have made – only keep it as small as possible as I don't want to pay too much tax.

Yours sincerely,

Don Lerr

Required:

(a) From the data provided by Mr Lerr prepare a business trading, and profit and loss account for the period ended 31 December and a balance sheet as at that date. Show clearly all your workings and assumptions as notes to the accounts.

(b) Write a short report to Mr Lerr highlighting what you consider to be the most important features revealed by the accounts you have prepared.

10.3 **Women in Lumber** is a sorority of female lumberjacks in the state of Idaho. They have established a branch organization in Nottingham and operate a shop selling beads, trinkets and perfume. The shop is organized as a limited company, but the sisters have failed to keep good accounting records. At the end of the first year of trading they write to you, as an accountant in practice, seeking advice. Their letter is as follows:

Dear Sheila

Thank you for agreeing to sort out the accounts of our Shop 'Women in Lumber' which commenced trading on 1 January. I have analysed the bank statements as shown below, but otherwise our accounting records are not very complete. The sisterhood in America sent us £60,000 in cash to pay for the issued share capital of the business, and this was used to buy a 20-year lease of shop premises for £30,000 and to pay for shop fittings, £20,000, and a van for £10,000. The fittings will last us eight years, but the van, which has already suffered four serious accidents, will be scrapped for £1,000 in two years from now.

Launch costs and publicity cost us £8,000, so we went into overdraft from the start of our trading year. Most of our sales are for cash, but we do have some trade customers to whom we sell on credit terms. The closing balance owed by them is £24,000 but we believe 10% of this money will never be received. Closing creditors are estimated to be £34,000 and closing stock £48,209.

Women in Lumber	Analysis of Bank Statements	Year ended 31 December
Receipts		*Payments*	

Women in Lumber		Analysis of Bank Statements		Year ended 31 December
Receipts		*Payments*	
Sales: cash shoptakings banked	180 000	Launch costs	8 000
Cheques banked from credit		Cheques paid to suppliers	170 000
customers	25 000	Shop rates	9 000
		Light and heat	4 000
		Motor expenses	14 000
		Bonus to shop assistant	2 000
		Bank interest	7 500

Before the shop takings were banked some expense items were paid:

Petty cash expenses	£1 410
Wages	£600 per week
Repairs	£975
Printing and advertising	£1 430
Insurance	£1 860
Goods for resale	£4 650

There was £432 in the till on 31 December together with an unpaid electricity bill for £550 and some cheques received from credit customers, not yet banked, totalling £480. These cheques were taken into account when we calculated the closing debtor balances above. The insurance period runs from 1 July for one year, and the rates cover an eighteen-month period to 30 September next.

Our sisters in Idaho are expecting a dividend of 10% on their share capital, so I hope you will be able to prepare some accounts for us soon.

Yours sincerely,

Cynthia

Required:

Prepare a trading and profit and loss account for Women in Lumber for the year to 31 December and a balance sheet as at that date

CHAPTER 11

Control Accounts and Other Practical Matters

THE AIMS OF THIS CHAPTER

To enable students to

- Appreciate the significance of control accounts
- Draft a control account for the debtors ledger and the creditors ledger
- Reconcile a cash book to a bank statement
- Adjust for book-keeping errors by using journal entries or a suspense account

CONTROL ACCOUNTS

In most businesses a number of suppliers provide materials on credit terms, and many customers purchase goods on credit. Thus the asset debtors and the liability trade creditors which appear in the balance sheet are the total figures for a number of debtor balances and a number of creditor balances. To record the individual accounts a subsidiary ledger is maintained for debtors, and another for creditors. The individual account of each debtor is kept in the debtors ledger, a personal ledger which is not part of the main book-keeping system, while the total figure for amounts owed by all the debtors is shown in a control account in the general ledger and appears in the balance sheet as a current asset. The personal account for each creditor is kept in the creditors ledger, but the total figure for amounts owed to all creditors is shown in a control account in the general ledger and the balance is a current liability in the balance sheet.

With many accounts for debtors or creditors, book-keeping mistakes are bound to be made, so the device of the control or total account is used in an attempt to reveal them. Suppose there are 5,000 customers of a business, all buying goods on credit terms, so that 5,000 individual debtor accounts must be maintained. Goods purchased by each customer will be debited to each individual's personal account and the sales account will be credited. Cash paid by customers, discounts allowed to them and goods returned by them will be credited to the personal account of each customer and debited to cash, discounts and returns. If the amounts for the goods sold, goods returned, cash received and discount allowed for all debtors are totalled and the total figure entered into a control account, the balance of this account must equal the total of all the balances of the individual debtor accounts. If it does not, then a book-keeping mistake has been made which must be sought and rectified. Total figures from the daybooks and cash books can be used to draft the control account, since they summarize the transactions entered from those books to the individual debtor or creditor accounts.

A total account can be used to control the situation wherever a large number of postings are made to the individual accounts in a subsidiary ledger, for example the cost ledger control, or the handwritten control used to check the accuracy of amounts entered into a mechanized or computerized book-keeping system. The balance on the control account will appear in the trial balance taken out from the general ledger, while the total of balances in the subsidiary ledger must be reconciled to this figure.

Why use Control Accounts?

The advantages of control accounts are:

1. **The localization of errors.** If the total balances of a section of the debtors ledger does not agreewith its control account balance, the extent of the difference is known, and the search for it can be concentrated on that section of the ledger. This saves much time and effort.

2. **They avoid delay in producing the financial statements.** The trial balance will balance using the control account balance from the general ledger. If mistakes have been made in the personal ledgers, these can be corrected later, after the accounts are produced.

3. **They provide a useful check against inaccuracy and fraud.** If the control account is written up as part of the general ledger, it will act as an independent check on the personal ledger account. Fraudulent activity by the clerk in charge of the personal ledger will be disclosed unless collusion has taken place between employees operating the personal and general ledgers.

Typical entries in a creditors ledger control account

Dr	Creditors Ledger Control Account	Cr
	£	£
Cash paid	Opening balance b/d	
Discounts received	Purchases	
Returns outwards		
Closing balance c/f		

The totals for the month are entered into the account from the following sources : purchases from the daybook, returns from the returns daybook (written up from credit notes received), cash and discounts from the cash book.

Typical entries in a debtors ledger control account

Dr	Debtors Ledger Control Account	Cr
	£	£
Opening balance b/d	Cash received	
Credit sales	Discounts allowed	
Dishonoured cheques	Returns inwards	
(written back)	Bad debts written off	
	Closing balance c/f	

The amounts entered in the account are totals for the month (hence the name total account) and are posted from the following books :

(a) cash received and discounts allowed from the cash book;

(b) returns inwards from the sales daybook or a separate book for credit notes if one is maintained;

(c) bad debts written off from the journal;

(d) sales from the daybook; and

(e) cheques written back from the cash book.

The procedure when a customer's cheque 'bounces' is to reverse the entry made when it was first received, credit the cash book and debit the customer's account in the debtors ledger. If the control account is to reflect the total of accounts in the personal ledger, then it too must be debited. At first glance this seems to be two debits for one credit, but the debtors ledger is treated as a subsidiary ledger for memorandum purposes only, to give a detailed analysis of the total debtors figure shown in the control account. It is this total figure which appears in the trial balance and which is used in the computation of accounting statements.

Example of a debtors ledger control account

Shaw and Steadfast Ltd keep a debtors control account in their general ledger, and maintain individual accounts for each customer in a subsidiary debtors ledger. There are 150 accounts in the debtors ledger. The first eight are as follows:

	Balance at 1 January £
T. R. Andrews & Co.	1 260
Arnold & Palmer	2 640
Ankler Ltd	200
Bageholt & Drew	–
Bell Garages Ltd	3 000
T. C. Belling	600
Bright & Co.	1 360
Broadbent & Neames	2 400

The total of the balances outstanding at 1 January (including the above) is £192,840. Transactions during January affecting these accounts were:

	Sales £	Returns £	Bad debts £	Cash received £	Cash discounts £
T. R. Andrews & Co.	2 800	–	–	1 260	–
Arnold & Palmer	–	–	–	2 000	–
Ankler Ltd	1 640	280	–	1 540	20
Bageholt & Drew	700	–	–	480	20
Bell Garages Ltd	–	–	–	2 940	60
T. C. Belling	–	–	600	–	–
Bright & Co.	1 280	–	–	1360	–
Broadbent &Neames	700	60	–	2360	40
All other accounts	135 600	1 740	840	148 620	2 060
	142 720	2 080	1 440	160 560	2 200

Step 1
Head up accounts for the debtors control and for the first eight accounts in the debtors ledger. Add a further account to represent all the other customers' accounts.

Step 2
Enter the above transactions.

Step 3
Balance all the accounts and check that the total of the balances in the debtors ledger agrees with the control account balance at 31 January.

Dr	T. R. Andrews & Co.		Cr
Balance b/d	1 260	Cash	1 260
Sales	2 800	Balance c/f	2 800
	£4 060		£4 060
Balance b/d	2 800		

Dr	Arnold & Palmer		Cr
Balance b/d	2 640	Cash	2 000
		Balance c/f	640
	£2 640		£2 640
Balance b/d	640		

Dr	Ankler Ltd		Cr
Balance b/d	200	Returns	280
Sales	1 640	Cash	1 540
		Discount	20
	£1 840		£1 840

Dr	Bageholt & Drew		Cr
Sales	700	Cash	480
Discount			20
Balance c/f			200
	£700		£700
		Balance b/d	200

Dr	Bell Garages		Cr
Balance b/d	3 000	Cash	2 940
		Discount	60
	£3 000		£3 000

Dr	T. C. Belling		Cr
Balance b/d	£600	Bad debts	£600

Dr	Bright & Co.		Cr
Balance b/d	1 360	Cash	1 360
Sales	1 280	Balance c/f	1 280
	£2 640		£2 640
Balance b/d	1280		

Dr	Broadbent & Neames		Cr
Balance b/d	2 400	Returns	60
Sales	700	Cash	2 360
		Discount	40
		Balance c/f	640
	£3 100		£3 100
Balance b/d	640		

Dr	All Other Accounts		Cr
Balance b/d	181 380	Returns	1 740
Sales	135 600	Bad debts	840
		Cash	148 620
		Discount	2 060
		Balance c/f	163 720
	£316 980		£316 980
Balance b/d	163 720		

Dr	Debtors Ledger Control		Cr
Balance b/d	192 840	Returns	2 080
Sales	142 720	Bad debts	1 440
		Cash	160 560
		Discount	2 200
		Balance c/f	169 280
	£335 560		£335 560
Balance b/d	169 280		

List of balances	£
T. R. Andrews & Co.	2 800
Arnold & Palmer	640
Bageholt & Drew	200
Bright & Co.	1 280
Broadbent & Neames	640
Others	163 720
Total debtors per personal accounts	£169 280

BANK RECONCILIATIONS

At the end of an accounting period a statement will be received from the bank showing all amounts paid into or drawn out of the business bank account. The balance on this statement represents the funds of the business held at the bank or the amount overdrawn. It is rare for the balance on the statement to agree with the balance in the cash book maintained at the office of the business. It may seem strange that two records made up from the same basic documents should disagree, but this is because certain items which appear on the bank statement are not in the cash book, and vice versa.

These items are:

1. Cheques drawn by a company in favour of its creditors and entered in its cash book, but *not yet presented* at its bank for payment by those creditors. A cheque is drawn, entered on the payments side of the cash book, and then put into an envelope and sent off to the creditor. There is a time lag while the cheque is in the post, while it is at the creditor's office and while it is filtering through the banking system from the creditor's bank, where it has been paid in, to the debtor company's bank, where it is presented for payment. Thus cheques not yet presented are payments made by a business but which have not yet been paid out of its bank account.

2. Cheques received from debtors and entered into the cash book on the receipts side, but *not yet entered* on the bank statement because of the time lag while they are entered on a paying-in slip, taken to the bank and deposited, and then entered by the bank on the appropriate bank statement page.

3. Receipts or payments made by banker's order, standing order or direct debit, are payments made not by cheque but by an instruction to a bank to make the payment. Thus the transaction is completed within the banking system by the transfer of funds from one bank to another. If no prime document is produced to inform the recipient business that the payment has arrived, it discovers this only when it receives its bank statement. In this case the bank statement itself acts as the document of prime entry which evidences the transaction and initiates its entry into the cash book.

4. Miscellaneous income of a business is collected by its bank and will therefore appear on the bank statement rather than in the cash book. Dividends from an associate company, or the interest on a loan, can be paid by a warrant sent directly

to the bank of the recipient, so that if no separate notice is sent to the office of the recipient no entry will be made in the cash book until the item is picked up from the bank statement. Many companies make routine payments by standing order, and these are posted from the bank statement to the credit side of the cash book and from there debited to the appropriate expense account.

5. Other items which are first notified to the company through its bank statement concern the costs of running the bank account itself, i.e. bank charges and interest charged on overdrawn balances. These amounts must be identified on the bank statement and entered from there into the cash book.

Dishonoured Cheques

When a cheque received from a debtor and banked is dishonoured, this too will appear on the bank statement but not in the first instance in the cash book. The company receives the cheque, enters it in the cash book (debit), and posts it from there to the credit of the debtor's account. The cheque is then banked and presented by the creditor company's bank for payment. If the debtor does not have sufficient funds in his account to meet that cheque his bank will return the cheque to the creditor company's bank marked 'refer to drawer'. This means that the cheque has 'bounced', i.e. that it has been returned from the debtor's bank. The creditor company's bank will therefore write it back out of their client's account, so that it appears on the payments side of the bank statement to contra its earlier appearance on the receipts side. The bank will notify its client of this action, but often such dishonoured cheques are found to be a source of difference between the bank statement and the cash book. The company will then debit the debtor and credit cash.

Thus the differences between the cash book and the bank statement have two main causes. These are:

(a) items not yet processed completely through the banking system, and

(b) items not yet notified by the bank to the business so that they are not in the cash book.

At the end of each month, when the cash book is closed, cross-cast and posted to the accounts in the general ledger, a bank reconciliation must take place. All the items causing a difference between the cash book and the bank statement must be identified, those not yet entered in the cash book must be entered, and the remaining difference must be set out in the form of a reconciliation statement so that no items are 'lost' between the bank and the business, and the cash book total as entered in the accounts shows the correct amount for cash belonging to the business. Such a reconciliation will also eliminate errors in the cash book.

Reconciliation Procedure

The procedure is a simple one.

Step 1
The items in the cash book and in the bank statement are checked off against one another to find the transactions which are not shown on both statements.

Step 2
A list of cheques sent out to creditors and entered in the cash book but not yet presented by their recipients can be computed and deducted from the bank balance or added to the overdraft.

Step 3
The amounts paid in before the end of the period but not yet shown on the bank statement must be added to the bank statement total, which should then agree with the cash book. Amounts paid in to the bank are sometimes termed 'lodgements'. It is important to list these outstanding amounts so that at the end of the next month it can be easily ascertained that they have gone through the system correctly and are not still outstanding for some other reason.

Step 4
Extraordinary items, such as cheques on the bank statement which do not correspond with the cheque number sequence used by the company, or standing orders not authorized by the company, can come to light as a result of this system, thus highlighting mistakes and fraud.

Example of a bank reconciliation

A book-keeper has written up the cash book of **Nolling Ltd** for the month of June, but the balance shown by his work does not agree with the corresponding amount on the bank statement. Your task is to check the cash book for errors, reconcile it to the bank statement and comment briefly on any matters you discover which might merit further investigation.

Dr				Cash Book of Nolling Ltd				Cr

	Receipts				Payments			
June	Account	£	June	Cheque	Accounts	Ref	£	
6	Dawson & Co	47.50	2		Opening balance	b/d	2 761.75	
7	James	29.29						
15	Shaw	10.00	6	473	T. Maint	M13	32.00	
24	Dingle Ltd	70.00	6	474	L. Brock	B7	25.00	
24	Weather Ltd	36.32	8	475	IKI Ltd	I2	18.20	
28	Mitchells	41.29	9	476	Clumber Ltd	C4	59.14	
28	Ronalds	88.00	13	477	Crackle Ltd	C7	40.00	
	Total lodgements	322.40	16	478	Lamp & Co	L17	39.98	
30	Balance c/f	2 496.59*	19	479	Print & Co	P42	100.25	
			20	480	Bandelle Ltd	M3	22.67	
			25	481	Petty cash	PC14	50.00	
			27	482	Crumble	C4	35.00	
			27	483	Anderton	A7	30.00	
			29	484	Nimble Ltd	N21	105.00	
		£3 318.99					£3 318.99	
			July					
			1		Opening balance	b/d	2 469.59*	

Eastmid Bank Ltd, Statement of Account with Nolling Ltd

Particulars		Debit £	Credit £	Date June	Balance £
Balance forward				2	2 761.75 (o/d)
Lodged			47.50	9	2 714.25
	476	59.14		10	2 773.39
	473	32.00			
SO		16.32		12	2 821.71
	477	40.00			
	475	18.20		13	2 879.91
Lodged			29.29	20	2 850.62
	478	39.98		22	2 890.60
SO		36.00		23	2 926.60
Lodged			70.00	24	2 856.60
CT			23.34	25	2 833.26
	481	50.00			
	9437	21.50		26	2 904.76
	482	35.00		29	2 939.76
CT			46.32	30	2 893.44

SO = Standing Order
CT = Credit Transfer

Note that the cash book shows payments in excess of receipts, which means an overdrawn account at the bank. The cash book balance has been computed in error. There has been a transposition of figures when the balance was carried down (*) and a casting error in the balance calculation. The correct balance carried forward should be £2,996.59 (£3,318.99 – £322.40).

Bank Reconciliation

	£	£
Correct balance per cash book (overdrawn)		2 996.59
Deducted lodgements not entered in cash book (credit transfers)	23.34	
	46.32	69.66
		2 926.93
Add payments not entered in cash book	16.32	
	36.00	
	21.50	73.82
Real balance per cash book (overdrawn)		3 000.75
Less cheques not yet presented	105.00	
	30.00	
	25.00	
	22.67	
	100.25	282.92
		2 717.83
Add lodgements not yet credited	36.32	
	10.00	
	41.29	
	88.00	175.61
Balance per bank statement		£2 893.44

Note that as this account is *overdrawn*, cheques not yet presented are deducted and lodgements not yet credited are added.

Task 11.1

What points would you investigate as a result of this bank reconciliation?

Solution

The following points should be noted:

1. Cheque 9437 is out of sequence on the bank statement. Enquire of the bank whether this is the correct number. Ascertain whether it is a Nolling cheque.

2. Reference C4 is used twice on the payments side of the cash book. Is there a misposting? The accounts of Clumber Ltd and Crumble are not likely to be on the same page in the creditors ledger.

3. £29.29 was received from James on 7 June according to the cash book but was not banked until 20 June according to the bank statement. Why was there a delay in banking funds when the account is overdrawn?

4. Check authority for standing orders.

5. Bandelle Ltd is posting folio M3 in the cash book. Is this correct? Should it not be a 'B' posting?

ADJUSTMENTS FOR ERRORS

Mistakes often occur in the accounting system, and when they are discovered the books and accounts have to be adjusted. Some adjustments will have an effect on the profit figure, some on items in the balance sheet, and some on both the position and income statements. In some cases a compensating error will be found, the adjustment of which shows no change in a figure on an accounting statement; for example if money received from debtor A is posted to debtor B's account, when this is adjusted the overall debtor figure on the balance sheet will not have changed. The major types of adjustment are as follows.

The capital/revenue allocation. Items which should be capitalized are often written off to the income statement as expenses. They are adjusted by increasing the asset in the balance sheet and reducing the charge in the income statement, thus increasing the profit for the period. If the fixed assets are increased, the depreciation charge for the period must be updated to include the newly capitalized amount, so an extra depreciation charge will reduce the profit figure. This type of adjustment occurs where a company uses its own labour to install a new machine. In this case the wages account must be credited and the asset account debited with the cost of labour so used.

Drawings of the proprietor charged in the salaries account. An amount drawn out by a proprietor is an appropriation of profit and not a charge against profit. Salaries must be reduced and thus profits increased, but at the same time drawings increased so that the amount of retained profit remains the same.

Prepayments or accruals omitted when the accounting statements were made up. An expense discovered, after the income statement has been completed, must be debited to the profit and loss account, thus reducing the profit and shown in the balance sheet as an accrual among the current liabilities. A payment such as rent or insurance premium, for a period other than this accounting period, must be credited to the profit and loss account, thus increasing the profit, and shown in the balance sheet as a prepayment or debtor among the current assets.

Credit sales understated. If sales made to some customers on credit terms have been omitted, the amount of such sales must be credited to the trading account, thus directly increasing the profit while debtors are similarly increased in the balance sheet. Note that the profit is increased by the full amount of this transaction, since the cost of goods has already been debited to the trading account as the closing stock was taken after the goods had been sold.

Goods on sale or return counted as sold. Such goods are placed with an agent in the hope that they will be sold, but until the agent sells them they are still the property of the business and should be counted in the closing stock shown in the balance sheet. The adjustment required in this case is to reverse the entries made, so that sales are reduced, stock is increased, and the profit figure is reduced by the profit margin on this transaction.

A stock write-down. If stock is old or has lost its value, a realistic value may be less than the figure shown in the balance sheet. Stock in the balance sheet is reduced and the amount of the reduction is written off against profit in the income statement.

Errors in the cash book. There are many errors which can be made when a cash book is written up, e.g. an amount of £86 posted as £68, in which case the appropriate increase must be made, or a payment posted on the receipts side, in which case the adjustment is to post double the amount to the payments side.

Loan interest outstanding. If this expense has been omitted it must be debited to the profit and loss account, thus reducing profit, and shown among the creditors on the balance sheet. Sometimes interest is paid half-yearly so that the first instalment may appear in the trial balance, but an accrual is needed for the remainder. The loan and interest rate must be checked to find out how much has been paid.

A debtor balance which goes bad after the accounting date. An extra provision must be raised to reduce the profit and to appear as a deduction from debtors among the current assets of the balance sheet.

Taxation omitted when the profit figure is struck. Sometimes an amount for taxation, due to be paid, is forgotten. The provision is debited to the profit and loss account, thus reducing profit retained, and the amount thus provided appears on the balance sheet among the creditors, since payment has not yet been made.

Debit balances listed as credits, or debits posted as credits. The adjustment in this case is to reverse the wrong posting, remembering to double the amount involved.

Casting errors. Pages in the ledger may be under- or over-cast, in which case the difference between the wrong figure and the right figure must be calculated, and this amount added to or subtracted from cost (and profit), or the appropriate asset account as the case may be.

The list of likely adjustments shown above is not exhaustive, since the practical application of double entry book-keeping produces many types of error. Suffice it to say that a cool head is needed to work out the impact of mistakes and see what is required to correct them.

JOURNAL ENTRIES

The means by which adjustments are made in the books is the journal entry. The journal is written up in a two-column ledger so that the dual aspect of each adjustment can be seen. It is customary to explain the reason for each adjustment by means of a 'narration' or 'narrative'. Only authorized persons are allowed to make journal entries, and a file of journal vouchers is maintained as a form of internal control.

A typical journal ruling is

Date	Narration	£	£
1.4.20 …	Plant and machinery Direct labour Being cost of own 　labour used to install plant, capitalized	1423	1423

Task 11.2

The balance sheet of **Harold Derby Ltd** as at 30 June is as follows:

	£ Cost	£ Depreciation	£
Fixed assets			
Buildings	400 000	—	400 000
Plant	220 000	110 000	110 000
Vehicles	90 000	60 000	30 000
	710 000	170 000	540 000
Current assets			
Stock		230 000	
Debtors		190 000	
Cash		90 000	
		510 000	
Current liabilities			
Creditors	275 000		
Tax payable	60 000		
		335 000	
Working capital			175 000
			715 000
Long-term loan at 12% p.a.			200 000
Net Assets			£515 000
Financed by:			
Share capital			485 000
Retained profit			30 000
			£515 000

The following information is discovered after the accounts are produced. It is *your task* to draft journal entries to deal with each item below, and rewrite the balance sheet

(a) The company's own workmen were employed to construct the foundation for a new machine. No adjustment has been made in the books for the labour cost of £29,300. Depreciation is at 10 per cent using the straight line method.

(b) Interest on the loan for the half year to 30 June is outstanding, and has not yet been recorded in the books.

(c) Goods costing £24,000 have been sent to an agent on a 'sale or return' basis. These goods have been invoiced at a mark-up of 25 per cent on cost and are included in sales for the year. The goods also appear in stock.

(d) A dividend of £5,000 is to be provided.

(e) A vehicle, four years old, has been sold at its written-down value, but no entry has been made in the books to record this transaction. The original cost of the vehicle was £16,000. Depreciation on vehicles is at 20 per cent using the straight line method.

(f) A debtor of the firm who owed £8,000 has gone bankrupt. Reliable evidence confirms that his estate is likely to pay 50p in the pound.

Solution

Harold Derby Journal

	Debits £	Credits £
(a) To plant	29 300	
By labour cost		29 300
Being capitalization of labour cost of constructing the foundation of a new machine		
To profit and loss	2 930	
By depreciation		2 930
Being depreciation on newly capitalized foundation		
(b) Loan interest	12 000	
Creditors		12 000
Being loan interest for the half year, due but unpaid		
(c) Sales (24,000 + 25 per cent)	30 000	
Debtors		30 000
Being goods on sale or return written back		
(d) Dividend	5 000	
Dividend payable		5 000
Being dividend provided for the year		
(e) Vehicle disposal account – written-down value	3 200	
Depreciation on vehicles	12 800	
Vehicle account		16 000

Being transfer of balances to disposal account		
Cash	3 200	
Vehicle disposal account		3 200
Being sale of vehicle at written-down value		
(f) Profit and loss account	4 000	
Provision for doubtful debts		4 000
Being provision for doubtful debt		

Harold Derby Workings

	£
Retained profit before adjustment	30 000
(a) Labour cost capitalized increases profit	29 300
Depreciation on capital asset	(2 930)
(b) Interest accrued	(12 000)
(c) Sales counted in error – written back	(30 000)
(d) Dividend provided	(5 000)
(e) Vehicle sold for book value – no profit or loss	–
(f) Provision for doubtful debts	(4 000)
Retained profit after adjustment	£5 370

Harold Derby Balance Sheet

	£ Cost	£ Depreciation	£
Fixed assets			
Buildings	400 000	–	400 000
Plant (+ 29,300 – 2,930)	249 300	112 930	136 370
Vehicles (−16,000 + 12,800)	74 000	47 200	26 800
	723 300	160 130	563 170
Current assets			
Stock		230 000	
Debtors (−30,000 − 4,000)		156 000	
Cash (+ 3,200)		93 200	
		479 200	
Current liabilities			
Creditors (+12,000)	287 000		
Tax payable	60 000		
Dividend payable	5 000	352 000	
Working capital			127 200
			690 370
Long-term loan			200 000
			£490 370
Share capital			485 000
Retained profit			5 370
			£490 370

SUSPENSE ACCOUNT

Where a trial balance will not balance, it is sometimes the practice to open a suspense account, entering therein the difference. As errors are found they can be posted to the suspense account and the difference will gradually be eliminated.

Task 11.3

At Naunton Knitwear the month-end trial balance will not balance, credits exceeding debits by £1,227.
Inspection of the ledgers discovers the following errors:

(a) A balance of £57 on a debtor's account has been omitted from the schedule of debtors, the total of which was entered as debtors in the trial balance.

(b) A small piece of machinery purchased for £1,138 had been written off to repairs.

(c) The receipts side of the cash book had been undercast by £400.

(d) The total of one page of the sales daybook had been carried forward as £3,209, but the correct amount was £3,292.

(e) A credit note for £271 received from a supplier had been posted to the wrong side of his account.

(f) An electricity bill for the sum of £78, not yet accrued for, was discovered in a filing basket.

(g) Mr Exe, whose past debts to the company had been the subject of a provision, at last paid £311 to clear his account. His personal account has been credited but the cheque has not yet passed through the cash book.

Your task is to write up the suspense account and make the entries to clear the balance thereon. State the effect of each error on the accounts.

Dr		Naunton Knitwear Suspense Account	Cr
	£		£
Opening balance	1 227	Debtor balance omitted	57
Sales omitted	83	Cash book undercast	400
(3,292 − 3,209)		Credit note posted to	
		wrong side (271 × 2)	542
		Cash posted to Mr Exe written back	311
	1 310		1 310

(b) A capital/revenue adjustment will not affect the trial balance.

(f) This item has not yet been entered in the books and so cannot affect the balance.

Effect of errors:

(a) Debtors increase in balance sheet

(b) Capitalize £1,138, assets increase, expenses decrease, so profits increase.
Remember to depreciate the new asset.

(c) Cash increased in balance sheet.

(d) Sales increase, profit increases.

(e) Creditors reduced in balance sheet.

(f) Cost increases, profit decreases.

(g) Cash increases in balance sheet. Provision against this debt can now be removed. Affects profit and balance sheet.

CONCLUSION

Accounting techniques can be used as part of the system of internal check to prove the amounts recorded in the ledgers. The personal accounts of debtors and creditors can be checked in total by control accounts, and the cash book entries can be reconciled to the bank account. Thus figures in the ledgers are substantiated and can then be entered into financial statements with greater confidence that they are correct. The trial balance must balance before figures can be drafted onto financial statements. The suspense account helps to achieve this balance as part of the system of rechecking to locate errors.

SEMINAR EXERCISES

11.1 A summary of the cash book of **Reconcile Ltd** for the year to 30 September is as follows:

Dr		Cash Book	Cr
	£		£
Opening balance b/d	912	Payments	175 638
Receipts	176 614	Closing balance c/f	1 888
	177 526		177 526

After investigation of the cash book and vouchers you discover that

(a) Standing orders appearing on the bank statement have not yet been entered in the cash book:
   (i) interest for the half year to 31 March on a loan of £30,000 at 8 per cent per annum;

(ii) hire purchase repayments on the managing director's car, 12 months at £61 per month;

(iii) Dividend received on a trade investment, £1,248.

(b) The company owes £789 to Midlands Electricity Ltd.

(c) A cheque for £112 has been debited to the company's account in error by the bank.

(d) Cheques paid to suppliers totalling £830 have not yet been presented at the bank, and payments into the bank of £780 on 31 May have not yet been credited to the company's account.

(e) An error of transposition has occurred in that the opening balance of the cash book should have been brought down as £921, and not as £912.

(f) A cheque received from a customer for £167 has been returned by the bank marked 'refer to drawer', but it has not yet been written back in the cash book.

(g) A cheque drawn for £69 has been entered in the cash book as £96, and another drawn for £341 has been entered as a receipt.

(h) Bank charges of £213 shown on the bank statement have not yet been entered in the cash book.

(i) A page of the receipts side of the cash book has been undercast by £400.

(j) The bank statement shows a balance of £516.

Required:

Produce well-presented statements to adjust the cash book in the light of the above discoveries, and reconcile the adjusted cash book to the bank statement.

11.2 The sales ledger supervisor of **Fisheries Ltd** has been taken ill and the inexperienced ledger clerk is having problems balancing the ledgers for the month of February. He presents you with the following information and asks for your help. The balances on the individual debtor accounts at 28 February are:

	£
R. Herring & Son	1 100
S. Newt Ltd	11 600
C. Lion & Co Ltd	28 350
Fish Food Ltd	4 900
The Eating Plaice	1 950
Fred's Restaurant	2 350
H. Addock	1 800
Trout Farms	7 300
	£59 350

The balance brought forward on the debtors ledger control account for 1 February is £68,300. The clerk says he has entered the following items on the customers' account cards to get the above balances:

	Sales	Cash received	Discount allowed	Goods returned
	£	£	£	£
R. Herring & Son	2 500	1 900		
S. Newt Ltd	4 900	9 600	400	
C. Lion & Co Ltd	3 650	7 450	150	1250
Fish Food Ltd	450	850		300
The Eating Plaice	–	250		
Fred's Restaurant	700	500		
H. Addock	2 300	300		
Trout Farms	5 100	2 900	300	
Total	£19 600	£23 750	£850	£1550

When he enters the above totals in the debtors ledger control account it does not balance to the total of the customers' accounts.

On investigation you find that

(a) The sales to S. Newt Ltd have been mistakenly entered on S. Newt's account in the creditors ledger.

(b) A contra has been entered on the account of Fred's Restaurant for £650 against his account on the creditors ledger. This has not been recorded on the control account.

(c) An invoice for £2,100 in respect of C. Lion & Co Ltd. has been omitted from the list of sales and is not included in the individual account balances on 28 February.

(d) The account for Mr C. Horse showing a balance of £1,650 has been removed from the sales ledger as the debt has been proved to be bad.

(e) The cheque from R. Herring & Son has been returned by the bank marked 'refer to drawer'.

(f) A credit note for £4,500 has been posted to the account of Trout Farms but not to the control account.

(g) The cash received from C. Lion & Co Ltd had not been entered on the customer account card.

(h) The chief accountant has been looking at the account of Codds Ltd. You have reason to believe the customer account card showing a credit balance of £1,850 is locked in his filing cabinet.

Required:

(a) Complete the debtors ledger control account.

(b) Reconcile the list of individual debtors' account balances to the debtors ledger control account balance.

CHAPTER 12

Disclosure

The Accounting Requirements of the Companies Act 1985 and Other Regulations

THE AIMS OF THIS CHAPTER

To enable students to

- Appreciate the format through which financial statements communicate information to shareholders
- Learn the rules for the legal minimum of information which must be disclosed
- Understand the principles on which the format and rules are based
- Draft accounts for publication

DISCLOSURE

Financial information disclosed to shareholders and the general public gives much less detail than is provided for managers.

The Companies Act of 1985 sets out rules as to the information which companies must disclose in their annual accounts. The requirements of the Act represent the legal minimum for disclosure, but many companies show more than is required by law. The 1985 Act lays down special formats in which company accounts are to be prepared. The company must select the form of balance sheet and income statement which it wishes to use, and use it consistently.

The information specified in the Act can be shown either on the face of the profit and loss account or balance sheet, or in the form of notes appended thereto. It is usual for companies to show their published profit and loss account and balance sheet as an austere statement with a few figures. The bulk of the information is provided in the form of notes appended to the accounting statements. Information concerning the previous year is always shown in published accounts, so that a comparison can be made. Accounts are prepared for use within the firm as in Chapter 8, and then these detailed statements are edited into a form which discloses only what is required by statute.

Principles and the True and Fair View

A requirement is written into the 1985 Act (section 228) that every balance sheet and profit and loss account shall give a true and fair view, and shall be based on certain accounting principles, i.e.

1. The company is presumed to be a going concern.

2. Accounting policies shall be applied consistently.

3. Items shall be determined on a prudent basis, e.g. only profits realized at the accounting date shall be included, whereas account shall be taken of liabilities and losses which are likely to arise in respect of the financial year. Relevant information which only becomes apparent after the end of the year but before the accounts are signed by the directors must be included.

4. Income and charges for the financial year shall be taken into account without regard to the date of receipt or payment (matching – the accruals principle.)

A note covering any departure from these principles with reasons must be shown. Thus the Act brings the accounting principles required by SSAP 2 (soon to be updated by a Financial Reporting Exposure Draft, FRED 21) into the legal requirements for company accounts. A further note must disclose the accounting policies adopted when the accounts were drafted. Financial statements can only be true and fair if they are in accordance with Generally Accepted Accounting Principles (GAAP). To achieve this they must follow the rules set down in Financial Reporting Standards. (FRSs) Thus the law supports accounting standards.

The true and fair view requirement overrides other legal rules in so far as extra information not required by statute must be disclosed if it is significant for a true and fair view. Where compliance with statute would inhibit a true and fair view, a statutory requirement can be ignored. The 'true and fair view override' only operates in special circumstances which must be noted in the accounts.

The 1985 Act specifies two alternative forms of balance sheet and four alternative formats for the profit and loss account. Companies must adopt their chosen format in subsequent years unless there are special reasons for changes, which must be noted. These formats are drawn from the 4th Directive of the European Commission. The formats specified are freely adapted by accountants, whose task it is to draft sensible statements. In the United Kingdom most companies use the format shown below. The profit or loss on ordinary activities before tax must be shown, together with amounts added to, or withdrawn from, reserves, and aggregate dividends paid and proposed. The legal requirements for the profit and loss account have been extended by Financial Reporting Standard 3, 'Reporting Financial Performance'.

THE PUBLISHED ACCOUNTING STATEMENTS

These are

(a) the profit and loss account;

(b) the balance sheet;

(c) the cash flow statement, using FRS 1 to be explained in Chapter 15;

(d) the statement of total recognized gains and losses accompanied by a note of historical cost profits and losses, and a reconciliation of movements in shareholders' funds all specified by FRS 3;

(e) the directors' report, a narrative statement which must be covered by the audit.

The Mega Group: *an example of published financial statements and notes*

The statements illustrated below are for a very large public company. The term 'consolidated' in front of the profit and loss account and balance sheet means that the statement consolidates into one account the results of many subsidiary companies in the group. Thus shareholders are able to see the result of a large international group of companies in which they hold an ownership interest. Clearly, segmental information added as a note to the accounts (SSAP 25) will enable shareholders to appreciate the performance of the broad divisions of this very extensive business entity. Items marked with an asterisk are explained later in the chapter.

FRS 3 stipulates that the group profit should be analysed for

(a) continuing operations;

(b) acquisitions (businesses bought during the year);

(c) discontinued operations (businesses sold during the year).

This is appropriate, since large groups hold a portfolio of different business investments, which they adjust from time to time with losses or gains from the sale of assets or whole companies. The cash flow statement must be in accordance with FRS 1, 'Cash Flow Statements', which will be explained in Chapter 15.

Comment on Mega Group's performance in Profit and Loss Account

There was less operating profit in 2002 than in 2001 (949 against 1027) but heavy losses from business terminations in 2001 (307 and 191) reduced earnings per share, and there was no transfer to reserve. Interest cost has fallen from 171 to 94.

The Mega Group

Consolidated Profit and Loss Account for the year ended 31 December 2002

	Notes	2002 £m	2002 £m	2001 £m	2001 £m
Turnover:					
Continuing operations		6 617		6 649	
Acquisitions		428			
		7 045			
Discontinued operations		868		2 099	
Total turnover	2,3		7913		8748
Operating costs	4		(6964)		(7721)
Operating profit:					
Continuing operations		865		895	
Acquisitions		37			
		902			
Discontinued operations		47		132	
Total operating profit	2		949		1027
Share of profits/(losses) of associates					
	17		16		10
			965		1037
Continuing operations					
Disposal of fixed assets	6	13		29	
Sale or termination of businesses	7	10		(1)	
Provisions for loss on sale					
or termination of businesses	7	(43)		—	
		(20)		28	
Discontinued operations					
Disposal of fixed assets	6	—		3	
Sale or termination of businesses	7	66		(307)	
Utilization of prior year provisions	7	53		49	
Provisions for loss on sale					
or termination of business	7	(45)		(191)	
		74		(446)	
			54		(418)
Interest	8		(94)		(171)
Profit on ordinary activities before taxation			925**		448
Taxation on profit on ordinary activities	9		(295)		(223)
Profit on ordinary activities after taxation			630		225
*Minority interests and preference dividends			(6)		(7)
Profit for the financial year			624*		218
Ordinary dividends	10		(246)		(218)
Transferred to reserves			378		—
*Earnings per share	11		30.6p		11.0p

The Mega Group

Consolidated Balance Sheet at 31 December 2002

	Notes	2002 £m	2002 £m	2001 £m	2001 £m
Fixed assets:					
Intangible assets	14		2 492		2 464
Tangible assets	15		2 638		2 764
Investments	16		713		851
			5 843		6 079
Current assets:					
Stocks	18	1 381		1 286	
Debtors	19	1 830		1 561	
Cash at bank and in hand		309		261	
		3 520		3 108	
Creditors – due within one year:					
Borrowings	20	(268)		(157)	
Other creditors	21	(2 097)		(2 135)	
		(2 365)		(2 292)	
Net current assets			1 155		816
Total assets less current liabilities			6 998		6895
Creditors – due after more than one year:					
Borrowings	20	(2 482)		(2703)	
Other creditors	22	(168)		(169)	
			(2 650)		(2 872)
Provision for liabilities and charges	23		(561)		(569)
			£3 787		£3 454
Capital and reserves:					
Called up share capital	25		526		515
Reserves	26				
*Share premium account		599		521	
*Revaluation reserve		666		861	
Profit and loss account		1 968		1 525	
			3 233		2 907
			3 759		3 422
*Minority interests			28		32
			£3 787		£3 454

Terminology Explained

1. **Minority interest.** In a group of companies, the parent company may not own 100% of its subsidiaries which make up the group. If the parent owns say 80% of the shares in another company, it will control that company, which will be consolidated in the group accounts, but 20% of the subsidiary will belong to the minority interest who are shareholders in the subsidiary but not shareholders in

the group. Thus the profit and loss account shows their share of the group profit and the balance sheet shows their share of the net assets of the group

2. **Earnings per share** (EPS). The profit available for dividend is divided by the number of ordinary shares which rank for dividend to give the EPS. The calculation is often a complicated one according to the rules of FRS 14, but the EPS is a significant figure for shareholders as it forms part of the price to earnings ratio.

3. **Share premium.** When a company issues shares, the investing public may be willing to pay more than the face value for those shares. The extra amount received by the company is the share premium. If a company issues 100,000 £1 shares for £2.50 each, the share capital increases by £100,000, and the share premium account stands at £150,000 (100,000 × (£2.50–£1)). This is a capital reserve, not available for distribution as a dividend, because it is part of the capital fund invested in the business.

4. **Revaluation reserve.** This item represents valuation increases derived from a revaluation of the assets, as explained in Chapter 6.

The Statement of Total Recognized Gains and Losses (STRGL)

The STRGL is not a statutory account but is required under the terms of FRS 3. It starts with the profit for the year, after tax and minority interests. It then shows other gains which are not available for dividend, such as property revaluation (a holding gain) and foreign currency adjustment made when investments abroad are translated back to pounds sterling for purposes of consolidation (SSAP 20). Disclosure of these items which are extra to the normal profit and loss calculation is designed to help users to understand the real performance of the business.

Financial Reporting Exposure Draft 22 (FRED 22) now suggests that in future the STRGL may be merged into a new format for the profit and loss account, to reflect all realized and unrealized gains and losses. A section for 'other gains and losses' will be added to the profit and loss account to contain the items now in the STRGL, together with profits or losses on disposal of fixed assets, hitherto shown as resulting from operating activitites.

The Mega Group

Statement of Total Recognized Gains and Losses for the Year Ended 31 December 2002

	2002 £m	2001 £m
Profit for the financial year	624*	218
Deficit on revaluation of investment properties in associate	(117)	–
Unrealized profit on sale of tenanted pub estate	–	23
Exchange adjustments on foreign currency net investments	(19)	(15)
Total recognized gains and losses for the financial years	£488	£226

*This figure is picked up from the profit and loss account.

Note of Historical Cost Profits and Losses

This note in the form of a statement shows in detail the difference between the profit figures in the accounts based on such revaluations as have taken place, and the profit figure which would have been disclosed if original historical cost amounts had been used.

The Mega Group

Note of Historical Cost Profits and Losses for the Year Ended 31 December 2002

	2002 £m	2001 £m
Profit on ordinary activities before taxation	925**	448
Realisation of property revaluation gains of prior years	76	392
Difference between the historical cost depreciation and the actual depreciation charge for the year calculated on the revalued amount	1	3
Asset provisions created (utilized) not required on an historical cost basis	(20)	(33)
Historical cost profit on ordinary activities before taxation	£982	£810
Historical cost profit for the year retained after taxation, minority interests and dividends	£425	£362

**This figure is picked up from the profit and loss account

Reconciliation in Movements of Shareholders' Funds

This statement provides detailed analysis of all items which have increased or decreased the shareholders' investment in the business during the year, not all of which appear in the profit and loss account.

The Mega Group

Reconciliation of Movements in Shareholders' Funds for the Year Ended 31 December 2002

	2002 £m	2001 £m
Profit for the financial year	624*	218
Ordinary dividends	(246)	(218)
Other recognized gains and losses relating to the year (net)	(136)	8
New share capital issued	151	77
Goodwill acquired during the year	(182)	(278)
Goodwill transferred to the profit and loss account in respect of disposals of businesses	126	214
Net additions to shareholders' funds	337	21
Shareholders' funds at 31 December 2001	3 422	3 401
Shareholders' funds at 31 December 2002	£3 759	£3 422

*This figure is picked up from the profit and loss account

THE PUBLISHED PROFIT AND LOSS ACCOUNT

Certain information, specified by statute, must be disclosed in the income statement or by notes thereto. Check the items with the statements shown above, and notes to the Mega Group accounts shown below.

1. **Turnover.** The amount of turnover (total sales or other income) and the basis on which it is computed must be disclosed, i.e. turnover of ordinary activities should be stated after deduction of trade discounts and VAT. Turnover and profit must be analysed for substantially different classes of business, and turnover for substantially different geographic markets, unless the directors consider that such disclosure would prejudice the interests of the company, in which case they must say so in a note to the accounts. See Note 2 to the accounts on segmental analysis shown below.

2. **Employees.** The average number of employees during the year must be noted, and analysed in categories of persons. The aggregate amounts of wages and salaries, social security costs and pension costs must be disclosed. See Note 12 to the accounts shown below.

3. **Directors' emoluments.** These must be divided between fees received as directors, amounts received for other services, e.g. salaries, and the cost of directors' pensions. The aggregate of all emoluments must be disclosed, including directors' and past directors' pensions, and compensation paid for loss of office. Where the total emoluments exceed £200,000, a note should reveal the emoluments net of pension contributions of the chairman and highest-paid director. The threshold figure of £200,000 is changed frequently by the UK government using an 'Order in Council' to amend the Act. See Note 13 below. Details of directors' share options should also be shown.

4. **Depreciation.** The amount provided for tangible or intangible fixed assets must be shown, together with additional provisions for temporary or permanent diminution, or amounts written back because no longer necessary. This requirement is usually covered by a note to the accounts concerning fixed assets and depreciation. See Note 15 below.

5. **Auditors' remuneration,** including expenses. It is important that the shareholders should be informed as to the amount paid to the auditors because, in theory at least, the auditors are employed by and report to the shareholders. It is interesting to see how much the auditors have earned from non-audit work, as this could affect the independence of their opinion.

6. Charges for the **hire of plant** or machinery.

7. Revenue from **rents** if material, net of outgoings.

8. **Interest** paid analysed between:

    (a) loans and overdrafts repayable by instalments within five years;
    (b) loans and overdrafts repayable other than by instalments within five years;
    (c) other loans.

9. **Income from investments** listed on a stock exchange. This will be part of 'other operating income' in the profit and loss account, so a note should provide the detail required.

10. **Taxation** on ordinary activities – the amount of:

    (a) UK income tax;
    (b) UK corporation tax;
    (c) tax imposed outside the UK.

    A note should cover any special circumstances affecting taxation, and the basis on which UK tax has been computed.

11. The aggregate amount of **dividend** paid and proposed. This is usually analysed by note to the various classes of capital.

12. **Reserves** – amounts set aside or withdrawn from reserves. The reconciliation of movements of shareholders' funds shown above contributes to this requirement.

13. **Exceptional items** – information must be disclosed to show

    (a) details of exceptional items, and the tax thereon, per FRS 3;
    (b) the effect of amounts charged or credited that relate to preceding financial years.

    Exceptional items are any items which although they are part of the ordinary activities of the company are exceptional because of their size or incidence – windfall gains or losses, closure and reorganization costs.

Task 12.1

In the segmental analysis shown below, relate net assets of £3,787 to the balance sheet on page 192, and the turnover of £7,913 and profit before tax of £925 to the profit and loss account on page 191.

Notes to the Accounts of the Mega Group shown above

2 Segmental Analysis

	2002 Turnover £m	2002 Profit £m	2002 Net assets £m	2001 Turnover £m	2001 Profit £m	2001 Net assets £m
Class of business:						
Continuing operations:						
Food	2 647	186	2 022	2 618	257	1 800
Drinks	2 858	505	1 815	2 471	451	1 534
Retailing	1 540	211	2 321	1 560	187	2 278
	7 045	902	6 158	6 649	895	5 612
Discontinued operations:						
Food	502	40	70	932	71	310
Drinks	–	–	–	318	26	–
Retailing	366	7	–	849	35	131
	868	47	70	2 099	132	441
	£7 913			£8 748		
Operating profit		949			1 027	
Other net income/(charges) less interest		(24)			(579)	
Profit before taxation		925			448	
Capital employed			6 228			6 053
Net borrowings			(2 441)			(2 599)
Net assets			£3 787			£3 454
Geographical area by country of operation:						
United Kingdom and Ireland	* 1 872	319	1 315	* 2 940	354	1 816
Continental Europe	* 1 292	117	747	* 862	104	557
United States of America	4 184	445	* 3 895	4 433	504	3 466
Rest of North America	185	19	152	216	20	128
Africa and Middle East	155	7	29	145	10	21
Rest of world	225	42	90	152	35	65
	£7 913			£8 748		
Operating profit		949			1 027	
Other net income/(charges) less interest		(24)			(579)	
Profit before taxation		925			448	
Capital employed			* 6 228			6 053
Net borrowings			(2 441)			(2 599)
Net assets			£3 787			£3 454

Comment on segmental information

An accountant would note that:

* Sales in the UK have fallen by 36% (2,940 – 1,872 ÷ 2,940).

* Sales in Europe have risen by 50% (862 – 1,292 ÷ 862).

* 62% of net assets are in USA (3,895 ÷ 6,228 × 100). This is up from 57% last year.

12 Employees

The average number of employees during the year was

	2002			2001		
	Full time	Part time	Total	Full time	Part time	Total
Continuing operations:						
Food	22 367	2 282	24 649	20 637	6 285	26 922
Drinks	12 135	458	12 593	10 451	301	10 752
Retailing	22 933	36 484	59 417	24 965	38 047	63 012
	57 435	39 224	96 659	56 053	44 633	100 686
Discontinued operations	5 053	693	5 746	18 131	3 361	21 492
	62 488	39 917	102 405	74 184	47 994	122 178

The aggregate remuneration of all employees comprised

	2002 £m	2001 £m
Wages and salaries	1 073	1 262
Employer's social security costs	138	135
Employer's pension and other post-employed benefits	(39)	(46)
	1 172	1 251

13 Directors
Emoluments

The emoluments of the directors, including pension contributions, were as follows:

	2002 £	2001 £
Non-executive directors – fees	206 083	163 875
Executive directors:		
Remuneration excluding bonuses	2 241 080	2 299 262
Annual bonus payments	399 879	615 019
Pension contributions	836 457	710 548
	£3 683 499	£3 788 704

The emoluments, excluding pension contributions, of Sir John Smith, the Chairman and Group Chief Executive, were £770,682 (2001 – £713,391). Sir John took no salary increase at 1 January 2003.

A shareholder might note that the Cadbury Code on corporate governance states that the post of chairman and chief executive should not be held by one person as it concentrates too much power with one individual.

THE BALANCE SHEET

The following information must be shown on the balance sheet or as a note. Check the items with the balance sheet of the Mega Group shown above.

Share Capital

The amounts for authorized and issued capital must be summarized. The authorized capital is the amount which the company is authorized to raise, under its memorandum and articles of association, and the issued capital is the proportion of authorized capital which has been issued to subscribers. Where 'redeemable' shares have been issued, the details of redemption dates, whether the redemption is optional, and any redemption premium which may be payable, must be shown. Such details are usually revealed in the form of a note including the number and aggregate nominal value of each class of shares allotted. Where shares are issued during the year a note must explain the reason for the issue, the numbers issued, their aggregate nominal value and the consideration received. A further note is required to give details of the aggregate amount recommended for dividend and any arrears of fixed cumulative dividend together with the arrears period.

Reserves and Provisions

Amounts transferred to or from reserves or provisions must be disclosed by note or as part of the reconciliation in movements of shareholders' funds. The sources from which increases in reserves and provisions have been made must be shown, as must the way in which any reduction of a reserve has been applied. A share premium account should be shown separately. It is a statutory reserve not available for distribution, and the uses to which such an account can be put are severely limited.

Transfers from a provision for a purpose other than that for which the provision was created must be explained.

Loans

Creditors must be analysed between amounts falling due within one year and after one year. Loans repayable more than one year from the balance sheet date must be separated from other loans. Amounts repayable in more than five years, by instalment and otherwise, must have the repayment terms and rate of interest shown. For loans raised during the year, the reasons, class, amount and consideration should be disclosed. Any loans or other liabilities which are secured on the assets of the company must be noted showing the assets concerned. Where there is a charge on the assets of the company to secure the liabilities of another person, this too must be stated.

Current Liabilities

The Act says little about how current liabilities should be shown except that amounts owed for tax and social security must be separated from other creditors, as must proposed dividends. Dividends proposed, but not yet paid, are a current liability.

Contingent Liabilities

These must be noted. They are not part of the balance sheet computation, since they are not owed at the balance sheet date. They relate to transactions which took place before the balance sheet date and which may or may not become liabilities after the balance sheet date, contingent upon some further circumstances which cannot be accurately forecast (e.g. damages in a future court case).

Capital expenditure authorized by the board and not yet contracted for, and capital expenditure for which contracts have been placed, should be noted.

Material contingent losses must be provided for where a future event may confirm the loss. A note must disclose the nature of the contingency, the uncertainties, and a prudent estimate of the financial effect of the contingent event if is practicable to make such an estimate.

Pension Commitments

A note is required to show particulars of provisions made and items for which no provision has been made.

Tangible Fixed Assets

The accounts must show the cost or valuation of fixed assets net of depreciation to date, analysed to disclose movements during the year: opening cost, plus or minus revaluations, plus acquisitions, less disposals, to give cost at the end of the year.

Cumulative depreciation is similarly analysed to show the provision at the beginning of the year, plus the provision for the year, less depreciation transferred to disposals account, leaving the cumulative provision at the end of the year. Usually one figure for net book value is given in the accounts, with an extensive note to provide the required analysis. Any significant difference between book value and real value must be mentioned in the directors' report.

For fixed assets carried in the accounts at a valuation rather than historical cost, details must be disclosed of the value and year of valuation. In the year of valuation the names and qualifications of the valuer and the basis of the valuation must be shown. Thus investors can assess the validity of any new value set upon the fixed assets of the business, and can see when they were last valued.

Land and buildings must be analysed between freehold, long leaseholds (50 or more years to run) and short leaseholds. A note concerning depreciation methods will appear with the other accounting policies. Note 15 on fixed tangible assets shown below relates to the Mega group balance sheet shown above.

15 Fixed assets: Tangible assets

	Land and buildings	Plant and machinery	Fixtures and fittings	Assets in course of construction	Total
	£m	£m	£m	£m	£m
Cost or valuation					
At 31 December 2001	1 885	1 031	293	258	3 467
Exchange adjustments	1	2	1	–	4
Additions	107	115	47	83	352
New subsidiaries	50	37	3	1	91
Disposals	(225)	(279)	(44)	(11)	(559)
Transfers	30	16	5	(51)	–
At 31 December 2002	1 848	922	305	280	3 355
Depreciation					
At 31 December 2001	138	444	121	–	703
Exchange adjustments	1	1	–	–	2
Provided during the year	58	117	31	–	206
Disposals	(27)	(148)	(19)	–	(194)
Transfers	1	(2)	1	=	–
At 31 December 2002	171	412	134	=	717
Net book value					
At 31 December 2002	1 677	510	171	280	2 638
At 31 December 2001	1 747	587	172	258	2 764

(i)   The total at cost or valuation for land and buildings comprises:

	2002	2001
	£m	£m
At 1988 professional valuation	863	984
At 1985 professional valuation	–	5
At cost	985	896
	1 848	1 885

The valuations were made on an open market existing-use basis except for specialized properties which were valued on a depreciated replacement cost basis.

(ii)   The net book value of land and buildings comprises freehold of £1,376m (2001 – £1450m), long leaseholds of £86m (2001 – £92m) and short leaseholds of £215m (2001 – £205m).

(iii) Included in the net book value of freehold property is £535m (2001 – £520m) in respect of public houses, and £303m (2001 – £356m) of land unrelated to those properties. Depreciation is not charged on these amounts.

(iv) Included in the total net book value of tangible assets is £31m (2001 – £28m) in respect of assets acquired under finance leases; depreciation for the year on these assets was £10m (2001 – £11m). There is also included £88m (2001 – £86m) in respect of assets held for the purpose of leasing out under operating leases; depreciation for the year on these assets was £1m (2001 – £3m).

Intangible Fixed Assets

Any amount not yet written off must be stated.
Notes must disclose:

1. **Capitalized development costs** – the reason for capitalising such costs and the period over which they are to be amortized.

2. **Purchased goodwill** – the amortization period chosen by the directors, which may not exceed the economic life of the goodwill, and reasons for their choice. This is a similar analysis to that for tangible fixed assets

3. **Brands** – the last revaluation date, the valuer and any impairment which has occurred.

Investments

Fixed asset investments are normally shown at cost, with notes to explain further details.

1. The amount of listed investments with a note as to their current stock exchange value or market value .

2. Investments carried at directors' valuation must be accompanied by an explanation of the valuation method

3. If the company holds more than 10 per cent of any class of another company's shares it must show the name and country of origin of the company, and the proportion held.

Stocks

Stocks are to be shown at the lower of net realizable value or purchase price or production cost. A note about the basis of the valuation will appear with other accounting policies.

The purchase price or production cost of stocks can be determined by an appropriate method chosen by the directors from those mentioned in the 1985 Act, i.e. FIFO, LIFO, weighted average and any similar method (see Chapter 7). At this point the Act is in direct contravention of SSAP 9, which does not allow the use of the LIFO method. If the amount shown differs materially from the replacement cost of the asset this difference must be noted. The Act also allows stocks to be included at a fixed quantity and value where this is not subject to material variation. This could be construed to permit the use of the 'base stock' method banned by SSAP 9.

Debtors

Amounts recoverable after more than one year must be disclosed separately from other debtors.

Example: from trial balance to published accounts

Grande plc has an authorized share capital of £3,750,000, consisting of ordinary shares of £1 each. The company prepares its accounts as on 31 March in each year and the trial balance, before final adjustments, extracted on 31 March 2002 showed:

	£	£
Goodwill	20 000	
Ordinary shares of £1 issued and fully paid		3 600 000
General reserve		180 000
Retained profit as on 31 March 2001		18 000
Secured long term loan 6 per cent		120 000
Unsecured loan stock 6 per cent		30 000
Freehold office premises:	3 000 000	
accumulated depreciation		12 000
Leasehold factory : cost at beginning of year	600 000	
accumulated depreciation		228 000
Plant and machinery : cost at beginning of year	260 000	
accumulated depreciation		105 000*
additions in year	30 000	
Interest on secured long term loan	7 200	
Interest on loan stock	1 800	
Directors' emoluments	506 000	
Auditors' remuneration	47 500	
Creditors and accrued expenses		518 000
Stock as on 31 March 2001	480 000	
Debtors and prepayments	582 000	
Balance at bank	204 000	
Sales : invoiced value less allowances		3 678 000
Cost of sales	2 100 000	
Distribution costs	250 500	
Administration expenses	400 000	
	£8 489 000	£8 489 000

You ascertain that:

1. The unsecured loan stock is repayable at par on 31 December 2003. The secured loan is secured on the leasehold factory and is repayable in ten years' time.

2. The lease of the factory is for 50 years, with 20 years expired. Freehold premises are split – £600,000 for the buildings and £2,400,000 for the land.

3. Directors' remuneration comprises (a) salaries of chairman, £130,000, managing director, £133,000, sales director, £103,000; (b) fee of non-executive director, £75,000; and (c) pension contributions, £65,000.

4. Annual depreciation is calculated as to:

   Leasehold factory and freehold building – 2 per cent on cost.

   Plant and machinery – 20 per cent on written-down value (WDV) at 31 March 2001 plus additions in year. Plant costing £20,000 was sold for its WDV of £5,000 cash on 31 March 2002, but no entry has yet been made in the books for this transaction.

5. Stock has been valued consistently at the lower of cost and net realizable value.

6. A dividend of 3.33 pence per share is proposed.

7. Corporation tax on the profit of the year has been computed at £120,000 and is payable on 1 January 2003.

8. The directors have placed contracts for new plant costing £75,000 and have authorized further expenditure on new plant costing £60,000.

9. Sales are at invoiced value less allowances.

10. The directors have decided to amortize goodwill to the profit and loss account over a five-year period starting this year.

You are required to prepare in a form suitable for publication and in conformity with the provisions of the Companies Acts:

(a) a balance sheet as at 31 March 2002;

(b) a profit and loss account for the year ended 31 March 2002; and

(c) notes to the accounts.

The **first step** is to calculate depreciation, according to notes 2 and 4 above. Note that freehold land is not depreciated.

(i) Freehold £600,000 × .2 = £12,000, an administration cost.

(ii) Leasehold factory £600,000 × .2 = £12,000 as cost of sales.

(iii) Plant at cost £260,000 less sold £20,000 plus additions £30,000 = £270,000.

For disposals. Cost of £20,000 - WDV £5,000 = cumulative depreciation of £15,000.
Depreciation in the trial balance £105,000 - £15,000 = £90,000*.
(£270,000 – £90,000) × .2 = £36,000

The **second step** is to compute the net profit. The figures for cost of sales, distribution costs and administration expenses must be calculated, picking up figures from the trial balance and the first step.

	Cost of Sales £	Distribution cost £	Administration expenses £	Finance charges £	Total £
Trial balance	2 100 000	250 500	400 000	7 200 1 800	
Depreciation – Lease	12 000				
Depreciation – Plant	36 000				
Depreciation – Office			12 000		
Directors' fees		103 000	403 000		
Audit fee			47 500		
Goodwill (£20,000 ÷ 5)			4 000		
	2 148 000	353 500	866 500	9 000	3 377 000
Sales					3 678 000
Net profit before tax					£301 000

The **third step** is to draft the accounts.

Grande PLC Profit and Loss Account for Year Ending 31 March 2002

	£	£
Sales		3 678 000
Less cost of sales		2 148 000
		1 530 000
Less distribution costs:	353 500	
Administration expenses	866 500	
Interest on loans repayable within one year	1 800	
Interest on loans repayable otherwise than by instalments in more than five years' time	7 200	
		1 229 000
Net profit before taxation		301 000
UK corporation tax based on profit for the year		120 000
* Net profit after taxation		181 000
Less: proposed dividend at 3.33 pence per share	119 880	
transfer to general reserve	30 000	
		149 880
Unappropriated profit for the year		31 120
Balance of unappropriated profit b/d		18 000
Balance of unappropriated profit c/f		£49 120

Earnings per share
*[£181,000 ÷ 3,600,000 shares] 5 pence per share

Note that earnings per share is calculated by dividing the net profit, *after* tax but *before* extraordinary items, by the number of shares at issue

Grande PLC Balance Sheet as at 31 March 2002

	Note	£	£	£
Fixed assets:				
Intangible assets : goodwill	2		16 000	
Tangible assets : land and buildings	2		3 336 000	
plant and machinery	2		144 000	
				3 496 000
Current assets: stocks			480 000	
debtors			582 000	
bank			209 000	
			1 271 000	
Creditors – amounts falling due within one year:				
** Unsecured loan stock 6 per cent		30 000		
Trade creditors		518 000		
Corporation tax		120 000		
Proposed dividend		119 880		
			787 880	
Net current assets				483 120
Total assets less current liabilities				3 979 120
Creditors falling due after more than one year				
6 per cent long-term loan	3			120 000
				£3 859 120
Capital and reserves:				
Called-up share capital	6			3 600 000
General reserve				210 000
Unappropriated profits				49 120
				£3 859 120

** The unsecured loan stock is now repayable within the next twelve months so it is a current liability.

The **fourth step** is to draft the notes.

Notes to the accounts:

1. **Accounting policies :** stock is accounted for at the lower of cost or net realizable value.
   Depreciation: freehold building: 2 per cent on cost on a straight line basis.
   leasehold building: 2 per cent on a straight line basis.
   plant: 20 per cent on net book value.
   Goodwill: the directors have decided to amortize it over a five-year economic life starting this year.

2. **Fixed Assets**

	Freehold land and buildings	Leasehold buildings	Plant	Goodwill	Total
	£	£	£	£	£
At cost 1 April 2001	3 000 000	600 000	260 000	20 000	3 880 000
Acquisitions	–	–	30 000	–	30 000
Disposal	–	–	(20 000)	–	(20 000)
Cost 31 March 2002	3 000 000	600 000	270 000	20 000	3 890 000
Depreciation					
Balance 1 April 2001	12 000	228 000	105 000		345 000
Provision	12 000	12 000	36 000	4 000	64 000
Disposals	–	–	(15 000)	–	(15 000)
Balance 31 March 2002	24 000	240 000	126 000	4 000	394 000
WDV	2 976 000	360 000	144 000	16 000	3 496 000

Freehold buildings cost £600,000.
The lease is a short lease.

3. The 6 per cent **long-term loan** is repayable in ten years' time and is secured on the leasehold property.

4. **Directors' emoluments**

	£
Salaries	366 000
Fees	75 000
Pension contributions	65 000
	506 000

Chairman – £130 000
Highest paid director – £133 000

5. **Capital expenditure**:contracts placed – £75,000

contracts authorised – £60,000

6. **Share Capital**

Authorized 3,750,000 £1 ordinary shares

Issued 3,600,000 £1 ordinary shares

THE DIRECTORS' REPORT

This is a formal statement that is appended to the published accounts. The auditor must certify that it is consistent with the financial statements. In the report the directors must set out a fair review of the development of the company during the year and its position at the end of the year. A minimum of information is required by the Companies Act, but many companies exceed these limits in the cause of good public relations.

Many companies now produce a chairman's statement as a public relations item, accompanying the published accounts. This statement is separate from the directors' report, the contents of which are specified in the Companies Act 1985. The report should cover the following matters:

1. A fair review of the development of the business of the company and its subsidiaries during the year, and their position at the end of the year.

2. The principal activities of the company and its subsidiaries during the accounting period, with details of any significant changes to those activities. For example, if a construction company acquires a bank as a subsidiary company during the year, this fact must be mentioned in the directors' report.

3. Details concerning the directors:

    (a) The names of all persons who acted as directors at any part of the accounting period.
    (b) The interests of directors in shares or debentures of the company, showing amounts at the beginning and end of the year. This information is to be given for each person who was a director of the business at the end of the financial year. As an alternative the directors' interests in shares or debentures may be given as a note to the accounts rather than being set out in the directors' report.

4. The amount of dividends proposed and paid during the year and the amount proposed to be transferred to or from the reserves.

5. A comment concerning future developments. This comment should give users of the accounts an idea of the board's future policy, but it is more often honoured in the breach than in the act, in that a bland but meaningless comment is made which fulfils the strict requirements but not the spirit of the law.

6. Details of any post-balance-sheet events which have taken place since the end of the accounting year but before the accounts are signed as approved by the directors.

7. If a company purchases or otherwise acquires its own shares during the course of the year, the directors must disclose the number of shares purchased, their nominal value, the aggregate consideration paid, and an explanation of the reasons for the purchase. If fewer shares are held at the end of the year than were held during the year, the maximum number and nominal value must be shown. The number and nominal value of shares disposed of or cancelled during the year, and any charge on the shares if they have been used as security, must be disclosed.

8. If the average number of employees in the business exceeds 250, the directors' report must state the company's policy as to the employment of disabled persons and the training, career development and promotion of disabled persons.

9. If the company employs more than 250 people in the UK, the directors' report must disclose policy and actions to provide employees with information on matters of significance to them, to consult with employees or their representatives and to operate an employee share scheme.

10. The total figure for political and charitable contributions made by the company during the year must be disclosed unless the combined total is less than £200. The amount given and the name of any political party, or persons paid, for each contribution for political purposes in excess of £200 must be shown.

THE SIGNIFICANCE FOR DISCLOSURE OF STATEMENTS OF STANDARD ACCOUNTING PRACTICE

Accounting standards usually fill in the detail of disclosure between the broad principles laid down by statute. Statements of Standard Accounting Practice (SSAPs) and the more recent Financial Reporting Standards (FRSs) specify methods of accounting practice approved by the major professional accounting bodies in the UK, for application to all financial accounts intended to give a true and fair view of the financial position, or profit and loss. Professional accountants, whether acting in the capacity of director, executive or auditor, must observe the requirements of these standards and explain departures from them as a note to the accounts. Failure to do this may lead to the qualification by an auditor of the certificate on a set of published accounts.

FRSs and SSAPs reflect best accounting practice, and often stipulate disclosures beyond what is required by statute. The requirements of some SSAPs have been incorporated into subsequent Companies Acts, and in one case at least an SSAP is in conflict with the law.

DISCLOSURE: THE WAY FORWARD

The Companies Act 1989 allows companies to send abbreviated accounts to shareholders. A large company may have many shareholders, and it is probable that the detailed notes to the accounts will not be appreciated by many of them. The published accounts must be meaningful to shareholders with a widely differing financial awareness. A full set of accounts with accompanying notes will be understood by a qualified accountant but may be unclear to a financially unsophisticated shareholder who owns, say, 100 shares. Some companies suggest that they should send their members an easily understood summary of full accounts, but perhaps this is wrong to cater to shareholders lack of knowledge about accounts by telling them less. Already much significant information is contained in the notes to the accounts, and to allow a summary to be distributed to shareholders could result in the publication of misleading information. The accounting statements should be presented in a more understandable form. The new suggestion is that shareholders will have to request a full set of accounts if they require more information than that given by the summary statement. So far detailed proposals for items to be included in the summary have not been very informative and there may be a considerable risk that important information could be missed from summarized accounts.

There seems to be a mismatch between the amount of information which reporting accountants and directors are required to make available, and the amount which shareholders can conveniently assimilate. Published accounts seem to have developed to the point where companies combine considerable public relations material with a technically complex set of financial statements and notes. Research evidence shows that many shareholders give their annual booklet only a cursory glance before throwing it away. The disclosure of financial information made at such a high cost by companies is proving ineffective to meet the disparate requirements of statute, the stock exchange, and the investors. Perhaps investors need a simple review in narrative form which explains key figures, ratios and transactions.

The reform of company law is under discussion, and the creation of a shareholder report designed to meet the needs of shareholders is at the forefront of this discussion. Perhaps a revised form of the 'preliminary announcement' made for stock exchange purposes would suffice, with the full report available for those who request it. The 'preliminary announcement', made as soon as audited accounts are finalized to pre-empt stock exchange rumour, has more effect on the share price than the eventual publication of the full accounts. A short narrative report free of jargon and publicity material would help shareholders, even though there are nearly 1,000 individual disclosure requirements for a complex group of companies in the Companies Acts, FRSs, and Stock Exchange regulations. Some commentators suggest that provided shareholders agree, a company could email the shareholder with notification that the published accounts are available on a web site.

Unfortunately only companies listed on the Stock Exchange produce a preliminary announcement, so shareholders in smaller limited companies do not have access to information in this way. Many companies now produce an 'Operating and Financial Review' (OFR) in order to help shareholders. This is sometimes merged with the chairman's annual statement rather than as a stand-alone document. There are no rules as to what should be included, and some OFRs now stretch to four pages. Clearly a workable compromise must be found to provide details for the financially sophisticated user, and a 'basic' message for the majority of shareholders.

Task 12.2

What is the minimum of information which you think should be provided for shareholders?

Solution

Your solution might include

- Summary income statement – to show turnover, gross profit, exceptional items, net profit after tax, dividend per share and earnings per share.
- Summary balance sheet – to show single figures for fixed assets, stock, loans, etc.
- Discussion of shareholder value – to show loans recruited and repaid, gearing, and working capital management
- Cash flow and liquidity.
- Acquisitions and disposals of companies in the group and major assets – to show goodwill purchased and losses on disposals

The shareholders need to judge whether the directors are managing the business effectively, the return on investment is adequate, and at what value a takeover bid should be accepted.

STATISTICAL SUPPLEMENTS TO PUBLISHED ACCOUNTS

Many companies present a statistical supplement to their published accounts. The purpose is to highlight the salient features of the accounts, to put current events in the company into perspective, and to provide background information to help shareholders and potential shareholders to interpret the accounting statements. Such statements can become a public relations exercise to ensure that the company's activities and performance are shown in the best possible light, to maintain the price of the shares.

Statistics of this type should be easy to assimilate. Companies often work to the nearest £1,000 and use percentages and ratios so that comparisons can be made easily, trends are revealed and key figures are accentuated. A good statistical supplement uses forms of visual presentation other than tables of figures, such as graphs, bar charts and pie charts. An international company may show a map of the world with a dot or company emblem in every area in which the group has an interest.

A pie chart is a useful device for showing the proportion of parts to a whole. An example of the use of such a chart is in demonstrating how the profit figure is appropriated. A large slice of the pie would go in taxation, another large slice would be ploughed back into the company, and a comparatively small slice would be dividend to the shareholders. Such a pie diagram might be useful in undermining the arguments of trade union officials for higher wages based on the large return achieved by the shareholders.

CONCLUSION

It is imperative that published accounts should disclose a true and fair view to investors if confidence in the share capital market is to be maintained. Accordingly company law sets out the statutory minimum of information which companies must disclose, and financial reporting standards amplify this will further detail. Companies publish this complex technical information in the Annual Report and Accounts, where it is combined with further public relations information which is not subject to an audit. The consequent mismatch between what must be disclosed and what the average shareholder can assimilate leads to costly inefficiencies in the system.

Discussion Topics

Thirty-minute essay questions:

1. Explain the mismatch between the financial information provided to shareholders in the published accounts, and the financial information which many shareholders require. Suggest action to solve this problem.

2. What segmental information is disclosed to shareholders. Explain why it is important and beneficial.

3. What statistical means are available to the accountant to supplement financial information disclosed in the published accounts.

SEMINAR EXERCISES

12.1 **Digger plc** is a manufacturer of gardening tools. Set out below is a trial balance extracted from the books of the company as at 31 December.

	Debit £	Credit £
Sales		3 815 900
Cost of sales	1 985 789	
Distribution costs	140 000	
Administrative expenses	699 269	
Debtors/creditors	489 531	201 122
Provision for doubtful debts		23 610
Directors' remuneration	551 500	
Audit fee	40 000	
Debenture interest paid	7 500	
Buildings at cost	700 000	
Plant and machinery at cost	185 000	
Provision for depreciation on plant and machinery at 1 January		65 000
Motor vehicles at cost (salesmen's cars)	64 000	
Provision for depreciation on motor vehicles at 1 January		34 000
Stock in trade and work in progress at 31 December	291 628	
Trade investment at cost	82 000	
Bank overdraft		275 382
Profit and loss account balance at 1 January		131 203
General reserve		240 000
Ordinary share capital		300 000
10 per cent debentures (2010) secured on premises		150 000
	£5 236 217	£5 236 217

The following information is also related to the accounts for the year to 31 December.

(a) The bad debt provision is to be increased to an amount which is equal to 1 per cent of the turnover for the year.

(b) The directors' remuneration is divided among the four directors of the company as follows:

	£
Salaries:	
Chairman	104 000
Managing director	160 000
Finance director	89 500
Sales director	78 000
	431 500
There are also directors'	
pension contributions of	£120 000

In addition provision must be made for directors' fees of £4,000 to each of the above directors.

(c) Depreciation is to be provided for the year as follows:

Buildings	2 per cent on cost
Plant and machinery	10 per cent on cost
Motor vehicles	25 per cent on written-down value

The only changes in fixed assets during the year were an addition to plant and machinery in early January costing £40,000, and the purchase of buildings for £700,000.

(d) A provision of £160,000 is to be made for corporation tax at 33 per cent based upon the profits for the year. This will be payable on 30 September next year.

(e) A final dividend of 6.5p a share on the ordinary share capital is to be provided in the accounts.

(f) The sum of £75,000 is to be transferred to general reserve.

(g) The authorised ordinary share capital is 600,000 50p shares. All shares in issue are fully paid.

(h) Administrative expenses include £4,134 interest on the overdraft.

(i) The value of the trade investment at current Stock Exchange price is £55,000. The investment consists of 20,000 20p ordinary shares in Fork plc, a company with an issued share capital of 200,000 ordinary shares.

(j) Investment income this year was £7,000 and has been credited to sales in error.

Required:

Within the limits of the above information, prepare the final accounts of Digger plc for the year ended 31 December in a form suitable for presentation to the members and which complies with the requirements of the Companies Act.

The required information should be shown as part of the accounting statements or by way of note, whichever is considered more appropriate.

CHAPTER 13

Audit

The Attest Function of the Accountant

THE AIMS OF THIS CHAPTER

To enable students to

- Understand the objectives and general principles of auditing

- Explain the existence of the 'expectations gap' and suggest ways to reduce the gap

- Recognize the source of audit risk, and steps which can be taken to reduce exposure to risk

- Draft an audit report

- Appreciate the rights, duties and liabilities of the auditor

- Demonstrate how internal control and internal check make the accounting system more effective

WHAT IS AN AUDIT?

A well-proven definition of an audit is 'the independent examination by an auditor of the evidence from which the income statement and balance sheet have been prepared, to ascertain that they represent a true and fair view of the transactions under review, and of the financial state of the organization at the closing date of the period'. An auditor is one who

(a) asks questions,

(b) listens to answers,

(c) checks facts,

(d) eventually forms an opinion about the correctness of the financial statements, and

(e) reports a view to shareholders of the company.

The auditor's opinion is contained in the audit certificate or report which is appended to the published accounts. The evidence on which this opinion is founded is derived from the accounting records, and especially the vouchers which provide the basic data from which the accounting records are prepared, e.g. invoices, goods received notes, orders, sales invoices, wage sheets and bank statements. All provide evidence to confirm that the books properly represent the transactions which have taken place and that the accounts are based firmly on those book entries. Apart from this paper evidence the auditors must examine the assets themselves, where possible, to ascertain that they really exist, that they belong to the business, and are correctly valued in the ledgers and the accounts. Justification is important to ascertain that the transactions which have been recorded have received the correct accounting treatment according to best accounting practice as expressed in accounting standards and the Companies Act.

One of the objectives of an audit is to reveal errors in the accounts, and to discover fraud, but another objective of equal importance is to prevent error and fraud from taking place. It is the professional duty of an auditor to report on the accounting systems in operation in the business. The system must be tested to ensure that it can account adequately for all transactions and that it is being operated properly. If the system is weak, or the operation of a good system is less than thorough, what is called a 'letter of weakness' is sent to the client. When auditing a company the auditor is employed by the shareholders to comment to them on the accounts prepared for them by the management, but the letter of weakness is sent to the management of the company so that they can act to put matters right.

In a leading case, *Fomento (Sterling Area) Ltd v. Selsdon Fountain Pen Co. Ltd* (1958) WLR45, Lord Denning, then Master of the Rolls, had this to say:

> An auditor is not confined to the mechanics of checking vouchers and making arithmetical computations. He is not to be written off as a professional adder upper and subtractor. His vital task is to take care to see that errors are not made, be they errors of computation or errors of omission or downright untruths. To perform this task properly he must come to it with an enquiring mind – not suspicious of dishonesty, but suspecting that someone may have made a mistake somewhere, and that a check must be made to ensure there has been none.

The audit forms an important part of the corporate reporting system. When the independent auditor certifies that the accounts are 'true and fair' he is supporting them with his own reputation, creating confidence in the statements and increasing their credibility in the eyes of all parties who may rely on them. The auditor must be satisfied that the accounts have been drawn up according to best accounting practice as expressed in the Financial Reporting Standards, and the statutory rules embodied in the Companies Act 1985. The relevance of accounting policies used, and the adequacy of notes to accounts in disclosing significant information, must be considered by the auditor before the audit certificate is signed off.

OBJECTIVE AND GENERAL PRINCIPLES
(Statement of Auditing Standards 100)

This standard produced by the Auditing Practices Board (APB) gives a professional view of the audit. The objective is to enable the auditor to give an opinion on the financial statements taken as a whole, and thus provide reasonable assurance that the statements are true and fair and prepared in accordance with statute and standard. To do this the auditor must

(a) carry out procedures which will obtain sufficient appropriate evidence to ascertain with reasonable confidence that the financial statements are free from material misstatement;

(b) consider the overall presentation of the statements to see whether they have been prepared in accordance with the Companies Act and accounting standards; and

(c) report, showing a clear expression of opinion on the financial statements.

Accounting statements are often imprecise because they concern matters which are inherently uncertain, which require judgements to make accounting estimates and select accounting policies which influence the figures. The auditor's opinion increases the credibility of the statements. Users cannot, however, assume that a clear audit report guarantees the future viability of the business, nor does it prove that the managers are working efficiently.

Responsibility for the preparation of the company accounts rests firmly with the directors. The auditor merely forms and expresses an opinion on the statements. The fact that the accounts have been audited does not relieve the directors of their responsibilities. The term 'reasonable assurance' is central to understanding the objective of an audit. Financial statements are based on a combination of fact (actual figures) and judgement (estimates, provisions and the selection of accounting policies), so it follows that no financial statement can be absolutely correct. The auditor must use judgement when framing the opinion, to

(a) gather evidence – what checks to apply, how often to apply them and the extent of the work to be done to check the evidence; and

(b) draw conclusions – how reasonable are the estimates made and how appropriate are the accounting policies selected when the statements are computed.

The task of the auditor has important ethical considerations. If shareholders and others are to be assured of a true and fair view the conduct of the auditor must be beyond reproach

Task 13.1

What ethical qualities do you consider an auditor should bring to his task?

Solution

Your solution might include the following points

- Integrity – honesty, trustworthiness and committment to matters of principle;
- Objectivity – fairness not influenced by personal feelings;
- Independence – not influenced by interested parties who seek to bias the accounting statements;
- Professional competence – only a good accountant will persuade other accountants to adopt his or her suggestions;
- Professional behaviour – working within the ethical guidance rules issued by professional accounting bodies;
- Confidentiality – the auditor knows much about the future plans of the business and must take care that this share price sensitive information remains secret until the directors decide to publicize it.

THE EXPECTATIONS GAP

In a company, the directors are responsible for the accounts and the auditor is appointed by the shareholders to give an independent opinion of those accounts. In fact, the auditor works closely with the directors to advise and negotiate changes to the figures to ensure an unqualified report – independence and professional competence are significant at this stage.

There is considerable discussion as to the position of the auditor where fraud is concerned. Some users of accounts believe that the auditor will be acting without using professional standards of care if fraud is not detected. Auditors, however, assert that their task is to comment on the accounts in the terms of the audit certificate. They will advise the directors where to strengthen the system and deter fraud or discover it, but this is a by-product of the audit and not its main concern. Thus there has developed an 'expectations gap' between the liabilities accepted by the auditing profession, and the items for which some users seek to hold auditors responsible. Much of this problem is derived from the lack so far of an agreed legal definition of the term 'true and fair'.

The expectations gap can be defined as the difference between the apparent public perception of auditors' responsibilities, which affects the assurance that their involvement provides, and the legal and professional reality. Misunderstandings about the nature of audited financial statements contribute to the gap, such as:

(a) The balance sheet shows a true and fair valuation of the assets and the business as a whole.

(b) Amounts in financial statements are precisely correct.

(c) The audit certificate guarantees the continued existence and survival of the business.

Further misunderstandings about the level of assurance provided by the audit compound the difficulty, such as:

(a) The auditors examine all or most of the transactions.

(b) A 'clear' audit report provides assurance that no fraud has occurred during the accounting period.

The APB have taken steps to reduce the expectations gap by providing more information about the duties and position of the auditor. The responsibilities of directors and auditors for the financial statements are now clearly differentiated and defined in the audit certificate, which has been enlarged to cover the responsibilities of the directors and the basis on which the auditor's opinion has been reached. This includes a clear statement that records have been examined on a test basis (not completely), that assessments have been made of estimates and judgements built into the figures, and that only reasonable assurance (not complete assurance) is given that the figures are free from misstatement.

An example of an audit report is shown below on page 225.

INTERNAL AUDIT

The internal auditor is an employee of the company and reports to its managers. The task is to

(a) review the systems set up in the business and ensure that they are efficient, and operating properly;

(b) comment on the security of the assets; and

(c) discover and prevent fraud where possible.

The work of the internal auditor is very detailed, involving much checking and vouching of prime documents, and is often closely connected to the systems design department. The relationship of the internal auditor and the external auditor is one of friendly co-operation. The external auditor can decide to ignore the work undertaken by the internal audit department. Usually, however, having tested the abilities and standards of the internal auditor, the external auditor is able to avoid the duplication of much detailed checking by relying on some of the work already completed by the internal auditor. The programmes of work undertaken by the internal audit department are usually designed after consultation with the external auditor.

'Vouching' is a term used to describe the substantiation of a transaction by the inspection of a voucher which provides evidence to support the entry made in the books. The Cadbury Report on Corporate Governance suggests that the non-executive directors of a company should form an audit committee so that the external and internal auditors have a right of access to very senior management to discuss or report matters of financial impropriety.

Small Company Audits

Small companies with a turnover of under £1m per year are excepted from the requirement to subject their financial statements to an audit. It is suggested that the limit should be raised to a turnover of £4.8m (the maximum permitted under European Union directives), but ineligible companies such as those in the financial services sector would still require an audit.

In the past, the Inland Revenue, banks, creditors and minority shareholders have seen the audit as essential for the small company. The government, however, wishes to reduce the administrative burden on small businesses. The banks now see accounts as less significant, as they usually take the directors' personal assets as security for a loan. In the small company there is often very little distinction between the directors as managers and owners. The company law review is currently suggesting that an Independent Professional Review (IPR) might be less burdensome for smaller companies, but still give assurance to banks, minority shareholders and others. The reporting accountants can provide negative assurance that they are not aware of any material changes to the accounts required to comply with statute and standards. This new quasi-audit has not met with acceptance from all auditors. Some suggest it will not give sufficient assurance to users, and others comment that it will create a second tier of audit work.

THE PROBLEM OF VOLUME

The audit of a large volume of transactions requires the application of special techniques. The auditor cannot check everything, since this would be too time-consuming. To save time, auditors have adopted two techniques, 'sampling' and 'depth-checking'.

Sampling is the selection of a statistical sample of the transactions which have taken place and the careful checking and vouching of the sample by the auditor. Auditors know that they can rely on this sample, if it is large enough, as being representative of the whole, so that if the transactions in the sample are found to be correct it is probable that the remainder, which have not been checked, are also correct. The success of sampling is largely dependent on the proper selection of the sample, and it should be ensured that the sample is large enough to be a significant guide to the whole 'population'. The auditor must use judgement to select a 'confidence level' appropriate to each item to be tested, which will in turn influence the size of the sample.

Depth-checking is a term used to describe the audit method whereby a single transaction is selected and checked in depth, which means that the auditor follows the transactions from beginning to end in great detail. For example, the auditor may select the purchase of a certain delivery of raw materials, and will check every prime document and every entry in the books needed to record that transaction from the moment that the purchase is requisitioned right through until the point at which the supplier is paid by cheque. This will show whether the system is operating correctly. If a large enough sample of transactions is selected to give confidence in the reliability of the remainder, depth-checking removes the need to check every transaction. It must be emphasized that the extent to which the auditor can rely on this work depends upon the selection and size of the sample.

THE AUDIT PROGRAMME

It is customary for an auditor to draw up a programme of the checks needed to complete the task. Thus if the work is interrupted, the audit programme ensures that nothing is missed, and if another auditor comes to finish the job, that person will know exactly what has been done to date. Auditing is a systematic and painstaking business; for example, careful notes are maintained in an audit file of questions asked and answers received, so that a comprehensive record is built up on which the auditor's opinion can be based. When an audit clerk initials a section of the programme, he is taking responsibility for its proper completion. The file contains the Internal Control Questionnaires (ICQs) completed at the beginning of the audit. The auditor will review the system of internal control in operation in the business and interview those responsible for its operation, gradually completing an ICQ which in time will form the basis of a letter of weakness.

AUDIT RISK

Legal claims against auditors for damages for implied negligence have now increased so much that the profession is very mindful of the risks it undertakes. Recently Coopers and Lybrand (Now Price Waterhouse Coopers) paid out £67 million for work for the business empire of Robert Maxwell, and in the United States Ernst and Young agreed a $335 million payout to Cendant Corporation for audit failures. The level of risk which is acceptable to the partners and their professional liability insurers is a matter of policy. Types of risk can be analysed to four categories:

(a) **Inherent Risk.** Some types of business or account balance are more susceptible by their very nature to a material misstatement. A cash-based business is more liable to theft than others, and this will affect whether the audit should be accepted and how the audit should be planned.

(b) **Control Risk.** If the internal control system is weak it may not detect errors or fraud. A detailed examination of systems and controls in a company will identify weaknesses, and this will influence the letter of weakness sent by the auditor, and the level of audit testing of transactions which must be built into the programme.

(c) **Detection Risk.** Collusion, or fraudulent misrepresentation by members of the client's staff, can lead to serious misstatements of some account items. The auditor must examine critically and with professional scepticism the information and explanations provided, and should not assume that they are correct.

(d) **Sampling Risk.** If the auditor test checks a sample of the transactions, the size of the sample will determine the possibility that errors or fraud will not be detected. The cost of checking large samples of transactions must be set against the risk of misstatement.

Reducing Exposure to Risk

Four steps which the auditing profession has taken to reduce the individual auditor's exposure to audit risk are:

(a) the introduction of statements of auditing standards which lay down the basic principles and practices which auditors are expected to follow in the conduct of an audit, thus helping auditors to maintain the necessary standard of work in areas addressed by the standards;

(b) the publication of an ethical guide which advises members as to the standards expected of them, as members of the profession, in key areas (e.g. independence, confidentiality, publicity and advertising, etc.);

(c) the encouragement of continuing professional development (CPD), which ensures that members of the accounting bodies keep themselves up to date and aware of important developments affecting their work, long after they have qualified by examination – the institution of peer reviews by other experienced practitioners raises standards;

(d) the fact that the professional accounting bodies will not grant members a practising certificate until they have gained satisfactory post-qualification experience.

The specific actions which an audit firm can take to minimize liability deriving from audit risk are as follows:

(a) Formal procedures should be established such that in making a decision to accept appointment or re-appointment as auditor to a particular client, due consideration is given to:

   (i) the audit firm's own independence;
   (ii) the ability to provide an adequate service to the client; and
   (iii) the integrity of the client's management.

(b) All members of audit staff should be aware of their obligations with regard to adherence to the requirements of the ethical guide.

(c) Quality control procedures should be established and enforced within the firm to ensure that at all times audit work is carried out in accordance with recognized best auditing practice. Staff members should initial the audit programme to take responsibility for work they have done.

(d) Suitable training should be provided for members of audit staff and the firm should employ personnel with the necessary specialist skills required to ensure that the firm can properly discharge its responsibilities. The audit team should be adequate for the task, and an effective system whereby queries are passed up the chain of command should be in place.

(e) Advice should be sought from outside the firm where this is felt to be necessary (e.g. making use of the accounting bodies' Practice Advisory Service).

(f) When it is felt to be necessary, use should be made of outside specialists.

(g) Both client and auditor should be made aware of their individual responsibilities. This is facilitated by issuing an engagement letter on appointment to any new audit client.

(h) Adequate professional indemnity insurance cover should be taken out with a reputable insurance company.

Task 13.2

As an auditor obtaining evidence, how would you verify the raw material stock figure on the balance sheet?

Solution

The task is to form an opinion as to the existence, and ownership, and whether the balance sheet value is appropriate.

- Plan the audit – assess the materiality of the stock figure and the risk of a misstatement.
- Ascertain the locations of the stock and the systems whereby stock movements are recorded.
- Attend the stocktake and observe whether the system is operating effectively.
- Test a sample of stock movements documents
  Order→Invoice→Stock→Requisition→Factory.
- Investigate differences between stock records and the physical stock count.
- Identify slow-moving or obsolete stocks which may be worth less than cost.
- Substantiate the values applied to various lines of stock, and test check the calculations to extend and cast the stock sheets.

APPOINTMENT OF AN AUDITOR

It is a matter of professional ethics that a new auditor of a company should ascertain from the retiring auditor whether there is any reason why he should not audit that company. The new auditor should not accept nomination for the post without written communication with the retiring auditor to ensure that all is well. This simple stratagem ensures that a new auditor is aware of any disagreements over the production of the accounts, or of any pressure put on the auditor to accept accounting policies which are considered to be undesirable. This will inhibit the ability of a board to change its auditors in order to gain acceptance of questionable accounting policies. The shareholders have a right to change the auditor at the annual general meeting, but they will often accept the advice of the board of directors when a change of auditors is proposed by the board.

The auditor has a right to act independently and must be able to form and express an opinion openly. This principle is supported in the appointment, rights and duties of auditors which are laid down in the various sections of the Companies Act 1985.

Section 384 of the Companies Act 1985, which deals with the appointment of auditors, states that

(i) The auditor shall be appointed by the shareholders at each annual general meeting.

(ii) The auditor holds the appointment from the end of that meeting until the end of the next annual general meeting so that an auditor can attend the AGM and speak if necessary, especially if another auditor has been appointed at that meeting.

(iii) If no auditor is appointed at the annual general meeting, the Secretary of State for Trade and Industry has the right to appoint.

(iv) The first auditor of a company may be appointed by the directors to serve until the end of the first annual general meeting.

(v) The directors are empowered to fill a casual vacancy caused by the death or retirement of an auditor during the accounting year.

The auditor's fee is fixed by the shareholders at the annual general meeting, unless the Secretary of State or the directors have made the appointment. The fee is, however, usually agreed with the board before the AGM. It is also stated in the Act (s.389) that only professional accountants who are members of accounting bodies recognized by the Department of Trade and Industry can act as auditors of a public company. The Companies Act 1989 allowed private limited companies to opt for an automatic reappointment of the auditor until the company or the auditor decide otherwise.

REGULATION OF THE AUDITING PROFESSION

The new regime of the regulation of auditors in the UK is in line with the EEC 8th Directive. Only 'registered auditors' are eligible for appointment as auditors of a company. A registered auditor can be either an individual or a firm, but must be supervised by a Recognized Supervisory Body (RSB). Individual auditors must hold appropriate qualifications, and an auditing firm must be controlled by qualified persons. Members of the existing recognized bodies under section 389 of the 1985 Act are deemed to hold an appropriate qualification.

Some persons are forbidden by law to act as auditors to public companies. Section 389 excludes an 'officer or servant' of the company from being its auditor. This term applies to directors, the company secretary and employees. The partner or employee of an officer or servant of the company cannot act as an auditor to that company. These measures ensure the independence of the auditor and prohibit the appointment as auditor of any person who owes a debt of loyalty to those running the company and who are the subject of the auditor's investigation. The separation in practice of auditing duties from consultancy work undertaken for a client is an important feature of this independence. A body corporate (another company) cannot act as an auditor.

RIGHTS AND DUTIES

The auditor has certain rights which are embodied in the Companies Act 1985.

(a) An auditor has a 'lien' on the books of the company for any unpaid audit fees. The auditor can withhold the books and papers of the company until the fee is paid.

(b) The auditor has a right of access to the books, accounts and vouchers of the business, and is thereby expected to use all available information. If necessary a previous opinion should be reviewed in the light of fresh information which becomes available.

(c) The auditor has a right to such explanations as are required from the officers and employees of the company, and must be invited to all meetings of the company. Any officer of a company who knowingly or recklessly makes a misleading statement to an auditor is guilty of an offence.

(d) When it is suggested that the auditor should be removed from office or replaced by another auditor, the rules protect the auditor from pressure from management. The auditor has the right to receive special notice of a resolution to appoint another person as auditor, or to remove the auditor before the expiry of the term of office. On receipt of such a notice the auditor can make written representations of a reasonable length to the company, and these must be sent out to all shareholders at the company's expense.

(e) Even after removal, an auditor has the right to attend the AGM at which the term of office would have expired, or a meeting held to fill a casual vacancy, and to be heard at such meetings.

(f) An auditor may resign by written notice, which must contain a statement to the effect that there are no circumstances connected with the resignation which should be brought to the attention of shareholders or creditors, or an appropriate statement. This statement must be circulated to all shareholders and the resigning auditor can convene an extraordinary general meeting to consider it.

In law, rights attract duties which must be undertaken, and standards which must be maintained. The auditor must make a proper investigation of the books and vouchers of the company, and form an opinion as to whether proper books have been maintained and whether the accounts are in agreement with those books.

THE AUDITOR'S REPORT

Having formed an opinion, the auditor has a duty to report clearly to the shareholders at the AGM that the accounts have been properly prepared in accordance with the law, and that they show a true and fair view. To quote Lindley LJ in the London and General Bank Case of 1895, 'He must be honest, that is, he must not certify what he does not believe to be true, and he must take reasonable care and skill before he believes that what he certifies is true.' In this case the auditor had informed the directors that provisions for doubtful debts were inadequate, but failed to report this to the shareholders.

A typical modern auditor's report might read as follows:

Directors' responsibilities in respect of *the preparation of the accounts*

The following statements, which should be read in conjunction with the statement of auditors' responsibilities included in this report of the auditors below, is made with a view to distinguishing for stockholders the respective responsibilities of the directors and of the auditors in relation to the accounts.

The directors are required by the Companies Act 1985 to prepare accounts for each financial year which give a true and fair view of the state of affairs of the Company and the Group as at the end of the financial year and of the profit and loss for the financial year.

In preparing the accounts on pages 26-51, the directors are required to select appropriate accounting policies, make judgements and estimates that are reasonable and prudent and state whether all accounting standards which they consider to be applicable have been followed. The directors are also required to use a going-concern basis in preparing the accounts unless this in inappropriate.

The directors have responsibility for ensuring that the Company keeps accounting records which disclose with reasonable accuracy the financial position of the Company and which enable them to ensure that the accounts comply with the Companies Act 1985.

The directors have general responsibility for taking such steps as are regularly open to them to safeguard the assets of the Group and to prevent and detect fraud and other irregularities.

Report of the auditors
To the members of the Company:

We have audited the accounts on pages 26-51.

Respective responsibilities of directors and auditors:
As described above, the Company's directors are responsible for the preparation of the accounts. It is our responsibility to form an independent opinion, based on our audit, on those accounts and to report our opinion to you.

Basis of opinion:
We conducted our audit in accordance with Auditing Standards issued by the Auditing Practices Board. An audit includes examination, on a test basis, of evidence relevant to the amounts and disclosures in the accounts. It also includes an assessment of the significant estimates and judgements made by the directors in the preparation of the accounts, and of whether the accounting policies are appropriate to the Group's circumstances, consistently applied and adequately disclosed.

We planned and performed our audit so as to obtain all the information and explanations which we considered necessary in order to provide us with sufficient evidence to give reasonable assurance that the accounts are free from material misstatement, whether caused by fraud or other irregularity or error. In forming our opinion we also evaluated the overall adequacy of the presentation of information in the accounts.

Opinion:

In our opinion the accounts give a true and fair view of the state of affairs of the Company and the Group as at 31 December and of the profit of the Group for the year then ended and have been properly prepared in accordance with the Companies Act 1985.

London

XYZ
Chartered Accountants
Registered Auditors

An auditor's report phrased in similar manner will be found appended to the published balance sheets of all public companies. Note how it is phrased to reduce the expectations gap mentioned above.

QUALIFICATION OF AN AUDITOR'S REPORT

A most powerful weapon in the armoury of the auditor is the threat to qualify the audit report. This is a public comment in the audit report on matters which are considered to be improper, unless the directors of the firm act to set matters right. When an auditor is not satisfied with an accounting policy, or a system, or certain transactions, it is a matter of duty to say so in the report, so that the shareholders and potential shareholders are made aware of factors which may adversely affect their interest.

Accounts not drawn up in conformity with recognized accounting principles will be qualified if the standard practices agreed by the Accounting Standards Board have been ignored; this must be mentioned. Not all companies agree with the standards, and their directors sometimes adopt non-standard practices when drawing up their accounts. The auditor must focus attention on this fact, even though a company which cannot be accused of accounting malpractice has chosen to account in ways not approved by an accounting standard. If accounts are qualified for this reason, the number of qualifications made in a year will increase, which reduces the impact of a more serious qualification made by the auditor of another company. In the past a qualification by the auditor was considered a very serious matter, but nowadays, as qualifications increase and are often the subject of a disagreement over the technical terms of an accounting standard, the significance of a qualification has been reduced.

If the auditor does not agree with the amount stated in the balance sheet for an asset, or with an item shown in the profit and loss account, a comment must be made. Qualifications of this nature often concern the directors' valuation of investments in subsidiary companies, or of fixed assets such as buildings. Another reason for qualification is where the accounts fail to disclose some information which the auditor feels is significant if a true and fair view of the position is to be read from the accounts.

The auditor must reveal any inconsistencies where, for example, a note to the accounts changes the view given by the accounting statements themselves. Qualifications should be concise, clear and specific, and should express the auditor's opinion in such a way that the comments cannot be misinterpreted.

LIABILITY OF THE AUDITOR

Because the auditor is considered a professional expert the work done must meet high professional standards. If an auditor does not bring to the work the normal skill expected of a professional, and this negligence causes another party to suffer, then the auditor may be liable to make good any loss. Auditing firms insure against this liability by taking out a professional indemnity policy.

Under common law the auditor is considered as an agent of the company and, as a professional person, must bring to the work a high standard of care, skill and diligence. In the *Kingston Cotton Mill* case [1896] CH 279, the stock was overvalued and profits thus inflated. In the course of his judgement, Lord Justice Lopes remarked that an auditor must use reasonable care and skill in the execution of his duties, but was not a detective, next making his now famous remark that the auditor is a watchdog but not a bloodhound. The relevance of this remark was that the auditor was justified in believing the trusted servants of the company in whom confidence is placed by the company, and is entitled to assume that they are honest. In later cases, however, it has been held that the auditor must, to the best of his ability, use all available information when forming an opinion, and should make an attempt to check the accuracy of information given by employees of the company. It is difficult in practice for an auditor to decide how far to go with an investigation when suspicions are aroused which may later prove to be unfounded.

Professional negligence cases rarely come to court as they are settled between the parties as part of a claim on the professional liability insurance carried by all practising accountants. The reasons why some auditors are willing to settle legal cases out of court are:

(a) adverse publicity is reduced;

(b) expensive legal costs resulting from prolonged litigation are avoided; and

(c) the matter is brought to a speedy conclusion, thus minimizing disruption to ongoing activities.

Recent legislation to allow the establishment of limited liability partnerships shelters the partners of auditing firms from large claims of negligence.

INTERNAL CONTROL AND INTERNAL CHECK

The term 'internal control' is given to the whole system of controls existing in an organization, established to ensure that the accounting records are reliable, and that the assets are adequately protected. Such controls are not only financial, but arrange the systems of working within the business to achieve these goals. A system of controls over stock, debtors and fixed assets with internal checks within the system will, together with an internal audit department, lead to an appropriate level of assurance to management that all revenue is received and recorded, and that no expenditure is made without proper authorization. If the assets of the business are adequately accounted for they cannot be lost, stolen or misused, and if liabilities are systematically recorded it will be difficult to ignore such claims or to fail to provide for known losses when the accounting statements are produced.

Internal check comprises the routine checks on the day-to-day transactions which operate as part of the system. A major feature of internal check is to ensure that the work of one person is proved independently, or is complementary to, the work of another, so that errors are found or prevented. It is impossible to prevent all fraud, but a well-planned system can reduce temptation, increase the difficulties encountered by the fraudulent employee, and improve the chances of detection. Internal checks define the responsibility of individuals and arrange work so that no one person can undertake all the activities involved in any one transaction. A single clerk who can order goods, check their receipt, pass the invoice for payment, and then draw a cheque, is in a position of great temptation, since it would be possible to pass fictitious entries through the ledgers and make payments to friends and accomplices. If more than one clerk is involved in the system, however, collusion must take place before fraud can be effected. If employees are frequently rotated within the system then any collusion will not last long.

Test checks can be built into the system so that one record provides an independent confirmation of another, e.g. comparison of order with invoice. A well-organized accounting system will ensure that costs are classified and coded so that they are entered in the correct ledger accounts, and that control accounts are maintained for sections of the books (especially the personal ledgers) to isolate mistakes or differences. If the debtors ledger control account is written up by a senior clerk, this acts as a check on the accuracy of the junior clerk who maintains the debtors ledger, and collusion must take place between the two before fraud can be accomplished. The simple tactic of putting serial numbers on invoice pads will highlight any missing documents, and colour coding will serve to show where a copy of an accounting record, say an order, has strayed to the wrong department.

Authorization is an important feature of internal check, since it limits the ability of employees to act irresponsibly with the company's assets. If all orders, discounts, cheques, bad debts written off, etc. must be authorized by the signature of a trusted employee, judgement will be exercised before the company is committed in any way. The safe custody of order pads, cheque books and receipt books is part of the system. A close check is particularly important at the points where transactions enter the accounting system. There must be a prime document to support each entry, and it must be authorized before an accounting record is made. The existence of the internal audit department will ensure that the system is regularly reviewed to test its efficiency, and to test that an efficient system, once established, is operated properly.

CONCLUSION

Auditing is an advanced function of the accountant, since it involves checking the work of other accountants, studying the accounting system for weaknesses, and reporting to shareholders. The existence of the expectations gap and the incidence of negligence claims has motivated accountants to examine audit risk and improve their performance to close the gap and reduce the risk. The auditor's opinion enhances the credibility of financial statements, but those statements are based on estimates and imprecise figures and also produced in accordance with regulations contained in statutes and standards. The format of the audit report underlines the independence which is so important for the credibility of the audit.

Discussion Topics

Thirty-minute essay questions:

1. Describe the misunderstandings of the public in relation to the nature of audited financial statements and the level of assurance provided by auditors which have led to the expectations gap.

2. Explain the actions of the auditing profession and individual auditors to close the expectations gap.

3. Explain the main categories of audit risk and show how auditors try to reduce the risks to which they are exposed.

4. Show how the rights and duties of auditors enhance that independence which is crucial for the assurance to shareholders that they can rely on financial statements.

5. Justify the significance of internal control and internal check for an effective accounting system.

PART THREE

Interpretation and the Importance of Cash

CHAPTER 14

The Interpretation of Financial Statements

THE AIMS OF THIS CHAPTER

To enable students to

- Understand the fundamental questions to be answered when financial information is used to interpret the position and performance of a business

- Calculate the major accounting ratios as an aid to the interpretation of financial statements

- Apply interfirm comparison and segmental analysis

- Comment sensibly on the position and performance of a business

WHO NEEDS ANALYSIS

The means by which an accountant is able to understand a set of accounts and reveal their meaning to a non-accountant are among the most advanced accounting techniques. A blend of skill and experience is required to explain the relative importance of the figures and the relationship between one figure and another. A good accountant can translate what the statements show to be happening to a company, and can comment on the significance of the figures for the efficient operation of the business. This is not always a matter of hindsight, since comment on future planned positions is also helpful.

The accountant must bear in mind who is to receive the interpretation when drawing out the meaning of a set of financial statements, as what is significant to one user may be less so to another. Comments may be made

(a) to management on the performance of various divisions or segments in a group of companies;

(b) as an extension of the annual accounts, providing helpful information for the shareholders.

The accountant may also be called on to comment on a business to potential investors, such as a city institution or the client of a stockbroker, or to managers when they are considering a takeover bid. The profit record, dividend cover and growth potential will be important to an investor, whereas the asset base and price/earnings ratio will usually be of greater interest in a takeover bid. When interpreting a set of accounts for a creditor or potential creditor, the accountant will comment on cash flow and the company's ability to repay a loan on the due date, to meet the interest required, or to provide security to cover the loan.

Interpretation is a costly activity, and thus it must provide users with comment and information from which they will derive a benefit in excess of that cost. Comparison is a significant element in the explanation of the meaning of financial statements either with the situation disclosed in a previous accounting period, or against a norm derived from an average for similar businesses, or the planned performance of the business under review.

THE BASIC QUESTIONS

There is a set of basic questions to which the interpreter will seek answers. The answer to each question will lead to further questions, so that gradually a picture of what is happening in the company will emerge. Primarily comment concerns the performance of the business and its financial position.

1. The first question usually concerns *profitability*. It is not enough to discover whether a profit or a loss is being made, since a measure of the adequacy of profit is needed. The return on capital employed (ROCE) should show whether profits are sufficient to warrant the amount of funds invested in a business, the risk taken by investing those funds, and whether a better return for the same class of risk could be earned by an alternative employment of the funds. This approach leads on to questions to determine whether the assets are employed in the right way or in the best combination and whether the company is on the threshold of a profit breakthrough after some lean years when reorganization has taken place.

2. The second question investigates *solvency*, or the ability of the firm to pay its way. Some argue that this should be the first question asked as sometimes a profitable business is brought to a halt through insufficient liquid funds. The interpretation of the solvency position focuses on the availability of cash to repay creditors and the adequacy of working capital resources to finance the level of activity required by management. The liquidity of the current assets, the rate of expansion of stocks and debtors to an 'overtrading' position, and the ability of the business to borrow are all significant in this part of the pattern.

3. The third major question concerns *ownership* of the business. One individual or group may control a firm through significant shareholdings, and thus may be in a position to influence management policy. The voting rights of various classes of capital are important in this case. Rights to dividend, and repayment of capital if the business is wound up, are important matters to a potential shareholder. Often the ownership of shares is obscured through the use of nominee holdings.

    Ownership, however, has a deeper significance, since it can be used to comment on the relative importance of the various groups who have supplied the funds utilized to finance the business. In this sense all those who have provided funds for use in the business, shareholders, long-term lenders and current liabilities, are seen as owners of the assets which their finance has helped to buy, especially since, if the firm ceased trading, they would expect to be repaid out of the proceeds of those assets. If, for example, the trade creditors become a significant provider of finance, they may begin to have more power over the destiny of the firm than its legal owners, the shareholders. When assets are charged as security for loans the actions of the managers may be inhibited, since they cannot dispose of certain assets without permission of the lender.

4. The fourth major question deals with *financial strength*. A weak company is one which has used up all its credit facilities and thus can borrow no more, or one which is overdependent on sources of finance outside the business. If a company has unused overdraft facilities or uncharged assets which can act as security for borrowings, it can use this extra finance to extricate itself from financial difficulties, or mount an expansion scheme. A different view of financial strength measures the amount of assets which the company controls year by year, so that growth in the assets, financed by increasing reserves from profits retained in the business, is seen as a healthy sign.

5. A fifth avenue of approach is to investigate *trends*. If the accounting statements for several years are expressed in columnar form and placed side by side, changes in the relative importance of certain items can be identified. For example, when all costs are expressed as a percentage of sales, the fact that one cost is becoming a larger proportion of the total as year succeeds year can be seen; or when all sources of finance are expressed as a percentage of total capital employed, the changing relative importance of the various classes of capital providers can be noted. When variations from a settled pattern are observed, an attempt should be made to discover the cause. If, for example, the proportion of debtors or stocks to total assets has increased, further investigation to establish the reason for such change should be initiated It is also possible to extrapolate the figures to forecast what is likely to happen if the present rate of change is maintained.

6. The last basic question concerns *cover*, a measure of security to reveal the adequacy of the margin of profits over a required rate of dividend, or the value of a secured asset over the principal of the loan. A loan of £1 million secured against a building worth £2 million is said to be twice covered by its security. Further questions concerning gearing are raised from this point to find the effect of a fluctuation in profit on the ability of the company to pay a dividend or to meet its liability for loan interest.

Once the answers to these six basic questions and their associated queries have been found, the accountant knows a great deal about the position of a business. Three techniques are used to answer these questions and to help form an opinion on a set of accounts. They are ratio analysis, a cash flow statement, and balance sheet criticism. These techniques are not used in isolation, but together, each providing evidence to support the conclusions drawn from another.

Task 14.1

As an investor what other questions would you ask to learn more about the profitability and position of a business?

Solution

Your questions might include:

- Turnover: are sales growing and is market share increasing, and have extra sales been achieved by reducing the profit margin?

- Exceptional items: how far have windfall gains or losses contributed to performance this year, and how does activity compare with previous years?

- Investment for the future: how much has management spent on new machinery, research to find new products, and training to improve staff skills?

- Strategy: what is the effect on profit of investments to buy new businesses to add to the group or to open up new markets?

- Changes: what parts of the business are expanding and what parts are contracting; are the profitable areas growing, and where is investment being channelled by managers?

RATIO ANALYSIS

A ratio shows the relationship of one figure to another and can be used in accounting to demonstrate the interplay between balance sheet items, or between features of the profit and loss account and the balance sheet. Ratios are useful in that they summarize a position and simplify an explanation of a complicated statement by its expression in one figure. However, a major disadvantage of their use is that they sometimes oversimplify a situation, and thus, without a proper understanding of the definition of the constituent parts, false conclusions may be drawn, e.g. the definition of net profit (before or after tax), or of capital employed, can seriously affect the return on capital employed.

Accountants often use ratios to focus attention on important items in accounting statements or to illustrate points made in reports, but these techniques must be treated with caution. Ratios should be used as a guide, not as a basis for definitive conclusions. Too much reliance should not be placed on the impression gained from one ratio alone. The findings should be checked against other ratios, and perhaps against a cash flow statement, until gradually a clearer picture emerges. Sometimes compensating changes in the constituent parts of a ratio can obscure the extent of the change that has taken place; for example, although profit and capital employed may double, this important change does not show up in the ratio of net profit to capital employed because the relationship remains the same. A change in both constituent parts at the same time will alter a ratio, but can cause confusion when the reason for the change is investigated; for example, if ROCE falls is it because net profit has fallen or because capital employed has increased?

Another use for ratios is as comparators. Absolute figures in an accounting statement are made more meaningful when they are put into perspective by comparison. Although the profit made by a company is always interesting, its significance is properly demonstrated only when it is measured against the capital employed in making that profit. An increase in profit may be considered as a good result until the extent of the extra capital employed to earn it is shown. The comparison of ratios of one company with those of another, or with the average ratios of a group of similar companies, is helpful. Comparison of the ratios of the same company at different time periods will reveal important changes from the established pattern for the company, which should prompt an investigation. Some companies treat ratios as guidelines or targets to be reached during the planning and budgeting operation. Because ratios reflect a relationship, they can transcend national barriers. The ROCE compiled from figures expressed in pounds, dollars or yen, enables international comparison to take place.

Ratios can be expressed

(a) as percentages, e.g. the rate of gross profit to sales, say 25%;

(b) as a relationship, e.g. current assets to current liabilities, say 1:7:1;

(c) as a multiple one figure related to another, e.g. the turnover of capital employed is, say, 2.4 times in a year;

(d) in terms of time, e.g. debtors to credit sales may reveal an average credit period of 60 days.

RATIO ANALYSIS: A TREE OR INTERRELATIONSHIP APPROACH

One approach to ratio analysis is to compute the ratios in Figure 14.1 and use their interaction to interpret the position of the company.

Return on Capital Employed (ROCE)

The primary ratio is the ratio of net profit to capital employed. It reveals the return on capital employed and comments on the efficiency of management in employing the funds placed at their disposal by shareholders and lenders. This ratio is often expressed as a percentage and can be used to compare performance with other companies in the same industry, or other industries, or in other economies, or at other time periods. The return on capital employed is seen by the investor as the return received for placing

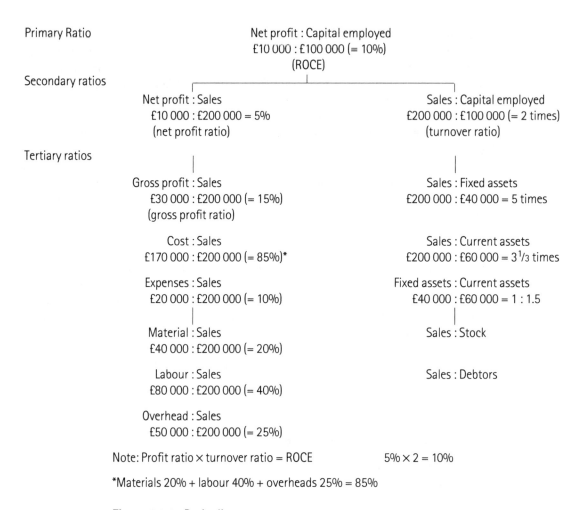

Primary Ratio

Net profit : Capital employed
£10 000 : £100 000 (= 10%)
(ROCE)

Secondary ratios

Net profit : Sales
£10 000 : £200 000 = 5%
(net profit ratio)

Sales : Capital employed
£200 000 : £100 000 (= 2 times)
(turnover ratio)

Tertiary ratios

Gross profit : Sales
£30 000 : £200 000 (= 15%)
(gross profit ratio)

Sales : Fixed assets
£200 000 : £40 000 = 5 times

Cost : Sales
£170 000 : £200 000 (= 85%)*

Sales : Current assets
£200 000 : £60 000 = 3 1/3 times

Expenses : Sales
£20 000 : £200 000 (= 10%)

Fixed assets : Current assets
£40 000 : £60 000 = 1 : 1.5

Material : Sales
£40 000 : £200 000 (= 20%)

Sales : Stock

Labour : Sales
£80 000 : £200 000 (= 40%)

Sales : Debtors

Overhead : Sales
£50 000 : £200 000 (= 25%)

Note: Profit ratio × turnover ratio = ROCE   5% × 2 = 10%

*Materials 20% + labour 40% + overheads 25% = 85%

Figure 14.1 Ratio diagram

funds at risk, and is compared with the return available for alternative investments in the same risk category.

The definition of capital employed remains the subject of discussion. The main alternatives are as follows:

(a) The ratio of **net profit to shareholders' funds** (share capital and reserves) expresses the return on the capital contributed by the legal owners of the business. This figure is a valuable guide to the profitability of the shareholders' investment, but, since it uses a limited definition of capital employed, cannot comment well on managerial efficiency.

(b) **Net profit to net capital employed,** defined as fixed assets plus working capital, is often used for ROCE in published accounts. It provides an acceptable figure, but of course does not set profit against all the capital employed, since current liabilities, an important source of capital employed, are ignored. It is argued that current liabilities provide finance for only a few weeks or months and should therefore be excluded, but when one current liability is repaid, usually another takes its place, so the total funds employed do not fluctuate very much. It seems wrong to calculate the ROCE after excluding bank overdraft and taxation awaiting payment as part of the capital employed.

(c) Some authorities prefer to set **net profit against gross capital employed** (fixed and current assets, or shareholders' funds, long-term liabilities and current liabilities) to show what surplus the management have really produced from all the assets at their disposal. This definition is incomplete if it uses historical values for assets derived from a balance sheet. Perhaps a fairer view of managerial efficiency is found by setting net profit against the current value of all the assets, but this of course presupposes that the current value can be determined easily.

Where net profit is set against the net capital employed, which includes long-term liabilities, there is a case for adding-back loan interest to the net profit figure so that a true return on the capital employed is shown. If this argument is carried to its logical conclusion, overdraft interest should be added back to profit if the gross capital definition is favoured. Whichever definition is chosen, it must be used consistently if true comparability is to be achieved.

A good management should minimize the tax burden on the company, and therefore net profit after tax shows what is available for dividend or reinvestment in the company, and this should be used to calculate ROCE.

ANALYSIS OF ROCE USING ACCOUNTING RATIOS (SEE FIGURE 14.1) PROFITABILITY VERSUS ACTIVITY

A good or bad ROCE can be caused by two main factors. Either (1) the profit on the activity is not large enough or (2) the capital employed is not worked hard enough. Further investigation of these reasons can be achieved by the use of *secondary ratios*.

(1) **Net profit to sales** shows the profitability of sales made, and can be expressed as a percentage or as so many pence of profit for every pound of sales. This ratio can be further analysed by the tertiary ratios. If net profit to sales is not satisfactory the cause may be the gross profit ratio affected by the pricing policy of the firm if the mark-up is insufficient, or the cost structure, if costs are too high. The difference between the percentage of net profit and gross profit to sales is the percentage of expenses to sales. When the gross profit margin is adequate, the reason for an unsatisfactory net profit to sales ratio should lie in the expenses structure, which can be further analysed by computing the percentage of various expense to sales, and revealing the changing position of the various cost headings, when compared with a previous period.

(2) Alternatively, if net profit to sales shows an adequate return, the reason for low ROCE could be that not enough sales are being made. In other words, the productive

capacity or assets of the firm are not working hard enough. The ratio of **sales to capital employed** (the turnover ratio) shows how many pounds of sales are earned by each pound of capital employed, or how many times the capital is turned over. Every time a firm turns over its capital it is said to make the net profit margin.

When the ratio of net profit to sales is multiplied by the turnover ratio, the result is equal to the primary ratio. If the turnover ratio is inadequate, further analysis to pinpoint that part of the asset structure where under-utilized capacity exists will investigate the ratios of sales to fixed assets, and sales to current assets (or sales to working capital if the net capital employed definition is used in the primary ratio). The ratio of fixed assets to current assets will show whether there is a preponderance of current or fixed assets. Too much plant and too little stock, or too much stock and too little plant, will not maximize efficiency. Sales can be set against the individual assets to reveal over-investment in any one classification. The ratio of stock to sales in this context shows how many pounds of sales are earned for each pound of stock held. In other circumstances stocks would not be set against sales since stock are at cost while sales include the profit margin.

How useful is ROCE?

Although ROCE is useful for making comparisons over time and between firms in different industries or difference economies, it is not without its disadvantages as a measurement of managerial efficiency.

(a) It is misleading if all capital employed is not included (brands and goodwill) and if profits are computed at current prices while the capital employed is stated at book value based on historical costs.

(b) Even when ROCE is computed fairly, a further appraisal must be made to establish the risk taken with the investment to measure whether the ROCE is adequate to compensate investors for that risk.

(c) The effect of factors outside the control of management must be defined before ROCE can be used to comment on managerial performance.

(d) Capital investment is a long-term operation, with projects which may have lives of ten years or more, and perhaps with the return not flowing in evenly over the years of this life. ROCE shows only the results of one year's transactions.

Efficiency is a loose term and means different things to different people, e.g. to the engineer, the cost accountant and the economist. To the engineer it might be the input/output ratio of a machine, to the cost accountant the difference between standard and actual cost, and to the economist the achievement of maximum output from a given input (productivity). Profit is the return that a management has made on the capital employed in the business, and it is right that their efficiency should be judged on the basis of this return. The risk incurred in the business must be taken into account, by computing a risk factor and applying it to the capital employed, to show how much profit should be made by a particular business. The success of ROCE as a measure of business efficiency also depends upon the objectives of the firm. Not all firms seek to maximize their profits: their objectives may be a satisfactory return on capital, or the provision of a good service, or growth to establish a market position.

Comparison between the operating units within a large organization may help the departmental management by showing how each department or division compares with others and by pinpointing areas in which improvement can take place. Such comparison may also help the central management in the firm, which is concerned with providing management advisory services to the constituent units. Intra-firm comparison on the basis of ROCE will help central management to judge whether the performance of operating units is satisfactory and will show where improvements can be made and central funds allocated. There are, however, certain points which must be discussed, such as what is meant by efficiency, how it is to be measured, what the causes of differences in efficiency are, and how much similarity is necessary before useful comparisons can be made between divisions. ROCE employed as a measure for comparison compares operating profit to capital employed and acts as a common denominator between firms when comparing the efficiency of managements in using available resources.

Task 14.2

What other comparison measures can be used to comment on efficiency in business?

Solution

You might suggest:

(a) the rate of growth of assets (depends on dividend and borrowing policy, not efficiency);

(b) profit alone (this has limited benefit unless related to capital employed);

(c) value added per employee (may depend on how much capital equipment supports the efforts of the employees);

(d) output per man- or machine-hour;

(e) sales per employee or per £ of payroll.

The last three measures may all show a favourable position while the firm itself is inefficient in other ways. As tests they are not valid, since they do not show an overall view of the business. ROCE is important because it shows whether adequate use is being made of the funds in the business, irrespective of the source of the capital. It must be established whether the funds have earned the return that should have been made from them. Any discussion of business efficiency and ROCE must take into account the fact that good management ensures continuity and expansion, and should not squeeze out extra profits in the short term, which will harm the long-term position of the business. Development periods for large-scale capital projects, when a low return is to be expected, must also be taken into consideration.

The Limitations of ROCE

Certain factors reduce the usefulness of ROCE:

1. Definitions of capital employed vary, and confusion may arise when return on capital is discussed unless terms are rationalized.

2. The return on capital is a misleading guide to efficiency unless assets are valued at current prices. Profits are counted in terms of current prices, so it will be misleading if they are compared with capital computed on a historical basis.

3. Comparison of efficiency between firms by means of return on capital employed will be difficult if they are not truly comparable businesses: e.g. one business may lease its plant, another may have new plant, while another may work with old-fashioned plant. Any device to reduce these differences to a common figure will introduce an element of unreality into the comparison.

4. ROCE does not take risk into account. Thus a business may appear to be making a high return, but the fact that a high return is necessary to compensate for risk taken is not considered.

5. Capital investment is a long-term phenomenon, and often a low return is experienced in the early years of a long-term project. It is therefore necessary that the return on the project over its full life, not just part of its life (say, a year), is used if a true conclusion about its profitability is to be reached. A business is a going concern, while accounting periods tend to be closed systems measuring the return on capital during only part of a full cycle. Difficulty is experienced in deciding what horizon is to be used in measuring efficiency. Some firms will accept low profits at present for larger returns in the future, while others will prefer high profits now and small returns later.

Use of ratio analysis: an example

The following abbreviated final accounts relate to firms X and Y, two businesses in the same industry. Using ratio analysis compare the financial situations of the two companies from the information available.

Profit and Loss Account

	X	Y
	£	£
Sales	2 200 000	2 400 000
Less cost of sales	1 760 000	1 680 000
Gross profit	440 000	720 000
Less expenses	286 000	552 000
Net profit	£154 000	£168 000

Balance Sheet

	X		Y	
	£	£	£	£
Fixed assets		200 000*		1 000 000*
Current assets:				
Stock	400 000		160 000	
Debtors	120 000		400 000	
Cash	40 000		40 000	
	560 000*		600 000*	
Less current liabilities:				
Trade creditors	260 000		400 000	
Working capital		300 000		200 000
Net capital employed		500 000		1 200 000
Less long-term liabilities		100 000		100 000
Net assets		£400 000		£1 100 000
Share capital and reserves –				
shareholders' funds (equity interest)		£400 000		£1 100 000

Note: 50 per cent of sales are on credit terms. All purchases are on credit terms. Opening stocks are : X, £500,000; Y, £100,000. (Using cost of sales and closing stock you can compute purchases as £1,660,000 for X and £1,740,000 for Y.)

	X	Y
The *primary ratio* profitability:		
(i) Net profit to net capital employed	154 000 : 500 000	168 000 : 1 200 000
Company X is the more profitable	30.8%	14%
(ii) Net Profit to total capital employed	154 000 : 760 000 *	168 000 : 1 600 000*
	20.2%	10.5%
(iii) Net profit to shareholders funds	154 000 : 400 000	168 000 : 1 100 000
	38.5%	15.3%

This underlines the importance of the definition of the ratio being used. Strictly speaking, the interest on long-term capital should have been added back to net profit for (i) and (ii). X is more profitable than Y.

	X	Y
The secondary ratios		
Net profit to sales	154 000 : 2 200 000	168 000 : 2 400 000
	7%	7%
Sales to net capital employed	2 200 000 : 500 000	2 400 000 : 1 200 000
Turnover ratio	4.4 times	2 times
Relate to the primary ratio	$4.4 \times 7 = 30.8\%$	$2 \times 7 = 14\%$

Both companies earn the same return on their sales, 7%, but X makes its capital work harder and is thus more profitable.

Further investigation of the asset structure reveals:

	X	Y
Sales to fixed assets	2 200 000 : 200 000	2 400 000 : 1 000 000
	11 times	2.4 times
Sales to working capital	2 200 000 : 300 000	2 400 000 : 200 000
	7.3 times	12 times
Fixed assets to working capital	200 000 : 300 000	1 000 000 : 200 000
	1 : 1.5	5 : 1

X is more efficient in the use of fixed assets, while Y makes working capital work harder. The larger proportion of fixed assets to working capital in Y perhaps shows underutilized capacity. Too much plant?

Further ratio analysis of the asset structure shows:

	X	Y
Sales to stock	2 200 000 : 400 000	2 400 000 : 160 000
	5.5 times	15 times
Sales to debtors	2 200 000 : 120 000	2 400 000 : 400 000
	18.3 times	6 times

A significant difference can be seen.

In Y the stocks work three times as hard as in X, whereas the debtors of X support three times as much sales as those of Y.

Both companies have the same profit ratio (7%), but what happens with further investigation?

	X	Y
Gross profit to sales	440 000 : 2 200 000	720 000 : 2 400 000
	20%	30%
Expenses to sales	286 000 : 2 200 000	552 000 : 2 400 000
	13%	23%

Company Y has a real advantage over X, either on mark-up or on cost of goods sold as shown by the gross profit ratio, but this is nullified by the impact of higher expenses in Y. Perhaps the higher expenses of Y reflect the impact of extra depreciation and maintenance on the extra fixed assets which it possesses.

Note that nothing is certain in this comparison. The ratios have been used to suggest further avenues of enquiry.

THE ALTERNATIVE APPROACH TO RATIO ANALYSIS

This approach investigates the firm's affairs one aspect at a time. Ratios can be used in groups to comment on solvency, earnings, stocks, capital, sales, etc.

Solvency

Two main ratios are used to generate comment on this important aspect of business affairs, and other ratios can be used to substantiate the situation. The first ratio is the **working capital ratio** or current ratio, which sets current assets against current liabilities. It expresses the surplus of current assets over current liabilities, or the amount of the firm's own funds used to finance short-term assets. It is also used by short-term creditors to assess the risk of lending to the firm, since a surplus of current assets over current liabilities means that there are sufficient current assets soon to be liquified as a fund from which to repay trade creditors and others. When current liabilities exceed current assets (negative working capital), it appears that short-term funds have been recruited to finance long-term assets – a danger sign.

Bracketed with the current ratio is the quick asset or **'acid test' ratio**, which sets those current assets which can be quickly turned into cash (debtors, investments and cash) against current liabilities. This ratio is a useful indicator of how well the firm can balance current liabilities against liquid assets, and a 1:1 relationship is considered prudent if a firm is to be able to pay its way. However, it must be made clear that this ratio is somewhat bogus, since the so-called quick assets often cannot be turned into cash in a short time, and in any case many of the current liabilities do not fall due immediately and may be payable in three or four months' time. Many companies are able to operate at a ratio far below the one-to-one norm. This is because they are in a cash trade, so that the inflows of cash are not delayed by waiting for debtors' payments, and/or the fact that the company may be in a strong market position. A strong company is able to take extended credit from its suppliers so that the operations can be financed using trade credit to a greater extent than is normal.

In the example of X and Y above, the current and quick asset ratios are computed as follows: Note the impact of stock on the liquidity of X.

	X	Y
Current ratio (CA:CL)	560 : 260	600 : 400
	= 2.15 : 1	= 1.5 : 1
Quick asset ratio (acid test QA:CL)	160 : 260	440 : 400
	= 0.6 : 1	= 1.1 : 1

X has a much stronger current ratio than Y because of its greater stock, but Y is better than X in liquidity terms because its debtors will soon pay and increase the cash. Clearly, the solvency position is affected by debtors, creditors and stocks. The **ratio of debtors to credit sales** comments on the average length of time that debtors take to pay their bills. The **ratio of trade creditors to purchases** reveals the average credit period taken by the company. Both these ratios can be computed in terms of time, as follows, using the figures for companies X and Y above.

	X	Y
Debtors to credit sales	$\frac{120\,000 \times 365}{1\,100\,000 \quad 1} = 40$ days	$\frac{400\,000 \times 365}{1\,200\,000 \quad 1} = 122$ days
Trade creditors to purchases	$\frac{260\,000 \times 365}{1\,660\,000 \quad 1} = 57$ days	$\frac{400\,000 \times 365}{1\,740\,000 \quad 1} = 84$ days

X collects its debts much faster than Y – this may be through more efficient credit control, or because Y gives trade credit to customers to encourage sales. Y takes more trade credit from suppliers. Furthermore, the **ratio of debtors to creditors** highlights the amount of trade credit given and received by the firm.

	X	Y
Debtors to creditors	120 000 : 260 000	400 000 : 400 000
	1 : 2.16	1 : 1

Company Y is in balance, while Company X is seen to use more credit than it gives, which reflects the position as shown by the quick asset ratio.

The ratio of bad debts to credit sales will show up reckless selling, if the volume of bad debts has reached an unacceptable level. The figures are not available in this example

Stocks

The purpose of stock ratios is to comment on the adequacy of stock levels in the light of the reason for holding the stock concerned. These ratios can be computed for different kinds of stock, usually in terms of time – stockholding days. Alternatively, the ratios can be expressed as a single figure representing the number of times the stock is turned over during the year. Further analysis of stock ratios is part of working capital management in Chapter 19. Ratios for companies X and Y disclose:

	X	Y
1. Stock/cost of sales × 365 Average stock holding period	£400 000 ÷ £176 000 × 365 = 83 days	£160 000 ÷ £1680000 × 365 = 35 days
2. Cost of sales/stock Stock turnover	£1 760 000 ÷ £400 000 = 4.4 times	£1 680 000 ÷ £160 000 = 10.5 times

Both calculations reveal the same situation. Company X holds stock for a longer period than Company Y, and therefore turns over its stock less often than Y.

Holding stock may be considered as a wasteful investment since the stock is waiting in idleness to play its part in the manufacturing process. This is a matter of working capital management.

Some companies compute stock ratios using the average stock calculated as opening stock plus closing stock divided by 2.

Capital

The main ratios used to explore this aspect of a firm's activity are as follows:

1. **Capital employed to total indebtedness.** This is the ownership ratio, which highlights the proportions of the assets financed by the legal owners and by lenders.

    Overdependence on finance from outside the firm is a sign of weakness, although in circumstances of inflation it can bring benefits. The ratio can take two forms:

    (a) total assets to long-term liabilities and current liabilities; and
    (b) long-term liabilities and current liabilities to share capital plus reserves.

    Ratio (b) is the **debt to equity ratio**, which examines the relative importance in the business of borrowed funds as opposed to the investment of the legal owners.

    Calculated for companies X and Y above it shows:

	X	Y
Debt : equity	360 000 : 400 000	500 000 : 1 100 000
	0.9 : 1	0.45 : 1

    Lenders are more significant in the capital structure of X, which increases the risk of that company. Investors in X would expect a higher return on their capital to reflect this extra risk.

2. **The gearing ratio,** which can be computed by a number of alternative formulae, points out the importance of fixed return capital in the capital structure. In a highly geared company the proportion of fixed return capital is high, so when profits exceed the amount required to service the fixed return capital the ordinary shareholders will benefit. An upward fluctuation of profits in these circumstances will lead to a more than proportionate increase in the return to the ordinary shareholders. The usual formulae are:

    (a) ordinary shares to preference shares and long-term liabilities; or
    (b) fixed return capital (L) to equity interest (S) plus fixed return capital:

    $$\frac{L}{L + S}$$

    Equity interest is share capital plus reserves – the shareholders funds.

    Calculated for companies X and Y above the gearing ratio (b) shows:

	X	Y
Loans	£100 000	£100 000
Loans plus shareholders' funds	£100 000 + £400 000	£100 000 + £1 100 000
	= 20%	= 8%

X is more highly geared than Y and is shown again to have a more risky capital structure, so that investors in X will expect a higher return on their funds to compensate for this extra risk.

3. Another capital ratio comments on the disposition of the assets financed by the capital employed. The **ratio of fixed assets to capital employed**, or of fixed assets to current assets, will highlight the proportions in which management have divided their investment of the funds at their disposal between long- or short-term assets. Some accountants hold the view that it is prudent to ensure that the fixed assets are covered by the ownership interest in the business, i.e. share capital and reserves, but others, with an eye to the advantage of raising the gearing and post-inflation repayment of long-term loans, are more flexible in their attitude.

Earnings

The managers, shareholders and potential investors all have an interest in these ratios.

1. **Net profit after preference dividend and tax, to equity interest** (ordinary shares plus reserves).

   The return earned on the ordinary shareholders' investment in the company must be sufficient to warrant the risk they are taking in entrusting their funds to the management. The funds involved consist in this case of the original investment in shares, and profits retained since the company began trading (reserves). The return on ownership capital invested shows whether the company is organized in such a way as to maximize the proportion of the net profit which belongs to ordinary shareholders, irrespective of how much of that profit is paid out to them as a dividend.

2. The **'pay out' ratio** sets profit available for dividend against dividend paid, to explore the dividend policy of the board and at the same time to comment on the ability and/or determination of the company to expand by ploughing back profits. Further analysis using the ratio of profit available for dividend to dividend required or paid shows the dividend cover position. If profits are sufficient to cover the dividend at a certain rate then there is greater security or certainty that the dividend required by a potential investor will be paid.

   The formula is

$$\frac{\text{Dividend}}{\text{Net Profit after Tax}} \times \frac{100}{1}$$

Example of cover

100,000 ordinary shares of £1 each are in issue. A dividend of 20 pence in the pound is required to meet the investors' calculations of the risk involved, so £20,000 is needed to pay a dividend. If the profit after tax is £40,000 then the required dividend is 'twice covered', and there is an ample margin for profit retentions.

The amount of profit to be retained in the business is often a very finely balanced decision. If too much profit is retained the dividends will be restricted and demand for the shares will be reduced. If too little is 'ploughed back' then, although dividends are high in the short term, development and replacement of capital equipment is cut back so that obsolescence follows and in time earning capacity is reduced. In either case a takeover bid could follow.

3. **Yield.** This ratio sets dividend paid per share against the current market price of the share and shows what return an investor can expect to receive as dividend from funds laid out in the purchase of a share. It suffers from the weakness that the dividend paid is only part of the earnings attributable to the shareholder.

    The formula is

    $$\frac{\text{Dividend paid per share}}{\text{Current share price}} \times \frac{100}{1}$$

4. Another ratio, the **P/E (price to earnings) ratio** is often used as an alternative. The earnings per share (EPS) are set against market price of the share to show the shareholder what return is being earned on the current value of the share, both as dividend and profits retained for reinvestment by the directors. The EPS are calculated by dividing the net profit after tax and preference dividend by the average number of ordinary shares in issue during the year.

    The formula is

    $$\frac{\text{Current share price}}{\text{EPS}} = ? \text{ times}$$

    The EPS should be shown as a note on the face of the published profit and loss account. Thus a potential investor can compare a P/E ratio for the company with that of similar companies, or with its own P/E for a previous year.

    The P/E ratio reflects the opinion of investors in the market who determine the share price. This opinion is based on their assessment of the future performance of the company.

THE GROSS PROFIT RATIO

This ratio is considered to be so important to accountants that it merits separate discussion. It is computed by setting the gross profit against sales, and is expressed as a percentage. Clearly, it can be used as a control device, since it brings together all the elements of the trading account. The gross profit is computed by adding opening stock to purchases and subtracting closing stock to show the cost of goods sold. This figure is then subtracted from sales to give gross profit. The mark-up or profit percentage added to cost when selling price is determined should be reflected by the gross profit percentage, and if there is a difference the accountant knows that some figure in the trading account contains an error.

Many factors can contribute to such a difference. Suppose, for example, that the closing stock figure is wrong. This will have an effect on the cost of goods sold and thus on gross profit. An error in the closing stock can be caused by

(a) miscounting the number of items in stock;

(b) pricing them at the wrong cost on the stock sheet; or

(c) miscalculating when the amounts are multiplied and added up on the stock sheet.

Alternatively, the sales figure may be wrong, perhaps because some sales have not been recorded, either by mistake, or on purpose if the cash received has been stolen. If stock has been stolen by customers or staff, the cost of the goods sold will increase and the gross profit percentage will not agree with the mark-up. Sometimes the "cut-off point" is the cause of an error. At the end of an accounting period stock is taken by a physical count, and the books should be closed at this point. If, however, purchases are entered after the cut-off point they will not be in stock, and the cost of goods sold will be distorted.

INTER-FIRM COMPARISON

Managerial ratios can be used to facilitate comparison of one firm with another, or of an individual firm with the average for other similar firms in the same industry. An inter-firm comparison (IFC) scheme may be operated by a trade association, or a firm of accountants who audit a number of businesses in the same trade. All participants in the scheme are encouraged to analyse costs according to a set pattern of analytical headings. These costs are then submitted on a pre-designed form to the authority organizing the IFC. Some schemes require participating companies to calculate their own ratios, but others ask only for the information. Clearly it is vital to the success of the scheme that the figures of individual businesses remain confidential and are not leaked to other participants in the scheme.

An average is found for the group for each ratio so that the ratios of one company can be compared to the average figures for the group, and managers at that company can see if their performance in various aspects of the business is above or below average. It is possible to calculate upper and lower quartiles and even upper and lower deciles to give each firm an idea of how far its performance is below or above the average for each ratio. The key ratios form a scoreboard to indicate the extent of the leeway to be made up, if any, by each firm. This is a management exercise in that managers must examine the position of their company *vis-à-vis* the average, and work out for themselves the reasons why their performance is above or below the norm. It is hoped that ideas to improve efficiency will result from this analysis.

IFC schemes are not without their problems. Difficulties are encountered when making inter-firm comparisons, as the outcome is meaningless unless like is compared with like. Terms must be defined and standardized, and considerable effort is involved in organizing and initiating a scheme. An exact comparison cannot be made between a firm, say, that owns its premises having bought them 25 years ago, with another

firm which owns premises bought last year and yet another firm which ᴄ
premises but pays rent under a lease. It is possible to make adjustments tᴏ
to bring such disparate firms into line, e.g. by charging a notional re
companies who own property, but when this is done the figures depart fɪ
and the validity of such a comparison is correspondingly reduced. Policy decisions
must be made within the scheme as to how to treat investment income which can
distort the profit figure. Usually, operating profits are used for IFC, thus neutralizing
the effect of non-operating incomes.

An example of the ratios which are likely to be used in an IFC scheme is shown
below, with comment as to the likely conclusions which can be drawn from the figures
disclosed.

Fragile Structures plc has joined an inter-firm comparison scheme for civil
engineering businesses. The scheme administrators have returned the following ratio
analysis for Fragile Structures for the current year to 31 December.

Management ratio
Q1 – 1st Quartile
M – Median
Q3 – 3rd Quartile

			Unit	Industry	Fragile Structures
1.	Operating profit / Operating capital	Q1	%	6.3	5.5%
		M		8.7	
		Q3		12.4	
2.	Operating profit / Sales	Q1	%	3.7	4.2%
		M		4.1	
		Q3		4.6	
3.	Sales / Operating capital	Q1	Times	1.7	1.3
		M		2.1	
		Q3		2.6	
4.	Admin. costs / Sales	Q1	%	2.1	3.3%
		M		2.5	
		Q3		3.2	
5.	Marketing costs / Sales	Q1	%	0.6	0.9%
		M		0.8	
		Q3		0.9	
6.	Sales / Fixed assets	Q1	Times	2.9	5.9
		M		3.6	
		Q3		5.1	
7.	Sales / Current assets	Q1	Times	2.5	2.5
		M		2.9	
		Q3		3.8	
8.	Fixed assets / Current assets	Q1	Times	0.82	0.42
		M		0.80	
		Q3		0.74	

9.	Stocks of materials	Q1	Days	51	60
	Materials used	M		64	
		Q3		82	
10.	Work in progress	Q1	Days	63	120
	Cost of production	M		84	
		Q3		91	
11.	Debtors	Q1	Days	30	90
	Sales	M		58	
		Q3		71	
12.	Plant £s	Q1	£	1 000	£950
	Production Employees	M		1 250	
		Q3		1 620	

Required:

(a) Draft a report to summarize the performance of Fragile Structures plc in relation to its competitors.

(b) Recommend aspects of Fragile Structures plc which merit investigation.

Points which might be included in the report are as follows: *relevant ratios are shown in brackets.* Fragile Structures plc (FS) has a ratio below the first quartile for ROCE (1). Reasons for this poor performance concern either a lack of activity or a lack of profitability or stem from both these factors.

Profitability. Operating profit to sales (2) shows an above average performance, but sales earned by capital employed (3) is very weak. This suggests that operating assets may be wastefully employed and that some assets of the business may lie idle, earning nothing. The strong operating profit to sales ratio (2) is satisfactory, but this advantage seems to be dissipated by ratios of administrative costs to sales (4) and marketing costs to sales (5), which are well above the average. For ratios such as this a location in the third quartile denotes inefficiency. If operating profit is 4.2 per cent of sales, and administration costs and marketing costs are 3.3 per cent and 0.9 per cent of sales, respectively, this implies that when administration and marketing costs are taken away from the operating profit there will be no net profit remaining (3.3 +0.9 = 4.2).

Activity. The turnover ratio of sales to capital employed (3) suggests a weak performance, but ratio (6) shows the fixed assets to be working very hard, since the figure for FS is well above the third quartile. This is an apparent sign of efficiency. Sales to current assets (7), however, shows performance just above the first quartile but below average. The suggestion is that FS has a problem in this area. Ratio (8), however, discloses an extreme imbalance in the asset structure in favour of current assets. The median position for the group is 0.8 to 1, but FS can only show 0.42 to 1 as the relationship of fixed assets to current assets. This must raise the question as to whether the company is using too few fixed assets and whether the suggested efficiency disclosed by ratio (6) is correct. It must be borne in mind that if a company is leasing plant on short-term hire agreements this plant will be working for the business but will not appear on the balance sheet to influence the ratios concerned.

Current assets. Ratio (9) suggest that the stockholding period for materials is slightly below average – a sign of efficiency. Work-in-progress stock (10), however, is well above average as a proportion of annual activity, which may suggest that the production processes used by FS are slow, perhaps because insufficient plant is employed. Ratio 12, which sets plant at balance sheet value against production employees, supports this view, because each employee working for FS is supported by only £950 worth of machinery, which is below the first quartile for the industry. The debtor ratio (11) suggests that too much credit is given to customers by FS. It appears that three months' credit is given as opposed to two months' as an average for the industry.

An analysis of what is meant by administrative costs in this inter-firm comparison may show that the administration costs of FS are artificially high because this figure includes interest on funds borrowed to finance the large stocks of work in progress and the abnormally high debtors.

Aspects of the business of Fragile Structures plc which might merit further investigation are as follows:

(a) Credit control – action must be taken to see if it is feasible to reduce the debtor balances. Perhaps FS is allowing customers a longer period to pay to underpin the sales effort.

(b) Work in progress – consideration must be given to completing jobs in less time to bring down the over-long time lag before work in progress is turned into a completed job. Earlier completion will lead to collecting the price for the work at an earlier date, which will economize on capital employed, reduce borrowing and cut the cost of interest.

(c) Control should be applied to the administration costs, which seem to be well above the third quartile, let alone the average for the industry.

(d) The production process must be investigated with a view to increasing the plant available on site. This may increase the speed with which jobs are completed. The point must be made, however, that extra plant must be financed, and since there is no net profit this year it may be necessary to borrow, or lease, in order to improve this aspect of the company's performance.

SEGMENTAL ANALYSIS

Many large groups of companies are organized into divisions which specialize in separate products or even industries. Investors need to know the contribution which each segment of the business is making to the overall performance, whether sales are increasing or decreasing and how much managers are investing in each segment. Accordingly a note to the accounts gives segmental information, and SSAP 25,

'Segmental Reporting', sets out best accounting practice for this matter. Interpretation of this information will disclose

(a) The proportion of total turnover, profit and assets employed, for each segment, and when compared with figures for the previous year, the growth or decline that has been experienced.

(b) Ratio analysis for net profit to assets employed, net profit to sales, and sales to assets employed, with comparators for the previous year.

(c) Comment on the relationship and changes that are shown.

Sometimes divisions of a group will trade with each other, so intersegment sales should be shown as part of the analysis. Divisions may use the central administrative services of the group, the costs of which together with finance costs will be paid centrally. Segmental analysis can also be arranged to focus on the various geographic areas in which the group operates.

Example of segmental analysis

The segmental information shown below is an extract from the corporate report of a large food and drinks group for 2004.

You are required to further analyse this information to interpret what it discloses about the operations of the group.

SEGMENT ANALYSIS	2004			2003		
Class of business	Sales £m	Profit £m	Net assets £m	Sales £m	Profit £m	Net assets £m
Continuing operations						
Food: branded	3 267	267	2 007	3 066	227	2 226
retailing	1 104	230	1 353	1 153	175	1 378
Drinks	3 371	520	1 657	3 418	563	1 856
	7 742	1 017	5 017	7 637	965	5 460
Discontinued operations	38	6	—	483	77	658
	7 780		5 017	8 120		6 118
Operating profit before exceptional items		1 023			1 042	
Associates before exceptional items		45	729		24	620
Exceptional items		(291)			(286)	
Interest		(123)			(155)	
Profit before taxation		654			625	
Capital employed			5 746			6 738
Net borrowings			(2 159)			(3 025)
Net assets			3 587			3 713

Solution

(1) Prepare a table showing the proportion of each activity to the whole for sales, profit and net assets.

(2) The percentage change from 2003 to 2004 can then be calculated.

(3) A further table will show ratios for profit to sales; profit to net assets; sales to net assets.

(4) Comment on what the tables disclose.

Proportion	2004						2003		
	Sales		Profit		Net Assets		Sales	Profit	Net Assets
	%	Change	%	Change	%	Change	%	%	%
Food branded	42	+ 6.5%	26	+17%	40	10%	38	22	36
Food retail	14	−4%	23	+32%	27	−2%	14	17	22
Drinks	43	−1%	51	−8%	33	−11%	42	54	30
Discontinued	1		—		—		6	7	12
	100		100		100		100	100	100

Ratios	Profit : Sales	Profit : Net Assets	Sales : Net Assets	Profit : Sales	Profit : Net Assets	Sales : Net Assets
Food branded	8%	13%	1.6 times	7.4%	10%	1.37 times
Food retailing	21%	17%	0.81 times	15%	12.6%	0.8 times
Drinks	15%	31%	2.0 times	16%	30%	1.8 times
Overall	13%	20%	1.6 times	12.8%	17%	1.32 times

Note
Exceptional items in 2004 are £291m – enquire what has made such a dent in profit.
Interest in 2004 cost £123m – a fall of 23% on 2003. Investigate the financial structure.

Calculation
Food branded sales % 3,267 ÷ 7,780 × 100/1 = 41.9%
Food branded sales change 3,267 - 3,066 = 201   201 ÷ 3,066 × 100/1 = 6.5%

Comment

1. The drinks division has the best return on assets (31%) and works the assets hardest (2 times). Food retailing has a good profit to sales (21%), but sales to net assets (0.81 times) shows considerable assets are required to earn each pound of sales. Food retailing has increased profit to sales and profit to assets since last year.

2. Branded food, with a $6\frac{1}{2}$ % increase in sales, has increased its proportion of total sales (42%), but this is the least profitable activity of the group (13%).

3. In 2003 drinks earned 54% of profit from 42% of sales and 30% of assets, but in 2004 it earned 51% of profit from 43% of sales and 33% of assets. Net assets have been reduced in branded foods (10%) and drinks (11%).

4. Food retailing has the best profit to sales ratio (21%) up from 15% last year, but it accounts for only 14% of group sales.

5. Discontinued items are much less in 2004 than in 2003. Perhaps there has been less disruption due to strategic change this year.

CONCLUSION

Interpretation of performance and position is a very useful accounting technique. Ratio analysis can be used to suggest interpretive comments, but the accountant must understand the constituent parts of each ratio and realize that conclusions drawn from ratios must be substantiated by other investigations. Inter-firm comparison and segmental reporting extend the ways in which ratios can be used to investigate and interpret. These techniques are as much a part of management accounting as of financial accounting

Discussion Topics

Thirty-minute essay questions:

1. 'Solvency is more important than profitability in business.' Discuss.

2. 'Overdependence on finance from outside the company is a sign of weakness.' Do you agree?

3. Discuss the advantages and disadvantages of ratio analysis as a tool of interpretation.

4. Explain the interaction of ratios in the diagram approach to ratio analysis.

5. Why is the gross profit ratio considered to be so important? What factors can cause this ratio to be different from the mark-up on goods sold by a company?

SEMINAR EXERCISES

14.1 **Puzzle Ltd** is a small manufacturing company with premises in the East Midlands. The balance sheet of the company is shown below, together with other significant figures extracted from the accounts.

Puzzle Ltd, Balance Sheet as at 31 March

	£	£	£
Capital:			2400000
Ordinary shares of £1 each,			
authorized and issued			
Reserves			4 800 000
			7 200 000
Long-term liabilities:			
10 per cent loan stock			8 000 000
Current liabilities:			
Creditors		2 000 000	
Tax		600 000	
Overdraft		3 000 000	5 600 000
			£20 800 000

	Cost	Depreciation	
Represented by:			
Fixed assets:			
Buildings	4 000 000	—	4 000 000
Plant	8 000 000	4 240 000	3 760 000
Vehicles	300000	60 000	240 000
	12 300 000	*4 300 000*	8 000 000
Current assets:			
Stock		4 800 000	
Debtors		7 200 000	
Investments		800 000	12 800 000
			£20 800 000

Sales £16 000 000   Gross profit: £3 200 000   Net profit: £1 600 000

Required:

Using simple ratio analysis, comment on the performance of this company for the year to 31 March.

14.2 **David** and **Charles** each carry on business as wholesalers of the same product. Their representative accounts for the year to 31 January are as follows:

Trading and Profit and Loss Accounts

	David		Charles	
	£	£	£	£
Sales		1 440 000		1 400 000
Cost of sales:				
Opening stock	280 000		32 000	
Purchases	1 240 000		1 216 000	
	1 520 000		1 248 000	
Closing stock	320 000		48 000	
Cost of sales		1 200 000		1 200 000
Gross profit		240 000		200 000
Selling expenses	72 000		28 000	
Administration expenses	81 600		95 000	
		153 600		123 000
Net profit		£86 400		£77 000

Balance Sheets at 31 January

	David £	Charles £
Freehold property	200 000	140 000
Fixtures, fittings and equipment	217 500	138 400
Motor vehicles	120 000	60 000
	537 500	338 400
Stock	320 000	48 000
Debtors	288 000	112 000
Bank	89 500	113 600
	£1 235 000	£612 000
Capital	1 080 000	308 000
Creditors	155 000	304 000
	£1 235 000	£612 000

Notes

(a) All fixed assets are at written-down value.
(b) You may assume that stocks increased over the year at an even rate.
(c) All sales are on credit terms.
(d) The amounts of creditors and debtors have not changed significantly over the year.

Required:

Compare the profitability and financial position of the two businesses by:

(a) Calculating at least eight suitable ratios for each business;
(b) Commenting on the significance of the results of your calculations

14.3 The proprietor of the **St Denys Press Ltd**, a small printing firm, has read about a scheme whereby significant accounting ratios are prepared on an average basis for the industry as a whole, and published as a yardstick against which individual firms can gauge their own performance and efficiency. He has acquired a set of ratios for firms in the class appropriate to his own, and now seeks to make a comparison, with your assistance. He provides you with the following information:

Significant Accounting Ratios for a Printing Business with a Turnover in the Range Appropriate

Return on net capital employed	14%
Gearing ratio	20%
Turnover ratio	2 times
Current ratio	1.6 : 1
Quick asset ratio	1.1 : 1
Gross profit ratio	14%
Net profit ratio	7%
Stock turnover period	30 days
Debtors collection period	30 days
Creditors payment period	60 days

St Denys Press Ltd Profit and Loss Account for Year to 31 December

	£	£
Sales (80% on credit terms)		2 880 416
Opening stock	168 271	
Plus purchases	1 804 630	
	1 972 901	
Less closing stock	220 412	
Material cost	1 752 489	
Labour	502 641	
Factory overheads	371 240	
Cost of sales		2 626 370
Gross profit		254 046
Expenses		180 731
Net profit before loan interest		73 315
Long-term loan interest		30 000
Profit available for distribution		£43 315

St Denys Press Ltd Balance Sheet as at 31 December

	£	£	£
Share capital			250 000
General reserve			296 000
Unappropriated profit			4 692
Equity interest			550 692
Long-term loan			300 000
Net capital employed			£850 692
Represented by:			
Fixed assets			468 207
Current assets:			
Stock		220 412	
Debtors		357 620	
Cash		4 838	
		582 870	
Current liabilities:			
Trade creditors	150 385		
Taxation	50 000		
		200 385	
			382 485
Net assets			£850 692

Required:

(a) Compute the appropriate ratios.

(b) Comment to the proprietor on your findings.

(N.B. Work to one decimal place.)

CHAPTER 15

The Cash Flow Statement

THE AIMS OF THIS CHAPTER

To enable students to

- Appreciate the importance of cash in business
- Understand the reasons for cash inflows and outflows
- Draft a cash flow statement in good form
- Use the statement to make interpretative comments
- Appraise a balance sheet with the eye of an accountant

THE IMPORTANCE OF CASH IN BUSINESS

Cash is the life blood of a business. Almost every transaction recorded by the accountant will lead eventually to cash flows in or out of the business. Adequate liquid resources held by a business reduce the risk involved as bills can be paid on the due date, perhaps earning a cash discount for early payment. Conversely, a business which is short of cash must constantly delay payment to creditors if it cannot draw down cash from lenders. Cash, however, lies idle waiting to be paid out and does not earn a profit like other assets, so managers must strike a balance between the need for cash as an insurance against insolvency, and the need to use assets in the business as intensively as possible. Efficient cash management maintains a liquid cash fund that is sufficient for the needs of the business yet not too large and thus wasteful of resources. The cash flow statement shows the major sources and uses of cash in a period so that investors and others can see the extent of the cash flow generated by the businesses, and decide whether there is sufficient liquidity in the business to finance its operations. The adequacy or inadequacy of cash resources is a significant factor when judging the riskiness of a business.

Cash is needed by a business for

(a) **the transactions motive** – to make planned payments in the near future for general business purposes;

(b) **the precautions motive** – to pay for unexpected costs or demands for early payment from suppliers; and

(c) **the speculative motive** – to take advantage of opportunities as they arise.

The Cash Flow Statement (CFS)

The balance sheet shows the sources from which funds have been recruited to finance the business, and the ways in which those funds have been invested in assets. The balance sheet, however, only discloses this position at a specific point in time. The CFS analyses the changes taking place between two balance sheet dates so far as cash flowing in and out is concerned. The statement identifies cash flows covered by changes in the capital structure (shares and loans, raised or repaid) and changes in the asset structure (machinery bought or sold) during a period. The CFS acts as a partner to the profit and loss account to explain the events which have led up to the most recent balance sheet. It is important to note that the position of a business is influenced by income (sales less expenses) as well as by the flow of cash in and out. It is possible for a company to make losses in the short run and survive if it remains solvent, whereas profitable operations can be brought to a halt by a lack of cash to pay wages and creditors in the immediate future. The CFS is a significant aid to interpretation and can be used in conjunction with accounting ratios.

Cash Inflows and Outflows

Cash flows into a business from the following sources:

(a) Cash generated by trading activities; cash received from sales less cash paid out for expenses – this is the cash flow from operations.

(b) Cash injected into a business on a long-term basis. These cash flows are derived from the issue of shares including a premium, and long-term loans.

(c) Cash released from long-term applications for use elsewhere in the business. These are cash flows derived from structural changes such as the sale of fixed assets or subsidiary companies and the repayment of loans previously made to subsidiaries or other businesses.

(d) Cash lent to the business on a short-term basis by trade creditors, or as bank loans and overdraft, or as tax waiting to be paid. The liquidation of short-term assets also generates cash inflows as stock or debtors are reduced, investments sold and cash deposit accounts closed.

Cash outflows arise for the following reasons:

(a) Trading losses occur when the payment of expenses exceeds income from sales.

(b) Cash is used to acquire permanent assets such as land, buildings, plant, vehicles, fixtures and fittings and long-term investments.

(c) Cash is paid away outside the business to repay long-term loans or to redeem share capital.

(d) Cash is invested outside the business in loans made to subsidiary companies.

(e) Cash is used to acquire assets of a short-term nature, stocks of material, work in progress and finished goods; trade credit is allowed to debtors who have not yet paid for goods sold to them; short-term investments are made as a temporary repository of idle funds; cash is paid to trade creditors and for tax and dividends.

Note that already with this simple analysis shown above, items concerning cash moved into and out of the business on a long-term basis are being mixed in with short-term movements, and the source and application of cash from changes in the asset structure. Cash leaking out of the business to pay tax and dividends is considered as a use of cash, the same as funds invested in assets.

The cash generated by trading operations can be computed as in item (a) in the first list above, but an alternative method of calculating the same figure is to take the net profit before tax and add back all non-cash costs that have been deducted in the profit calculation. A good example of a cost which has not caused an outflow of cash during the year is depreciation, because it is a means of spreading over a period of years the cash spent when a fixed asset was originally purchased. The term cash flow is often used for net profit plus depreciation and any other non-cash costs identified during the year.

Sources

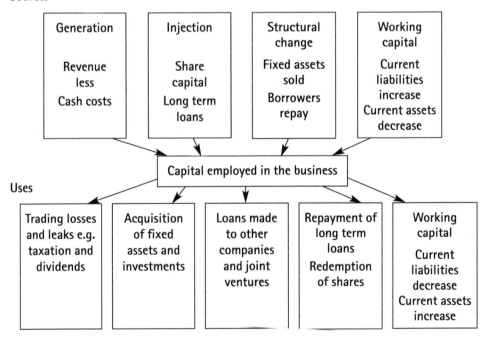

Figure 15.1 Cash flow diagram

The 'cash employed' in Figure 15.1 acts as a reservoir into which cash flows from four major streams. The funds are then tapped off as a result of managerial decisions to irrigate the five fields shown, and any remaining in the reservoir will be represented by the bank balance. If, however, outflows exceed the inflows the reservoir will run dry and, unless extra short-term credit can be arranged at short notice, some of the activities will not receive all the funds they need, and the business will suffer as a result. Cash, like water, can run in different directions, so funds from any source can be used to finance any use, although it is imprudent to use short-term funds to acquire fixed assets, unless long-term funds will be raised to cover the position quickly. Circumstances such as these would be highlighted in a cash flow statement.

Objectives of the CFS

Shareholders, creditors and others are interested in the liquidity situation of a company in order to assess its ability to survive by paying liabilities on the due date. A business is able to change course when the need arises if it has liquid resources or the ability to borrow to invest in new activities. Profit is an important concept to stakeholders in a business, but the generation of positive cash flows is equally vital to free the business from overdependence on outside finance and to promote the independence of its investment programme.

The objective of the CFS is to assist stakeholders to assess the vital characteristics of a business. They are:

(a) the liquidity of the business – can it pay its liabilities when they fall due?

(b) the viability of the business – can it survive in the long run by raising enough long-term finance to pay for those investments in products and assets that maintain competitive ability?

(c) the adaptability of the business – can it take advantage of opportunities and new ventures, and the need to change to keep abreast of market movements?

Sophisticated commentators use the CFS to estimate the future generation of adequate cash flows which can be used to pay future obligations, dividends and interest, and to fund growth by the acquisition of subsidiary companies. Companies hesitate to publish forecasts of cash flows, but details of past cash flows can be of assistance to analysts if they reflect future conditions. The CFS provides figures against which to check previous forecasts for accuracy and the validity of assumptions. The reconciliation of the profit figure for a period with cash flows from operations during that period reveals interesting information about the short-term finances of the business.

Format of the Cash Flow Statement

To be of maximum assistance to the users of the corporate report the cash flow statement should classify the flows according to the various activities undertaken by the business. Useful headings in a cash flow statement are specified by Financial Reporting Standard 1 (FRS 1), 'Cash Flow Statements', as follows. Outflows are shown in brackets.

CASH FLOW STATEMENT   Year Ending ....

	£	£
1. Net cash inflow from operating activities		–
2. Returns on investment and the servicing of finance		
Interest received	–	
Interest paid	( )	
Preference dividend paid	( )	
Interest element of lease rentals	( )	( )
3. Taxation		( )
4. Capital expenditure and financial investment		
Purchase of fixed assets	( )	
Sale of plant	–	
Sale of trade investments	–	( )
5. Acquisitions and disposals		
Purchase of subsidiary	( )	
Net overdraft acquired with subsidiary	( )	
Sale of business	–	
Purchase of an interest in a joint venture	( )	( )
6. Equity dividends paid		( )
7. Cash outflow before use of liquid resources and financing		
8. Management of liquid resources		
Cash withdrawn from deposit		
Purchase of govt securities	(–)	
Sale of corporate bonds	–	
9. Financing		
Share capital issued	–	
New secured loan	–	
Increase in short-term borrowings	–	
Capital element of finance lease	( )	–
10. Net cash flow		

The items shown in the statement are defined as follows:

1. **Cash flow from operating activities,** to include cash flowing in from sales, set against cash flowing out to pay suppliers, expenses and employees.

2. **The net cash flow from returns on investment and the servicing of finance.** This part of the statement discloses the cost to the business of interest paid out to lenders, and dividends paid out to preference or fixed-return shareholders set against the cash inflow from dividends received by the business from the investments which it has made in other companies. Interest paid on leasing deals is included here.

3. **Taxation.** This item is considered to be so important that it has a line of its own in the cash flow statement, to show the actual cash paid out during the period.

4. **Cash flows from capital expenditure and investing activities,** including outflows for the purchase of fixed assets and trade investments, stated together with inflows consequent upon the sale of fixed assets or investments.

5. **Acquisitions and disposals.** Groups of companies regularly buy and sell subsidiary companies or their interest in other businesses or joint ventures. This is all part of the group's investment strategy to achieve a satisfactory portfolio of business ventures.

6. **Equity dividends** are the cash payments to ordinary shareholders. This item shows how much cash leaks away out of the business to provide ordinary shareholders with an income, and to maintain shareholder confidence which in turn influences the market price of shares.

7. **A sub-total** at this stage shows the net cash inflow or outflow experienced by the business for the year before attempting to raise fresh long-term funds by the issues of shares or debentures, or short-term treasury tactics.

8. **Liquid resources.** Many companies operate a 'treasury' department whose function it is to ensure that company funds temporarily not being used in the business are invested for a short term to earn an income. These items are of a semi-cash nature since although they are invested for up to three months they can be disinvested quickly if the treasury department identifies a need for cash.

9. **Cash flow from financing activities.** This section of the statement discloses inflows or outflows from the issue or redemption of share capital or the issue and re-purchase of long-term loans including the expenses paid in connection with such financial operations. Finance leases are treated as borrowings.

10. The net total of all the above items is shown at the bottom of the statement as the **increase or decrease in cash** during the year.

FRS 1 argues that cash flow information provided by the form of statement set out above will be relevant to the investment decisions of shareholders and lenders. The statement will also fulfil the stewardship function of the corporate report, in that it discloses details of performance in terms of insolvency and liquidity.

The disclosure of the amount of loan facility, not so far drawn down, compared with loan repayments and interest due soon after the accounting date, would be of great importance in a highly geared business. Managers object to the disclosure of such sensitive information, which might affect confidence in the business, but if such information is sensitive then perhaps shareholders and creditors have a right to be informed on a regular basis. The fact that such information must be disclosed might restrain some managers from overborrowing and thus prevent the sudden collapse of the business when the situation is eventually exposed. When issuing FRS 1, the Financial Reporting Council had to make a political decision as to how much useful cash flow information could be disclosed without generating protests and counter-arguments from company managers to reduce the cost of disclosure.

FRS 1 provides users of the corporate report with a standard calculation across all companies which shows the cash generated and cash absorbed by the business during a period. Such historical cash flows may help users of the corporate report to make their decisions as to the amount, timing and degree of certainty of future cash flows, and to understand the relationship between profitability of the business and its ability to generate cash.

DRAFTING A CASH FLOW STATEMENT

Many figures in the CFS are derived by comparing the items shown in the opening and closing balance sheets. Follow the figures through this example to produce a CFS for Bradmore Bakeries plc.

The balance sheet of **Bradmore Bakeries plc** for the last two years is set out below:

	Last Year			This Year		
	Cost £	Depreciation £	Net £	Cost £	Depreciation £	Net £
Fixed assets:						
Freehold land and buildings	265 000	—	265 000	215 000	—	215 000
Plant and machinery	250 000	120 000	130 000	320 000	125 000	195 000
Vehicles	50 000	20 000	30 000	40 000	20 000	20 000
	£565 000	£140 000	425 000	£575 000	£145 000	430 000
Joint venture			100 000			—
Trade investments			—			170 000
Current assets:						
Stock	79 896			95 300		
Debtors	60 104			86 210		
Short-term deposits	97 100			66 000		
Cash	39 646			—		
		276 746			247 510	
Less current liabilities:						
Trade creditors	74 321			62 503		
Current taxation	12 000			14 000		
Dividend payable	10 000			12 000		
Overdraft	—			2 811		
		96 321			91 314	
Working capital			180 425			156 196
Total assets less current liabilities			705 425			756 196
Long-term liabilities:						
8 per cent debentures		108 000			38 000	
Unsecured loan		—	108 000		35 000	73 000
			£597 425			£683 196
Capital						
Ordinary shares of £1 each fully paid			510 000			560 000
10 per cent redeemable preference shares			22 000			—
Reserves:						
Share premium account			—			5000
General reserve			60 000			85 000
Unappropriated profits c/f			5 425			33 196
			£597 425			£683 196

Investigation into the balance sheet figures produces the following significant information:

(a) A freehold building was sold during the year for £75,000.

(b) Plant which originally cost £30,000 was sold during the year for its written-down value of £5,000 and replaced by new machinery which cost £100,000.

(c) Some old vehicles which originally cost £10,000 were sold during the year for £750, at a book loss of £1,250.

(d) Current taxation in the balance sheet represents tax on the profits for that year.

(e) The joint venture was sold for its book value.

(f) Sales were all on credit terms, being £630,000 for the year. Interest paid out during the year totalled £8,000 and investment income received amounted to £6,000.

(g) Cash paid to suppliers is £301,516 and to employees £230,685. Tax and pension for employees was £30,000.

(h) The trading profit for the year is £55,021 after charging depreciation of £38,000.

You are required to:

1. Compute a cash flow statement for the company, from the data given above.

2. Prepare a memorandum for submission to the managing director, commenting briefly on the information revealed by the statement.

Computation of the Figures

Step 1: Calculate operating cash flow

There are two methods which can be used for this calculation.

1. **The Direct Method.** This calculation takes the cash inflow from customers, deducts cash paid to suppliers and cash paid to and on behalf of employees to derive the cash flow from operations. Cash received from customers is calculated using opening debtors plus sales less closing debtors to find the amount. In the Bradmore Bakeries example the figures are:

	£
Cash received from customers	603 894
[Opening debtors £60,104 + Sales £630,000 (f) –	
closing debtors £86,210]	
Less cash paid to suppliers (g)	(301 516)
Less cash paid to and on behalf of employees (g) (£230,685 + £30,000)	(260 685)
	£41 693

FRS 1 says that this calculation 'may' be disclosed, but as managers often do not wish to show this information, the direct method, specified in the USA, is hardly used at all in the UK.

2. **The Indirect Method.** This calculation is the reconciliation from operating profit to operating cash flow which is specified by FRS 1. Starting with the trading profit, add back interest paid and deduct investment income received to derive an operating profit. Then add back all non-cash costs to find the cash generated by operations. Next adjust the figure for changes to working capital items, during the year.

In the Bradmore Bakeries example the figures are:

	£
Trading profit (h)	55 021
Add back interest paid (f)	8 000
Deduct investment income received (f)	(6 000)
Operating profit	57 021
Add back the non-cash cost depreciation (h)	38 000
Adjust for working capital items	

- Deduct the increase in stock during the year – cash used up (£95,300 – £79,896) – see balance sheet (15 404)
- Deduct the increase in debtors during the year – cash used up (£86,210 – £60,104) – see balance sheet (26 106)
- Deduct the decrease in creditors during the year – cash paid out (£62,503 – £74,321) – see balance sheet (11 818)

£41 693

Step 2: Use the notes to calculate cash movements during the year

Note (a): The balance sheet shows that a building costing £50 000 has been sold (£265 000 – £215,000), but note (a) says the price was £75,000, so a profit of £25,000 has been made.

Notes (b) and (c): This information helps with Task 15.1 below but also shows that plant was sold for £5,000 and vehicles for £750 and plant was purchased for £100,000.

Note (d): The current liability for tax in the balance sheet at the end of the year is the profit and loss account charge for tax that year waiting to be paid (£14,000). Therefore the opening liability for taxation (£12,000) must be the amount of cash paid out during the year.

Step 3: Compare balance sheet figures for the beginning and end of the year to find other cash movements

Note (e): The *investment* in a joint venture has been sold for £100,000 and a trade investment purchased for £170,000. There was no profit on the sale of the joint venture.

- **Dividends** paid out in cash. The current liability for dividends payable in the balance sheet at the beginning of the year was £10,000, and this will have been paid during the year as a cash outflow. The current liability for tax payable in the balance sheet at the end of the year (£12,000) is the amount provided in the profit and loss account for this year.
- **Short-term deposits** have fallen from £97,100 at the beginning of the year to £66,000 at the end of the year. This implies that these deposits have been liquidated during the year to give a cash flow of £31,100 for use in the business.
- **The 8% debentures** stand in the balance sheet at £38,000 at the end of the year as against an amount of £108,000 at the beginning of the year. Clearly £70,000 of cash has flowed out of the company to repay the loan. Since unsecured loans were nothing at the beginning of the year but £35,000 at the end of the year, this amount of long-term loan has flowed back into the business in the form of cash.
- **Redeemable preference shares** stood at £22,000 at the beginning of the year, but are not included on the balance sheet at the end of the year. This implies that this capital has been repaid in cash.
- **Ordinary shares** have increased from £510,000 to £560,000 during the year, and the share premium account has risen from nothing to £5,000. This suggests that 50,000 £1 ordinary shares have been issued at a premium of 10 pence per share, creating a cash inflow of £55,000.

All these figures have a place in the framework of the CFS. Once they have been calculated it is a simple matter to fit them into the format of the CFS shown in Step 4 below.

Step 4: Draft the cash flow statement

Note that by convention outflows are shown in brackets

Bradmore Bakeries plc Cash Flow Statement

	£	£
Cash flow from operating activities		41 693
Cash flow from Investments and the servicing of finance		
Investment income received	6 000	
Interest paid out	(8 000)	(2 000)
Taxation		(12 000)
Capital expenditure and financial investment		
Sale of fixed assets (£75,000 + £5,000 + £750)	80 750	
Purchases of machinery	(100 000)	
Purchase of a trade investment	(170 000)	(189 250)
Acquisitions and mergers		
Sale of joint venture		100 000
Equity dividends paid		(10 000)
Net cash flow before use of liquid funds and financing		(71 557)

Management of liquid resources			
Short-term deposits			31 100
Financing			
Ordinary shares issued at a premium		55 000	
Preference shares redeemed		(22 000)	
Debentures repaid		(70 000)	
Unsecured long-term loan		35 000	(2 000)
Net cash outflow			£(42 457)

Task 15.1

Can you substantiate the net cash outflow as £42,457?

Solution

Cash reduced £39,646 + Overdraft £2,811 – Check these figures with the balance sheets at the beginning and end of the year.

Task 15.2

Can you substantiate the figure for depreciation charged for the year as £38,000, shown in note (h) of the example?

Solution

Depreciation can be calculated as follows by analysis of the fixed assets in the opening and closing balance sheets. This is an incomplete records technique to find the balancing figure.

Plant £(000s)	Cost	Depreciation	Net	
Opening balances	250	120	130	
Less sale at written-down value	(30)	(25)	(5)	Note (b)
Remainder	220	95	125	
Purchases	100			Note (b)
Balancing figure=depreciation	—	30*	70	
Closing balances	320	125	195	Balance sheet
Vehicles £(000s)				
Opening balances	50	20	30	
Sold during year	10	8	2	(written-down value)**
	40	12	28	
Balancing figure=depreciation	—	8*	8	
Closing balances	40	20	20	Balance sheet

**Cash £750 + Loss £1,250 = WDV £2,000 – Note (c)
*Depreciation on plant and vehicles for the year is £38,000.

Task 15.3

Can you substantiate the figure for trading profit given in note (h) as £55,021?

Solution

An income statement is not provided, but you can work back to the appropriate account from the balance sheet. The trading profit is the balancing figure. Profit is appropriated in three directions: to provide for taxation, to provide for the dividend, and to increase the general reserve of the business.

Dr		Profit and Loss Appropriation Account		Cr
	£			£
Appropriated to general reserve B/S	25 000	Opening balance b/d B/S		5 425
Appropriated to taxation (note (d))	14 000	Profit on sale of building (note (a))		25 000
Appropriated to dividend	12 000	Trading profit		55 021
Loss on sale of vehicle (note (c))	1 250	(balancing figure)		
Closing balance c/f	33 196			
	£85 446			£85 446

The provision for tax and dividend can be found as current liabilities in the closing balance sheet (£14,000 + £12,000), and the amount appropriated to the general reserve is calculated by the increase in that item in the balance sheet since last year (£85,000 - £60,000 = £25,000). The profit or loss on the sale of assets can be picked up from notes (a) and (c) to the question. Buildings are reduced from £265,000 to £215,000, so an item which cost £50,000 has been sold, and note (a) gives the price as £75,000, thus disclosing a profit of £25,000 on the sale.

The trading profit of £55,021 is calculated above after payment of interest and the receipt of investment income. To find the net profit from operating activities, the items in note (f) must be adjusted to the trading profit. The calculation is £55,021 + £8,000 – £6,000, giving a figure of £57,021. Clearly, the profit on the sale of buildings and the loss on the sale of vehicles cannot be considered as part of the cash flowing from operating activities.

Interpretation of the Cash Flow Statement

Some points which should be included in the explanatory memo to the managing director of Brademore Bakeries plc are as follows:

1. No certain conclusions can be drawn from such sketchy evidence, but the figures in the statement can lead an accountant to form an opinion which can be confirmed by further questioning.

2. The liquidity position of the company has been drastically reduced. Nearly £40,000 of the firm's assets stood idle as a cash balance at the beginning of the year, but these have now been utilized in the business, and overdraft of nearly £3,000 has also been drawn on. Short-term deposits have been liquified in the sum of £31,100 and these funds have been employed.

3. Funds generated (£41,693) and funds injected (negative £2,000) are insufficient to finance the net long-term application (£89,250), so £50,000 of cash and deposits have been used to fill the gap.

4. The purchase of plant and an increase in stocks and debtors suggest an expansion. It is odd that buildings and vehicles have been sold at such a time.

5. The expansion has been financed by several sources: the sale of a freehold, the liquidation of some deposits, and operating cash flow.

6. The expansion has taken place at a time when long-term funds (debentures and preference shares) have been repaid. It is financially imprudent to repay long-term funds when they are needed to finance the expansion scheme.

7. Why have trade creditors been reduced during the expansion period, when stocks and presumably purchases have increased?

8. The gearing ratio has changed. Fixed-return capital has been repaid (debentures and preference shares) and fresh ordinary shares have been raised. The unsecured loan is probably at a fixed rate of interest and thus it also will affect the gearing of Bradmore Bakeries and its perceived riskiness.

9. What has to be paid out in the immediate future? Dividend and taxation amount to £26,000. In the absence of cash resources to meet these payments more overdraft will be needed. Will the bank manager be willing to lend more to the company?

BALANCE SHEET APPRAISAL

The CFS is founded on the opening and closing balance sheets and gives a 'cash' perspective to the information they disclose. To an experienced accountant each item on the balance sheet of a company has a certain significance which leads to further enquiries. These questions are largely a matter of trying to discover the reality of the situation and to ascertain that all is as it should be. The following are some enquiries an accountant might make to discover the significance of various items in a balance sheet.

1. **Capital.** Has the issued capital been completely called up, and if not, what calls are outstanding? A prospective purchaser of partly called shares should be warned that he will be liable if the remaining calls are made. To a lender the uncalled capital represents a form of security, since if the company is wound up such capital can be called up by the liquidator to meet amounts owed to creditors.

   The relative voting rights of different classes of share capital are of interest to a prospective purchaser. The existence of convertible loan stock can change the voting pattern of a company in the future. If there are any arrears of preference dividend they may need to be made good before a dividend on ordinary shares can be paid.

2. **The reserves.** It is important to discover whether they are available for dividend or are of a capital nature. Reserves created by the issue of shares at a premium reflect

the confidence of investors, and reserves built up from the revaluation of fixed assets give an indication of the accuracy of the figure for those assets shown elsewhere in the balance sheet. Capital reserves can be used to 'pay up shares' for a bonus issue, and their existence makes that tactic a possibility, if not a probability. The size of revenue reserves shows the financial strength of a company, but the rate at which they are increasing reflects the ploughback/payout policy of the directors and the ability of the company to grow by retaining its profits. A potential lender to the company may suggest that revenue reserves are capitalized before the loan is made, since this tactic will prevent the payment of a dividend from such reserves, using the cash that the lender has injected.

3. **Long-term loans** are significant for the gearing of the company. Where debentures are concerned, an accountant automatically asks

   (a) whether they are secured;
   (b) whether the security is adequate;
   (c) when is the redemption date;
   (d) how they are going to be redeemed; and
   (e) how the rate of interest on them compares with the current market rate for such securities.

   Redemption in the near future can mean an outflow of cash unless the firm intends to reborrow on the market, where higher interest rates on the replaced funds could mean an increase in costs.

4. The significance of adequate **working capital** is covered in Chapter 19 . The existence of liquid funds in the balance sheet can suggest either an undynamic management which is unable to put all the company's assets to work, or that management are liquefying their assets with some strategic move in view. A company with unutilized cash resources might be a takeover prospect, since profitability can be improved by employing all the assets in the business, and the share price is likely to be depressed by the impact of low profits on dividends.

5. The **trade creditors** deserve analysis to discover, if possible, whether any of them are secured and so are first to be repaid if the company is liquidated, to the detriment of the claims of other creditors. The existence of a few large creditors who can join together to form a pressure group on the management is important, but if trade creditors are a large disparate group of individuals to whom only small amounts are owed, such co-ordination and pressure are less likely to occur.

6. The size of the **overdraft,** together with amounts owing to other creditors, highlights any overdependence on financial sources other than the owners, and the extent of unused overdraft facilities shows the freedom of action remaining to management.

7. The amount owed to the **Inland Revenue** is always of interest. The amount may be an amalgam of corporation tax, VAT, Schedule E deductions, etc., each with a different payment date.

8. The **fixed assets** should be investigated to find the extent to which the balance sheet figures reflect their market value, and whether the depreciation written off in the

past has been sufficient to charge the profit computation with a true amount for the fall in the value of the asset. The impact of inflation on fixed assets, especially property, can be hidden if those assets are shown at historical cost, or were last revalued some years ago. Shareholders could be misled as to the true value of their assets, and may accept a takeover bid for their shares at a low price. If fixed assets are undervalued the depreciation charge will be insufficient and profits will be overstated, and where goodwill has been computed on the basis of these past profits it will also be overstated. If the fixed assets are pledged as the security for a loan, managers may be inhibited in the flexibility with which they manage these assets.

The precise description of fixed assets is interesting, to separate such items as freehold and leasehold property.

Task 15.4

Where a company occupies premises held on lease, what terms of the lease would you investigate?

Solution

(a) When is the next rent review?

(b) What will be its impact on the costs of the company?

(c) How long has the lease to run?

The adequacy of fixed assets in relation to the business of the company is important. The historical cost of the plant will not be a good guide to its value in a period of inflation. If the plant is well written-down this implies that it is nearing the end of its working life, is likely to be expensive in terms of repair bills and perhaps will have to be replaced in the near future. If plant resources are small relative to the turnover, it could mean that machinery is leased rather than owned, in which case the terms of the lease should be investigated.

9. **Current assets** raise a separate set of questions. Apart from the adequacy of *stock* levels and the cost of funds tied up in stock, the accountant also considers the efficiency with which the stock has been counted at the year end, and the basis used to value stocks once they are entered on the stock sheets. Any mistake in counting, calculation or valuation will not only invalidate the balance sheet figure but will also distort the profit measurement. The computation of the amount for stock of work in progress is also interesting, since some overhead expenses may be wrongly allocated to stocks and carried forward in the stock figures from one accounting period to another, with a consequent effect on profit.

    The item *debtors* is significant when compared with credit sales. The adequacy of the provision for doubtful debts, which has an impact on profit, must be borne in mind. Further investigations using an 'ageing debtors list' may show up some important slow payers.

10. **Intangible assets** shown in a balance sheet will always raise questions about their valuation, and whether their existence as assets can be substantiated. Goodwill is an example of an asset which must be treated with caution. Its existence depends on an estimate of future super-profits made by the company. The accountant considers whether the present and future profitability is sufficient to support the goodwill figure. The valuation of brands or product development costs should be queried.

11. A debit balance on the unappropriated profit account means that losses have been made in the past. The accountant is alerted by these past losses and asks

    (a) whether they are likely to continue;
    (b) what has been done to bring the company into a profit situation; and
    (c) whether the past losses must be made good before a dividend is paid.

12. **The notes to the accounts** showing an analysis of balance sheet figures and an explanation of accounting policies are very helpful in providing some answers to these questions. It must be realized, however, that the balance sheet shows the position at a specific point in time, and it may not be representative of the current situation. Some significant items appear in the notes rather than on the face of the balance sheet, e.g. information concerning contingent liabilities and future capital commitments.

CONCLUSION

The interpretation of the profit and loss account and balance sheet give an important insight in to the position and performance of a business, but information about cash flows is of equal importance to stakeholders who have financed its operations. The ability to generate sufficient cash to pay liabilities gives confidence to investors, and they in turn provide the long-term injection of funds which enables managers to renew fixed assets and plan the long-term strategy of the business. The CFS furnishes much of the information on which investors and lenders base their decisions. The reconciliation of operating profit to operating cash flow brings a further dimension to the interpretation of financial statements, and links comment to working capital management.

Discussion Topics

Thirty-minute essay questions:

1. 'Cash is the life blood of a business and as such accountants recognize its significance and accord it appropriate importance in their reporting procedures.'
    Explain the need for cash flow information and show how the cash flow statement meets that need.

2. The cash flow statement has been required as a part of the financial statements of quoted companies since 1992.

   (a) Explain why this document is considered to be important when the profit and loss account and balance sheet provides a comprehensive record of the financial position of the company and its activities since the previous balance sheet date.
   (b) Set out the format of a cash flow statement as presented to meet current requirements under FRS 1.

3. Explain the objectives of the cash flow statement.

SEMINAR EXERCISE

15.1 The **Bridgford Bassinette and Perambulator Company Ltd** (BBPC) has extended its activities into the field of general engineering. Draft financial statements for the year to 30 June this year with comparative information for last year are as follows:

Balance Sheet £000s

		This year		Last year	
Fixed assets	Premises (note 1)		1 550		1 650
	Plant (note 2)		1 470		1 420
	Vehicles (note 3)		56		61
			3 076		3 131
Investments (note 4)			1 130		600
Current assets	Stock	600		150	
	Debtors	700		360	
	Deposits	–		350	
	Cash	20		100	
		1 320		960	
Current liabilities	Creditors	650		280	
	Overdraft	320		–	
	Tax	20		100	
	Dividend	80	1 070	40	420
Working capital			250		540
			4 456		4 271
Long-term loans (debentures 18%)			600		500
			£3 856		£3 771
Capital					
	Ordinary shares		2 400		1 900
	Share premium		100		–
	Preference shares 8%		–		600
	Retained profit		1 356		1 271
			£3 856		£3 771

Profit and loss a/c £000s

	This Year
Trading profit	460
Loss on sale of investments	(100)
Loss on sale of vehicles	(25)
Profit on sale of premises	80
Interest	(230)
Net profit before tax	185
Tax	(20)
Net profit after tax	165
Dividend	(80)
Retained profit for the year	£85

Note 1   Premises were sold during the year at a profit of £80,000.

Note 2   Plant was sold during the year at book value.

Note 3   Vehicles were sold during the year at a loss of £25,000.

Note 4   The only trade investment owned at 30 June last year was sold during the year at a loss of £100,000 and replaced by an interest in a joint venture.

Note 5

Plant   £000s

	Cost	Depreciation	Net
30 June last year	2 730	1 310	1 420
Disposals	(1 562)	(980)	(582)
Acquisitions	850	–	850
Charge to P/L	–	218	(218)
30 June this year	2 018	548	1 470

Note 6

Vehicles £000s

	Cost	Depreciation	Net
30 June last year	175	114	61
Disposals	(60)	(30)	(30)
Acquisitions	40	–	40
Charge to P/L	–	15	(15)
30 June this year	115	99	56

Required:

(a) Draft a cash flow statement for BBPC Ltd for the year ended 30 June this year.

(b) Comment on the information revealed by your statement.

15.2 The directors of **Alco plc** are preparing to draft the corporate report for this year. They require a cash flow statement to accompany the draft profit and loss account and balance sheet. The following information concerning Alco plc is available:

Draft Profit and Loss Accounts for the years to 31 December

	Last year	This year
	(£000s)	(£000s)
Operating profit	9 400	24 360
Interest paid	–	(280)
Interest received	100	40
Profit before taxation	9 500	24 120
Taxation	(3 200)	(5 600)
Profit after taxation	6 300	18 520
Dividends		
Preference (paid)	(100)	(150)
Ordinary: final proposed	(3 300)	(6 000)
interim paid	–	(2 000)
Retained profit for the year	£2 900	£10 370

Draft Balance Sheets at 31 December

Fixed assets		
Plant, machinery and equipment at cost	17 600	25 570
Less accumulated depreciation	(9 500)	(9 750)
Trade Investment	8 000	–
Interest in a joint venture	–	4 000
	16 000	19 820
Current assets		
Stocks	5 000	12 000
Trade debtors	8 900	22 100
Cash at bank and in hand	100	–
Government securities	–	5 000
Cash on deposit	500	–
	14 500	39 100
Less current liabilities		
Bank overdraft	–	6 200
Trade creditors	6 800	11 000
Taxation	3 200	5 600
Dividends	3 300	6 000
	13 300	28 800
Total assets less current liabilities	17 300	30 120
Long-term loans		
3-year bank loan (11%)	–	(5 000)
15% debentures	(8 300)	(4 750)
Net assets	£9 000	£20 370
Capital		
Ordinary shares of £1 each	5 000	5 000
10% preference shares of £1 each	1 000	2 000
Retained profits	3 000	13 370
	£9 000	£20 370

Additional information:

(1) During this year fixed assets originally costing £5,500,000 were sold for £1,000,000. The accumulated depreciation of these assets as at the end of last year was £3,800,000; the effects on profit and taxation of this transaction have been included in the draft profit and loss account shown above.
(2) During this year the trade investment was sold for £10,000,000 and an interest in a joint venture was purchased for £4,000,000.
(3) Early this year the cash on deposit was liquidated to finance working capital requirements. Surplus funds at a later stage in the year were invested in short-dated government securities.

Required:

(a) Prepare a cash flow statement for this year using the format laid out in Financial Reporting Standard 1 (see page 264) including a reconciliation of operating profit to net cash flow from operations.
(b) Comment on the position disclosed by your statements, identifying two major items of interest to users of the corporate report.

CHAPTER 16

The Cash Budget

THE AIMS OF THIS CHAPTER

To enable students to

- Appreciate the advantages of a cash budget
- Draft a cash budget
- Explain the difference between a cash budget and a profit and loss account

THE ADVANTAGES OF A CASH BUDGET

The cash budget is not part of the information disclosed to shareholders and others. As a forecast it is difficult to audit and as a plan it is too confidential to expose to rivals. A matter of such importance as the amount of liquid funds available to a business cannot be left to chance. Cash planning or budgeting means that the accountant as a member of the management team will forecast the flows of cash into and out of the business bank account. This budget may be part of the general budgeting system or it may act as a stand alone statement to show what is planned for the cash resources of the business. A cash budget can be prepared on a monthly or even a weekly basis according to the needs of the management and the situation of the company. The main benefits derived from a cash budget are:

1. A business cannot operate without cash available to pay wages, suppliers, expenses and tax. To know well in advance what the cash balance will be at each month end, for as much as twelve months ahead gives managers an assurance that the business can make these imporant payments, especially if the business has an overdraft and wishes to ensure that the limit placed on this loan by the bank is not exceeded.

2. If a surplus of cash is revealed by the budget, managers can plan how to use these funds in the business to improve profitability, or, alternatively, put the surplus on deposit to earn a rate of interest.

3. Any excess of payments over receipts should be identified well in advance so that action can be taken to provide for a shortfall of cash. Thus managers avoid a panic

approach to the bank at short notice to plead for an increase to the overdraft. Finance cannot be raised quickly without extra expense. It is preferable to make arrangements in good time so that funds are available when required. A useful tactic when approaching a bank for overdraft facilities is to furnish the bank manager with a cash budget, but be sure that you can substantiate the figures in your statement. Evidence of good financial planning and control will improve the creditworthiness of the business in the eyes of the bank.

4.   If receipts and payments are set out in a statement which shows movements each month, it gives managers the opportunity to adjust activities to fine-tune the system with the object of improving the month-end cash balance. Action can be planned to slow down payments, hasten receipts and delay capital expenditures, and alternative stratagems can be compared.

5.   A cash budget which discloses the amount of future overdrafts will focus attention on the cost of interest to pay for these funds. This in turn encourages the consideration of alternative sources of finance.

6.   The cash budget allows managers to see the effect of operations planned by them on the liquidity situation of the business. This may enable them to recognize the limits on expansion of the business imposed by the availability of cash. If a large investment is planned in say six or eight months' time, the action needed to accumulate cash to make this payment can be organized using the cash budget.

The Technique of Cash Budgeting

The technique of cash budgeting is a simple one. The accountant needs to forecast the receipts and payments of cash which are likely to take place in the future, and the dates on which they will occur, so that an estimate of the balance at the end of the month or week can be computed. The accountant must estimate the length of the lead-time between incurring an expense and paying for it, and the time-lag between making a sale and collecting the price from debtors. The art of cash budgeting is to forecast accurately the timing of receipts and expenditure. If, for example, a firm takes two months' credit on its purchases, materials delivered in January will need to be paid for in March. The same applies to cash collected from credit sales.

If a firm gives three months' credit to its customers, then cash from January credit sales should be received by the end of April. Care must be taken in this forecast to take into account the likely percentage of bad debts which will reduce the cash received, and to separate cash sales from credit sales, since these will be banked at once. Cash discounts may also affect this figure.

With **labour costs** the timing is a little more predictable, but computation may be difficult, since some companies pay a week in arrears. This means that in a monthly cash budget, each quarter, divided into 13 weeks, must be analysed for the number of weeks in each month. If January and February each contain four pay days then March will cover five weeks of wage payments. If the firm pays one week in arrears the cash

Task 16.1

A business makes sales of £250,000 in January. Payment is received according to the following pattern:

(a) 40% of sales are made to cash customers.

(b) 30% of sales are made to trade customers who take advantage of a $2\frac{1}{2}$% cash discount to pay within one month.

(c) 30% of sales are to trade customers who pay within three months, but 5% of these sales are expected to be bad debts.
When will cash be received from sales made in January?

Solution

- Sales in **January** £250,000 – 40% cash in January   £100 000

- 30% pay in **February**, net of $2\frac{1}{2}$% cash discount
  (£250,000 × .3 = £75,000) × .975   £73 126

- 30% pay in **April** less 5% bad debts
  £75,000 × .95   £71 250

The cash discount and bad debts would appear in the profit and loss account as costs.

paid out in February will equal one week of January's wages ($\frac{1}{4}$) and three weeks of February's wages ($\frac{3}{4}$), whereas in March the wages paid out will be a quarter of February's labour cost and four-fifths of March's labour cost. It must be remembered that in cash budgeting the actual wages sheets are not available and figures must be assessed from estimates of monthly costs. Tax and National Insurance deductions will not be paid in cash at the same time that wages are paid.

Expenses are usually easier to forecast, since they are often paid one month in arrears, e.g. salaries. Certain expenses are paid quarterly, e.g. rent, or half-yearly, e.g. loan interest, or annually, e.g. insurance premiums or annual bonus. Some expenses, such as depreciation, do not cause an outflow of cash and therefore should be ignored for cash budgeting purposes.

Care must be taken when budgeting for **miscellaneous items**, both receipts and payments. Dividends received from an investment should be allotted to the correct month, together with projected receipts from the sale of fixed assets, while the amount and date of capital expenditure and payments of tax and dividend should be entered on the statement. It then remains only to set off the receipts against the payments each month to compute the surplus or deficit, and to show the impact of this cash flow on the bank balance or overdraft. A columnar approach facilitates the compilation of a cash budget. Once the cash budget is compiled, managers can use it to adjust transactions and reduce the overdraft of the business.

Cash Budget versus Profit and Loss Account

Three groups of transactions can cause a difference between the cash flow and the profit figure.

1. **Timing differences.** Accruals and prepayments are used to adjust the profit figure for costs incurred but not yet paid for, or costs paid out but not yet incurred, e.g. annual insurance premiums. Sales made on credit terms are counted as revenue at once, even though payment has not been made. Receipts and payments will eventually catch up with revenue and expense, but taken on a monthly basis wide differences can occur, which will affect the balance of cash or overdraft.

2. **Non-cash items.** Some costs, e.g. depreciation, are provisions and are therefore notional charges which do not flow out in cash. A provision for doubtful debts acts as a cost in one year but may not affect the cash book until a subsequent year when payments expected from a debtor are not received. The allocation of central administration costs to departments does not result in a flow of cash, being only a 'paper' transaction.

3. **Matters of principle.** Capital expenditure or the raising of share and loan capital does not form part of the profit and loss account, but does have an effect on the cash budget. Appropriations of profit for tax and dividend will appear in both statements, but not necessarily in the same period.

Computing a Cash Budget

The format of the cash budget can be designed to meet the needs of the managers who will use it. Usually there is a column for each month with cash receipts (inflows) above, and payments (outflows) below. A surplus or deficit of cash flow can be calculated each month, and this amount when added to or subtracted from the opening cash balance or overdraft will disclose the bank balance at the month end. The closing balance for one month is the opening balance for the following month. If the budget reveals an overdraft, the interest charge for the month can be calculated and added to the overdrawn balance.

Example

This is a step-by-step example of a cash budget extended to show the relationship of the cash budget to the profit and loss account.

Belvoir Conservatory Products Ltd will commence business on 1 January to sell conservatory furniture. A cash budget is required to cover the first six months of the business. The following transactions are planned:

(a) 50,000 £1 ordinary shares will be issued for cash on 1 January. A long-term loan of £100,000 will be raised on 1 April, with interest at 11% payable every six months.

(b)   Sales are expected to be £90,000 in February, £120,000 in March, £250,000 in April and growing at 15% each month thereafter. Sales will be 20% of the total for cash each month, with 40% of customers paying after one month for a $2^{1}/2\%$ discount. The remainder will pay in the third month but 8% will be bad debts.

(c)   Purchases are planned to be £60,000 in January, £90,000 in February, £120,000 in March and increasing at £10,000 per month thereafter. Suppliers allow two months credit. A closing stock of £95,000 is planned at the end of June.

(d)   Wages and salaries will cost £25,000 per month for January, February and March and £30 000 per month thereafter. Tax deductions of 20% of labour costs will be paid to the Inland Revenue one month after the deduction

(e)   Insurance for the year will cost £40,000 payable in January. Rates for January to June will cost £25,000 payable in March. Rent of £60,000 per annum will be paid quarterly in advance. Administration will cost £12,000 per month, payable one month in arrears.

(f)   Advertising will cost £8000 each month, but there will be a special expense of £20,000 in January to launch the business – all payable one month in arrears.

(g)   Special vehicles costing £40,000 will be purchased in January and paid for in that month net of 20% retention, which will be released after three months. These vehicles will have a working life of five years with no scrap value at the end.

(h)   The bank manager has offered overdraft facilities at an interest rate of 13% per annum.

The cash budget will be computed as follows:

Step 1: Calculate cash flows from sales.

Step 2: Draft a format for the cash budget statement.

Step 3: Enter cash receipts on the statement from Step 1 and transaction (a).

Step 4: Work through the transactions and enter items on the statement. Identify accruals and prepayments for the profit and loss account and balance sheet.

Step 5: Calculate the closing balance each month and the interest paid if there is an overdraft, e.g. overdrawn £4,000 × .13 ÷ 12 = £43 interest for a month at 13% per annum.

Step 1:

Calculate cash flows from sales as follows

	January £	February £	March £	April £	May £	June £	Notes
Sales	–	90 000	120 000	250 000	287 500	330 625	* Total sales £1,078,125
Less cash sales 20%	–	18 000	24 000	50 000	57 500	66 125	
Sales on credit	–	72 000	96 000	200 000	230 000	264 500	
Credit sales 40%	–	36 000	48 000	100 000	115 000	132 250	** £132,250 debtors
Discount 2$\frac{1}{2}$%	–	900	1 200	2500	2 875	3 306	* £7,475 cash discount
Cash after 1 month	–	35 100	46 800	97 500	112 125	128 944	
Credit sales 40%	–	36 000	48 000	100 000	115 000	132 250	** £347,250 debtors
Bad debts 8%	–	2 880	3 840	8 000	9 200	10 580	* Bad debts £6,720
Cash after 3 months	–	33 120	44 160	92 000	105 800	121 670	* Provision for doubtful debts £27,780
Paid		May	June				

*See profit and loss account

**See balance sheet

- Debtors of £347,250 are unpaid sales for April £100,000, May £115,000 and June £132,250.

- Bad debts are £2,880 + £3,840 = £6,720.

- Bad debts in April, May and June have not yet occurred as these months will be paid for after June. As the bad debts are expected they must be the subject of a provision in the profit and loss account (£8,000 + £9,200 + £10,580 = £27,780).

- Cash discount is a cost but only four months count in the profit and loss (£7,475). June discount is suffered in July.

Steps 2–5:

Cash Budget for Belvoir Conservatory Products Ltd

	January £	February £	March £	April £	May £	June £	Notes
Receipts							
Share capital	150 000	–	–	–	–	–	Balance sheet
Long-term loan	–	–	–	100 000	–	–	Balance sheet
Cash sales	–	18 000	24 000	50 000	57 500	66 125	
Credit sales	–	–	35 100	46 800	97 500	112 125	£132,250 debtors
Credit sales	–	–	–	–	33 120	44 160	£347,240 debtors less provision £27,780
	150 000	18 000	59 100	196 800	188 120	222 410	
Payments							
Purchases	–	–	60 000	90 000	120 000	130 000	£140,000 + £150,000 creditors Purchases £690,000
Wages	20 000	20 000	20 000	24 000	24 000	24 000	
Tax Deducted	–	5000	5 000	5 000	6 000	6 000	£6,000 creditors
Rent	15 000	–	–	15 000	–	–	
Insurance	40 000	–	–	–	–	–	Prepaid £20,000 debtor
Rates	–	–	25 000	–	–	–	
Administration	–	12 000	12 000	12 000	12 000	12 000	£12,000 creditors
Vehicles	32 000	–	–	8 000	–	–	Depreciation to be calculated
Advertising	–	28 000	8 000	8 000	8 000	8 000	£8,000 creditor
	107 000	65 000	130 000	162 000	170 000	180 000	
Opening balance	–	43 000	(4 043)	(75 755)	(41 399)	(23 531)	
Surplus / (Deficit) that month	43 000	(47 000)	(70 900)	34 800	18 120	42 410	
Balance	43 000	(4 000)	(74 943)	(40 955)	(23 279)	18 879	
Interest that month	–	(43)	(812)	(444)	(252)	–	£1,551 in P/L
Closing balance	43 000	(4 043)	(75 755)	(41 399)	(23 531)	18 879	Balance sheet

N.B. There might be some overdraft interest in June.

Managers can use this cash budget to negotiate overdraft facilities rising to £76,000 in March with £24,000 still needed in June. If the long-term loan is raised in March, the need for overdraft would be avoided for that month, but 11% on £100,000 for one month is greater than the £812 of overdraft interest shown in the cash budget.

Step 6:

This example can now be extended to draft a profit and loss account for the first six months trading of the business, and a balance sheet at 30 June. The figures can be picked up from the cash budget, Step 1, or the transactions in the question.

Belvoir Conservatory Products Ltd Profit and Loss Account to 30 June

		£	£
Sales			1 078 125
Cost of sales	Opening stock	–	
	Purchases	690 000	
	Closing stock (c)	(95 000)	595 000
Gross profit			483 125
Expenses –	Wages (d)	165 000	
	Rent (e)	30 000	
	Insurance (e) (£40,000 ÷ 2)	20 000	
	Rates (e)	25 000	
	Administration (e) (6 × £12,000)	72 000	
	Depreciation (g) (£40,000 ÷ 5) × $^{6}/_{12}$	4 000	
	Interest on overdraft	1 551	
	Interest on loan – accrued (£100,000 × .11 × $^{3}/_{12}$)	2 750	
	Advertising (£8,000 × 6 + £20,000)	68 000	
	Bad debts (Step 1)	6 720	
	Provision for doubtful debts	27 780	
	Cash discount (Step 1)	7 475	430 276
Net profit			£52 849

Belvoir Conservatory Products Ltd Balance Sheet at 30 June

	£	£	£
Fixed assets – Vehicles (£40,000 – £4,000)			36 000
Current assets			
Stock (c)		95 000	
Debtors – 1 month (Step 1)	132 250		
– 3 months (Step 1)	347 250		
Less provision (Step 1)	(27 780)	451 720	
Prepayments – Insurance (e)		20 000	
Cash		18 879	
		585 599	
Current liabilities			
Trade creditors (cash budget)	290 000		
Loan interest	2 750		
Accruals – Tax	6 000		
– Adverts	8 000		
– Administration	12 000	318 750	
Working capital			266 849
			302 849
Long-term loan			100 000
Net assets			£202 849
Financed by:			
Share capital			150 000
Retained profit			52 849
			£202 849

Cash Budgeting for a Single Contract

The technique of cash budgeting can be used in the construction industry to forecast the requirement of a building project for funds, and the impact of finance costs on profit. The budget is a plan, and it can be used to plan tactics to reduce borrowing and consequent interest costs.

Careworn Contractors plc has successfully tendered for a job to build a warehouse with attached office facilities.

The price is £960,000 with a start date of 1 April 2004 and scheduled completion by 30 September 2005. The company needs to know how much extra finance to negotiate with its bank in order to fund work on this job. Overdraft facilities are costing the company 17% interest, computed at the end of each month.

1. You are required to compute a cash budget for the warehouse and office contract.

2. Having completed the cash budget, how would you use it to assist the management of Careworn Contractors plc?

Cost information is as follows in £000s:

	April	May	June	July	August	September
Materials	20	40	70	80	100	100
Labour	35	40	50	50	50	30
Subcontractors	–	12	21	28	30	35
Plant hire	1.5	2.4	3.7	3.8	4	4
Certificates	–	100	150	170	240	300

Other data:

(a) Material suppliers allow two months' credit from the date of delivery. In September, half of the materials come from one particular supplier who allows only one month's credit.

(b) Labour is paid in the month the cost is incurred except that PAYE tax deductions are paid one month later. PAYE is estimated to be 15 per cent of the labour cost.

(c) Plant for the site is to cost £90,000 and will be paid for in April. It is usual to retain 10% of the cost of such plant for two months. It is expected that all this plant will be sold at the end of the job for £40,000, to be received in November. The accountant of Careworn Contractors advises you that the plant should be depreciated using the straight-line method over a three-year life with no scrap value.

(d) Subcontractors are paid monthly, one month in arrears, subject to three months' retention of 10% of the cost.

(e) Plant hire companies allow one month's credit.

(f) Site administration costs £8,000 each month. Fifty per cent of this cost relates to salaries paid to site staff each month. The balance is payable in the month following.

(g) In the Careworn Group, the administration costs of the head office organization are charged out to sites at the end of each quarter. These charges are calculated at 5% of turnover.

(h) Insurance for the site costs £4,000 for six months, payable on 1 April.

(i) Certificates are issued by a quantity surveyor to certify that a proportion of the work is completed. The client then makes a progress payment to the contractor based on the amount certified. Progress payments will be made two months after a certificate is issued, net of 10% retention. Total retention will be released six months after completion.

It is essential to understand the 'periodicity' of this problem and to enter cash movements in the right month. Depreciation (c) will not form part of the cash budget, as it is a non-cash cost. Note (g) is also a false clue, since no cash will leave the group as a result of a head office charge.

Warehouse Contract Cash Budget

	April	May	June	July	Aug	Sept	Oct	Nov	Dec	Mar
Revenue										
Cash from certificates	–	–	–	90 000	135 000	153 000	216 000	270 000	–	96 000
Sale of plant	–	–	–	–	–	–	–	40 000	–	–
	–	–	–	90 000	135 000	153 000	216 000	310 000	–	96 000
Costs										
Material	–	–	20 000	40 000	70 000	80 000	150 000	50 000	–	–
Labour	29 750	34 000	42 500	42 500	42 500	25 500	–	–	–	–
PAYE	–	5 250	6000	7 500	7 500	7 500	4 500	–	–	–
Subcontractors	–	–	10 800	18 900	25 200	27 000	31 500	–	–	–
Retention	–	–	–	–	1 200	2 100	2 800	3 000	3 500	–
Plant:	81 000	–	9 000	–	–	–	–	–	–	–
Depreciation	–	–	–	–	–	–	–	–	–	–
Plant hire	–	1 500	2 400	3 700	3 800	4 000	4 000	–	–	–
Site admin.	4 000	8 000	8 000	8 000	8 000	8 000	4 000	–	–	–
Head office charge	–	–	–	–	–	–	–	–	–	–
Insurance	4 000	–	–	–	–	–	–	–	–	–
	118 750	48 750	98 700	120 600	158 200	154 100	196 800	53 000	3 500	–
Surplus (deficit)	(118 750)	(48 750)	(98 700)	(30 600)	(23 200)	(1 100)	19 200	257 000	(3 500)	96 000
Balance b/f	–	(120 432)	(171 579)	(274 108)	(309 025)	(336 932)	(342 821)	(328 206)	(72 218)	(78 982)
Balance on which										
interest is charged	(118 750)	(169 182)	(270 279)	(304 708)	(332 225)	(338 032)	(323 621)	(71 206)	(75 718)	17 018
Interest at 17%	(1 682)	(2 397)	(3 829)	(4 317)	(4 707)	(4 789)	(4 585)	(1 009)	(3 264)*	–
	(120 432)	(171 579)	(274 108)	(309 025)	(336 932)	(342 821)	(328 206)	(72 218)	(78 982)	17 018

* Interest in December (£3,264) includes January and February to calculate the balance brought forward on 1 March.

The cash budget could be used:

1. To negotiate overdraft facilities. The maximum required is £343,000 in September, but £300,000+ is required from July to October. An overdraft of £79,000 must be financed from December until the retention is released in March.

2. To find the total cost of interest on this contract and thus measure a true profit: £30,579 interest takes up 64% of the operating profit on the job. Is the remaining profit of £17,018 sufficient to warrant the risk taken, and other resources committed to this job? Note that the cash flow surplus equals profit at the end of the contract.

3. To plan means whereby cash flow can be improved and interest can be reduced, e.g.

    (a) bring forward progress payments;
    (b) bring forward payment for plant sold;
    (c) take more credit from suppliers;
    (d) delay payment for plant by one month or extend the retention period.

CONCLUSION

An adequate cash balance is important for the efficient operation of a business, and in some circumstances for its very survival. Accordingly it is important to know what the cash balance or overdraft is likely to be in future months so that managers can plan their activities to avoid insolvency and reduce the cost of interest. The cash budget is a useful management tool, but those who use it must understand how it differs from a profit and loss account.

Discussion Topics

Thirty-minute essay questions:

1. Outline the advantages of a cash budget.

2. Explain the differences between a cash budget and a profit and loss account.

SEMINAR EXERCISE

16.1 **Trent Electronics** has developed a new computer-based game called the Wizzbang. The company is currently overdrawn by £30,000 and it believes it can make greater profits by switching some capacity from its existing game, Plugman, into Wizzbang production.

In the short term this may mean increasing the borrowing from the bank to buy machinery, and some disruption to the factory for three months while the Plugman machinery is removed.

Sales of Wizzbang at £80 each are expected to start at 500 per month for the first three months and 1,000 each month thereafter.

Sales of Plugman have been 1,000 per month up to now but are expected to fall immediately to 500 each month. The selling price of Plugman is £20 each.

Twenty five per cent of all sales are to cash customers; the remainder of customers are given 60 days credit. The company regularly suffers bad debts of 1% of credit sales.

Total costs equal 75% of Wizzbang's sales value and 90% of Plugman's sales value. These costs are payable 30 days after the sale date.

The new machinery will cost £30,000, with payment being made in two equal instalments in months 2 and 4.

Required:

(a) Prepare a cash budget for the next six months of Trent Electronics Ltd production, clearly showing the maximum overdraft that might be required.

(b) The bank manager says that she is not prepared to lend the amount of overdraft that the business is planning to ask for (on the basis of the budget in (a) above). What advice would you offer to the directors of Trent Electronics Ltd?

PART FOUR

Financing
the Business

CHAPTER 17

Capital Structure and Gearing

THE AIMS OF THIS CHAPTER

To enable students to

- Understand the principles which lead to an efficient capital structure for a business

- Explain the differences between elements of the capital structure: ordinary shares, preference shares, debentures

- Appreciate the significance of capital gearing

- Calculate the weighted average cost of capital

CAPITAL STRUCTURE

Assets earn the profits which create shareholder value, but effective financing enables the business to invest in these assets. The funds used to finance the assets of a company can be recruited from several sources; usually a combination of share capital and reserves, long-term loan capital and short-term facilities is used. The capital structure of a business is the combination of these sources, which should be the subject of careful board decisions. A well-balanced capital structure will attract present and potential providers of finance. It is important that a significant proportion of the finance is provided by ordinary shareholders, who are the legal owners of the business. The existence of a sizeable fund of permanent capital invested in the business will increase the confidence of other lenders, whereas overdependence on finance provided by sources other than the legal owners is seen as a sign of weakness.

The authorized capital of the business is the number of shares stated in its memorandum of association which it has authority to issue to investors. The proportion of that capital which has been sold to the public is termed the issued capital, and is usually in the form of ordinary or preference shares. A public limited company (plc) can issue shares to the public at large, and does so through its 'listing' on a stock exchange. A private limited company is not quoted on a stock exchange and is thus restricted as to the marketability of its shares.

FUNDS: LONG TERM VERSUS SHORT TERM

The funds needed to finance a business can be divided between fixed capital and working capital. The fixed element of the capital employed is normally sunk into fixed assets such as machinery and buildings. The working capital is turned over in the short term, in a cycle from cash to stock, to work in progress, to finished goods, to debtors and back to cash again. Some funds will be provided to finance current assets from bank overdrafts and trade creditors for goods supplied, thus reducing the amount of funds from the firm's own resources needed to finance stocks, debtors, etc. The level of fixed assets, stocks and debtors engaged in the business may fluctuate over time and seasonally (see Figure 17.1), but usually an amount below which it will not fall can be established. It is necessary, therefore, when reviewing the capital structure of a business, to compute the amount of funds which will be needed permanently in the business and thus discover the extra amount of funds needed during peak periods of activity only.

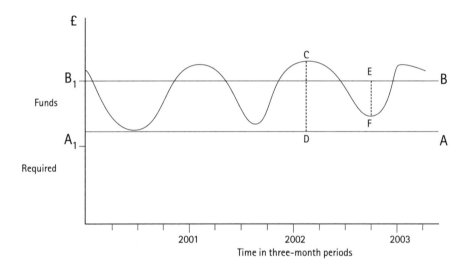

Figure 17.1

The business must determine whether to raise long-term funds up to level A^1A or B^1B (Figure 17.1). If long-term finance is raised up to level A^1A then the amount DC will be needed as short-term funds at peak periods of activity. In the situation where short-term borrowing is more costly than long-term finance, this could be expensive. However, if long-term funds are borrowed up to level B^1B, while the expensive short-term requirement is reduced, some of the long-term finance may lie idle during periods when business activity slumps (FE). Even though they are not utilized to earn a profit, such funds will still need to be serviced by way of interest. The decision as to the form of the company's financial structure is one in which the flexibility of expensive short-term finance must be set off against the cost of servicing long-term funds during periods when they are not fully employed. Another factor which influences this decision is the ability of the business to raise short-term funds at the precise time when they are needed, and the availability of assets to act as security for long-term loans. Capital gearing and its effect on the riskiness of the business as perceived by potential shareholders is also significant for this decision.

The cost of long-term finance will vary according to when it is raised. If it is raised at a time when interest rates are high, the company, once it is committed, will have to pay these rates for many years. It may therefore be preferable to borrow short-term and delay a long-term commitment until rates improve.

Task 17.1

What four fundamental questions should managers examine when considering the financial structure of their business?

Solution

Your response might cover the following:

1. *Can we raise adequate finance for our activities when we need it?*

   A business must convince capital providers (owners plus lenders long and short term) that it is a secure investment with good prospects, to such an extent that it can draw down finance when it is required. A hint that the company is desperate for funds will discourage investors, and funds may not be available at a time of crisis or opportunity. Investor confidence and the reputation of the business are significant for this question. The ability to offer adequate security reduces the risk to lenders.

2. *Can we pay an adequate price for the funds as dividend or interest, and can we repay when necessary?*

   The cash flow statement and cash budget are important when this question is considered, but of paramount importance is the return to be earned on the funds. Managers must ensure that capital projects earn a rate of return in excess of the cost of capital invested in them when the decision as to which projects to support is made. Thus they need to know the cost of capital for their business.

3. *Can we employ all the funds raised, all the time?*

   Idle funds must still be serviced with interest or dividend, so it is crucial that the recruitment of funds into the business is co-ordinated to the investment programme to acquire assets.

4. *Who shall we raise funds from?*

   At this stage managers must consider the relative advantages of owners versus lenders, and long-term funds versus short-term funds. The capital gearing ratio and debt to equity relationship focus on the risk of borrowing from outside the business rather than using permanent shareholder funds. Overdependence on outside finance is a sign of weakness, because such funds may be withdrawn when they are most needed.

Ordinary Shares

An ordinary share is a fixed unit of the common fund of the company, and it gives its holder a right to a proportionate interest in the profit or loss, and the return of capital in the event of a winding-up. When a business ceases to operate, a liquidator will wind up the business; the assets are realized and the funds used first to repay claims on the business, by creditors and lenders, and only then to repay shareholders. Thus the term '**equity shares**' means that ordinary shareholders have a right to share, pro rata to their holdings, the profits made and any surplus available on a winding-up. Most ordinary shares carry with them the right to attend and vote at all meetings of the company. The shareholders elect the board and the auditors, and approve or disapprove the level of dividend which is proposed by the board. They can also vote to accept or reject a takeover offer made by another company. There are, however, some ordinary shares known as 'A' shares, which do not possess voting rights. Some companies have ordinary shares and 'A' ordinary shares in issue at the same time. Another class of shares is called '**founders shares**'. These are issued to members of the family which built up the business before it changed from a private to a public company, or others who founded the company. Such shares usually carry enhanced voting rights such as ten votes per share, and are used as a means whereby a small group of people can maintain control over an old family business after it has expanded. Needless to say, the Stock Exchange disapproves of these various classes of shares with different voting rights, and encourages the issue of shares on a one vote per share basis.

The ordinary shareholders with their **votes** can approve or disapprove the board's policy and vote to remove the directors from office. Anyone who possesses over 50% of the voting shares is said to have a controlling interest in a company, while the other shareholders in this instance comprise the minority interest. It is, of course, possible to maintain control of a company by owning a share stake with less than 50% of the votes if the other shares are disposed over a large number of small holdings whose owners find it difficult to join together to formulate concerted action.

The ordinary shareholder has a right to sell his shares on the market, and the company has a duty to record this transfer in its share register and issue the appropriate share certificate. The marketability of shares in a private limited company is restricted, since such shares cannot be traded on the Stock Exchange. Financial managers see the issue of ordinary shares as **advantageous**, since there is no need to repay the investment and the rate of dividend can fluctuate with profits. If losses are made, the ordinary share dividend can be 'passed', i.e. not paid, but this may cause shareholders to sell their shares so that the market value of the business falls and a takeover bid may follow. Holders of ordinary shares possess the right to participate in all surpluses remaining after prior right capital (preference shares) has been satisfied. This means that the reserves belong to the ordinary shareholders. Any increase in the value of ordinary shares on the market gives capital growth to the shareholder. The main **disadvantage** of issuing ordinary shares is that the creation of extra votes may change control in a company and give more investors the chance to join in the distribution of profits.

Bonus Shares

Bonus shares are extra shares issued to ordinary shareholders pro rata to their holdings. These shares are not paid for, since they represent reserves which are already part of the equity interest of the business. Directors have 'ploughed back' profits by reinvesting rather than distributing the profit as a dividend. Thus the reserves belong to the ordinary shareholders and can be used to 'pay up' (create) new shares for the bonus issue. A bonus issue is a means by which the share capital of a company can be brought more into line with the value of assets owned by the company, since reserves which are not available for distribution can be used to 'pay up' the issue. A bonus issue is sometimes called a 'capitalization' issue for this reason.

How a bonus issue works

Bonus plc has the following balance sheet

	£
Fixed assets	1 200 000
Current assets	800 000
Current liabilities	(200 000)
Net assets	£1 800 000

Financed by:	
Share capital 1,000,000 £1 ordinary shares	1 000 000
Share premium account	250 000
General reserve	550 000
	£1 800 000

The company decides to make a bonus issue of three new shares for every ten shares held by each shareholder. The new shares are to be paid up out of the reserves, using the share premium account first as it cannot be distributed to shareholders as a dividend.

30% of 1,000,000 shares = 300,000 new shares

The share premium account will fund 250,000 £1 shares, so the remaining £50,000 will be financed from the general reserve. There is no change to the net assets of the business, but the capital section of the balance sheet will now show

	£
Share capital 1,000,000 + 300,000 £1 ordinary shares	1 300 000
General reserve (£550,000 − £50,000)	500 000
	£1 800 000

The shareholders have been given nothing except what was already theirs, but they may benefit if the existing rate of dividend is maintained on the new increased share capital.

Preference Shares

Another class of shares is preference shares. These shares are so called because shareholders have a **preferential right** to receive their dividend (if profits exist) and to repayment of capital before other shareholders. The exact rights of preference shareholders will be found in the articles of association of the company. The dividend on such shares is limited to a fixed percentage of the face value (nominal or par value) which is stated on the share certificate. We can thus speak of 8% £1 preference shares, being shares whose owner has a right to a divided of 8% (8 pence) each year, but not more,. If a company has issued 10,000 8% £1 preference shares, and has made a profit of only £800, then the preference shareholders will have a right to receive their dividend before any payment is made to the ordinary shareholders, who in this case receive nothing. The same rule normally applies in the event of a winding-up, so that the preference shareholders are repaid the face value of their shares before any money is repaid to ordinary shareholders.

Thus preference shares give investors a steady return with a high degree of safety. However, the ordinary shareholders have a right to all the profits that are made after the preference dividend has been paid (the reserves belong to the ordinary shareholders), and a right to divide equally among themselves the entire value of the business on a winding-up after the preference shareholders have received the face value of their shares. Thus the ordinary shareholders take the greater risk, since they are the last group to receive their share of profit or their money back on a winding-up, although they do have a right to all the surplus that is earned. This is why ordinary shares are considered as risk capital. Preference shares also suffer by restriction of their **voting rights**. Normally they carry no right to vote at a general meeting of the company, but if an extraordinary meeting is called to discuss matters which prejudice their preferential rights, e.g. a capital reorganization scheme, then it is usual for preference shareholders to be allowed to vote.

Some companies issue **cumulative preference shares** to avoid the difficulty which occurs in a year when profits are too small to pay either the preference or ordinary share dividends. In this case a preference shareholder will receive nothing, and will have to wait until next year for a normal fixed percentage dividend. The holder of a cumulative preference share will, in a subsequent year, receive arrears of dividend which have accumulated in the past, before any dividend is paid on the ordinary shares.

Yet another variation of the preference share is the **participating preference share**. A holder of such a share has a right to a fixed preference dividend, and then has a further right to participate in exceptionally high profits when they are made and divided. The terms of issue of such a share usually state that when the ordinary shares have a received a dividend of, for example, 30%, the participating preference shareholders will receive an extra X% for every further Y% paid to the ordinary shareholders. Thus the preference shareholder is in a safer position than the ordinary shareholder because of these preferential rights. Less risk means lower returns. The equity interest in the business comprises the ordinary share capital and the reserves which belong to the ordinary shareholders.

Redeemable Shares

Section 159 of the Companies Act 1985 permits a company to redeem (pay back) preference or ordinary shares on condition that one class of non-redeemable shares remains in issue. This means that part of the capital sum can be repaid by the company to the shareholders. The normal rules for such a redemption state that it can be

(a) financed by reserves available for distribution; or

(b) financed by a fresh issue of shares.

If the redemption is financed out of reserves, then a **capital redemption reserve** must be established by law. Part of the reserves available for dividend is transferred to a capital redemption reserve, which is a reserve not available for dividend. Thus if a company repays parts of its share capital without raising fresh capital it must establish a reserve not available for distribution to replace the share capital repaid, so that the right of the creditors to be repaid before shareholders is not prejudiced in any way. The use of the capital redemption reserve is restricted, only to pay up shares which can be issued as bonus issue, or to offset the effect of writing off preliminary expenses or the premium paid on the redemption of a debenture.

How the redemption of shares works

The balance sheet of **Redeem plc** is as follows:

	£	£
Fixed assets		2 500 000
Current assets	1 300 000	
Less current liabilities	900 000	
Working capital		400 000
		2 900 000
Long-term liabilities		1 000 000
Net assets		£1 900 000
Capital		
£1 ordinary shares		1 000 000
£1 17% preference shares		300 000
General reserve		600 000
		£1 900 000

The company decides to redeem the preference shares at par £300,000. The transaction is to be funded partly by the issue of 100,000 £1 ordinary shares at par.

The shares are issued so net assets (cash) increase by £100,000. The preference shares are redeemed by paying out £300,000, so the net assets now stand at £1,700,000.

Redemption of £300,000 is only partly funded by the issue of fresh share capital, so £200,000 must be transferred from general reserve (available for distribution) to a statutory capital reserve, capital redemption reserve. The capital in the balance sheet would then show:

		£
Capital		
	£1 ordinary shares	1 100 000
	Capital redemption reserve	200 000
	General reserve	400 000
		£1 700 000

Debentures

A debenture is the written acknowledgement of a debt; it is a contract made under seal of the company, providing for a fixed rate of interest to be paid on the sum loaned to the company and specifying terms for the repayment of that sum at the end of the period. The company often has the option of repaying on a date of its own choosing within a period – say 2007–2010. The debenture is, therefore, a long-term loan. There is, however, some confusion about terminology. In the legal sense the term debenture is used to describe any long-term loan, evidenced by a deed or contract, whether it is secured or not, but the financial press use the term debenture to cover long-term loans which are secured against the assets of the business. Unsecured long-term loans are called loan stock. A debenture deed has a trustee whose task it is to protect the interests of the debenture holders or lenders. The interest will be paid on the due date regularly each quarter or half-year as specified in the agreement. If the interest is not paid, then the trustee must demand its payment or demand the repayment of the debenture holders' loan if the company is liquidated.

Security and debentures

If the debenture is secured, on liquidation the trustee can take charge of the assets which comprise the security and sell them to provide funds from which the debenture holders will be repaid. Often the security will be fixed on a specific asset of the company, e.g. the buildings. Sometimes the security is of a floating nature, which means that the trustee can liquidate any asset of the business to repay the loan. A floating security is useful in cases where the assets of the business are unsuitable for a fixed charge, or where the assets of the business fluctuate on a day-to-day basis. If a company has few fixed assets such as property or plant but carries a large volume of stock, this can be taken as security for a debenture. The value of the stock will fluctuate and may be uncertain at the time when the debenture is issued. A floating charge is subject to the further disadvantages that

(a) a supplier of stock may 'reserve title' until payment is made, or

(b) a fixed security may already exist as a prior charge on certain assets.

In both of these cases the floating charge will not attach to the assets concerned. A naked debenture (loan stock) is one which has no security at all. The holder of a naked debenture will rank *pari passu* with the ordinary creditors of the business at the time of a winding-up.

Status of debentures

A debenture holder is not a member of a company, but a creditor thereof with a claim against the business. As such the fixed interest is paid on this debt whether or not a profit has been made, and this interest is considered a charge against, not an appropriation of, profit. Therefore interest is considered by the Inland Revenue to be an expense of the business, allowable as a deduction against profits for corporation tax purposes. In effect the burden of debenture interest will be borne partly by the state, since for every pound of interest paid, taxable profit will be reduced and corporation tax at, say, 31% in the pound will be saved. Thus it is cheaper to finance the business by means of fixed-interest debentures, whose holders are not members of the company, than by the issue of fixed-return preference shares which do not have this tax advantage. The real rate of interest on a 15% debenture is $15\% \times (1 - 0.31) = 10.35\%$ after tax is taken into account.

Task 17.2

Calculate the post-tax cost of 9% interest paid on a debenture and 13% interest paid on an overdraft if the corporation tax rate is at 31%.

Solution

Debenture $9\% \times (1 - .31) = 6.21\%$

Overdraft $13\% \times (1 - .31) = 8.97\%$

The investor sees a debenture with its priority right and certainty of interest and repayment as much less risky than preference or ordinary shares. A debenture holder can sell a holding on the market, but the price offered for a fixed-return security will fluctuate with the general rate of interest. Debentures with a coupon rate of 7% will be worth $^7/_5$ of their face value when the market rate of interest is at 5%. But if the market rate rises to 9% the 7% debentures will only be worth $^7/_9$ of their face value. Debenture holders do not possess voting rights, so there will be no dilution of control with the issue of debentures. The need to repay the debt eventually, and the cost of interest up to that time, may prove a burden if profits fall, and will act to reduce cash flow.

Sometimes a debenture carries with it the right to convert to an ordinary share at the option of the holder. Conversion rights state a date or dates by which the option must be exercised, and the number of ordinary shares to be acquired for each £100 worth of debentures. Usually fewer shares are offered as succeeding dates are passed. The debenture holder gains the advantage that, if the company has good growth prospects, the investment can be switched to equity, or, if there is doubt about future results, the investor can stay safe with loan capital. In return for this advantage a slightly lower rate of interest is usually paid.

Task 17.3

What factors should managers consider when deciding whether to raise more capital by issuing ordinary shares or committing the business to a long-term loan?

Solution

1. The administration and legal *costs* of raising shares as opposed to loans – share issue costs are expensive.

2. The cost of *servicing* the finance – a certain rate of interest versus a fluctuating and non-mandatory dividend.

3. The *tax* 'shield', whereby interest is a tax allowable expense.

4. The *voting* implications. A block of ordinary shares issued to one party may upset the balance of control in the business. Debenture holders do not have votes.

5. Can the company offer suitable assets as *security* for a loan. Do managers wish to keep assets 'uncharged' so that they can sell them without affecting the security needed to underpin the capital structure?

6. Loans will eventually be *repaid*, or refinanced at their maturity date, but ordinary shares are issued in perpetuity unless the company wishes to redeem them.

7. What do potential shareholders *expect*? If the market is confident shares can be issued at a premium, and the prospect of capital growth will attract investors. The dividend yield and price to earnings ratio are important for this consideration.

8. The capital *gearing* ratio after the issue of shares or loan, and its effect on the perceived riskiness of the business.

Task 17.4

What factors should investors consider when deciding whether to lend, or invest as a shareholder?

Solution

1. **The risk.** With a loan the interest is certain, and capital repayment may be covered by a security. Dividends depend on profits and may fluctuate.

2. **The ability to disinvest.** Shares may be sold on a stock exchange, but long-term loans are more difficult to sell.

3. **Capital growth.** The value of a shareholding can fluctuate, but over time the market price of a share will rise if the company is well managed. Loans are repaid at their face value.

4. **Votes.** The number of votes controlled by a small investor does not give much power. The shareholder who controls a block of shares (say 5%) can use them strategically to vote for or against a takeover bid or some other suggestion. Where the opposing groups are finely balanced, a small block of shares can have a significant impact. Loans give no voting power.

CAPITAL GEARING

Gearing, or 'leverage' as the American textbooks call it, is the relationship between the fixed-return capital and equity capital used to finance the business. It is sometimes expressed as a ratio whereby fixed-return capital is set against equity, or alternatively against the aggregate of fixed-return and equity capital. There is some debate among accountants as to the precise definition of the parts of this ratio. Fixed-return capital is generally taken to mean preference shares, debentures and loan stock, all of which are serviced by a fixed rate of dividend or interest. Some authorities argue that bank loans and overdrafts receive a fixed rate of return and should be included in the definition. There is some degree of acceptance for this idea, but much less for the suggestion that loans from trade creditors should be included, since they are of a fluctuating nature and bear no interest charge at all. Some authorities use the term 'prior right capital' instead of 'fixed-return capital' to focus on investors who have a right to preferential treatment. Equity capital is sometimes included as the face value of ordinary shares only, but in most cases the reserves are added to this amount to change it to the equity interest in the business.

Gearing is said to be high when there is a large proportion of fixed-return capital in the capital structure of a company, and low when the equity interest comprises a large proportion of the capital. The following example shows the effect on the return to equity of profit fluctuation in a highly geared situation.

How Gearing Works

Step 1: Calculate the gearing ratio

Company A has a share capital of 400,000 £1 ordinary shares, 40,000 £1 14% preference shares, and £60,000 of 16% debentures. Company B has a share capital of 200,000 £1 ordinary shares, 40,000 £1 14% preference shares, and £260 000 of 16% debentures.

The capital structure is

	A	B
	£	£
Ordinary shares	400 000	200 000
14% preference shares	40 000	40 000
16% debentures	60 000	260 000
Net capital employed	£500 000	£500 000

	Gearing	$\dfrac{\text{Fixed return capital}}{\text{Total capital}} \times \dfrac{100}{1}$	$\dfrac{100}{500} \times \dfrac{100}{1}$	$\dfrac{300}{500} \times \dfrac{100}{1}$
			20%	60%
			Low	High

Step 2

Assume that in year 1 each company makes a profit before interest but after tax of £125,000. The return on capital employed for both companies is 125/500 × 100/1 = 25%.

In year 1 the profit would be allocated as follows:

	A £	B £
Net profit before interest but after tax	125 000	125 000
Interest and dividend to fixed return capital		
Debentures (16%)	(9 600)	(41 600)
Preference shares (14%)	(5 600)	(5 600)
Profit available for ordinary shareholders	£109 800	£77 800
Earnings per share (EPS) (£109,800÷400,000 shares)	27.45 pence	
(£77,800÷200,000 shares)		38.9 pence

Shareholders in B receive a better return on their investment than those in A. B is a highly geared company and has recruited a large proportion of its funds at 16%, which have been invested to earn a ROCE of 25%. This surplus belongs to the shareholders and boosts their earnings. The situation changes in year 2, when as profit increases by 20% the benefit of high gearing is felt by the shareholders of company B.

Step 3: Increase profit by 20%

	A £	B £
Net profit before interest but after tax	150 000	150 000
Interest and dividend to fixed-return capital		
(as before)	15 200	47 200
Profit available for ordinary shareholders	£134 800	£102 800
Earnings per share	33.7 pence	51.4 pence
Increase in EPS over year 1	6.25 pence	12.5 pence
Increase in EPS as a percentage of year 1	22%	32%

Profits have risen from year 1 by 20% but shareholders in highly geared company B benefit by an increase of 32% in their EPS. All the increased profit belongs to ordinary shareholders, since the return to prior right capital is already covered, but in B there are fewer shareholders to divide up the increase.

Now assume that in year 3 the profit of both companies falls by 33% from £150,000 to £100,000.

Step 4: Reduce profit by 33%

	A	B
	£	£
Net profit before interest but after tax	100 000	100 000
Interest and dividend to fixed-return capital (as before)	15 200	47 200
Profit available for ordinary shareholders	£84 800	£52 800
Earning per share	21.1 pence	26.4 pence
Percentage fall in EPS	34%	48.6%

In B, a fall in profit of one-third causes a near 50% reduction in shareholders' earnings. High gearing seems to be advantageous when profit is increasing, but ordinary shareholders may be penalized if profit falls. Remember that in B, if in year 4 profit falls below £47,200, the ordinary shareholders will have earned nothing, but shareholders in A would still have an EPS of 8 pence per share (£47,200 − £15,200 ÷ 400,000 shares).

Fundamental Principles of Gearing

1. This example shows that a disproportionate increase in the profit available to one class of capital providers is the consequence of the highly geared capital structure. Profit is earned by the fixed-return funds invested in the business, and any surplus of that profit over the interest required to service the fixed-return capital is available to increase the return on the ordinary shares. Another benefit is that debenture interest is a tax-deductible expense, and the cost net of tax is much less than the coupon rate.

2. If the management of a company are able to raise the gearing by recruiting fresh fixed-return capital, and make more in profit from the use of that capital than is needed to service it, then the surplus will increase the return available to ordinary shareholders. The equity interest will thus benefit when gearing is raised.

3. What if profits fluctuate in a downward direction? The fixed-return capital would still need to be serviced, and if, as in year 4 of the above example, there was no surplus after interest had been paid, then the dividend would be passed. Real problems would follow if profit in one year was not sufficient to cover the fixed return, as interest must be paid whether or not a profit is earned. Although the ordinary shareholder who bears the risk in the company receives all the super profits when they are made, he will also be the first to suffer if profits fall away.

4. Gearing influences the repayment of capital and the risk borne by the ordinary shareholders. When the gearing is raised by increasing fixed-return capital, perhaps using the fixed assets as security, this new group of lenders now has a prior right to interest out of profit, and repayment of principal before the claims

of ordinary shareholders are met. Because this group now stands in front of the ordinary shareholders, the risk borne by those shareholders has increased and thus the return they would expect for taking a greater risk would also need to increase. High gearing brings high risks.

Managing the Capital Structure

In the UK, property companies have traditionally been highly geared businesses. In property the rent is fixed in advance by the terms of the lease, so income does not fluctuate. The property itself forms a good security for the loan. Under these conditions it was not uncommon to see property companies borrowing to finance their assets with gearing up to 65% and beyond. With the onset of recession, however, tenant businesses began to close down, rents were not paid and properties remained empty. Meanwhile, at the property companies, interest on the highly geared loan finance was becoming difficult to cover from profits. Most worrying to the lenders was the fact that the value of the property which formed their security was falling. This situation has caused many property companies to go into liquidation in recent years, as victims of their own capital structure policies.

Debt will reduce the overall cost of capital because it is cheaper than equity. Debt carries no risk premium required by ordinary shareholders, and interest payments are tax deductible. Thus gearing should be increased but not up to the point where the risk borne by ordinary shareholders is increased. A gearing ratio of 30% is often seen as the threshold between high and low gearing, but much depends on the circumstances of the company. Equity is more flexible than debt because interest is mandatory, but dividends can be varied by board decisions. A company that relies too heavily on debt finance is at risk for its cost and availability in a 'credit squeeze'. Financial managers should observe the following rules:

1. **Danger.** Do not combine high gearing with high business risk or fluctuating profits. The stability of profits and cash flows must govern the ability to commit the business to more borrowing.

2. **Security.** Asset-based companies can pledge assets to lenders, and raise gearing levels.

3. **Tax.** Loan interest brings a tax advantage, but is this worthwhile when measured against the administrative costs of borrowing, the increased risk to shareholders, and the loss of flexibility to manage assets given as security?

4. **Competitors.** Other companies with lower gearing have a competitive advantage when interest rates are high.

5. **Flexibility.** Do not borrow up to the limit of a company, as there is then no spare financial capacity to be drawn down when new opportunities arise.

THE COST OF CAPITAL

Every business seeks to maximize the wealth of shareholders in the long run, so the management should only invest in projects which give a return in excess of the cost of investment funds used to finance such projects. If the capital employed in the business has been recruited from a range of sources, it may be difficult to determine the cost of funds applied to individual projects.

The measurement of the likely return from an investment before funds are committed is dependent upon an estimate of cash flows throughout the life of the investment. It is only profitable to invest in a project if cash flowing in from the project during its life exceeds cash flowing out when the project is established. Since flows in are experienced over a period of years, they must be discounted to show their present value, in order to be accurately compared with cash flowing out at the commencement of the project. The discount factor which is usually applied in this calculation of present value is the cost of capital to the firm. If a project earns a total cash inflow which exceeds the outflows and covers the cost of capital tied up in the project, then a profit is assured. The cost of capital is difficult to define because a business will recruit funds from various sources, so a weighted average cost of capital is calculated based on the capital structure of the firm. Risk, which is influenced by gearing, will in turn influence the cost of capital of the various types of finance in the capital structure. Tax must of course be taken into account where it is relevant.

The Cost of Equity

Shareholders will expect a dividend on their investment, but they also require growth. The cost of equity is therefore the dividend yield necessary to satisfy investors in the market, plus a factor to account for capital growth expectations Expressed as a formula this amount can be calculated as

$$\text{Cost of Equity} = \frac{\text{Expected Dividend}}{\text{current share price}} + \frac{\text{Growth}}{1}$$

For example, assume that a company has issued £1 ordinary shares on which it is currently paying a dividend of 10 pence per share, and that these shares are currently priced in the market at 150 pence each, with an expected growth factor of 10%. Shareholders will expect a dividend of 11 pence next year so when the formula is applied to these figures the calculation is:

$$\frac{11 \text{ pence}}{150 \text{ pence}} \times \frac{100}{1} = 7.3\% \text{ yield}$$

7.3% yield + 10% growth = 17.3%

Retained earnings, the reserves in the business, generated from past profits, have the same cost of capital as ordinary shares, because if a company wants shareholders to leave profits in the business then a similar return to that earned on the shares must be made on these shareholders' funds.

The Cost of Debt

The cost of debt is the rate of interest adjusted for the fact that interest is an allowable expense for corporation tax purposes. Assuming debentures with an interest rate of 16% and applying a corporation tax rate of 31%, the formula is

$$Cost = Interest\ (1 - tax\ rate) = 16 \times (1 - 0.31) = 16 \times 0.69 = 11.04\%$$

The same logic can be applied to overdraft or other short-term bank loans. Assuming a short-term bank loan of 18%, the formula gives the cost of capital as 12.42 per cent for this part of the company's capital structure.

The Weighted Average Cost of Capital

The next step is to apply these rates to the capital structure of the company weighted for the various types of capital. Assume that the company has issued 8 million ordinary shares of £1 each, that it has retained earnings of £5 million, 16% debentures of £4 million and a short-term bank loan of £3 million at a rate of 18%. The following computation will calculate the weighted average cost of capital for this business.

	Capital Structure		Weight	×	Cost	=	Weighted cost
£8 000 000	£1 ordinary shares	8/20	40%		17.3%		6.920
£5 000 000	Retained earnings	5/20	25%		17.3%		4.325
£4 000 000	16 per cent debentures	4/20	20%		11.04%		2.208
£3 000 000	Bank loan on 18 per cent	3/20	15%		12.42%		1.863
£20 000 000			100%				15.316

As an approximation a cost of capital of 16 per cent could be used

CONCLUSION

The financial structure of a company must be carefully adjusted to achieve the correct balance between long- and short-term funds, and between fixed-return and equity capital. Financial managers must appreciate the advantages of ordinary shares, preferences shares and debentures from the viewpoint of the company and that of the potential investor. Alternative structures combine these elements in different ways which change the capital gearing and which in turn affect the perceived risk of the business. The tax shield on debenture interest reduces the real cost of this element of the capital structure and its effect on the weighted average cost of capital which managers must cover by the profits of business activity.

Discussion Topics

Thirty-minute essay questions:

1. 'The decision as to the form of the company's capital structure is one in which flexibility of expensive short-term finance must be set off against the cost of servicing long-term funds during periods when they are not fully employed.'

   Discuss the optimum capital structure of a business with reference to the significance of gearing, the tax system and the cost of capital.

2. Some research students have made a significant discovery and now intend to set up a limited company to exploit their new technology
   (a) Explain to the researchers the principles of capital gearing and support your explanation with a brief computation.
   (b) Discuss the significance of the cost of capital for the capital structure of a business with reference to capital gearing.

3. Explain the differences between ordinary shares, preference shares and debentures in the capital structure of a company.

SEMINAR EXERCISES

17.1

Required:

(a) Explain the term 'financial structure', with reference to **Careworn Contractors plc.**

(b) The balance sheet of Careworn Contractors plc at 31 March is as follows:

	£000s		
	Cost	*Depreciation*	*Net*
Fixed assets			
Freehold property at cost	5 500	550	4 950
Plant and vehicles	3 000	1 500	1 500
	8 500	2 050	6 450
Current assets			
Stock of materials and work in progress		600	
Debtors (progress payments outstanding)		1400	
Cash		10	
		2010	
Current liabilities			
Trade creditors	750		
Tax on profit for the year	170		
Dividend proposed	280		
Overdraft	1 000		
		2 200	
Working capital			(190)
Total assets less current liabilities			6 260

Long-term liabilities

12% Unsecured loan stock	2 000
Net capital employed	£4 260
Share capital – ordinary shares of 50p	2 000
Retained profits	2 260
	£4 260

The market price of the shares currently stands at £1.40 per share. The 12% unsecured loan stock is repayable in September at par. The overdraft is costing the company a 20% interest rate. The dividend proposed is for the full year to 31 March. Corporation tax is at 31%. The freehold property was purchased ten years ago.

Required:

Comment on the capital structure of Careworn Contractors plc.

Your solution might be based on ratios for working capital, gearing, yield, p/e and interest cover.

No profit figure is given in the question, but you know that tax on profit is £170. £170 ÷ 0.31 = £548

17.2

Croxton Kilns Ltd owns and operates a factory making speciality bricks in the Vale of Belvoir. Your employer is considering an investment of £1 million in this business by the purchase of 250,000 new ordinary shares of £1 each at a price of £4 each.

The most recent financial statements of the business are stated on the balance sheet.

Required:

(a) Comment on the capital structure of Croxton Kilns Ltd.
(b) Relate your comment to the investment which your employer is now considering.

Croxton Kilns Balance Sheet as at 31 December

	£000		
	Cost	Depreciation	Net
Fixed assets			
Factory buildings	2 000	–	2 000
Plant and machinery	1 654	782	872
Vehicles	216	130	86
	3 870	912	2 958
Current assets			
Stock		520	
Debtors		1698	
Cash		111	
		2 329	
Current liabilities			
Creditors	457		
Overdraft	1 654		
Tax	240		
Dividend	180		
		(2 531)	
Working capital			(202)
			2756
Long-term loans (repayable in 5 years' time, secured on the factory)			(1 400)
Net assets			
			£1 356
Share capital – ordinary shares of £1			1 000
Revaluation reserves			300
Retained profit			56
			£1 356

Profit and Loss Account for year ending 31 December

	£000s	£000s
Sales (all on credit terms)		5 094
Costs		(3 986)
Operating profit		1 108
Less interest – Long-term loan	252	
– Overdraft	280	(532)
Net profit before tax		576
Tax		(240)
Net profit after tax		336
Dividend		(180)
Retained profit for the year		£156

The most recent share price in the somewhat limited market for this company's shares is 360 pence each. The factory buildings were revalued last year.

CHAPTER 18

Sources
of Finance

THE AIMS OF THIS CHAPTER

To enable students to

- Understand the market for finance and the effect of risk on the investor
- Appreciate the significance of financial institutions in that market
- Identify long- and short-term sources of finance
- Explain the operation and advantages of leasing

THE MARKET FOR FINANCE

Whatever is invested in business must be provided by an investor, who must forgo consumption and save to provide the funds. Savers and users of their funds come together in the market for finance, where the normal rules of supply and demand apply unless there is government interference with interest rates. In the UK, it is a committee under the chairmanship of the Governor of the Bank of England which sets a rate in response to economic pressure – the need to control inflation. The price of money is the rate of interest paid for its use. If the demand for investment funds is greater than the funds offered for investment by savers, then the rate of interest will rise until people in the economy are induced to forgo consumption and make their savings available for investment. The money market is worldwide, and is limited only by communication difficulties and problems of transferring funds from one economy to another. Within each country the money market tends to be concentrated in one place, where the important institutions of the market have their offices, e.g. in the City of London there is the Stock Exchange, the banks, and pension and life assurance companies. However, finance is also local; for example, the banks have established a network of branches nationwide.

The mechanics of the market for finance are not as simple as, for example, a local country market for eggs or butter, where buyers and sellers meet. The market for finance involves the use of many intermediary institutions such as banks, stockbrokers, unit trusts, pension funds and life assurance companies, whose function is to accept the savings of many individuals and channel them to the businesses which need the funds for investment. Savers can invest their funds in a wide range of different industries and companies, and at different levels of risk. They can also choose from many types of investment, e.g. an ordinary share in or a loan to a company, or a deposit in a bank, which is lent in turn by the bank to a company in the form of an overdraft or loan. In this way the saver may not be directly connected to the business which uses his or her money. An important influence in the financial market is the government, which borrows in advance of tax revenue, and sometimes in excess of tax revenue, in order to pay for its current expenditure.

RISK AND THE INVESTOR

A small business may be limited to the amount of money that the proprietor can invest in it. If it is to expand, extra funds must be recruited from elsewhere, and the return on these funds must be met out of profits. The proprietor may offer a share of the business and its profits to tempt a saver to entrust funds to the firm. On the other hand, the saver may prefer to lend money to a firm on the understanding that the interest is to be paid whether a profit is made or not, and that the funds can be disinvested and repaid on a certain date. This depends perhaps on the investor's need to use the funds at a future time, or perhaps on psychological characteristics, i.e. the investor is a risk-seeker or a risk-averter.

The risk encountered in business can be caused by natural hazards such as drought, flood or the death of a key employee, or calamities such as war or revolution. Other risks encountered are of an economic nature, for example a fall in demand for a product because of a change in taste or fashion, or losses as the consequence of inefficient management, bad product design, or strikes caused by poor industrial relations. The causes of some types of risk are thus outside the control of the business, while others are a direct consequence of circumstances within the business. If an investor is to take a risk there must be the chance of high reward as well as the chance of failure. The trade-off of risk against return will help the investor to decide whether to commit funds.

PROFIT RETENTION AS A SOURCE OF FUNDS

A large and well-established business will have access to the market of the Stock Exchange as a means of raising funds, since, as a public company, it can offer its shares to investors in general. Despite the presence of this wide market for funds, the fact remains that the most significant source of capital for British industry is ploughed-back profits, or profits retained in the business. The appropriation of profit is in three main directions

(a) a proportion is paid to the Inland Revenue as corporation tax;

(b) a proportion is paid out to the shareholders as dividends; and

(c) the remainder is reinvested in the business.

Profits retained in the business are shown in the balance sheet as reserves, and the funds they represent are invested in the general assets of the business. The board of directors decides how much of the profit available for dividend is to be paid out. This decision is important, since it involves a fine calculation of the amount needed to satisfy the shareholders and thus maintain the price of the shares, while ensuring that sufficient funds are reinvested in the business to maintain its financial health. If too little profit is retained, shareholders get a good dividend but the business may find itself starved of funds and be unable to expand or modernize. Profits may then fall and the company could be the subject of a takeover bid. If a large proportion of profit is retained, the dividend payment to shareholders will be small, and they may express their dissatisfaction at the annual general meeting or by selling their shares and reinvesting in another company. If this happens the price of the shares on the Stock Exchange will fall, and, although the company is financially healthy, it may be the subject of a takeover bid, since the share price undervalues the assets involved. The profit-retention decision is thus a difficult one, since the need to modernize or to finance the present level of activity during an inflationary period must be balanced against the need to maintain the confidence of the shareholders.

THE LONG–TERM CAPITAL MARKET

A public limited company (plc) can raise fresh capital from the market by an issue of shares, debentures or loan stock. Sometimes loan stock is issued with a conversion right which allows the lender to convert the stock to ordinary shares at a future date. The factors which influence the decision by a company to issue shares or loans are:

(a) the ability to provide security for the loans;

(b) the need to retain control so that the issue of voting shares is avoided, and

(c) the effect of the new issue on the gearing of the business;

(d) the investors' perception of future prospects.

Issuing Shares

Issuing shares on the market is an expensive operation, involving the services of an issuing house, an underwriter, a bank and solicitors. Merchant banks in the City of London can provide some or all of these services. The company must be 'introduced' to the market, where brokers will be willing to 'list' the shares and buy and sell them.

If the shares of a public limited company are to be traded on the Stock Exchange, it is necessary to ensure that sufficient shares are available to 'make a market' and that those shares are not concentrated in the hands of relatively few shareholders who may not wish to buy or sell on a regular basis. Marketability of the shares is important to a company seeking an 'introduction' to the market. The company will need to supply the information required by the Stock Exchange. The issuer must disclose all material facts in the 'listing documents', and compensation may be payable to investors for false or misleading statements. To be successful in an application for listing, the company should have at issue £700,000 of equity shares, but in fact companies applying for listing usually have a market capitalization of at least £5,000,000. A further rule is that a minimum of 25% of any class of ordinary shares in a company must be in the hands of the public to ensure that there is a fair market in the shares. A good trading record over a five-year period preceding the application, and the possession of significant assets, are other requirements for a successful introduction.

The 'secondary market' is available to young growing companies to recruit share capital for expansion. Its rules are less demanding than the main stock exchange, but because there is a chance that expanding companies may collapse, investors see this as a high risk market, and normally only specialist investors operate there.

Many growing companies prefer to achieve quotation on 'the secondary market' and then, having grown some more, transfer their listing to the main Stock Exchange. A common procedure is to combine an introduction onto the Stock Exchange with a public issue of shares. A company may expand by using short-term finance (bank loans or overdraft), which it later replaces by a 'funding operation'. Long-term funds are raised by issuing shares or debentures and used to repay the short-term finance, which is then available to be reborrowed in the next stage of expansion.

THE INSTITUTIONAL INVESTORS

There seems to be a size beyond which companies cannot grow without an injection of long-term funds, but sometimes there is a gap between the size to which they can grow by the use of their own resources and the size which they need to be before they are big enough to make a public issue of shares. To help small companies to expand across this gap or step (the MacMillan gap), other financial institutions have been developed to assist the small company to grow until it becomes large enough to go public. Foremost among these are the *merchant banks*. The shares of some merchant banks can be bought and sold on the Stock Exchange, while others are owned by the large commercial banks. As their name implies, they used to be involved in the finance of foreign trade by means of bills of exchange. Although the bill market is still important, they are now more involved in the provision of finance to growing businesses. Most merchant banks have an issuing house department, and some provide an underwriting service. They also provide advice and financial assistance in takeover battles on the sides of both the attacker and the defender. A merchant bank likes to make contact with a small growing company early in its existence and help it to expand by providing loan capital or by taking a stake in its shares. Sometimes a merchant bank will appoint a director to the board of the company to watch over its interests and to provide helpful financial advice. When the company has grown large enough to cross the gap and apply to the Stock Exchange for a public quotation of its shares with a view to making a public issue, the issuing house department of its merchant bank will organize the issue. Later in the life of the company, when amalgamations or takeover negotiations take place, the merchant bank gives help and advice.

A similar institution in the finance market is the *investment trust*, which is not a trust in the normal sense of the word, but is really a public company whose shares can be traded on the Stock Exchange. An investment trust is a company which holds the shares of other companies. Its task is to invest its funds in a portfolio of other companies, both large and small, so that it spreads its risk and makes a profit from the investment expertise of its directors.

Task 18.1

What is an underwriter?

Solution

A merchant banker who will contract with a company which is about to issue ordinary shares, that for a fee, the underwriter will take up any of the shares not applied for by the public. To the company underwriting is a form of insurance to make certain that the share issue is a success. To the underwriter, it is the application of expertise to judge whether a new issue of shares will attract investors. If the underwriter has misjudged the market he will be left with the shares, which may take some time to sell on the market without depressing the price.

There is often no clear line of demarcation between merchant banks and investment trusts, since both will operate what are called 'city nurseries', where a number of small but profitable private businesses are encouraged to expand and then are helped to go public.

Unit trusts are institutions within the finance market whose task it is to channel savings from their many unit holders to be invested in companies. The unit trusts, the life assurance companies and the pension funds collect the savings of many people and convert them to investment by buying shares and debentures both privately and on the market. These institutions spread their risk and do not want to dominate any company in which they invest, but during a takeover bid the institutions, with their large block holdings of shares (say 5%), are the ones whose votes are most significant in deciding whether or not the bid is successful. When a merchant bank has a block of shares to place, it contacts unit trusts, assurance companies and pension funds, and is usually able to place the shares with them without much difficulty.

VENTURE CAPITAL

Capital of this type is provided by an institution or individual to a small but growing firm and usually takes the form of a share stake in the business. Such growth situations are inevitably risky, and the venture capitalist seeks a good return in a relatively short period by selling the investment after the company has made significant progress. Venture capital can take the form of 'start-up' funds for a new business, assistance for young companies after they have traded successfully, and development capital for specific situations in established companies. The venture capitalist may also assist in a management buy-out. An entrepreneur running a profitable private limited company may be unable to finance the growth required from the retention of profits and may find that the more traditional providers of finance are too cautious to invest in a high-growth/high-margin situation. In this situation the proprietor/manager may be forced to consider offering a minority share stake to a venture capitalist in return for funds which are desperately needed by the business.

To be successful in raising funds from a venture capitalist, a small firm must be able to demonstrate that it has certain qualities:

(a) a competent and skilled management team which is motivated to work hard and achieve high growth;

(b) a product capable of making progress in the market;

(c) ability to keep up with technological change and to compete adequately with other companies in the same business; and

(d) the absence of dependence on suppliers or other financial institutions.

A feasible venture investment will also be equipped with an exit route, whereby the venture capitalist can recoup the investment either when the company goes public by a listing on the Stock Exchange, or perhaps if it is likely to be acquired by a larger company in a takeover bid. A significant factor in a venture capital proposal is that the company should have developed a sound business plan providing the information which the venture capitalist requires about its products, management, operations, marketing methods and financial situation.

MANAGEMENT BUY-OUTS (MBOS)

This is a specialist form of transaction, whereby a group of managers combine to make an offer for a part, or the whole, of a business. Finance to pay for the purchase is partly provided from the managers' own resources, but most of the funds are derived from long-term loans furnished by financial institutions (merchant banks or venture capitalists). Accordingly, the resulting company is owned by its former managers but is encumbered by a significant measure of debt. Such a capital structure is highly geared, and, for this reason, MBOs are often referred to as 'leveraged bids'.

An MBO will take place

(a) when a large company reviews the significance of a segment of the business for the overall group strategy with the intention of concentrating on core activities;

(b) when a receiver sells a failed business as a going concern; or

(c) when major shareholders in a private company wish to retire and sell their controlling interest in the business.

In these circumstances the existing managers are well placed to gauge the likely success of the business they are buying, and to make a bid. The vendor company may wish to divest itself of a division of the business which does not fit well into the core activity of the group, and to release funds to finance the development of the core. A group of companies will regularly review the portfolio of its investments, or may wish to sell part of a business which it has recently purchased. For example, a firm of publishers taken over by a large newspaper company might have an academic publishing division, which is not in line with the core activity of the new group. Such a division will be hived off and sold.

Participation in an MBO is a risky activity for the managers concerned, since they stand to lose a significant part of their private fortune if the new company fails. However, the bid is based on their confidence in their own ability to run the business successfully and the desire to build a private fortune. The financier will be satisfied with an investment at favourable rates, probably secured on the assets of the business, and perhaps with a part of the equity of the business included to give growth potential. A management 'buy-in' is where an enterprising manager sees an investment opportunity in another company, and organizes the finance to buy a share of that company for himself or herself.

OTHER SOURCES OF FINANCE

There are other ways in which a company can finance the purchase of an asset which it needs without raising capital.

Sale and Lease-back

A company may undertake a sale and lease-back operation, which is a financial technique to set free some funds that are tied up in fixed assets so that they can be used elsewhere in the business. For example, suppose a company owns a large office block as its headquarters, and wishes to invest £500,000 in new plant for its factory. The company may contact a city institution or property company with a view to selling its headquarters office block to the institution, a term of the contract of sale being that the company can lease back the premises for the payment of rent. In this way the manufacturing company can continue to use the building, while at the same time it now has the funds it needs to purchase the machinery. The property company or city institution has a good investment, since it now possesses a prime piece of property let to a reputable company at a fair rental, and it also gains any increase in value achieved by the property because of inflation or other reasons. This technique thus has advantages for both parties. If the company had mortgaged its office block it could have borrowed the required funds and retained ownership of the building, but the payment of interest and repayment of the loan may have created cash flow problems. Sale and lease-back releases the full market value of the asset, whereas a mortgage only raises funds equal to a proportion of this value. The mortgage alternative does, however, mean that the company retains the ownership of the property, so any increase in value falls to the company rather than the financier.

Leasing

The practice of leasing is another method whereby a company can gain the use of an asset without investing a capital sum. The lease is a contract between the owner of an asset (the lessor) and the user of the asset (the lessee), whereby in return for a rental the lessor buys the asset and allows the lessee uninterrupted use of the asset. This form of finance is an alternative to raising a loan to buy an asset and paying interest. With a lease, the finance company, which is usually a subsidiary of a bank, owns the asset, and the rental charged has in its calculation an element of interest on the funds used to buy the asset and an element of capital repayment.

Short-term leases known as 'operating leases' allow the lessee to rent the asset for only a part of its economic life, and then return the asset to the lessor. The operating lease concerns cars, computers, office fixtures, etc. A 'finance lease' is a long-term contract whereby the user stipulates a significant capital asset and the financier provides that asset exclusively to the user for all or almost all of its economic life. The rentals paid on such a lease must cover the repayment of the capital sum used to buy the asset and interest on that sum. Legally, the asset belongs to the lessor, but in practice it is no different from other assets owned and used by the lessee. The rental payments may be phased over a primary period which is shorter than the working life of the asset, and a secondary period up to the end of that life at a nominal rental. Some manufacturers of plant and machinery offer leasing deals to customers as an alternative to the sale of the asset.

The Accounting Treatment of Leases

Operating leases have the simple treatment of charging the rentals to the profit and loss account. With a finance lease the company must account for the economic substance over the legal form of the transaction. As lessee the company does not own the asset but has an unrestricted right to use the asset during its economic life, so the asset should appear on the lessee's balance sheet, and depreciation should be charged to the profit and loss account. The lessee also has the liability to repay the cost of the asset to the lessor as part of future rentals, and thus this amount should be shown as a long-term liability. The rental paid each year should be apportioned between interest charged to the profit and loss account, and capital repayment which will reduce the amount of the long-term liability. Note that the cash flows for interest on leases and capital repayment on leases are disclosed in different parts of the cash flow statement on page 264.

This accounting treatment will have a considerable effect on the ROCE and the gearing ratio since outstanding lease balances count as long-term liabilities in the calculation. To the lessor bank, the lease represents a long-term debt rather than a tangible fixed asset, and that debt is partially repaid from every rental payment received. The bank as legal owner of the asset receives the tax writing-down allowances on the asset, but may pass part of this benefit to the lessee within the terms of the rental to be paid.

The Advantages of Leasing

The large banks have developed leasing subsidiaries, until leasing is now a significant source of finance for businesses seeking to acquire fixed assets for one or two years, or for their entire working life. The advantages of leasing to the borrower (lessee) can be stated as follows:

(a) The amount of borrowing can be tailored to fit exactly the amount needed to finance the asset which is required.

(b) The asset will pay for itself from its earnings as rentals occur over the life of the asset. Thus cash flows can be ascertained well in advance and fitted into a cash-planning exercise.

(c) Leasing enables a business to expand without committing its capital resources and without recourse to the normal methods of raising long-term loans.

(d) With leasing, the asset concerned is the security, so the other assets of the business are not mortgaged, and can thus be managed with greater flexibility.

(e) Leasing is a useful source of finance when other sources are exhausted, and other assets are already committed as security for loans. The leasing industry would like to see all leases treated as 'off balance-sheet finance', arguing that the leased asset does not legally belong to the lessee, and that future rentals are not a liability on the day of the balance sheet. The accounting profession, when issuing SSAP 21 on leases, took the view that the economic substance of the transaction was more important than the legal form, and that finance leases should be disclosed. It is wrong to permit managers to commit a business to a long-term leasing contract without disclosing this event to shareholders and other lenders. The capital element of a finance lease should appear as a loan in the gearing calculation.

(f) With a loan there is a heavy outflow of cash at the end of the contract, or the business has to refinance by borrowing elsewhere. This is avoided by a finance lease as the rentals contain an element of capital repayment as well as interest.

Hire Purchase

A business can enter into a high purchase agreement with a finance company, whereby it can pay for assets which it uses, not before it possesses them but out of the profits earned while it is using them. With hire purchase a series of payments are made, say over 24 months, and the asset becomes the property of the user when this payment sequence is completed. With leasing the asset remains the property of the lessor unless a purchase clause is inserted to allow the lessee to buy the asset at the end of the contract. Under Inland Revenue rules capital allowances can be claimed by the user business for hire purchase assets, but only by the lessor for leased assets.

Government Grants

It is government policy to encourage the modernization of industrial plant, to promote business activity in areas of high unemployment, and to nurture the growth of small businesses. To promote these goals a whole series of schemes have been established whereby government grants and other financial incentives are available. These schemes should always be considered as potential sources of capital when an investment in plant or premises is under consideration.

SHORT-TERM FINANCIAL REQUIREMENTS

There are several sources of short-term capital available to companies.

Overdraft

The commercial banks provide short-term funds to finance working capital items, either by loans repayable at short notice or by overdraft facilities. An overdraft is usually considered to be preferable to a loan, since interest is payable only on the overdrawn amount, whereas with a loan, interest is payable on the whole amount, whether or not it is used in its entirety in the business. The rate of interest payable on such short-term facilities offered by the banks depends on the creditworthiness of the borrower, and is also linked to the minimum lending rate of the Bank of England. In some cases commercial banks require security for such a short-term loan, and with a small business it may be that the security needed is a guarantee on the part of the proprietor to repay the loan if the business fails to do so. In this way the banks can avoid the difficulties they would encounter if, once they had lent money to the company, the owner of the company claimed protection as a shareholder under the limited liability rule when the company went into liquidation. The large commercial banks have been criticized for not supporting industry by advancing funds for the long and medium term. They have, however, introduced medium-term and variable interest rate loans, as well as taking a significant share of the hire purchase and leasing markets through the operation of subsidiary companies.

Trade Credit Advanced by Suppliers

This is usually governed by the terms of trade in a particular industry, and by the contract between the purchaser and supplier of goods. The amount of credit advanced to a company by its suppliers depends on their view of the company's creditworthiness, and whether the company is an important customer. Trade credit is often viewed as being a source of interest-free funds, since apparently there is no rate of interest attached to it. This is not always true, since if a cash discount is offered by the supplier, the fact that the customer does not pay early, net of the discount, shows the amount he or she is prepared to forgo in order to extend the payment period. Although a business should try to maximize the amount of trade credit it takes from its suppliers, there is a limit beyond which its reputation as a good payer begins to suffer, and at which the creditors begin to emerge as a significant pressure group in the running of the business. Both bank finance and trade credit are important sources of finance for the small firm, but they can also be the reason for its sudden demise if this financial support is withdrawn at a crucial moment. The Inland Revenue is also a provider of short-term funds in that the tax on business profits is not payable until some months after the end of the accounting year, and during the intervening period funds needed eventually to pay tax can be used for business operations.

Invoice Discounting or Factoring

If a company makes sales to a number of customers on credit terms it will have to wait for two or even three months before its debtors pay what they owe. This means that the debtors must be financed by the company. The idea of factoring is to pass over the finance of debtors from the selling company to a special factoring or finance company. The factoring company, after reviewing the amount of the debts and the credit-worthiness of the debtors, will pay the selling company, at the end of the month in which the sales were made, the amount it can expect to receive from the debtors (less a percentage). In this way the selling company receives its money one or two months earlier than would normally be the case. The factoring company will then collect the debts from the selling company's customers when they fall due. A company with sales of, for example, £20,000 a month can release up to £40,000 of working capital for use elsewhere in the business if it sells its debts to a factoring company. However, debt factoring has some disadvantages, such as:

(a)   The expense of the discount charged by the factoring company.

(b)   The procedures whereby the factor collects the debts from debtors who are not its customers. The factor may not be too courteous in the way it collects the money and therefore an element of goodwill on the part of the selling company may be lost.

(c)   Factoring companies are very particular about what debts they are willing to buy, and will often only accept balances owed by the larger and more reputable customers, so the selling company may be unable to factor all its debtor balances, and will also have to bear the cost of all bad debts involved.

(d)   Some companies like to hide the fact that they factor their debts in case this harms their financial standing, while others factor their debts with a company which not only undertakes collection later, but also takes on the task of recording sales and book-keeping.

CONCLUSION

There is a range of facilities open to a company to raise finance in both the long and short term and it is up to managers to select the source of funds which is cheapest and/or most convenient for the business. Cost and convenience cannot always be used as criteria, for once the cheapest and most suitable source has been utilized, if the business needs yet more finance the less suitable and more expensive sources must be used. Some methods such as leasing or factoring do not resemble the traditional methods of borrowing money, but they must be recognized as sources of finance and accounted for accordingly.

Discussion Topics

Thirty-minute essay questions:

1. Why is the decision about how much profit to retain in the business an important one?

2. Outline the institutions which operate in the long-term capital market.

3. Why is the finance lease such a useful source of finance?

4. What facilities are available in the market to meet the short-term financial requirements of a business?

5. A business acquaintance owns and operates a small construction company. You meet him for lunch, and he tells you that he has interviewed his bank manager that morning, with a view to increasing the overdraft facilities extended to his business. The bank manager said 'Your business is under-capitalized and the gearing ratio is too high; you must control the situation before the overdraft limit can be raised; why don't you try factoring your debtors?' But your friend does not understand financial jargon.

   Explain the bank manager's comment, and advise your friend of the action he must take to improve the financial position of his business.

6. You decided to start your own company to manufacture components for the motor trade.
   (a) Estimate your requirements for finance.
   (b) Discuss the sources from which such funds may be recruited.

SEMINAR EXERCISES

18.1

   (a) 'The nature of the capital structure of a company has important implications for financial management purposes, and in this respect the gearing is an important consideration.' **Discuss** this statement.
   (b) **George & Sons Ltd** are considering expanding their operations. Several alternative strategies are being discussed for financing this expansion. The latest balance sheet of the company at 31 December 2004 is as follows:

George & Sons Ltd Balance Sheet at 31 December 2004

	£	£
Tangible fixed assets		
Land and Building (market value £150 000)		80 000
Plant and equipment		180 000
		260 000
Current assets		
Stocks	100 000	
Debtors	80 000	
Cash	10 000	
	190 000	
Creditors:		
Amounts falling due within one year	50 000	140 000
Total assets less current liabilities		400 000
Creditors:		
Amounts due after more than one year		
12% loan repayable 2010		180 000
		£220 000
Financed by share capital and reserves		
Ordinary shares of £1 each		100 000
Profit and loss account		60 000
8% cumulative preference shares at £1 each		60 000
		£220 000

Operating profit before tax and interest was £50,000 in 2004.

The board of directors has identified the following possible alternative ways of obtaining an additional £100 000 required during the following year to finance planned expansion.

(a) Issue additional ordinary shares.

(b) Issue additional 8% preference shares.

(c) Raise an additional long-term loan at 12%.

Required:

Discuss the company's existing capital structure in terms of its gearing, and examine the advantages and disadvantages of each alternative method of financing the expansion plan.

18.2 **A plc and B plc** are both companies in the construction industry. Their financial statements in £000s for the year ended 31 March are as follows:

Profit and Loss Account

	A £000s	B £000s
Turnover	12 000	6 000
Cost of goods sold	9 600	4 800
Gross profit	2 400	1 200
Less: Operating expenses	750	390
Interest charges	385	287
Net profit before tax	1 265	523
Tax	500	220
Net profit after tax	765	303
Dividend	300	100
Retained profit for the year	£465	£203

Balance Sheet

		A £000s		B £000s
Fixed assets (net of depreciation)		3 000		1 500
Current assets				
Stock and work in progress	2 400		1 500	
Debtors	1 656		800	
Bank	100		50	
	4 156		2 350	
Less current liabilities				
Trade creditors	(2 650)		(600)	
Overdraft (18%)	(984)		(316)	
Net current assets		522		1 434
Total assets less current liabilities		3 522		2 934
Long term loans				
15% debentures secured on fixed assets		(1 000)		(1534)
Net assets		£2 522		£1400
Shareholders' funds				
£1 ordinary shares		1 000		500
Reserves		1 522		900
		£2 522		£1 400

Required:

(a) Compare and contrast the capital structure of A plc and B plc with the aid of appropriate accounting ratios

(b) Calculate the weighted average cost of capital for A plc and B plc. A has provided a dividend of 30p a share and B 20p a share. The market expects growth of 5% p.a. from A and 8% from B. Share prices currently stand at 250p for one ordinary share in A or B. Corporation tax is at 31%.

(c) Both A and B plan to invest £750,000 in a new long-term project. What advice would you give to each company as to how best to raise funds for this project?

CHAPTER 19

The Management of Working Capital

THE AIMS OF THIS CHAPTER

To enable students to

- Understand the nature and significance of working capital

- Calculate the amount of working capital required

- Appreciate the conservation of business resources and interpret the working capital position of the business

- Apply working capital trade-off strategies

THE NATURE OF WORKING CAPITAL

The working capital of a business is computed by deducting the current liabilities from the current assets at any point in time. It is sometimes expressed as a ratio of current assets to current liabilities. The current assets of a business, as shown on the balance sheet, consist of:

- stock, valued at the lower cost or net realizable value;

- debtors, less a provision for doubtful debts;

- short-term investments;

- prepayments;

- amounts of cash and bank deposits.

The current liabilities show the sources from which short-term funds have been recruited by the business, and are:

- trade creditors,
- accrued charges,
- short-term loans,
- amounts owed to the Inland Revenue,
- bank overdraft,
- any dividends which are payable in the near future.

The amount owed to the Inland Revenue may consist of corporation tax to be paid within 12 months, or amounts of value added tax, or income tax deductions made from wages paid to employees, which are collected by the company and later paid over to the revenue authorities. Thus the working capital of a business shows:

(a) the amount of the firm's own funds which have been used to finance the current assets after short-term borrowings have been deducted;

(b) the extent to which the business relies on short-term finance to pay for its current assets;

(c) the potential future cash flows as current assets are converted to cash within a few weeks or months of the balance sheet date – to a creditor or potential creditor the existence of working capital indicates a safety margin of current assets over current liabilities which is a pool of liquidity from which short-term creditors will be repaid;

(d) the existence of negative working capital, which means that current liabilities exceed current assets – the implication of this imprudent situation is that current liabilities have been used to finance fixed assets which cannot easily be liquidated to provide funds for repayment.

In the past the working capital ratio of current assets to current liabilities has been considered satisfactory if a relationship of 2 : 1 existed. This was thought to be a safe margin of current assets over current liabilities, but now it is considered that the extent of a satisfactory margin depends upon the situation of the company concerned, the usual conditions of a certain trade, the season of the year, and other factors. A financially strong company can persuade trade creditors and banks to offer short-term finance, so a ratio of 1.3:1 for retailers and 1.8:1 for manufacturers is considered normal.

The 'acid test' ratio of quick assets to current liabilities is considered a useful measure of liquidity as it does not include stocks. This ratio should be at 1:1 if trade creditors and others are to feel secure that there will be enough future cash flow to pay the amounts owed to them.

Working capital is often viewed by accountants as that portion of the finances of the firm which is used to 'oil the wheels of business'. The funds employed as fixed assets are directly concerned with the production of goods which the business sells, but it is the function of working capital to facilitate that production and selling activity. For example, working capital invested in stock eases production problems, since production without stock would be difficult, and working capital invested in debtors allows the sales force of the company to support their activities by offering trade credit.

DISADVANTAGES OF INSUFFICIENT WORKING CAPITAL

The importance of adequate working capital for a business is demonstrated by the disadvantages suffered by firms which operate with insufficient working capital. Such firms are in a financial straitjacket, as their operations are hindered and their growth stunted by a lack of funds to finance extra stock and debtors. The weakness of such firms is also demonstrated by their dependence on short-term sources of funds to finance their operations, since at times of great dependence the providers of funds may begin to dictate the policy of the business and, in extreme cases, may bring profitable operations to a halt by calling a creditors' meeting and appointing a liquidator. A business must always have adequate funds to finance the continuity of its operations. If it can be proved that the directors or managers authorized the company to borrow money at a time when they knew it was already insolvent, they can be charged with fraud.

The disadvantages suffered by a company with insufficient working capital are as follows:

1. The company is unable to take advantage of **new opportunities** or adapt to changes. Since it does not have sufficient financial elbow room, it is unable to finance the development of new products or the alteration to production techniques needed when new opportunities occur. A company which has used up all its overdraft facility is unable to take advantage of a cheap line of raw material when a supplier offers it.

2. **Trade discounts are lost**. A company with ample working capital is able to finance large stocks and can therefore place large orders. The bigger the order the more generous the trade discount offered by the supplier, who uses it as a method of reducing the price so that the company is induced to place an order. If a company is unable to place large orders it will find that prices it has to pay for raw materials and components are higher than those paid by its rivals, so it is at a competitive disadvantage in the market. Large stocks also act as a cushion against the disruption of production consequent upon a 'stock out', if there are supply problems.

3. **Cash discounts are lost.** Some companies will try to persuade their debtors to pay early by offering them a cash discount off the price owed. Discounts of $2\frac{1}{2}$% for cash in one month (instead of taking two or three months' credit) or even 4% for cash within seven days are not uncommon. A discount of $2\frac{1}{2}$% for payment one month early is equivalent to an annual rate of interest on the money of about 30%.

i.e. $\dfrac{2\frac{1}{2}}{97\frac{1}{2}} \times 12 = 30.67\%$

Inadequate working capital means that cash is short and payment must be delayed.

4. The advantages of being able to offer a **credit line** to customers are forgone. If the sales force can support their efforts by making credit available to the customer, this will give them an advantage over rival organizations whose credit facilities are less extensive. In the case of contracts for large items of heavy engineering plant where the goods offered for sale are of equal efficiency, the credit line may be the deciding factor. Insufficient working capital to support the current asset debtors creates this problem.

5. **Financial reputation is lost.** A company with ample working capital is able to pay its bills to suppliers and other creditors in good time. Thus it achieves a reputation as being a good payer, and this will enhance the goodwill of the business. A company with a good reputation can expect co-operation from trade creditors at times of financial difficulty; for example, it would be possible for a firm that is well known in the trade to negotiate with suppliers as much as two or three months' extra credit at a time when funds are short because a large item of capital equipment has been purchased. Suppliers will value their connection with a company with a good reputation and may be willing to offer advantageous prices to maintain the connection. Conversely, a company with a bad reputation can expect credit controllers in the trade to be on their guard if it attempts to exceed the credit limits they have set. At such times, a credit controller may cut off supplies of raw materials to a factory, thus seriously disrupting production.

6. **Insolvency.** There may be concerted action by creditors. If the working capital of a business is grossly inadequate it will be forced to finance its operations more and more by short-term borrowings such as overdraft and trade credit. Eventually the point will be reached beyond which the short-term lenders are not willing to extend credit, and it is at this point that the policy, and indeed the continuation of the business, is dependent not on the wishes of the owners, shareholders or directors, but on the actions of the creditors. Even though the business is a profitable one, at this weak stage in its development a creditors' meeting can decide that, in the absence of repayment, the creditors will apply to the court to appoint a liquidator or force the company to commence a voluntary winding-up.

OVERTRADING

Overtrading is often the reason for the development of adverse credit conditions in a business. In simple terms, to overtrade means to attempt to finance a certain volume of production and sales with inadequate working capital. If the company does not have enough funds of its own to finance stock and debtors it is forced, if it wishes to expand, to borrow from creditors and from the bank on overdraft. Sooner or later such expansion, financed completely by the funds of others, will lead to a chronic imbalance in the working capital ratio. At this point the creditors and the bank may withdraw their support and a creditors' meeting will take place. A careful scrutiny of the working capital and acid test ratios of a business may enable the accountant to predict the onset of financial distress. A business which changes its suppliers to raise extra credit, whose payments to creditors, including the Inland Revenue, are rarely made on the due date, and whose overdraft facilities are fully committed, is a business in which the slightest breath of change on the part of current liabilities can blow down the fragile credit structure which supports its operations.

CONSERVING THE RESOURCES OF CAPITAL EMPLOYED IN A BUSINESS

A much-used measure of the profitability of a business is to set net profit against the capital employed and show it as a percentage thereof. This is known as the return on capital employed (ROCE). A good accountant or financial manager will attempt to manage the resources of the business in such a way that the capital employed is used efficiently and not wasted. If the capital employed can be reduced and profit maintained, then an improved ROCE will be achieved. Conversely, if the capital employed in current operations is reduced, funds are released for use in other activities, and the profit on capital employed is increased. The financial manager should review the asset structure of the business to seek out idle, under-utilized and non-profitable assets, so that they can be turned back into cash which can then be re-employed in the business, or elsewhere, at a much greater return. Fixed assets are as important in this operation as are current assets, since when they are squeezed, liquidity, or funds for use elsewhere in the business, is the result. Some fixed assets, especially plant of a specific nature, may not be easy to sell unless at a price well below book value, and there will also be redundancy payments if staff are involved.

The **land and buildings** used by the company should be investigated. The accountant must attempt to find out whether they are fully utilized, and to discover idle or underused space, or space being used for wasteful or unprofitable purposes. Discussions with the technical experts in the business will indicate ways to rearrange the factory area, to re-route goods and stocks of work in progress which travel round the factory so that some space is released. Such space can then be sold, rented out, or used to house a new operation; any of these courses of action should improve the cash flow of the business.

A review of **machinery** used in the business should be made, to discover the level of idle time experienced each week or day by individual machines. This survey will reveal:

(a) whether the plant and machinery is working at full capacity;

(b) whether the same volume of work could be produced from a smaller number of machines;

(c) how much extra work could be undertaken using the existing plant and machinery.

Once again, the level of spare capacity, if it exists, will be shown, so that it can be put to work or sold. Care must be taken in such economy reviews that 'back up' capacity is seen not as an idle resource, but as a form of insurance against breakdown.

Vehicles should also be brought under scrutiny. Investigation, with the transport manager, into routes and mileages driven per week or per month would pinpoint those vehicles which do not earn their keep, and perhaps produce ideas so that fewer vehicles can be used to undertake the work of the company.

Investments made by the business also tie up capital, and therefore they too should be analysed. The return received from an investment should be set against its current value to determine whether it is worthwhile. In cases of low return, perhaps the investment is held for strategic reasons, e.g. a share stake in a supplier or customer company. It is difficult to quantify such strategic benefits, but an attempt should be made to find out whether the benefit is considered to be worth tying up the amount of capital in the investment. Perhaps the same strategic benefit could be gained by holding a smaller share stake, thus releasing some funds for use elsewhere in the business.

CONSERVING FUNDS INVESTED IN CURRENT ASSETS

Stocks

A review of the current assets should also be made to ascertain whether levels of stocks and debtors could be the subject of economy measures.

The stocks of a manufacturing business are usually of three types. They consist of:

(a)   stocks of raw material waiting in the store to be used in the productive process;

(b)   stocks of work in progress or semi-finished goods being worked on in the factory;

(c)   stock of finished goods waiting to be sold.

The computation of ratios is a useful device to determine the stockholding period.

In the case of **raw material**, the stock should be set against the usage of each material. If the amount of stock is divided by the average weekly issue, a figure for the number of weeks' usage held in stock will emerge. This figure can be compared with the 'lead time' between placing an order and receiving delivery in order to find out whether the stock held is excessive. For example, if one can buy raw material at a fortnight's notice, it seems wrong to finance two months' usage of that raw material in stock. The executive responsible for this is the buyer and, if the raw material stockholding period is increasing, this manager must be called to account for the change. It may be that the rate of production has slowed down while purchasing of materials has continued at the same rate, or that purchasing is not coordinated properly to production quantities. On the other hand, the buyer may be attempting to build up stocks in anticipation of a forthcoming seasonal demand or as a hedge against inflation.

The ratio is calculated as

$$\frac{\text{Raw material stock}}{\text{Annual usage}} \times \frac{365}{1}$$

will show the average number of days that material is waiting in the stores before it is issued to production.

Task 19.1

A company has a raw material stock of £960,000 and uses £3,000,000 of raw material in a year.
   Calculate the average stockholding period, and comment.

Solution

(£960,000 / £3,000,000) × 365 = 117 days

Materials wait nearly four months in the store before they are issued to production. This is committing nearly a million pounds of capital employed to stock, so there must be a good reason for the investment – perhaps a large trade discount for a bulk purchase? The period of 117 days must be compared to the lead time. Some managers consider money tied up in stock is 'dead money' because it is earning nothing. The 'just in time' system attempts to reduce stock to a minimum by planning deliveries of materials to coordinate with their issue to production. If this material can be replaced two weeks after ordering, there should be good strategic or cost reasons to justify this overstocking situation.

The ratio of stocks of **work in progress** to the cost of production when computed as a number of days or weeks will show how long it takes for semi-finished articles to progress through the factory. This time period must be compared with the normally expected production cycle and discrepancies analysed. If, for example, there are 50 working weeks in the year and it takes a week to complete the production process, but work-in-progress stock is $^4/_{50}$ of the production cost for a year, then there is too much work-in-progress stock in the factory, and the bottlenecks which are disrupting production must be discovered and eliminated. This will reduce the working capital cycle.

   The ratio calculated as

$$\frac{\text{Work-in-progress stock}}{\text{Cost of production}} \times \frac{365}{1}$$

will show the average number of days work in progress spends in the factory before it is completed.

Task 19.2

A company has a work-in-progress stock of £1 600 000 and a cost of production of £7 000 000. Calculate the average work-in-progress period and comment.

Solution

$(£1,600,000 / £7,000,000) \times 365 = 83$ days

This average period should be compared with the length of the production cycle. If this is say 30 days, there is a bottleneck in the production process which must be removed to speed up production and reduce the work-in-progress stock. If the number can be cut from 83 days to 40 days, the work-in-progress stock would be $^{40}/_{365} \times £7,000,000 = £767,000$ a saving of £833,000 of working capital. If this money is borrowed on overdraft at say 13% interest, a cost of £108,000 would be avoided.

The ratio of **finished goods** to the cost of goods sold will, when expressed as a time period, show how long the finished goods wait in the stores before they are sold. In this way one can discover whether production is coordinated properly to sales, or whether the factory goes on producing at its normal rate while sales are falling away.

The ratio is calculated as

$$\frac{\text{Finished-goods stock}}{\text{Cost of goods sold}} \times \frac{365}{1} = \text{Days}$$

Task 19.3

A company has a finished-goods stock of £3 million and sales of £10 million. The gross profit rate is 12%. Calculate the average stockholding period for finished goods and comment.

Solution

Sales £10 million less gross profit 12% = Cost of goods sold, £8,800,000 (10 million × .88)

$(£3,000,000 / £8,800,000) \times 365 = 124$ days

This is four months, a very long stockholding period, which could be reduced if production was coordinated to sales. Just think how much interest could be saved if this period was reduced to one month.

$^{1}/_{12} \times £8,800,000 = £733,333$ as finished-goods stock

£3,000,000 − £733,333 = £2,266,667 saved

Interest on £2,266,667 borrowed at say 13% = £424,666

The comments made in tasks 19.1, 19.2 and 19.3 are often relevant when the accountant is called on to interpret the working capital situation of a business.

The Stock Level Trade-Off Decision

The establishment of a correct stock level is a decision affected by many different factors. The management team must trade off the advantages of holding large stocks against the disadvantages. The advantages of holding large stocks can be summarized as follows:

(a) large orders can be placed with suppliers so that trade discounts are secured;

(b) there is a reduction of buying costs if orders are placed less often;

(c) a smooth flow of production is maintained, since a large buffer stock of raw materials will reduce the possibility of a 'stock out';

(d) constant quality is achieved from large batches purchased.

The disadvantages of holding a large stock of raw materials stem from the costs of financing and maintaining the stock:

(a) interest paid on overdraft to finance the stock;

(b) the cost of running the stores, i.e. rent, rates, light, heat, insurance;

(c) the costs of spoilage, spillage and pilferage;

(d) the losses inherent in the operation of breaking bulk;

(e) the fear of obsolescence, followed by stock write-down.

These disadvantages must be set against the advantages shown above to find the optimum stock level for the business.

The accountant must ensure that stocks are examined to discover slow-moving and obsolescent items so that quantities involved can be reduced to realistic levels and funds released. Any action taken to improve the flow of products through the factory will reduce the time-lag involved in the conversion of raw material to a sold product. Capital is invested during that period, and if those funds have been borrowed as an overdraft, the cost of interest will reduce profits.

The Working Capital Cycle

The working capital cycle can be expressed in terms of the number of days it takes to store raw materials, to convert raw materials to finished goods, to store finished goods and then after they are sold to collect the price from the company's debtors. Such a computation will reveal the time period for which the company must finance the working capital cycle. From this period it is possible to subtract the period of credit received from suppliers. For example, if the raw material waits 30 days in the stores before being used, is then transferred to the factory for a ten-day production cycle, then waits for 15 days in the finished-goods store before being sold, and the person to whom the goods are sold delays a further 60 days before the bill is paid, it will take 115 days to change the funds invested in raw materials back into cash or liquid resources. This means that the company will have to finance this period, but if the company in turn takes 60 days of credit from the supplier of raw materials, the period to be financed is reduced to 55 days. Thus the amount of working capital tied up in raw materials for this transaction will be the cost of 55 times an average day's usage of raw materials.

Example

	Days
Storage	30
Production	10
Finished-goods store	15
Payment delay	60
	115
Less credit from suppliers	60
Days to finance	55

This simple sum emphasizes the importance in the working capital cycle of the management of stock, debtors and creditors. If debtors can be induced to pay sooner and creditors can be persuaded to wait for their money, the amount of the company's own funds tied up in the transaction will be reduced. Any other factor which can shorten the time period, such as a shorter production cycle or a reduced lead time between the delivery and use of raw material stocks, will also reduce the amount of working capital required. Thus planning and the reduction of production bottlenecks can help to turn over stocks faster and allow the same amount of money to finance more transactions, and earn more profit margins, in an accounting period.

How Much Working Capital is Required

The working capital cycle can be used to calculate the amount of working capital needed to finance a certain volume of activity, and this information can be used to find how much will have to be borrowed and focus attention on the cost of that borrowing.

Example

You are a member of the management team of a transport authority which has recently installed a new tramway system. The authority is about to sign a contract with **Windowstox Ltd**, to supply window units for the new tram fleet, but there are rumours that Windowstox is short of funds and that it may not be able to finance this contract. Your authority wishes to judge the adequacy of the working capital of Windowstox, and as a first step you have been asked to evaluate the amount of working capital required to support the activity of Windowstox at normal capacity. Windowstox have informed you that they have £2m available for working capital and that the Croesus Bank have offered them overdraft facilities at 14% p.a. interest if more is needed.

Investigation reveals that Windowstox plan for a turnover of £32m next year, with raw material purchases expected to be £9m, direct labour costs £7m, and variable factory overheads limited to 15% of sales revenue.

The company operates a 50-week production year. Opening and closing stocks of raw material are budgeted to be equal to eight weeks' usage of raw material. The closing stock of finished goods will be equal to four weeks' cost of production. There are no stocks of work in progress.

All sales are on credit terms of payment after one month, and two months' credit is taken from material suppliers.

Calculate:

(a) the amount of working capital which Windowstox will need to support this level of activity;

(b) how much Windowstox will need to borrow from the Croesus Bank; and

(c) the annual cost of this borrowing.

Solution:

Windowstox Working Capital Requirements

		£
Raw Material Stock		
Opening and closing stock are the same,		
so usage will equal purchases		
£9m ÷ 50 weeks × 8 weeks		1 440 000
Finished-goods stock		
Material cost	£9.0m	
Labour cost	£7.0m	
Overhead cost (32m × .15)	£4.8m	
Production cost	£20.8m	
£20.8m ÷ 50 weeks × 4 weeks		1 664 000
Debtors		
£32m ÷ 12 months		2 666 666
		5 770 666
Less creditors		
£9m ÷ $^2/_{12}$ months		1 500 000
(a) Working capital required		4 270 666
(b) Funds available		2 000 000
(c) Overdraft needed		£2 270 666

Interest at 14% on £2,270,666 = £317,893

Note: If the finished-goods stock period could be reduced to two weeks, £832,000 of overdraft would not be required. If a further two weeks of credit can be negotiated with creditors (£9m × $^2/_{50}$), an extra £360,000 of trade credit would be available. These two tactics would reduce the overdraft by £1,192,000 and save £166,880 of interest each year

DEBTORS AND CREDITORS

To conserve the working capital of the company the accountant must approach debtors with some caution. There is less control over debtors than, for example, over stock, since the period of credit which the company must give depends to some extent on the activity of the other party to the transaction, i.e. the customer. The volume of funds required to finance debtors may grow without an increase in the volume of transactions, merely because in a period of inflation prices rise and more capital is needed to finance the same number of transactions, or because in a recession customers may take longer to pay their bills.

Many companies employ a **credit controller** in an attempt to economize on their working capital tied up in the form of debtors. The credit controller has four main tasks:

(i)   To vet new customers and set a credit limit (an amount beyond which goods will not be sold to the customer without the payment of previous bills).

(ii) To review the credit position of old customers and set new credit limits for them

(iii) To ensure that credit limits are not exceeded.

(iv) To hasten the slow payers by means of carefully worded letters encouraging them to pay.

The credit controller is in a delicate position, since money must be collected from the firm's customers, but without rudeness while collecting the money, since this may discourage them from buying from the company in the future. Thus the credit controller is the rope in the tug of war between the accounting department, who wish to collect debts and reduce working capital wastefully tied up in debtors, and the sales department, who wish to extend the credit line and maintain customer goodwill. A useful device in the control of trade credit is the **ageing debtors list**. This is merely an analysis of all debtor balances to show how long they have been outstanding. Thus the poor payers are revealed and the credit controller can try to make them pay. The danger with debtor balances which are four or five months or more overdue is that they may, unless the credit controller is careful, become bad debts.

Another aspect of the management of working capital which a financial accountant must monitor with care is the amount of trade credit which the company can take from the suppliers of raw materials. The general rule is to take as much as possible, since it is free, but not too much, since slow payment of bills harms the reputation of the company and its goodwill, and may affect future prices charged to the company for raw materials. Long delayed payment may result in a stop on the delivery of vital raw materials to the factory. Some companies adopt the policy of always paying promptly where they are offered a cash discount, while others, through careful programming with their suppliers, organize the deliveries to coordinate with the needs of the factory and thus reduce the stockholding period (just in time).

Cash balances, or funds lying in the bank, are considered by many companies to be idle assets, since they are earning nothing. They are, however, a useful safety margin to ensure that urgent bills can always be paid. Forward planning in the form of a cash budget can show up the impact of future transactions on the cash balance, so that when an overdraft is required it can be requested well in advance.

Interpreting the Working Capital position

Ratio analysis is a sensible starting point for this interpretation, which can be developed with comment based on the ratios calculated.

Task 19.4

What ratios can be used to comment on the working capital position of a business?

Solution

The following ratios may prove helpful:

(a) Working capital	Current assets to current liabilities
(b) Acid test	Quick assets to current liabilities
(c) Stock turnover in days	Materials stock ÷ usage × 365 or
	Materials stock ÷ purchases × 365
	Work-in-progress stock ÷ cost of production × 365
	Finished-goods stock ÷ cost of sales × 365
(d) Debtors payment period	Debtors ÷ sales × 365
(e) Creditors payment delay	Creditors ÷ purchases × 365

Example

A finance director is about to start negotiations with the company's bankers to increase the overdraft. She is convinced that the company has adequate working capital, having calculated the working capital ratio from the following extract from the balance sheet.

Current assets	£
Stock of materials	3 641 209
Stock of work in progress	4 262 532
Stock of finished goods	3 205 000
Debtors	8 758 163
Cash	217 860
	£ 20 084 764
Current liabilities	
Trade creditors for materials	1 458 270
Tax payable	570 652
Proposed dividend	342 000
Overdraft	7 648 095
	£10 019 017

Turnover for a year is £16 million with a gross profit rate of 16%.
Material purchases for a year are £9,438,925. Overdraft interest is at 11%.

Required:

> (a) Explain the working capital position of the company.
> (b) Suggest improvements to the working capital management of the business.

Solution (a):

> (i) Working capital ratio CA:CL = £20,084,764 : £10,019,017 = 2:1
>
> Acid test   QA:CL = £8,976,023 : £10,019,017 = 0.9:1
>
> The working capital position looks good, but this is distorted by the large stocks which are the least liquid of the current assets. Accordingly the acid test discloses a worrying liquidity position with 90 pence of quick assets to provide cash to pay each £1 of current liability. Cash of £217,000 is not enough to pay the dividend or the tax, and the bank will not be keen to advance funds for such payments.
>
> If the stocks can be turned quickly into finished goods and then into sales this will produce much-needed cash flow. The bank manager is in a dominant position, since if he loses confidence in the business, the overdraft might be reduced with serious consequences.
>
> (ii) Stock control.
>
> | Material stock | £3,641,209 / £9,438,925 × 365 = 140 days |
> | Work in progress | £4,262,532 / £16m × .84 × 365 = 116 days |
> | Finished goods | £3,205,000 / £13,440,000 × 365 = 87 days |
>
> Stocks are out of control. Raw material storage time, and the work in progress period, are too long. Finished goods are made nearly three months before they are sold.
>   Purchases are used for the material stock ratio because a usage figure is not available. Work in progress is set against cost of sales as a cost of production figure is not given.
>
> (iii) Debtor control: £8,758,163 / £16m × 365 = 200 days – 6$\frac{1}{2}$ months
>
> A very long period of credit is allowed to customers – is this necessary? Could the same sales be made with a 3-month period?
>
> Creditor control: £1,458,270 / £9,438,925 × 365 = 56 days – 8 weeks
>
> The company is paying its suppliers after a comparatively short period of credit.
>
> (iv) Debtors : Creditors £8,758,163 : £1,458,270 reveals 6:1.
>
> The business is financing its customers much more than trade associates are supporting the company. Overdraft interest must be a crippling cost (£841,290). The largest liability is the overdraft. If the bank manager is supportive, the business will survive, but it seems risky to press for more overdraft at this stage.
> £7,648,095 × .11 = £841,290, if the overdraft is constant at this amount throughout the year.

Solution (b):

Working capital management

(i) Stocks. Coordinate purchases to production, and production to sales. Investigate the reason for the large work-in-progress stock. If the raw material stock is purchased in large volume to earn a trade discount, ascertain whether this discount is greater than the cost of overdraft interest paid to finance this stock.

(ii) Debtors. Appoint a credit controller to reduce the investment in debtors, but take care not to upset any credit arrangements which underpin potential sales.

(iii) Creditors. Steps should be taken to increase the credit period taken unless a lucrative cash discount is allowed.

(iv) Reduce material stocks by 80 days.

$60 / 365 \times £9,438,925 = £1,551,603 - £36,412,109 \quad = £2,089,605$

Reduce work in progress by 50 days

$66 / 365 \times £13,440,000 = £2,430,246 - £4,262,532 \quad = £1,832,285$

Reduce finished-goods stocks by 30 days

$57 / 365 \times £13,440,000 = £2,098,848 - 3,205,000 \quad = £1,106,152$

Reduce debtors by 90 days

$110 / 365 \times £16m = £4,821,917 - £8,758,163 \qquad = \underline{£3,936,246}$

Total working capital saved $\qquad = \underline{\underline{£8,964,288}}$

The overdraft can be repaid, without taking more credit from suppliers, which will save the cost of interest. Control and the application of reasonable targets can transform what was a very badly managed business.

WORKING CAPITAL TRADE-OFF STRATEGIES

Working capital management comprises a trade-off or constant effort to balance the advantage achieved by a certain strategy against the costs of securing that advantage.

Assume that a sales organization allows two months' (60 days') credit to its customers. The company decides to offer a 4% discount for cash within ten days of sale, i.e. payment 50 days sooner than at present. Then

$$\frac{4}{96} \times \frac{365}{50} = 30.4\%$$

is the annual rate of interest which this strategy costs the company, and this cost must be balanced against the overdraft interest avoided because the money is collected sooner, or the profit which can be earned if that money is put to work in the business for 50 days. From the customer's point of view it would be profitable to borrow on overdraft at 18%, in order to pay bills 50 days early, and earn a discount giving an annual rate of 30%.

An alternative strategy might be to allow improved credit terms to customers in an attempt to increase sales. The profit from the extra sales must be set off against the cost of providing finance for the extra period to new and existing customers. An extension of the period before payment may also increase the number of bad debts experienced by the business, and the costs of accounting for extra customers.

The Situation

(a) A company has annual credit sales of £6 million and earns a gross profit of 20% on those sales.

(b) Customers pay within one month of their purchase so debtors at present are

£6m ÷ 12 = £500,000.

(c) Bad debts at present are at 1% of sales – £60,000.

(d) Overdraft finance is available at 13% interest.

The Scheme

The marketing manager suggests that customers should be allowed to extend their credit period from one month to two, and estimates that sales will increase by 30% as a result of this strategy. The credit controller comments that the scheme may cause bad debts to increase to $2^{1}/_{2}$% of sales and that an extra clerk at £15,000 p.a. would be required. The accountant reminds managers that debtors are financed by overdraft.

The Trade Off

		£
Revenue from extra sales (£6m × .3 × .2)		360 000
Less Admin costs – an extra clerk		(15 000)
Less Bad debts – At present (£6m × 0.01)	£60 000	
– Will be (£6m × 1.3 × 0.025)	(£195 000)	
		(135 000)
Less interest on increased debtors		
Debtors now (£6m ÷ 12) 1 month	£500 000	
Debtors will be (£6m × 1.3 ÷ 6) 2 months	£1 300 000	
Extra debtors to finance	£800 000	
£800,000 × 0.13 interest		(104 000)
Surplus		£106 000

Affirmative – the strategy is worth adopting. The surplus would have been even greater if the post-tax cost of overdraft interest had been used in the calculation.

$$13\% \times (1 - 0.31) = 8.97\% - \text{say } 9\%$$

CONCLUSION

A good manager will have a proper understanding of working capital – its impact on profit and its influence on customers and lenders. If stocks, debtors and creditors are well managed, overdraft interest will be kept to a minimum. Expansion without appropriate consideration of extra finance required may cause solvency problems for a business as overtrading leads to a loss of confidence by lenders and perhaps to liquidation. Proper control over stocks will reduce the amount of money lying idle in stocks to a safe minimum. Control over debtors is less certain than stock control, because debtors themselves influence the decision to pay. The credit controller in a business works to regularize debtor payments, eliminate poor credit risks and reduce the incidence of bad debts.

Discussion Topics

Thirty-minute essay questions:

1. What is working capital and why does a trade creditor see it as a significant figure on the balance sheet?

2. What disadvantages are suffered by a business which does not have an adequate fund of working capital?

3. What is the working capital cycle and how can an accountant use an understanding of this cycle to benefit the firm?

4. Explain the task of a credit controller with special reference to the pressures which are part of the job.

5. Your managing director has recently returned from a meeting with the company's bank manager, at which they discussed an extension to the overdraft. The managing director does not understand the bank manager's comments. He remarks, 'The bank manager said our working capital ratio was deficient at 1:1 and that we are in danger of overtrading. All this jargon is meant to confuse the honest borrower.' Draft a memorandum to the managing director which
   (a) explains the nature of working capital and the meaning of 'overtrading'; and
   (b) suggests how the company could improve its working capital situation.

SEMINAR EXERCISES

19.1 From the two balance sheets of **Ginger Ltd** shown below, calculate the change in working capital over the year and show how this change has arisen

Ginger Ltd Balance Sheets

	£	£		£	£
	1 Jan	31 Dec		1 Jan	31 Dec
Share capital	60 000	65 000	Freehold land and buildings	22 000	25 000
General	4 000	5 000	Plant and machinery	38 000	40 000
Profit and loss balance	9 000	11 000			
Long-term loan	–	50 000			
				60 000	65 000
Current liabilities :			Current assets:		
Trade creditors	12 000	14 000	Stocks	17 000	70 000
Tax	11 000	12 000	Debtors	7 000	10 000
Proposed final			Cash		
dividend	6 000	8 000		18 000	20 000
	£102 000	£165 000		£102 000	£165 000

19.2 **Unimix Ltd** are suppliers of ready mixed concrete to the building industry in the East Midlands. You have recently joined the business as assistant to the managing director. The corporate plan for this business forecasts an increased turnover of 40% in the next three years. Fixed assets are under-utilized at present, and can cope with this expansion.

Required:

(a) Draft a brief report to the managing director to explain the financial problems consequent upon such expansion, and outlining possible sources of finance for the company.

(b) The sales director of Unimix Ltd suggests that turnover would increase if credit limits imposed on customers were to be relaxed, and that sales invoices should be payable by customers after taking two months' credit instead of one month as allowed at present.

Currently, sales are steady at £300,000 per month, with a gross profit margin of 15%. If two months' credit is allowed to customers, it is forecast that sales will increase to £360,000 per month, but that bad debts will rise from 1% of turnover to 2%, and sales accounting costs will increase by £12,000 p.a. The company is at present using its overdraft facilities to the limit, but the bank has indicated its willingness to finance the scheme at 18% p.a.

Evaluate the proposal of the sales director.

19.3

(a) A company budgets for a sales turnover of £30 million in the forthcoming year and plans to purchase £14,400,000 of raw material and pay wages of £5,250,000. Production overheads will be limited to 15% of sales. Activity is spread evenly over the year. The company plans an opening and closing stock equal to thirty days' consumption of raw material and twenty days' production of finished goods. There is no stock of work in progress.

Eight weeks' credit is allowed by suppliers, while 80% of sales are on credit terms of payment after twelve weeks.

Calculate the amount of working capital needed to support this level of activity.

(b) A company spent £12,750,000 on purchases last year, and had a turnover of £21 million. Closing debtors were £4,442,307, and closing creditors £1,225,962. Overdraft interest is at 12%.

If the company budgets to achieve the same level of activity in the forthcoming year, **advise the directors** of the cost saving to the business if credit allowed to debtors is reduced by one week and credit taken from suppliers is increased by one week.

PART FIVE

Regulation and Accounting Theory

CHAPTER 20

Regulation

THE AIMS OF THIS CHAPTER

To enable students to

- Explain the standard-setting system in the UK

- Understand the need for and scope of standard accounting practices

- Appreciate the development of International Standards

THE NEED TO STANDARDIZE

Financial statements need to be easily assimilated by users, and comparable between companies and time periods. This aim will be more easily achieved if accounting standards codify methods and prohibit doubtful practices. Accounting principles, unlike the laws of natural science, are artificial, and they rely for their authority on the fact that accountants accept each principle as correct and a matter of good practice.

Business practice constantly evolves, and accounting principles slowly change to adjust to new conditions. Standards will reflect such changes, and persuade accountants through discussion to recognize and accept change. Standards also give accountants and auditors some means of protection from those who may try to pressurize them into accepting methods of which they do not approve.

ACCOUNTING STANDARDS AND THE LAW

Accounting standards are based on the reporting system established by company law. It is part of their function to fill in the details where statute is incomplete, or when the law is silent on a particular point. In the USA the law mandates the Securities and Exchange Commission which in turn delegates the Financial Accounting Standards Board to set standards on its behalf. In the UK the law has established an agency to oversee the standard setting procedures. This is the Financial Reporting Council (FRC) set up under the Companies Act 1989. This act also stipulated that company accounts should show a true and fair view which is only possible if they are in accordance with generally accepted accounting practice as expressed by the accounting standards.

There is a rebuttable presumption that companies must follow the standard practices if their accounts are to be true and fair. The onus is on the company to rebut this presumption, and argue, in court if necessary, that any departure from standard practice in its accounts has made those accounts truer and fairer.

In the UK accounting standards are debated and set by the Accounting Standards Board (ASB), and officially promulgated by the FRC, its parent body. The task of the ASB is to develop principles as a framework within which accounting judgements can be exercised, and to express those principles in Financial Reporting Standards (FRSs). The ASB works within certain guidelines:

1. To be objective in order that standards represent the underlying commercial activity.

2. To ensure that standards are clearly expressed and supported by reasoned analysis.

3. To encourage research, public consultation and careful deliberation as standards are developed.

4. To maintain regular liaison with international standard-setters.

5. To ensure consistency of one standard with another, and between accounting standards and the law.

6. To weigh the perceived costs of following a standard practice against the expected benefits of its application.

COMPONENTS OF THE UK STANDARD–SETTING SYSTEM

Accounting standards were set by the Accounting Standards Committee from 1970 to 1990. These old standards are known as Statements of Standard Accounting Practice (SSAPs), and some of them are still in issue. Since 1990 Financial Reporting Standards have replaced the old standards. The institutions responsible for FRSs are shown in Figure 20.1 and their roles in the system are as follows.

Figure 20.1

The Financial Reporting Council (FRC)

This is a policy-making body which plans the work programme of its three subsidiary committees and raises finance for the expensive task of standard-setting. It issues

Financial Reporting Standards under its own authority. The FRC has a chairman appointed by the Department of Trade and Industry after consultation with the Bank of England and the accounting profession. Half of the membership of the FRC is appointed on the recommendation of the accounting profession to represent practice, industry, commerce and the public sector, while the remaining members are drawn from the Stock Exchange, institutional investors, users, employees and government observers. The FRC derives its authority from the Companies Act 1989.

The Accounting Standards Board (ASB)

This board works through a number of subcommittees and working parties to review existing standards and develop new standard accounting practices. The ASB is developing a significant output of discussion documents concerning the objectives and format of the corporate report. It has a full-time chairman and a technical director who are supported by a full-time executive and a secretariat. Thus it is hoped that considerable expertise and continuity will be devoted to the task of setting accounting standards, while at the same time the expertise of the accounting profession can be used in the working parties and subcommittees.

The Financial Reporting Review Panel (FRRP)

This panel meets to consider cases of non-compliance with standards. The FRRP is able to initiate its own enquiries or receive cases referred to it by auditors and other interested parties. It expects the cooperation of directors and accountants and is able to force companies to revise their financial statements or to make extra disclosures if this is considered appropriate. It is at this point in the system that the 'rebuttable presumption' that standards must be followed if the accounts are to be true and fair comes into play. The representatives of large companies whose accounts are suspected of departing from standards must justify their accounting treatment before the FRRP's experts, to rebut the legal presumption that they are not true and fair unless standards are followed. If the FRRP is not convinced by the arguments put forward, the company must adjust its accounts or risk being taken to court under the 1989 Companies Act. No company has yet refused to follow the advice of the FRRP, but commentators remark that if the FRRP is forced into litigation this could be very expensive, and in the event of its losing a legal action the reputation of the standard-setting system as a whole would be seriously impaired.

In a recent case a company was forced to restate its accounts by millions of pounds for the last five years, turning each one to a loss. The dispute with the panel over revenue recognition and development costs changed its profit of £25m in one year to a loss of £9.9m.

The Urgent Issues Task Force (UITF)

This deals with current issues which cannot wait for normal standard-setting procedures. New practices can develop which can change the effect of the established rules and the UITF reviews and pronounces on such issues. Its views are expressed in 'abstracts' which comment on current practices that require reinterpretation and the settlement of 'brushfire problems'.

Abstract 26 clarifies the position of 'dotcom' businesses which barter free advertising space with each other and then value the transaction to add it to annual turnover.

STANDARD-SETTING: THE PROCEDURES

The programme of work for the ASB is generated by discussion within the FRC. Issues are targeted by the secretariat, problems emerge, and the matter is referred to the ASB. This body then selects a subcommittee or working party to begin preliminary discussions. The working party will produce a discussion paper which is published for distribution to interested parties. The paper sets out the issue which is under review, with the alternative practices which are currently in operation, and then discusses the difficulties and poses specific questions to which interested parties are asked to respond. After an interval for debate the subcommittee reviews the responses it has received, weighing the evidence and formalizing proposals in an 'exposure draft'. These documents are known as FREDs (Financial Reporting Exposure Drafts). A FRED is a formal proposition for what is likely to become a standard practice. The draft is exposed for a six-month period, and after the closing date further comments are analysed by the subcommittee. A formal standard practice (FRS) is then drafted. The standard practice must then be approved by the FRC. These procedures are designed to generate discussion over a fairly lengthy period, and then to persuade accountants to accept recommendations for what is termed 'best accounting practice'.

STATEMENTS OF RECOMMENDED PRACTICE (SORPS)

Although the procedure to draft a SORP is similar to that for the development of a FRS, the SORP does not have the same mandatory status given to a standard. A departure from a standard must be justified by a note to the accounts and may necessitate an adverse comment by the auditor in the audit report. In the case of a SORP, non-compliance need not be disclosed. SORPs are issued to cover matters of limited application, or matters which have widespread application but which are not of fundamental importance, e.g. pension scheme accounts – SORP 1. The standard-setter uses the device of a SORP to give guidance to accountants on problems which are specific to a certain industry, or which are of less central importance to the development of accounting practice.

THE ECONOMIC CONSEQUENCES OF STANDARDS

An accounting standard can have considerable economic consequences because it will determine the form and substance of information disclosed by company accounts, and could therefore influence the decisions made by users of those accounting statements. It follows that some parties to those accounts will be winners and others will be losers, if the standard allows information to be slanted in a certain direction. There may be considerable political pressure, and lobbying, to influence the standard-setters in favour of one accounting treatment over another. It is therefore important to ensure that the standard-setters can resist such pressures, and that those who sit on the standard-setting committees are unbiased.

If the supporters of one point of view can get themselves appointed to a working party, or influence members of the working party, they can 'capture' the standard-setting process, and slant standards in a direction suitable to their interests. In the face of powerful pressure groups arguing different points of view, there is a temptation for the standard-setters to compromise and draft a standard which seeks a consensus to ensure acceptance of the rules. Unfortunately, such attempts to damp down controversy produce standards which do not work well. 'Consensus-seeking' takes time and may delay the production of a standard. For example, SSAP 9 took 60 months to finalize and even then was the cause of much dissension and argument among accountants and others.

A technique called 'opinion-shopping' is now being used by some directors to influence the opinions of their auditors. If, for example, directors seek to treat a transaction in a certain way, and the auditors do not agree with this treatment, the board may then shop around other firms of accountants, seeking to find an opinion that agrees with their own. Once they have found a second opinion with which they can agree, they will use this opinion in an attempt to influence their own auditors to accept a practice which may not be quite correct. The proper ethical conduct in such a situation is for the accounting firm whose opinion is sought by a board to contact the company's auditors and fully discuss the situation.

Standard Practices

A review of the current standards gives an insight into the range of work covered by the standard-setters. From 1970 to 1990 the Accounting Standards Committee issued 25 Statements of Standard Accounting Practice (SSAPs). Some of those standards are still in operation. They are:

SSAP 4   Accounting for Government Grants (1974 revised 1988)
SSAP 5   Accounting for Value added Tax (1974)
SSAP 9   Stocks and Work in Progress (1975 revised 1986)
SSAP 13   Accounting for Research and Development (1977 revised 1988)
SSAP 17   Accounting for Post Balance Sheet Events (1980)
SSAP 19   Accounting for Investment Properties (1981)
SSAP 20   Foreign Currency Translation (1983)
SSAP 21   Accounting for Leases (1984)
SSAP 25   Segmental Reporting (1989)

From 1991 to 2001 the ASB has issued 19 Financial Reporting Standards. They are :

FRS 1   Cash Flow Statements (1992)
FRS 2   Accounting for Subsidiary Undertakings (1992; states rules for
          consolidated accounts)
FRS 3   Reporting Financial Performance (1993; extension of the profit and loss
          account – The STRGL and figures for continuing and discontinued
          operations|)

FRS 4   Capital Instruments (1993; clarifies debt and equity to foil schemes which seek to issue debt without raising the gearing)

FRS 5   Reporting the Substance of Transactions (1994; rules to support substance over form and reduce off balance sheet finance)

FRS 6   Acquisitions and Mergers (1994; rules to distinguish between merger and acquisition. Merger accounting avoids the creation of goodwill.)

FRS 7   Fair Values in Acquisitions Accounting (1994; rules for the calculation of goodwill)

FRS 8   Related Party Disclosures (1995; rules to disclose transactions with related parties which have hitherto been hidden)

FRS 9   Associate Companies and Joint Ventures (1997; rules to consolidate non-subsidiary businesses – the equity method)

FRS 10   Goodwill and Intangible Assets (1997; purchased goodwill should be capitalized and amortized)

FRS 11   Impairment of Fixed Assets and Goodwill (1998; impairment reviews to find when the recoverable amount is less than book value)

FRS 12   Provisions, Contingent Liabilities and Contingent Assets (1998; rules for the establishment of provisions, made to frustrate 'big bath accounting')

FRS 13   Derivatives and Other Financial Instruments (1998; disclosure rules)

FRS 14   Earnings per Share (1998; calculation rules – conforms to International Accounting Standard 33)

FRS 15   Tangible Fixed Assets (1999 rules for measurement, value and depreciation)

FRS 16   Accounting for Current Taxation (2000)

FRS 17   Retirement Benefits

FRS 18   Accounting Policies

FRS 19   Deferred Taxation

There is a discussion paper – 'Leases: A New Approach' – now issued to stimulate discussion.

The UITF have issued 26 abstracts so far since 1991. For example, Abstract 11 shows how directors share options should be disclosed in the corporate report.

International Accounting Standards

Industry and commerce now takes place on an international scale, not only in terms of trade but with the existence of multinational groups and multinational lenders. There is not however one accounting language across the world as different countries have their own rules for treating certain transactions. Globalization means that large companies seek to raise capital in many countries, but to do this their shares must be traded on different local stock exchanges. National accounting standards with differing rules make it difficult to report to investors on an international scale, and the need to prepare extra accounts for cross-border listings is a costly deterrent.

Competition between exchanges, anxious to increase their share of international business, encourages national regulators to accept international standards. Some developing countries adopt international standards as a ready-made set of rules acceptable to multinational companies, who seek to avoid the cost of preparing accounts according to several different sets of rules.

The International Accounting Standards Committee (IASC) was formed in 1973 with the following objectives:

1. To formulate and publish accounting standards and to promote their worldwide acceptance and observance.

2. To work for the improvement and harmonization of regulations, standards and procedures.

Currently the IASC has a membership of 153 accounting bodies from 112 countries representing over 2 million accountants. There are now over forty international standards. Member bodies publish IASC standards in their own country and use their best endeavours to ensure compliance by persuading governments, securities markets, standard-setters and auditors that local published financial statements should comply with international standards. In the UK, the ASB incorporates the requirements of international accounting standards (IASs) into FRSs as far as possible and adds a paragraph to explain the relationships to an IAS. Harmonization is the keynote of the system, since IASs are not allowed to dominate accounting and overrule local standards. The IASC uses the discussion paper and exposure draft system, but a two-thirds majority of the board is required to grant status as a standard.

A new constitution for the IASC which is operative from 2001 will underline its independence and hopefully increase its funding. Membership of its committees will now be on the basis of technical competence rather than geographical representation. The credibility of international standards was greatly increased in 2000 when the International Organization of Securities Commissions (IOSCO), which represents stock exchanges throughout the world, endorsed IASs as a suitable basis for the accounts of companies whose shares are traded on those exchanges. This is a significant step towards a core set of rules which have international acceptance, providing comparability, transparency and full disclosure for corporate reports. To maintain their position the IASs must be rigorously interpreted and applied.

CONCLUSION

Standards are vital to underpin the confidence of investors in financial statements, so most developed countries have an accounting standard-setting system. Financial reporting operates on an international scale, so harmonization is vital for multinational businesses to enable them to raise capital in financial markets around the world, and appraise foreign businesses for takeover purposes.

Discussion Topics

Thirty-minute essay questions:

1. Explain the system of setting accounting standards which operates in the UK with reference to the components of that system.

2. Discuss the need for global harmonization of standard accounting practices.

CHAPTER 21

Accounting

A Theoretical Approach

THE AIMS OF THIS CHAPTER

To enable students to

- Understand the basic theoretical tenets which underpin accounting

- Explain the conflicting ideas of the relative importance of the balance sheet and profit and loss account

- Realize the interplay of capital, income and value

- Appreciate the interface of economics and accounting

INTRODUCTION

It is now clear to readers that financial reporting mainly serves equity investors and lenders, who are concerned with the economic evaluation of business performance and decision-making. If the balance sheet, the profit and loss account and the cash flow statement are to provide these users with useful information, measurement by current valuation and future prospects are more helpful than historical cost valuation and past results.

If matters which are material to economic decisions should be disclosed, problems arise for the accountant.

(a) **Recognition** problems – to ascertain what is meant by an asset, a liability, a revenue and an expense, and how to disclose the true economic substance of transactions; for example, to identify off balance sheet finance and the creation of a liability. FRSs have addressed these problems.

(b) **Measurement** problems – historical cost is now seen to have little relevance for a current balance sheet or profit and loss account. The capital maintenance theory holds that a profit can only be properly measured after charging the costs of maintaining the capital employed. This leaves the problem of measuring the capital employed and agreeing how to set aside an amount out of profit to maintain it. Thus impairment and provisions are significant.

THE RECOGNITION OF REVENUE

The measurement of income uses the accruals principle, by which the costs of a product are matched against the revenue from its sale. Care must be taken, to differentiate between, on the one hand, cash received during a period and that part of the cash which can be counted as revenue and, on the other hand, cash expenditure which is not always an expense of the period. The measurement of income depends on the point in a transaction at which profit can be considered as earned and taken to the profit and loss account. A good accountant will not wish to show a profit for a period unless certain that the profit has been earned, and that circumstances which may transpire in a later period will not reduce that profit. If a dividend is paid out of a profit which is later found to be illusory, the capital of the business will be depleted.

The earning of profit is a gradual process. A manufacturer will change raw materials into finished goods, then transport, store and sell them. At the point of sale an asset, stock, is exchanged for another asset, debt, the difference between the values of the two being the profit. The debt is eventually collected and thus the asset, stock, is translated into cash. The recognition of revenue concerns the definition of the point in the cycle at which profit will be recognized and considered to have been earned, and there is certainty that all costs concerning the transaction have been taken into account. Some accountants hold that the point in that cycle when the most critical decision has been made or the most difficult task completed is the point at which profit can be recognized, and this is usually taken to be the time of sale. At this point profit has been earned, since the revenue-earning activity is complete, and the profit can be measured objectively since it has undergone the test of the market.

The Certainty Theory

This theory holds that revenue can be recognised at the point beyond which there is no further uncertainty about the completion of the transaction. Three rules can be applied by the accountant to determine whether certainty exists.

(a) The revenue has been earned by a change in value.

(b) The revenue-earning activity has been accomplished.

(c) The transaction must be capable of objective measurement. This means that an external comparator must be used to verify the amounts concerned in a transaction, e.g. a sale made across the market.

Critical Event Concept

This theory holds that for every transaction there is a critical event in the cycle which acts as a decision point for the recognition of revenue from the transaction.

EXCEPTIONS TO THE GENERAL RULE

The first exception to the general rule concerns **long–term contracts**. In the civil engineering industry it could take five years or more to complete a job for a client. It is wrong to take all the profit on a five-year job at the end of the five-year period, since if in any one accounting year no jobs are completed then no profit will be shown that year; but in another year, when more than one job is completed, profits will be high. Thus fluctuations in profit will occur unless the profit is spread over the years of the contract. The price for the work is usually determined in advance, so once part of the contract is completed it is possible to take profit on that part. The quantity surveyors in the building industry will decide with the architects how much of the contract is completed, and the management will be given technical advice about what could go wrong on the contract before it is finalized, so that an estimate of profit to date can be made. If acceptance by the architect is considered to be the critical event, then the profit on work to date covered by an architect's certificate can be recognized.

A second exception concerns **accretion**, where the value of work in progress increases gradually through natural growth or an ageing process. Examples of this are timber, which gradually increases in value as it grows year by year, animals, for the same reason, and commodities such as brandy or whisky, which mature over a long period. It is possible to value the stocks of such items at the beginning and end of an accounting period and to gauge the increase in value achieved during the year. This increase is an income even though it has not arisen from transactions, and has yet to be realized. Such an income cannot be made available for distribution, but this does not mean that it cannot be recognized and communicated to shareholders.

A third exception concerns **sales made on instalment or hire purchase terms**. The sale is made at one point in time and the customer is obligated to pay for the goods over a period. Revenue could be recognized at the time of sale, but since customers are sometimes poor credit risks it is more conservative to spread the profit over the period of the instalments. In practice this is usually accomplished by the use of percentages, i.e. when 70% of the total price has been paid, then 70% of the profit to be made from the transaction can be credited to the profit and loss account.

A fourth exception is that in some cases revenue is recognized only when **cash is received** from a sale. This is an extension of the third exception, but occurs in slightly different conditions. If the customer has a poor credit rating, or if circumstances outside the control of the parties to the transaction can interfere with the payment of the price, the critical event for the transaction must be considered to be collection of the price. In this case it is conservative not to recognize the revenue until the price is paid.

In some transactions **payment is made before delivery of the goods**, but this is not a case for the recognition of revenue, since a successful delivery, and in some cases production of the goods, must take place before the transaction is completed. In this case it is not payment, but delivery, which is critical. An example of this case is **subscriptions to a monthly magazine**. Such subscriptions are usually purchased a year in advance and then the magazine is printed and delivered monthly throughout the period of the subscription.

THE BALANCE SHEET: A CRITICAL APPRAISAL

1. This statement has been criticized for many reasons, not least that it shows up the position of the company at one point in time, and this can be very different from the position only a few days earlier or later than the balance sheet date. The balance sheet is a type of photograph catching the image of the business for a fleeting moment only. Some photographs are not always truly representative of their subject matter. The term 'window dressing' is used to describe the action taken by a company to temporarily improve its balance sheet position near to the year end, with a view to showing a healthy balance sheet in the published accounts. SSAP 17 on post-balance-sheet events requires that adequate notes should explain significant events which have taken place soon after the balance sheet date, but which affect a proper understanding of the accounts, or reverse significant transactions undertaken during the year.

The balance sheet:
   (a) gives no information about the past or the future;
   (b) does not tell the reader how the business reached its present position;
   (c) provides little information from which a trend can be deduced unless comparison is made with the figures from previous years.

2. This historical record is not a statement of current worth of the assets, but many investors confuse the book value of the assets with their real or market value. Companies revalue their assets from time to time so that their balance sheets are updated to meet changes in the value of assets, but such valuations are expensive and liable to personal bias on the part of the valuer. The asset values shown in the balance sheet soon become outdated again, and the assets can represent values at different points in time all added together unless all the assets are revalued at the same time. The value of shares in a business depends upon the financial climate in the market and the potential which a likely buyer sees in the business. The figure for general reserve is an amalgam of accretions over the years when profits have been ploughed back at varying price levels.

3. Not all the 'assets' of a business are shown in the balance sheet. Intangible assets which cannot be quantified such as good labour relations, know-how, or a team of hard-working executives, are ignored, unless included in the figure for goodwill. Some liabilities are also excluded; for example, the rentals due in future years on a lease will be excluded since they are not outstanding at the balance sheet date, but if the business were to cease, the other party to the rental contract would expect the amounts due under the contract to be paid at the proper times. SSAP 21, on the financial accounting treatment of leases, is a cure for this situation, but this does not apply to 'operating leases'.

4. Accountants often disagree about matters of accounting policy for the treatment of items in the balance sheet. They may have opposing views about

   (a) the treatment of intangible assets – development costs treated as an asset;
   (b) the valuation of freehold property – the person and the valuation method;
   (c) the rate for plant depreciation – life and method;

(d) the method by which stocks of raw materials or finished goods are to be valued – *fifo/lifo*

(e) the valuation of unquoted investments owned by a business – will they recover their value soon?

(f) the provision for doubtful debts – judgement.

When such differences occur (usually between the auditor and the company accountant) they undermine the general public's confidence in the veracity of the position statement.

THE INCOME STATEMENT: A CRITICAL APPRAISAL

1. The income statement is criticized since it shows the profit or loss that has been made, but makes no mention of the risk taken to make that profit or the potential of the business in terms of what profit could or should have been made. Nor does it give any forecast for the future to assist those who have to decide on future policies. The idea of the accounting year could also be considered as a limitation of the income statement, since a year is hardly a long enough period over which to make a worthwhile comment about a capital project with a life of perhaps 10 or 15 years.

2. The profit calculation is affected by the accounting policies adopted and by the estimates made in its computation. Accountants using different bases could produce different profit figures for the same period for the same business. The rate and method of depreciation, the basis of stock valuation and the treatment of advertising or research and development expenditure are all matters where the judgement applied by the accountant can have an impact on the profit figure.

3. The application of the principle of prudence leads to further differences. There are often sharp disagreements as to the amount of a provision to meet hazards which are expected to affect the business in the future.

PROFIT VERSUS POSITION: A CHANGE OF EMPHASIS

In recent years a dynamic view of accounting has moved the published profit and loss account into a more central position of attention than the balance sheet. The shortcomings of the balance sheet, where fixed assets, long-term liabilities and share capital are shown at historical monetary values, stocks and work in progress may be valued on a number of bases, and the reserves are a combination of accretions over a number of years at varying price levels, reduce its utility. The concept of conservatism only accentuates these shortcomings, while in an economic climate of inflation investors will pay more attention to the profit and loss account, since this shows performance from which a price/earnings ratio can be computed. Profit is the motivating force of business, and therefore the profit and loss account can be expected to assume major importance for those who have risked their funds and are seeking a return. While the balance sheet is a 'snapshot' of the financial position at one point in time, the profit and loss account summarizes the figures for a whole period and is a better vehicle for the extrapolation of trends. The appropriation section reveals the policy of management so far as the payment of dividend and the retention of profits in the business is concerned.

These two statements should be considered together with a cash flow statement to properly interpret what has happened in the business during the accounting year. The market value and book value of a company are very different, so what is shown in the balance sheet is of secondary importance to investors, but if the value of a business is computed as the present value of future profits, then a statement which reveals current profits will be of some interest. Recent accounting standards have done much to restore the credibility of the balance sheet, to reduce the opportunities for off balance sheet finance and install a system of measuring the impairment of fixed assets and goodwill.

REPORTING FINANCIAL PERFORMANCE: FRS 3

Investors concentrate their attention on the bottom line of the profit and loss account, to see the dividend or the earnings per share This means that investors may miss many of the items of significance in the computation of the profit figure before the bottom line is reached. It is now recognized (FRS 3) that losses made when parts of the business are sold, reorganized or cease production are normal rather than abnormal. The rules show a 'layered' approach to the profit and loss account. The income from normal continuing operations, acquisitions during the year and discontinued operations is separately disclosed so that investors can see the effects on profit of such changes.

FRS 3 also specifies a statement of total recognized gains and losses. Thus, unrealized gains and losses which would normally be taken directly to reserves, avoiding the profit and loss account (or perhaps not recognized at all), are now disclosed clearly for shareholders to see. It is necessary to consider all gains and losses recognized in a period when assessing the financial performance of a company. Such unrealized gains and losses will have an effect on the reserves or the shareholders' funds. This standard practice automatically assumes that the accounts will show up-to-date values for the assets of the business and it also recognizes that there may be a need to reconcile the profit figure disclosed to a truly historical cost profit on ordinary activities before tax.

THE POSITION STATEMENT VERSUS THE INCOME STATEMENT: AN ACADEMIC VIEW

The Sheet of Balances

Some academics see the balance sheet as merely a sheet of balances left in the books after the measurement of income has taken place. For them accounting theory stems from the income statement, with the accruals or matching principle as the most important part of the entire system. They reject the economist's view of income as the increase in the owner's interest during a period, preferring to match cost against revenue in the profit and loss account to show a profit on a *transactions* basis. These accountants seek to divide the flow of costs by channelling some of them into a pool to be deferred and used up in a future period (assets), while the balance of the flow is channelled into the income statement. According to this theory the balance sheet is created as a by-product of the matching process, and the assets shown therein are merely items which are not yet required as costs in the income statement. The opponents of the 'sheet-of-balances' view hold that income is best measured as a change in value during a period, and that the accruals principle leads to nothing more than a set of estimates made in an attempt to match costs with revenue. Such estimates, they say, are value judgements, depending on individual preference and bias, and cannot be part of a consistent theory. Matching to them is not a principle but a system which is adopted because it works. Its success depends upon the ability of the accountants who operate it, so rules such as conservatism have had to be made as parameters within which the accountant is able to exercise judgement.

The Statement of Financial Position

An alternative view considers the balance sheet to be more important than the profit and loss account. The balance sheet shows the assets and liabilities of the business. An asset can be defined as an item owned by the business from which future economic benefits or rights will be derived. Its value depends on what those benefits are currently considered to be worth. Liabilities are defined as obligations to convey assets or perform services at a future time. Liabilities, it is said, arise from past transactions which have to be settled at some future date. This concept of assets and liabilities goes much further than the view of them as merely balances remaining in the books. The net assets of the business can be equated to the owner's equity, and when during a period the net assets increase, the consequent change in owner's equity is seen as the income of the business. Thus the measurement of income, it is argued, is dependent upon the measurement of the value of assets and liabilities. Transactions therefore should be analysed in terms of their effect on the assets, the liabilities and the owner's equity of the business, so the revenue account is needed only as an analysis of the sources from which income is received.

The balance sheet as a vehicle for the interpretation of the financial position is far more important than a mere dumping-ground for surplus balances remaining in the books at the year end. The revenue account is a summary of only one class of transactions – revenue and cost. The true measurement of income thus depends on the measurement of assets, and it follows that the concept of income is dependent upon the concept of assets and liabilities as shown in the position statement. The counter-argument is that the balance sheet is a summary of stocks or residual items left after the measurement of income has taken place. This argument is supported by the belief that the value of an asset depends on the future income it can provide and that current earnings are the best guide to this future income. Thus it is argued that the concept of assets is dependent upon income, and the position statement is therefore of secondary importance to the income statement.

A balance sheet which shows assets at contemporary values, when combined with a profit and loss account which shows how those values have increased during the course of the year, and set alongside a cash flow statement, will be of the greatest assistance to users of the financial statements of business.

CAPITAL, INCOME AND VALUE

These items have different meanings for accountants and economists.

Capital: changing ideas

1. To an investor, capital is the amount of wealth committed to a certain economic project and from which an income is expected to flow. The investor has given up control over the use of funds and sees profit as the return for risk, and use forgone. This is the 'stock and flow' concept, with capital as the stock and income flowing from it.

2. The accountant sees capital as the amount invested in an enterprise by its legal owners (share capital plus reserves saved up out of profits), or lent to the firm over a long period (debentures). This concept of capital is derived from the assets owned by providers of finance to whom reports are made. Assets are recorded on the basis of the transaction undertaken to own them, i.e. historical cost or book value. Capital, then, is the book value net of liabilities of those debit balances left on the books after the income measurement exercise has taken place. It represents payments not matched as expenses against revenue, but left over after the profit figure is struck. All assets become expenses when they are used up by the business.

3. In economics, capital is considered to be the present value of future earnings derived from an asset or the enterprise as a whole, so capital and income are again linked together. An economist might prefer a broader definition of capital employed, and might suggest that some assets, such as human resources, are omitted by accountants because they cannot be quantified and recorded in the books. The accountant measures capital with reference to more tangible assets whose existence, ownership and costs can be verified. To the economist capital is an expression of the potential future earning power of the enterprise, and is measured in order to derive income from the change in capital between two points in time. If the capital value of the business has increased during the year this is an income, and should be included when profit is measured.

4. Accountants are drawing closer to the position of economists so far as assets are concerned. It is more important to account for the substance of a transaction than for its legal form, and an improved definition of what is an asset or a liability has generated clear thinking on the commercial reality of a transaction. An asset is a probable future benefit controlled by and accruing to a particular company as a result of past transactions or events. This idea is a significant departure from traditional accounting beliefs. It assumes that when a machine is shown in the balance sheet, as an asset, it is not the physical item which justifies its presence there, but rather the fact that economic benefits are expected to be derived from the physical item. It is the present value of future expected income flows which supports the machine as an asset of the business. Many users of accounting statements would prefer a predictive valuation derived from future expectations, but such a valuation based on estimate would be unreliable and difficult to audit. Management accountants are not inhibited by these supposed disadvantages.

Income

The concept of income is a significant point of difference between the accountant and the economist. Accountants measure income and try to ensure that their measurements are as accurate as possible. All relevant transactions must be included, at values which reflect the current market. Income is seen as a determinant of company dividend policy, since the rights of creditors might be prejudiced if a dividend was paid when losses had been made. Accounting income is a surplus derived from business activity and is measured by the use of the matching principle, when cost is set against revenue for a given time period. This is an 'ex-post' measurement, since it is made from objectively recorded amounts after the event has taken place.

Economists and accountants see profits as a guide to future investment in a business, using the past to assess future prospects. The best investment, of course, is the one which leads to the greatest future benefits, and these can be discounted and measured at their present value using the cost of capital as the discount factor. Thus capital investment is orientated towards the improvement of the present value of future receipts from the investments made by the company. From this premise it is only a short step for the economists to regard income as growth in the present value of future receipts, or the capital value of the business.

The Hicksian Concept of Income

Sir John Hicks defined income as the maximum amount an individual could consume during a period while remaining as well off at the end of the period as at the beginning. This idea depends upon the definition of the term 'well off', which can mean possession of capital, or wealth. Income, therefore, is the amount by which capital or net worth has increased during a period plus what has been withdrawn for consumption, less new capital that has been introduced into the business. For the economist, then, the net worth of the business is the capital value of expected future receipts, and any increase in the present value of those future receipts will be a profit. This valuation-based idea is very different from the accountant's view of net assets, which is the unexpired portion of the capital cost, stemming from recorded transactions.

Economists believe the accountants' definition of income is of little use as a measure of business success, because it ignores value changes, other than to write off depreciation and adjust stock values downward if required. Unrealized profits are ignored by accountants unless there is a certainty of their permanence, since it would not be conservative to distribute them. The accountant, however, might ask the economist:

(a) how to compute a profit figure from the concept of present value;

(b) how far into the future receipts are to be forecast;

(c) how accurate such a forecast should be;

(d) the criterion for the selection of the discount factor on which the present value calculation is based.

Nevertheless the STRGL accounts for some non-traditional items.

The Hicksian concept of income can be linked to the idea of maintaining the capital invested in the enterprise. If income is defined as the maximum amount that can be consumed in a period without a reduction in the expected level of consumption in the next period, it follows that the capital of the business must be maintained. Thus depreciation is a common factor in the definition of income by both accountant and economist.

The two views can be reconciled by formulae. If Y_e is economic income, C is consumption and S is savings

$$Y_e = C + S$$

This formula can be expressed as

$$Y_e = C + (K_N - K_{N-1})$$

K is the notation for capital, and N stands for time, i.e. now. K_{N-1} will therefore represent capital a year ago. Income is what has been consumed plus the increase in wealth during the year. Accounting income can be expressed in the same way:

$$Y_a = D + (R_N - R_{N-1})$$

In this expression D stands for dividend paid and R stands for reserves. Thus income equals the dividend paid out and the increase in reserves (profit ploughed back) during the year. The influence of the Hicksian concept is that the true growth in reserves can only be measured after an amount has been set aside out of profit to maintain the capital of the business. Thus the principle of capital maintenance (as well off at the end of the year as at the beginning) acts in part to reconcile the views of accountants and economists on income measurement. Depreciation is one method which accountants use to maintain the capital of the business.

Value

When a value is attributed to an asset, the asset is appraised and ranked in order of preference against other items which have greater or lesser values. These preferences are expressed in money terms, so value allows us to measure an asset against others in terms of the amount of purchasing power we must sacrifice to possess the valued item. Money shows what must be paid to exercise economic choice and to show a preference for one item over another, since money spent cannot be used to purchase alternatives which are competing for scarce purchasing power.

The accountant records the value laid out to purchase an asset, i.e. historical cost. Current market value is used if it is lower than historical cost for reasons of conservatism (the 'lower of cost or market value' rule for stocks). If a permanent increase in value above historical cost is established (a building revalued), this will be recognized and recorded in the books. Many accountants do not trust value, since it implies a subjective judgement or estimate which may be influenced by bias on the part of the valuer and may not be permanent. It should be remembered, however, that accountants themselves make subjective judgements when providing for doubtful debts or accrued expenses and when fixing a rate of depreciation.

The capital value of an asset is the present value of the future income stream expected to be derived from the asset. The price of the asset is the value set on it in the marketplace by the interaction of supply and demand. This is an exchange value for the asset whereby its worth is expressed in money, so that when the price is compared with the price of other assets its worth can be measured. The economic value computed for an asset simply reflects the expectations of the directors and sets the maximum price they would be willing to pay for it on the market. Therefore individuals with different expectations of the potential of an asset to produce income would value it at different amounts.

An asset may have different values according to the purpose for which the valuation is made. For example, the following are different ways of valuing a ship – say an oil tanker:

(a) Scrap value, i.e. what it is worth at break-up value. This reflects the intrinsic value of its parts less the cost of dismantling them.

(b) Going-concern value, i.e. what it is worth to the shipping company that owns it. The company intends to operate it together with other ships in its fleet and other assets which it possesses (docks, know-how, etc.). This value approaches economic value, as it may be an estimate of the present value of the expected income stream.

(c) Historical cost. This is an input value – what was spent when the asset was acquired. This value is soon outdated and does not represent earning potential.

(d) Book value, i.e. the asset as recorded in the books. Usually this is historical cost less depreciation to date, the unexpired portion of the capital cost. The depreciation profile adopted by the enterprise may not reflect the real fall in value from use and/or the passage of time.

(e) Net realizable value or market value. This is an exit value, since it represents what another shipowner would be willing to pay for the tanker as part of a fleet. It is impractical, however, to put assets up for sale simply to value them. The market price of specialized assets with a narrow market will not be easy to establish. The difference between this value and (b) above is the difference in the expectation of future income between its present owner and the potential buyer, and the cost of transaction. Supply and demand will affect this value. Net realizable value represents the view taken by the market as a whole, but replacement value concerns only the view of an asset by an individual business.

(f) Replacement value, i.e. the cost of another tanker to do the same job – an entry value. It will be difficult to establish price for an exactly similar asset, and also to appraise the amount to be deducted for years of expired service since the tanker is not new.

(g) Opportunity cost. This is a value based on the returns expected from the asset in its next best alternative use, for example as a floating oil reservoir by an oil rig in offshore production.

CONCLUSION

Accounting principles are a set of ideas, accepted by accountants because they work well in practice. Theory attempts to substantiate principles by suggesting reasons why they work so well. With so many alternative views there is ample scope to choose, but informed choice based on comprehension is most likely to be successful. The measurement of income, the definition of assets and liabilities, the idea of capital maintenance and the Hicksian concept give the accountant useful tools which can be used to solve practical problems.

Discussion Topics

Thirty-minute essay questions:

1. What conditions should exist for the recognition of revenue and what exceptions are there to the basic rule.

2. Some accountants see the balance sheet as just a sheet of balances and therefore of secondary importance to the profit and loss account. Others seeks to discredit the accruals principle arguing that a theory of assets and liabilities gives weight to the balance sheet. Explain.

3. Explain the Hicksian concept of income.

Appendix A

Drafting Accounts from a Trial Balance with Adjustments

This project is similar to one used by a large construction company to help accounting trainees. Take your time to work through the adjustments

The **Able Construction** division, a division of Megacorp plc, currently has *one* contract with a client, the health board, for the construction of a new hospital wing. The contract value is £5m including gross profit of £350k. Work began in September 2003 and is forecasted to be completed in September 2004. (The abbreviation 'k' stands for 1000.)

At 31 March 2004, the following trial balance was extracted from the division's nominal ledger.

Nominal ledger account	Debit £(000)	Credit £(000)
Sales: work certified complete		2 500
Materials	635	
Subcontractors	1 000	
Labour	500	
Plant hires	85	
Site overheads (GEs)	150	
Staff costs	50	
Rent and rates	40	
Repairs	5	
Bad debts – written off	5	
Bad debts – provisions	10	
Bank interest received	–	50
* Fixed assets – land and buildings	50	
* Fixed assets – plant	20	
Trade debtors	500	
		10
Trade creditors		190
Cash and bank	200	
Previous periods profit/loss		300
** AB plc loan account		200
Totals	3 250	3 250

* Land and buildings and Plant are shown in the trial balance net of depreciation charged to 1 April 2003.
** Head office funds advanced to the division as capital.

The following items have been identified by the assistant divisional accountant:

1. Repairs to replace a security gate in an existing store at a value of £10k has been incorrectly capitalised in Land and buildings.

2. One year's depreciation charge has to be made on the straight line basis on:

    2.1. Land and buildings – cost £100k – over 10 years;

    2.2. Plant – cost £25k – over 5 years.

3. A review of the ageing debtors list showed that:

    3.1. A two-year-old trade debt amounting to £20k has to be written off.

    3.2. Included in debtors was a retention by a customer amounting to £5k that is now doubtful – the debtor is in the receiver's hands and a provision is required.

4. A materials received reconciliation has been carried out on one creditor balance that is over three years old, and the supplier has confirmed that it no longer expects payment. The divisional accountant has instructed that the £40k creditor balance should be written back against materials.

5. A difference of £25k existed on the creditor control account reconciliation between the control account and the list of balances. The difference relates to cash received in respect of debtors   that has been incorrectly posted to creditors.

6. Two adjustments are required resulting from differences noted in the bank reconciliation:

    6.1. Bank interest received at a value of £45k had not been entered in the cash book.

    6.2. A cheque to a subcontractor amounting to £10k has not been cashed – it is over 6 months old and has to be cancelled and written back.

7. Rent and rates include an invoice of value £30k for the period from January to June 2004.

8. The following cost accruals were received from site:

    8.1. Value of delivery tickets (materials) with no invoices/lists – £5k;

    8.2. Subcontractor commitments – £10k;

    8.3. Plant hire – £15k.

9. The site manager has informed the assistant accountant that sales include an item of £100k that has to be deducted from sales and included as a separate creditor called Contingencies.

10. At a management meeting the forecast to completion had been reviewed. It was found that expected buying advantages are not being achieved and that there was a contingency required for unexpected delays. This has resulted in additional costs

forecasted at completion of £250k. Gross profit to 31 March 2005 therefore requires to be adjusted to reflect the forecasted break-even position at completion. A £50k reduction in sales is to be reported in the balance sheet as a provision for losses creditor at 31 March 2004.

Required:

Complete the outstanding information on the following pro-forma schedules for

(a) the journal entries resulting from the above adjustments

(b) the profit and loss account and balance sheet to 31 March 2004 for the division

(c) the notes to the accounts which support key figures.

An extended trial balance is provided as a clue to the solution.

Journal Entries Pro Forma

Jrnl No.	Nominal ledger account and description	£(000)	£(000)
1	Office repairs Fixed assets – Land and buildings Being: repairs incorrectly charged to Land and buildings		
2	Depreciation 2.1. Fixed assets – Land and buildings 2.2. Fixed assets – Plant Being: one year's straight line depreciation charge		
3.1	Bad debts – written off Trade debtors Being: bad debt write off		
3.2	Bad debts – provisions (P&L) Bad debts debtor provision Being: bad debt provision due to receivership		
4	Trade creditors Materials Being: write-back of creditor balance no longer due		
5	Trade creditors Trade debtors Being: Correction of debtor cash incorrectly posted to creditors		
6.1	Cash and bank Bank interest received Being: bank interest charge omitted from the bank overdraft		

6.2	Bank overdraft Subcontractors Being: out-of-date cheque written back to subcontractors		
7	Prepayments Rent and rates Being: prepaid rent and rates at 31 March 2004		
8	8.1. Materials 8.2. Subcontractors 8.3. Plant Accruals Being: site accruals at 31 March 2004		
9	Sales Creditors – contingencies Being: front loaded rates/measure		
10	Sales Creditors – provision for losses Being: adjustment to reflect nil margin at forecast to complete		

Profit and Loss Account

For the period ended 31 March 2004	Notes	£(000)	£(000)
Sales			
Direct costs:			
Materials			
Subcontractors			
Labour			
Plant			
Site overheads		_____	
Gross margin		_____	
Overheads			
Staff costs			
Rent and rates			
Depreciation			
Repairs			
Bad debts		_____	
Operating loss		_____	
Bank interest			
Pre-tax loss		_____	

Balance Sheet

As at 31 March 2004	Notes	£(000)	£(000)
Fixed assets:			
Land and buildings			
Plant			_____
Current assets			
Debtors			
Less creditors		═══════	═══════
Capital employed			
Net debt:			═══════
Cash and bank			
Previous period profit/loss			
Current period profit/loss			
AB plc loan account			
Capital employed			_____
			═══════

Notes to the Accounts

1. Fixed assets

At 31 March 2004	Land and buildings £(000)	Plant £(000)	Tool £(000)
Cost:			
Beginning of period			
Item not capitalized			
End of period			
Accumulated depreciation:			
Beginning of period			
Period charge			
End of period			
Net book value:			
Beginning of period			
End of period			

2. Debtors

    At 31 March 2004   £

    Trade debtors

    Bad debt debtor provision

    Prepayments

3. Creditors

    At 31 March 2004   £

    Trade creditors

    Overmeasure

    Loss provision

    Accruals

4. Bad debts

    At 31 March 2004   £

    Bad debts – written off

    Bad debts – provision

Extended Trial Balance

£	Trial Balance	
	Dr £	Cr £
Sales		2 500
Materials	635	
Subcontractors	1 000	
Labour	500	
Plant hire	85	
Site overheads	150	
Staff costs	50	
Rent and rates	40	
Depreciation	-	
Repairs	5	
Bad debts – written off	5	
Bad debts – provisions	10	
Bank interest received		50
Fixed assets – Land and buildings	50	
Fixed assets – Plant	20	
Trade debtors	500	
Bad debt debtor provision		10
Prepayments		
Trade creditors		190
Creditors – contingencies		
Creditors – loss provision		
Accruals		
Cash and bank	200	
Previous period profit/loss		300
Current Period profit/loss		
AB plc loan account		200
Totals	**3 250**	**3 250**

	Journal Entries		Profit and Loss Account		Balance Sheet	
Journal Ref	Dr	Cr	Dr	Cr	Dr	Cr
	£	£	£	£	£	£
9, 10	100 + 50			2 350		
8, 4	5	40	600			
8, 6, 2	10	10	1 000			
			500			
8	15		100			
			150			
			50			
7		15	25			
2	15		15			
1	10		15			
3.1	20		25			
3.2	5		15			
6.1		45		95		
1, 2.1		10 + 10			30	
2.2		5			15	
3.1, 5		20 + 25			455	
3.2		5				15
7	15				15	
4, 5	40 + 25					125
9		100				100
10		50				50
8		30				30
6.2, 6.1	10 + 45				255	
						300
				50	50	
						200
	365	365	2495	2495	820	820

Appendix B

A Practice Examination Paper with Solutions

This is an examination paper set at a level appropriate to first-year undergraduates specializing in accounting. The questions are slightly above the level of the first professional paper set by CIMA, the Certified Accountants and AAT. There are eight 25-mark questions, so you need to choose four for a three-hour test.

Examination practice is crucial for success. Students must learn to assimilate the requirements of the questions quickly and thus plan their approach to a paper by selecting the questions they intend to answer. Timing is also important to the plan.

100 marks to be earned in 180 minutes equals 1.8 minutes for each mark, so a 25-mark question should take 45 minutes. Remember this is 45 minutes of very hard work. There is no time to stray from the point as no marks are available for non-relevant information in solutions.

If you do not have a three-hour slot available, practice on the questions at 45 minutes each. Solutions are printed after the paper, so that you can assess your progress.

The rubric of the examination paper is:

Time allowed – 3 hours

Answer four questions

All questions carry equal marks

QUESTIONS

Question 1

Willoughby Woollen Mills Ltd is a medium-sized business in the knitwear trade. The company belongs to a trade association which operates an inter-firm comparison scheme. The most recent report from the trade association contains the following table from companies which are comparable in size to Willoughby Woollen Mills.

Ratio analysis	Average for participants
Return on total capital employed	24%
Sales to total capital employed	2.3 times
Gross profit percentage	20%
Current ratio	1.7:1
Stock turnover	32 days
Debtors turnover	30 days
Fixed assets to current assets	1.5:1

The latest accounts of Willoughby Woollen Mills are as follows:

Profit and Loss Account			£000s
Sales			3 970
Cost of goods sold			(3 120)
Gross profit			850
Selling and distribution cost			(170)
Administrative expenses			(120)
Financial charges			(60)
Net profit			£500
Balance Sheet			
Fixed assets			2 500
Current assets	– Stock	510	
	– Debtors	552	
	– Cash	20	
Current liabilities	– Creditors	(640)	
Working capital			442
Long-term liabilities			(1 250)
Net assets			£1 692
Share capital and reserves			£1 692

Required:

Calculate the ratios for Willoughby Woollen Mills and compare the business with the average for the inter-firm comparison scheme. Suggest action to the Willoughby managers.

(25 marks)

Question 2

(a) You are to attend a management meeting in the near future which will discuss the treatment of depreciation in the company's accounts. The newly appointed managing director, who is an engineer, does not appreciate the need for depreciation. At a previous meeting he has said "Why should we depreciate if at the same time we spend money to maintain the efficiency of our machinery. The money has already been spent to buy the machine, and we can save up later to buy a replacement."

Draft some notes for submission to the managing director to explain the rationale of depreciation and the relationship of depreciation to the replacement of fixed assets.

(10 marks)

(b) Your company purchased a machine in 1995 for £200,000, expecting it to have a scrap value of £40,000 at the end of its projected eight-year working life, in the year 2003. In 1997 the machine was overhauled at a cost of £20,000, and a new fitting which cost £30,000 was added to it. This fitting was expected to increase the range of operations which the machine could undertake. In 2001 the machine was revalued at £130,000, and it was then expected to work until the year 2008, when it would have a scrap value of £30,000. In 2004 the machine is declared to be obsolete, and sold for £20,000.

Required:

Calculate and explain the depreciation charge for each year of the life of this machine.

(15 marks)

Question 3

Horace Ltd sells to a range of customers and the managing director, fearful that not all debtors will pay, has decided to make a provision for doubtful debts of 2% of existing debtors at the year end. The balance sheet date is 31 December and outstanding debtor balances at 31 December 2001 were £1,860,000.

Credit sales in 2002 were £10,000,000 and cash from debtors £9,757,700

Credit sales in 2003 were £12,000,000 and cash from debtors £10,278,100

Credit sales in 2004 were £13,000,000 and cash from debtors £12,772,000

Bad debts incurred in the years to 31 December are:

    2001   £34,500

    2002   £37,800

2003   £41,900

2004   £38,000

The MD decided to reduce the provision to 1% of debtors at the end of 2003 since he believes the provision has been overestimated.

Required:

(a) Write up appropriate ledger accounts to record these transactions.

(13 marks)

(b) Calculate the amount charged to profit and loss account each year for bad and doubtful debts.

(6 marks)

(c) Explain how the provision for doubtful debts contributes towards the true and fair view of the financial statements, and comment on the trend in debtors at Horace Ltd.

(6 marks)

Question 4

Control Equipment Ltd operates a debtors ledger control account. On 1 November the debtors balances totalled £16,048 and £114 on the credit side. The creditors ledger control account on the same day showed a balance of £12,470 and a debit balance of £210. The balance of £114 occurred when a customer returned goods for which payment had already been made. The balance of £210 concerned an overpayment to a supplier.

Balances from the books for the month of November were

	£
Sales	127 456
Purchases	79 948
Cash from debtors	110 424
Cash to creditors	74 614
Discounts received	2 950
Discounts allowed	4 656
Returns inwards	2 004
Returns outwards	1 070
Bad debts written off	652
Cash received in respect of debit balance in creditors ledger	210
Balance in debtors ledger settled by contra against creditors ledger	868
Cash received for debt previously written off as bad	188
Allowances to customers for damages in transit	424

Required:

    (a) Write up for the month of November:
        (i)   Debtors ledger control account
        (ii)   Creditors ledger control account

(19 marks)

    (b) Explain the advantages of using control accounts.

(6 marks)

Question 5

The Dalby Dairy Ltd owns and operates a factory making speciality cheeses in the Vale of Belvoir. Your employer is considering an investment of £1.5 million in this business by the purchase of 500,000 new ordinary shares of £1 each at a price of £3 each.
    The most recent financial statements of the business are as follows:

Balance Sheet	£000	£000	£000
Fixed Assets	*Cost*	*Depreciation*	*Net*
Factory buildings	3 800	–	3 800
Plant and machinery	2 964	1 430	1 534
Vehicles	420	280	140
	7 184	1 710	5 474
Current Assets			
Stock		1 150	
Debtors		3 641	
Cash		280	
		5 071	
Current Liabilities			
Creditors	1 086		
Overdraft	3 418		
Tax	420		
Dividend	340		
		5 264	
Working capital			(193)
			5 281
Long-term loans (repayable in two years secured on the factory)			(3 000)
Net assets			£2 281
Share capital – ordinary shares of £1			2 000
Revaluation reserves			240
Retained profit			41
			£2 281

Profit and Loss Account for Year Ending 31 December

			£000s	£000s
Sales (all on credit terms)				11 230
Costs				(9 219)
Operating Profit				2 011
Less interest	– long-term loan	510		
	– Overdraft	600		(1 110)
Net profit before tax				901
Tax				(420)
Net profit after tax				481
Dividend				(340)
Retained profit for the year				£141

The most recent share price in the somewhat limited market for this company's shares is 288 pence each.

The factory buildings were revalued last year.

Required:

(a) Comment on the capital structure of the Dalby Dairy Ltd.

(19 marks)

(b) Relate your comment to the investment which your employer is now considering.

(6 marks)

Question 6

Saltby Ltd is a medium-sized manufacturing business. The most recent accounting statements in £000s are as follows:

Balance Sheet as at 31 December

			Last Year		This Year
Fixed assets	– Plant		47 000		59 000
	– Joint venture		—		25 000
	– Trade investment		20 000		—
			67 000		84 000
Current assets	– Stock	9 642		10 129	
	– Debtors	4 738		9 607	
	– Deposit account	5 000		—	
	– Cash	550		—	
		19 930		19 736	

Current liabilities	– Creditors	(5 704)		(6 229)
	– Tax	(1 108)		(2 619)
	– Dividend	(726)		(931)
	– Overdraft	–		(2 460)
Working capital			12 392	7 497
			79 392	91 497
Long-term loans – Debentures at 12%			(14 000)	(25 000)
Net assets			£65 392	£66 497
Share capital			60 000	60 000
Reserves			5 392	6 497
			£65 392	£66 497

Profit and Loss Account for the Year to 31 December This Year   £000s

Operating profit	18 581
Profit on sale of plant	3 000
Loss on sale of investment	(15 000)
Interest	(1 926)
Tax	(2 619)
Dividend	(931)
Retained profit	£1 105

Note 1: Fixed assets

	Cost	£000 Depreciation	Net
Balance 31.12. last year	68 000	21 000	47 000
Acquisitions	20 000	–	20 000
Disposals	(15 000)	(10 000)	(5 000)
Depreciation for the year	–	3 000	(3 000)
Balance at 31.12. this year	73 000	14 000	59 000

Note 2: Investments

During the year the trade investment was sold at a loss of £15 million. An interest in a joint venture was purchased for £25 million.

Required:

(a) Draft a cash flow statement for the year to 31 December this year.

(19 marks)

(b) Interpret the situation disclosed by your statement.

(6 marks)

Question 7

(a) Explain the importance of cash in a business.

(10 marks)

(b) **Blundell Construction Ltd** has the following entries in its cash book for the month of November.

Blundell Ltd – Cash Book £000s

Nov 1	Balance b/d	548	1	Wages and salaries	6 292
6	A B plc	6 886	1	Petty cash	110
6	C D plc	2 292	8	Wages	6 212
10	E F plc	1 276	8	Petty cash	78
10	G H plc	1 024	15	Wages	6 058
10	I J plc	8 348	15	Petty cash	156
14	K L plc	2 852	21	B C Ltd	1 858
14	M N plc	1 774	21	D E Ltd	268
21	O P plc	2 404	21	F G plc	154
25	Q R plc	5 750	21	H I Ltd	526
25	S T plc	1 964	22	J K Ltd	3 564
28	U V plc	2 006	22	L M Partnership	460
28	W X plc	1 444	26	Wages	6 434
28	Y Z plc	4 922	26	Petty cash	182
30	Balance c/d	28	26	N P plc	52
			26	P Q Ltd	1 736
			26	R S plc	214
			29	T U Ltd	1 332
			29	V W plc	224
			29	Wages	6 382
			29	Petty cash	104
			30	X Y Ltd	1 122
		<u>43 518</u>			<u>43 518</u>
				Balance b/d	28

Croesus Bank plc Statement of Account with Blundell Construction Ltd

Nov		Payments	Receipts	Balance
	Balance			2 270 Cr
1	Cheque	110		
1	``	6 292		
1	``	842		4 974 Dr
2	``	146		
2	``	310		5 430 Dr
6	``	424		5 854 Dr
9	Lodgements		9 178	
9	Cheque	6 212		
9	``	78		2 966 Dr
12	Lodgement		10 648	7 682 Cr
16	``		4 626	
16	Cheque	156		
16	``	6 058		6 094 Cr
23	Lodgement		2 404	8 498 Cr
26	Cheque	6 434		
26	``	182		
26	``	3 564		
26	``	268		
26	``	1 858		
26	Lodgement		7 714	3 906 Cr
27	Cheque	460		
27	``	526		
27	``	154		2 766 Cr
29	Lodgement		8 372	
29	Cheque	104		
29	``	6 382		
29	``	52		4 600 Cr
30	Dividend on Investment		5 456	
30	Cheque	1 332		
30	Bank Charges	1 872		6 852 Cr

Required:

Using the bank statement

(i) Reconcile the Cash Book to the Bank Statement at the beginning of November

(ii)   Complete the cash book for November

(iii) Reconcile the Cash Book to the Bank Statement at the end of November

(15 marks)

Question 8

Your friend has inherited a significant amount from an aunt's will and is considering making an investment in **Redmile Racers Ltd**, a business which manufactures go-karts for enthusiasts. He is concerned about the working capital situation of Redmile Racers Ltd.

Required:

(a) Explain the significance of working capital for the effective financial management of a business.

(15 marks)

(b) Comment on the working capital position of Redmile Racers Ltd, using the financial information set out below.

Current assets	Stock	Materials	5 186 370
		Work in Progress	12 273 415
	Debtors		12 845 620
	Cash		350 211
			£30 655 616
Current liabilities	Trade Creditors		2 283 749
	Tax		893 278
	Dividend Payable		520 000
	Overdraft		12 560 421
			£16 257 448

These figures are extracted from the most recent balance sheet. Turnover for the year to the balance sheet date was £32 million with a gross profit rate of 14%, so cost of sales was £27,520,000. All sales were on credit terms.

Material purchases on credit terms were £20,815,683.

(13 marks)

SOLUTIONS

Solution 1

Ratios	Willoughby	IFC
Return on total capital 500 / 3,582	14%	24%
Sales to total capital (3 970 ÷ 3 582)	1.11 times	2.3 times
Gross profit (850 / 3 970 × 100)	21.4%	20%
Current ratio (1 082 ÷ 640)	1.69:1	1.7:1
Stock turnover (510 / 3 120 × 365)	60 days	32 days
Debtors turnover (552 / 3 970 × 365)	51 days	30 days
Fixed assets to current asserts (2 500:1 082)	2.3:1	1.5:1

Willoughby is not as profitable as the average, being 10% behind. Even when financial charges are added back to profit (560 / 3,582 = 15.6) the position is not improved very much. Willoughby has a gross profit rate above average, so its poor ROCE must be caused by idle capacity. The sales to total capital ratio shows assets not working very hard.

Stock is held twice as long as the average. Debtors are given three weeks longer to pay, and despite this the fixed assets to current assets ratio suggests over-investment in fixed assets. Stock control, debtor control and a review of fixed assets is needed.

The current ratio is the same as the IFC, but this fails to disclose a seriously illiquid situation. The acid test ratio (572 : 640) is .89:1, and only £20,000 of cash is available. Managers must reduce stock, collect debts and sell idle fixed assets to avoid insolvency.

N.B. Total capital is 2,500 + 510 + 552 + 20 = 3,582.

Solution 2

(a) Your solution should include

- Definition of depreciation – capital expenditure versus revenue expenditure
- Allocation and profit measurement
- Capital maintenance and replacement

(b)

		£	
1995 Machine purchased for		200 000	
Depreciation ((200 – 40) ÷ 8)	1995	(20 000)	
	1996	(20 000)	
Written-down value		160 000	
((160 + 30 – 40) ÷ 6)	1997	(25 000)	Overhaul is not capitalized
	1998	(25 000)	
	1999	(25 000)	
	2000	(25 000)	
Written-down value		60 000	
Revaluation surplus to reserve		70 000*	
New value		130 000	
((130 – 30) ÷ 8)	2001	(12 500)	
	2002	(12 500)	
	2003	(12 500)	
Written-down value		92 500	
Scrapped and sold		20 000	
Deficit		72 500	
Transfer from revaluation reserve		(70 000)*	
Charge to profit and loss	2004	£2 500	

Solution 3

(a)

Debtors

2001	Balance	1 860 000	W/o to Bad Debts		34 500
			Balance c/f		18 25 500
		1 860 000			1 860 000
2002	Balance b/d	1 825 500	Cash		9 757 700
	Sales	10 000 000	W/o to Bad Debts		37 800
			Balance		2 030 000
		11 825 500			11 825 500
2003	Balance b/d	2 030 000	Cash		10 278 100
	Sales	12 000 000	Bad Debts		41 900
			Balance c/f		3 710 000
		14 030 000			14 030 000
2004	Balance b/d	3 710 000	Cash		12 772 000
	Sales	13 000 000	Bad Debts		38 000
			Balance c/f		3 900 000
		16 710 000			16 710 000
	Balance b/d	3 900 000			

Bad debts

Debtors	34 500	Profit and loss account	34 500
Debtors	37 800	Profit and loss account	37 800
Debtors	41 900	Profit and loss account	41 900
Debtors	38 000	Profit and loss account	38 000

Provision for doubtful debts

Provision c/f	40 600	Profit and loss account 2001	36 510
		Profit and loss account 2002	4 090
	40 600		40 600
Provision c/f	37 100	Balance b/d	40 600
Profit and loss 2003	3 500		
	40 600		40 600
Provision c/f	39 000	Balance b/d	37 100
		Profit and loss 2004	1 900
	39 000		39 000
		Balance b/d	39 000

(b)

		Bad debts and provisions = Profit and loss	
Charge to profit and loss	19.1	34,500 + 36,510	= 71,010
	19.2	37,800 + 4,090	= 41,890
	19.3	41,900 – 3,500	= 38,400
	19.4	38,000 + 1,900	= 39,900

(c) Solution would cover:

(i) The need to provide for doubtful debts – an estimate.

(ii) The matching concept / the prudence concept.

(iii) The trend in debtors at Horace Ltd is dangerously upwards.

Debtors have risen from £1,860,000 to £3,900,000 in 3 years – an increase of $((3,900,000 - 1,860,000) \div 1,860,000)$ 110%.

Solution 4

(a)

Debtors Ledger Control

Balance b/d	16 048	Balance b/d	114
Sales	127 456	Cash	110 424
Bad debts written back	188	Discount allowed	4 656
Balance c/f	114	Returns inwards	2 004
		Bad debts	652
		Settlement per contra	868
		Cash from bad debt	188
		Allowances for damaged goods	424
		Balance c/f	24 476
	143 806		143 806
Balance b/d	24 476	Balance b/d	114

Creditors Ledger Control

Balance b/d	210	Balance b/d	12 470
Cash	74 614	Purchases	79 948
Discounts received	2 950	Overpayment refunded	210
Returns outwards	1 070		
Settlement per contra	868		
Balance c/f	12 916		
	92 628		92 628
		Balance b/d	12 916

(b) Advantages of control accounts would include:

- the localization of errors;

- the avoidance of delay in drafting accounts;

- a check against inaccuracy and fraud.

Solution 5

(a)

1. The business is highly geared $\left[\dfrac{3000}{3000 + 2281} \right]$ at 56%, and

   Debt to Equity ratio ((5,264 + 3,000) : 2,281) 3.6:1 indicates over-reliance on outside finance. High gearing can be dangerous if profits fluctuate. Of the shareholders' funds, (240/2,281) 10% is revaluation reserve. The business is under-capitalized.

2. The long-term loan is only covered 1.26 times by its security, the factory, and is repayable in two years' time. It may be difficult to re-finance this loan even at an interest rate of (510/3,000) 17%.

3. Interest is only covered twice by the operating profit. This is not enough for a highly geared business.

4. The payout ratio is 71% (340/481) leaving only £141 as profit ploughed back into the business. Even after this, retained profit in the balance sheet is only 41, so there must have been accumulated losses of 100 at the beginning of the year.

5. There is negative working capital .96:1 and the acid test ratio shows .74:1. There is not enough liquid cash in the balance sheet Survival of this business could depend on the support of the bank and the speed with which debts can be collected.

6. The business is too dependent on the bank, and should take more credit to reduce the overdraft. Suppliers may not wish to give credit to a business which is in such an illiquid solvency position. Debtors are allowed 4 months' credit (3,641/11,230), and this is too long.

7. The dividend is 17p per share (£340,000 ÷ 2,000,000 shares) giving a yield of 6% (17/288). The P/E is 12 (£481,000 ÷ 2,000,000 shaes = 24p per share); (288 ÷ 24 = 12). A low yield, but the high P/E shows that the market believes there is potential for growth, or a takeover bid from a rival.

8. The business is profitable this year with a ROCE of 38% (2,011/3,000 + 2,281), but the impact of interest costs from the under-capitalized financial structure reduces this to ROI of (481/2,281) 21%.

(b) should cover:

500,000 ordinary shares gives a share stake of 20% (500/2,500), but this may not be enough to control the business.

£1½ million injected into Dalby could reduce the gearing, help to repay the long-term loan, and repay part of the overdraft. This would considerably reduce the lack of liquidity and reliance on outside finance, but it would not buy any more assets to increase the profits.

How much profit increase is expected as a result of the injection of £1½ million, and what return can the investor expect, especially if profits fluctuate?

The long-term loan is paid interest at 17% (510/3,000). Is this a better return than a potential shareholder could earn (dividend now 340/2,000 = 17 pence a share)? 17 pence on a £1 share which has cost £3 only gives a yield of 5.6%. What is the potential for capital growth?

Solution 6

(a)   £

Working	Operating profit	18 581	
	+ depreciation	3 000	
	Stock increase	(487)	(10 129 – 9 642)
	Debtors increasc	(4 869)	(9 607 – 4 738)
	Creditors increase	525	(6 229 – 5 704)
	Cash flow from operations	£16 750	

Cash flow statement

Cash flow from operations		16 750
Cash flow to service finance – interest		(1 926)
Taxation		(1 108)
Capital expenditure — Plant sold (5,000 + 3,000)	8 000	
— Plant Purchased	(20 000)	
— Investment sold (20,000 – 15,000)	<u>5000</u>	(7 000)
Acquisition – Joint venture		(25 000)
Dividends		<u>(726)</u>
Deficit before financing		(19 010)
Treasury operations – Deposit liquidated		5 000
Financing – Long-term loan		<u>11 000</u>
Net cash outflow (cash 550 + overdraft 2,460)		<u>£(3 010)</u>

Comment

1. Expansion – plant 12,000 + stock 487 + debtors 4,869 and the joint venture 25,000 = 42,356. Paid for with very little extra investment from shareholders.

2. Depreciation 3,000 + deposit 5,000 + creditors 525 + long-term loan 11000 + investments sold 5,000 + overdraft and cash 3010 + net cash flow (16,750 – 1,926 – 1,108 – 726).

3. Liquidity reduced and gearing increased.

4. Strategy – trade investment changed to joint venture.

5. Debtors doubled – new payment policy?

Solution 7

(a)

Most transactions are settled in cash sooner or later. Adequate liquid resources enable a business to pay its way. This reduces the risk involved and enhances the reputation. Cash management balances the need for a cash balance to meet normal payments and emergencies against too much cash lying idle without earning a profit.

The transactions motive, the precautions motive, the speculative motive.

(b)

(i) Opening reconciliation	- Bank statement		2 270
	- Oct. cheques banked in Nov.	842	
		146	
		310	
		<u>424</u>	<u>1 722</u>
	- Cash book		<u>548</u>

(ii)   Cash book

Dividend received	5 456	Balance overdrawn	28
		Bank charges	1 872
		Balance c/f	3 556
	<u>5 456</u>		<u>5 456</u>
Balance b/d	3 556		

(iii)

	Balance per bank statement		6 852
	Cheques not yet presented	1 736	
		214	
		224	
		<u>1 122</u>	<u>3 296</u>
	Balance per cash book		<u>£3 556</u>

Solution 8

(a) Your solution should cover:

- Definition
- Working capital shows
    (i) Business's own commitment
    (ii) Extent of reliance on others
    (iii) Fund available to repay creditors
    (iv) Situation of negative working capital
- Disadvantages of insufficient working capital
- Overtrading

(b) Ratio analysis

CA : CL	30,655,616 : 16,257,488	1.88:1
QA : CL	12,845,620 + 350,211 : 16,257,488	0.81:1
Material Stock	5,186,370 / 20,815,683 × 365	91 days
WiP Stock	12,273,415 / 32,000,000 × .86 × 365	163 days
Debtor Days	12,845,620 / 32,000,000 × 365	146 days
Creditor Days	2,283,749 / 20,815,683 × 365	40 days

Working capital looks good at 1.9:1, but this is not so, as the acid test shows 0.81:1. This is a dangerous situation with insufficient liquid cash to meet future payments. The stockholding period for materials is three months – this is too long unless there is a good reason to buy materials in bulk. The work in progress situation suggests a dramatic lack of control in the production processes, if it takes nearly six months to complete this type of product.

Debtors are allowed 5 months' credit while only 40 days, credit is taken from suppliers. Unless sales depend on credit allowed to customers, and unless a considerable cash discount is given for early payment by suppliers, these figures should be controlled.

The bank manager is the dominant element in this working capital situation. If the overdraft was called in, Redmile Racers would be in financial difficulties.

When you consider the interest cost on this overdraft, managers should reduce stocks and debtors to repay the overdraft and cut the cost of interest.

Solutions to Seminar Exercises

3.1   Balance Sheet Company A at 31 December

	£	£	£
Fixed Assets	Cost	Depreciation	Net
Land and buildings	95 000	10 000	85 000
Plant	25 000	6 000	19 000
**Vehicles	8 000	–	8 000
	128 000	16 000	112 000
Investments – Shares in Company X			7 000
Current Assets			
Stock		29 941	
Debtors		19 487	
Nottingham Bonds		8 000	
Payments in Advance		904	
Bank		8 186	
Cash		1 270	
		67 788	
Less Current Liabilities			
Creditors	43 614		
Wages payable	1 102		
Taxation owed	13 000	57 716	
Working Capital			10 072
Total Assets less current liabilities			129 072
Long Term Loan			20 000
Net Assets			£109 072
financed by			
Share Capital			50 000
*Retained Profits			59 072
Ownership Interest			£109 072

* A – L = C Share Capital is £50 000 so the balancing figure £59 072 must be retained profits held as a general reserve

** You should investigate why no depreciation has been charged on vehicles

3.2

(a) Increase capital, a liability; increase cash, an asset.

(b) Cash reduced; current liability 'wages payable' disappears

(c) Increase stock, an asset; reduce cash, an asset

(d) Increase stock, an asset; increase creditors, a liability

(e) Reduce freehold land and buildings, an asset; increase cash, an asset

(f) Reduce cash, an asset; reduce creditors, a liability

(g) Increase cash, an asset; but the asset 'Nottingham Bonds' disappears

(h) Reduce cash, an asset; reduce taxation owed, a liability.

3.3

(a) Balance Sheet for Company B at ?

	£	£	£
Fixed Assets			
Land and Buildings (at valuation)			156 000
Plant and Vehicles (at valuation)			64 000
			220 000
Investments			18 000
Current Assets– Stock		74 000	
Debtors		52 000	
Bank		36 000	
Cash		8 000	
		170 000	
Current Liabilities Trade Creditors	80 000		
Inland Revenue	40 000	120 000	
Working Capital			50 000
			288 000
Long Term Liability– Mortgage (secured on land and buildings)			70 000
Net Assets			£218 000
financed by:			
Share Capital			100 000
General Reserve – Retained Profit			118 000
Ownership Interest			£218 000

Notes

* No date for the balance sheet is given in the question
* The fixed assets are shown 'at valuation' not at cost less depreciation
* The loan is not set off against the land and buildings but a note discloses its security
* The investments could be a long term asset for strategic purposes or a current asset to set funds to work in the short term

(b) If the net assets are £218 000 and share capital is £100 000, then retained profit must be £118 000.

A – L (£218 000) = C the ownership interest.

SEMINAR EXERCISES 4

4.1   (a)

		£
(i)	£2430 in closing balance sheet as stock	35 282
(ii)	£360 is stock and £3840 is a creditor	3 480
(iii)		800
(iv)	Opening balance sheet creditor paid	–
(v)		230
(vi)	£180 is a payment in advance	180
(vii)		1 790
(viii)	Depreciation (a non cash cost)	1 000
(ix)	Accrued expense, creditor in balance sheet	380
		43 142
(b)	Net profit	1 858
	Sales	£45 000

(c)

Opening Balance Sheet

	£		£
Capital *	6 413	Equipment	4 000
Creditors	937	Stock	800
		Debtors	2 100
		Cash	450
	£7 350		£7 350

* Balancing figure A – L = C

(d)

Cash Book

	£		£
Balance at beginning	450	Payments	
Receipts		Goods £(37 712+937)	38 649
Sales	45 000	Wages	230
Debtors	2 100	Insurance	360
		Expenses	1 790
		Balance at end	6 521
	£47 550		£47 550

(e)

Closing Balance Sheet

	£		£
Opening capital	6 413	Equipment (net of depreciation)	3 000
Add profit	1 858	Stock £(2 430+360)	2 790
	8 271	Debtors	Nil
Trade creditors	3 840	Payment in advance	180
Accrued expense	380	Cash	6 521
	£12 491		£12 491

(f)

(i)   No capital has been introduced or withdrawn

(ii)   The opening debtors have all paid

(iii)   The business is a going concern, so it is correct to depreciate the equipment

(iv)   Stock will be sold at least for its cost so that no element of loss is ignored in its valuation

4.2   M A Tellow

		£	£
(a)	Opening cash (£20 000 + £10 000)		30 000
	Add sales		10 800
	Less payments:		
	Rent	500	
	Expenses	980	
	Insurance	1 200	
	Suppliers	7 000	
			(9 680)
	Closing cash		£31 120

		£	£
(b)	Sales		53 000
	Cost of sales (£47 000 – £15 000)		32 000
	Gross profit		21 000
	Less expenses:		
	Electricity	50	
	Insurance	100	
	Rent	250	
	Expenses	980	
			(1 380)
	Net profit		£19 620

Can you now compute a balance sheet as at 31 January? It should balance at net assets of £49 620 because Capital £30 000 + Profit £19 620 = £49 620

SEMINAR EXERCISES 5

5.1   Albert

Assets	+	−	Liabilities	+	−
Cash	1 000	4 000	Capital	20 000	
	20 000	25 000	Creditor	10 000	
Building	25 000				
Office equipment	4 000	30 000			
Stock	10 000	5 000	Add profit (iii)	500	
Debtor	4 500	_____			
	64 500	34 000			
	34 000				
	£30 500			£30 500	
Expenses			Sales		
Cost of sales	5 000		Customer 1	1 000	
	_____		Customer 2	4 500	
	£5 000			£5 500	

(i)   Overdraft facilities only become a transaction when used – Jan 4

(ii)   An order is not recorded as a sale until the goods are delivered

(iii)   Sales £5500 less expenses £5000 = Profit £500 – belongs to owner, Albert so add to his capital

Assets = Liabilities + capital

5.2 Granges capital comprises all the assets he has injected into the business whether in cash or as assets

Opening Journal Entry	£ Dr	£ Cr
Warehouse	24 000	
Fixtures and fittings	17 000	
Car	2 800	
Van	900	
Bank	8 500	
Capital account		53 200
Being assets injected into the business as capital		
Stock	1 446	
Collie and Co		471
Lot and Mee		360
Edmunds Ltd		615
Being goods bought for stock on credit terms		

If an account is opened for each of these amounts the nucleus of a set of accounts is formed. The next task is to enter the transactions in the daybook and write up cash and bank accounts. A separate book could be used for returns, but in this case they are merged with purchases in the daybook.

Purchases Daybook

			£
1 September	Apple Ltd	Typewriters	360
5 September	J Lewin	Goods	171
7 September	J Lewin	Returns	(20)
9 September	Edmunds Ltd	Goods	280
			£791
		Debit purchases	£451
		Debit fixtures	£360
		Credit returns	(£20)
			£791

Purchases are credited to the supplier's personal accounts

Sales Daybook

			£
2 September	T Veron	Goods	627
2 September	K Jones	Goods	460
6 September	T Veron	Returns	(127)
7 September	H Same Ltd	Goods	430
10 September	H Same Ltd	Goods	165
			£1 555
		Credit sales	£1 682
		Debit returns	(£127)
			£1555

Sales are debited to the customers' personal accounts

		Petty Cash					Bank Account			
	£		£		£			£	
1 September bank	250	4 September wages	83	1 September journal	8 500	1 September stationery		174
		8 September wages	76	3 September sales	165	1 September petty cash		250
		8 September office expenses	18	8 September sales	431	2 September packing		61
		10 September drawings	5	9 September Veron	475	2 September cleaning		16
		11 September bank	18	11 September petty cash	18	5 September Collie and Co		300
		11 September balance c/f	50			5 September Edmunds Ltd		600
	£250		£250			7 September rent		181
12 September balance b/d	50					9 September insurance		160
						10 September Lot and Mee		200
		Discount Received				11 September carriage		29
	£		£			11 September telephone		23
		5 September, Edmunds Ltd	15			11 September balance c/f		7 595
							£9 589		£9 589
		Discount Allowed		12 September balance b/d	7 595			
	£		£					
9 September, Veron	25							

Next post the opening journal entries, the total and individual items from the daybooks, and items from bank account and petty cash. Remember that bank (the cash book) and petty cash are daybooks as well as ledger accounts. Note that trade discount is deducted from the price of goods but cash discount is the subject of a separate account because it is a cost of the business.

The vehicle transaction on 7 September should go through the journal, but it has been posted direct to the vehicles account.

Warehouse

	£		£
1 September, journal	24 000		

Fixtures and Fittings

	£		
1 September, journal	17 000		
11 September, purchases daybook	360		
	17 360		

Vehicles

	£		£
1 September, car	2 800	7 September, van to car sales	900
1 September, van	900	11 September, balance c/f	5 600
7 September, van from car sales	2 800		
	6 500		6 500
12 September, balance b/d	5 600		

Capital Account

	£		£
		1 September, journal	53 200

Collie and Co.

	£		£
5 September, bank	300	1 September, journal	471
11 September, balance c/f	171		
	471		471
		12 Sept balance b/d	171

Stock

	£		£
1 September, journal	1 446	Balance c/f	1 446
	1 446		1 446
12 September, balance b/d	1 446		

Purchases

	£		£
11 September, purchases daybook	451	8 September drawn	53
		11 September balance c/f	398
	451		451
12 September, balance b/d	398		

Returns Outwards

	£		£
		11 September, purchases daybook	20

Lot and Mee

	£		£
10 September, bank	200	1 September, journal	360
11 September, balance c/f	160		
	360		360
		1 September, balance b/d	160

Sales

	£
3 September, bank	165
8 September, bank	431
11 September, sales daybook	1 682
	2 278

Returns Inwards

	£
11 September, sales daybook	127

Car Sales Ltd

	£		£
7 September, vehicles	900	7 September vehicles	2 800
11 September, balance c/f	1 900		
	2 800		2 800
		12 September, balance b/d	1 900

Stationery

	£
1 September, bank	174

Packing

	£
2 September, bank	61

Edmunds Ltd

	£		£
5 September, bank	600	1 September, journal	615
5 September, discount	15	9 September, purchases daybook	280
11 September, balance c/f	280		
	895		895
		12 September, balance b/d	280

Apple Ltd

	£
1 September, purchases daybook	360

J Lewin

	£		£
7 September, purchases daybook	20	5 September, purchases daybook	171
11 September, balance c/f	151		
	171		171
		12 September, balance b/d	151

T Veron

	£		£
2 September, sales daybook	627	6 September, sales daybook	127
		9 September, bank	475
		9 September, discount allowed	25
	627		627

Office Expenses				K Jones	
	£				£
2 September, bank, cleaning	16			2 September, sales daybook	460
8 September, cash, miscellaneous	18				
	34			**H Same**	
					£
Rent				7 September, sales daybook	430
	£			10 September, sales daybook	165
7 September, bank	181				595

Insurance				Wages	
	£				£
9 September, bank	160			4 September, cash	83
				8 September, cash	76
Carriage					159
	£				
11 September, bank	29			**Drawings**	
					£
Telephone				8 September	53
	£			10 September, cash	5
11 September, bank	23				58

All daybook items are now posted. If every debit has a credit a trial balance extracted at this stage will balance, but first accounts should be closed off and balances brought down. You should check the entries for all items in the exercise.

Trial Balance of Brian Grange as at 11 September

	Debits	Credits
	£	£
Warehouse	24 000	
Fixtures and Fittings	17 360	
Vehicles	5 600	
Capital		53 200
Stock at end	1 446	
Purchases	398	
Returns outwards		20
Sales		2 278
Returns inwards	127	
Creditors :		
Car Sales Ltd		1 900
Collie and Co		171
Lot and Mee		160
Edmunds Ltd		280
Apple Ltd		360
J Lewin		151
Discount allowed	25	
Debtors:		
K Jones	460	
H Same	595	
Discount received		15
Wages	159	
Drawings	58	
Stationery	174	
Packing	61	
Office expenses	34	
Rent	181	
Insurance	160	
Carriage	29	
Telephone	23	
Petty Cash	50	
Bank	7 595	
	£58 535	£58 535

SEMINAR EXERCISE 6

6.1 IRA MAIDEN – Points to cover in the solution.

- Purposes of depreciation:

    (i) to allocate cost to the years of useful economic life and measure a true profit;
    (ii) to retain funds in the business and maintain capital invested

- Danger if no depreciation – capital depletion. Company Law states that fixed assets must be depreciated

- The cost of any asset with a finite useful life in excess of one accounting year should be allocated to those accounting periods for which it contributes to the profits – matching concept. To write off a machine at once, if it has a five year life, will distort the profit figure.

- It is the responsibility of management to select a method of depreciation which is suitable to the assets concerned and to apply that method consistently and systematically.

- There is no magic about five years – depreciation should cover the useful economic life of the asset. Many companies select a life for a group of assets and apply it as a matter of accounting policy.

- Depreciation is to replace the funds invested in fixed assets as they are used up. These funds may be used for replacement but it is up to the managers how the money is spent. Replacement by a similar asset is comparatively rare because of the pace of technological change.

- Disclosure: CA 1985 – for each class of asset;

    (i)   the methods used/UELs or ratios applied;
    (ii)   the charge for the year, the gross amount of the assets; and
    (iii) the accumulated depreciation to date.

6.2   Ledger Accounts for Task 6.3

Plant A/c

2002 Cash	850 000	2008 Revaluation	940 000
2004 Cash	90 000		
	940 000		940 000
2008 Revaluation	450 000	2010 Disposal	450 000

Depreciation A/c

2 008 Revaluation	557 500	2002 P/I	100 000
		2003 P/I	100 000
		2 004 P/I	115 000
		2005 P/I	115 000
		2006 P/I	63 750
		2007 P/I	63 750
	557 500		557 500
2010 Disposal	150 000	2008 P/I	75 000
		2009 P/I	75 000
	150 000		150 000

Revaluation A/c

2008 Plant	940 000	2008 Depreciation	557 500
		Balance	382 500
	940 000		557 500
Balance	382 500	2008 Plant	450 000
2008 Reserve	67 500		
	450 000		450 000

Disposal A/c

2010 Plant	450 000	2010 Depreciation	150 000
		Cash	200 000
		Deficit	100 000
	450 000		450 000
2010 Deficit	100 000	2010 Reserve	67 500
		2010 P/I	32 500
	100 000		100 000

Revaluation Reserve

2010 Disposal	67 500	2008 Rev A/c	67 500

SEMINAR EXERCISES 7

7.1 Marmalade Ltd Stock Valuation

(a) First in first out method

Date	Stock		Issues	Price £	Cost £
1 November 2001	200 × £150				
24 November 2001	200 × £150	}			
	600 × £156				
8 December 2001	40 × £150	}	160	150	24 000
	600 × £156				
16 January 2001		{	40	150	6 000
			240	156	37 440
	360 × £156				
11 April 2002	360 × £156	}			
	300 × £160				
18 June 2002			260	156	40 560
	100 × £156	}			
	300 × £160				
		{	100	156	15 600
			120	160	19 200
	180 × £160				
15 August 2002	180 × £160	}			
	300 × £170				
29 October 2002		{	180	160	28 800
			100	170	17 000
	* 200 × 170				
		Cost of material used			£188 600

* Closing Stock per Balance Sheet £34 000

(b)   Last in first out method

Date	Stock	Issues	Price £	Cost £
1 November 2001	200 × £150			
24 November 2001	200 × £150 600 × £156 }			
8 December 2001		160	£156	24 960
	200 × £150 440 × £156 }			
16 January 2002		280	£156	43 680
	200 × £150 160 × £156 }			
11 April 2002	200 × £150 160 × £156 300 × £160 }			
18 June 2002		260	£160	41 600
	200 × £150 160 × £156 40 × £160 }			
6 July 2001		{ 40 160 20	£160 £156 £150	6 400 24 960 3 000
	180 × £150			
15 August 2002	180 × £150 300 × £170 }			
29 October 2002		280	£170	47 600
	*180 × £150 *20 × £170 }			
		Cost of material used		£192 200

*Closing stock per balance sheet = £30 400

(c)   Weighted average method

Date	Stock	Issues	Price £	Cost £
1 November 2001	200 × £150			
24 November 2001	800 × £154.5			
8 December 2001		160	£154.5	24 720
	640 × £154.5			
16 January 2002		280	£154.5	43 260
	360 × £154.5			
11 April 2002	660 × £157			
18 June 2002		260	£157	40 820
	400 × £157			
6 July 2002		220	£157	34 540
	180 × £157			
15 August	480 × £165.125			
29 October 2002		280	£165.125	46 235
	*200 × £165.125			
				£189 575

*Closing stock per balance sheet = £33 025

Workings	Quantity × £		£		
24 November 2001	200 × 250	=	30 000		
	600 × 156	=	93 600		
	800 ÷		123 600	=	154.5
11 April 2002	360 × 154.5	=	55 620		
	300 × 160	=	48 000		
	660 ÷		103 620	=	157
15 August 2002	180 × 157	=	28 260		
	300 × 170	=	51 000		
	480 ÷		79 260	=	165.125

7.2 Mr Spice

	Workings Tonnes	Price/Tonne £	Cost £	Sale
Purchases	20	114	2 280	100 × 130 = £13 000
	30	120	3 600	
	25	105	2 625	
	40	126	5 040	
	15	129	1 935	
	10	132	1 320	
	140 tonnes		£16 800	

Stock at 30 June 2003 is 40 tonnes

(a)	(i)	FIFO	10	132	1 320
			15	129	1 935
			15	126	1 890
			40		£5 145
	(ii)	LIFO	20	114	2 280
			20	120	2 400
			40		£4 680

(iii) Average : Average price on 30 June 2003 is $\dfrac{£168\,800}{140}$ = £120/tonne

Stock Valuation 40 × £120 = £4 800

(b)

	FIFO £	LIFO £	Average £
Purchases	16 800	16 800	16 800
Less Stock 30 June 2003	5 145	4 680	4 800
Cost of Sales	11 655	12 120	12 000
Sales	13 000	13 000	13 000
Trading Profit	£1 345	£880	£1 000

(c) Stocks are accounted for in the balance sheet and profit and loss account at the lower of cost or net realisable value as part of the concept of conservatism in accounting. This concept holds that no profit is shown until it is certain that it has been made, but that losses which could arise are taken into account at an early stage. Thus a profit figure does not contain any elements of profit yet to be realised, and stocks are normally shown at cost, and not at the selling prices which may be achieved in the future when they are sold.

However, in cases where it seems likely that stocks will be sold at prices below their cost it is assumed that the loss has already been incurred although the sales have not yet been made, and the stocks are written down to net realisable value. This is considered prudent since losses foreseen and taken into account at an early stage, do not affect profits of a later period when the stock is sold. The term 'net realisable value' is the likely selling price of the stock, less the costs of selling and any other costs to be incurred in bringing the stock to a saleable condition.

7.3   Simoco

1 (a) Stocks are valued at the lower of cost or net realisable value. This follows the convention of conservatism or prudence. The idea is to carry forward this asset at an amount which takes no account of the profit made if the stock is worth more than its cost on balance sheet day, but to account immediately for any loss suffered if the stock is currently worth less than its original cost.

The fact that stock values are deducted in the Trading account, when the cost of goods sold is calculated, conforms with the Accruals (Matching) principle. This concept stipulates that a true profit can only be measured if the cost of goods sold is matched with revenue from their sale, by carrying forward the cost of goods not yet sold as an asset in the balance sheet. Clearly the prudence concept overrides the matching concept, because conservative values are selected for use in the matching process.

(b)

CAR	A	B	C	D
NRV				
Conservative selling price	3 600	1 600	5 400	3 500
Less 'cost' to bring to saleable condition	40	–	60	80
	3 560	1 600	5 340	3 420
COST				
Cost of car	2 750	1 500	4 800	3 450
Plus 'cost' incurred so far to repair	300	180	80	100
	3 050	1 600	4 880	3 420
Stock value	3 050	1 600	4 880	3 420

(c)

Stocks accumulate from purchases made throughout the accounting year, perhaps at a range of prices. Unless goods sold on a certain day can be traced back to a particular purchase, the actual cost of goods remaining in stock cannot be accurately identified. To cope with this problem companies can apply the FIFO, LIFO and AVCO methods to value the stock.

FIFO assumes that all materials purchased are used up in chronological order. Thus in a period of inflation, the earlier purchases, (at lower prices), would be charged against sales in the profit calculation and the later or higher cost batches would appear in the balance sheet as stock. This method leads to profit being overstated.

LIFO assumes that the most recent purchases are used first, so that in a period of inflation the higher priced purchases will be charged against profits, and the earlier batches will be carried forward as stock. This system leads to a lower profit figure than that disclosed by FIFO.

AVCO prices material usage at a weighted average cost, and thus leads to a profit figure in between the two extremes of FIFO and LIFO

SEMINAR EXERCISES 8

8.1 (a) Sally and Denise, Profit and Loss Account for the Year Ended 30 April (£000s)

	£	£	£
Receipts from customers			4 510
Less :			
Materials used up (140 + 400 − 152)		388	
Wages (1080 + 40)		1 120	
Depreciation:			
Buildings	10		
Equipment	300		
Furnishings	146		
		456	
Cleaning expenses		160	
Directors salaries		40	
Heat, light and power		480	
Rent (490-70-40)		380	
Salon expense		920	
Doubtful debts		12	
Telephone		210	
			4 166
Net profit before tax			344
Less corporation tax			90
			254
Less proposed dividend			120
Retained profit added to reserves in balance sheet			£134

Balance Sheet as at 30 April (£000s)

	Cost £	Depreciation £	£
Fixed assets:			
Freehold land and buildings	860	90	770
Equipment and machines	1 500	600	900
Salon furnishings	1 460	576	884
	3 820	1 266	2 554
Current assets:			
Stock (160 – 8)		152	
Debtors less provision		238	
Prepayments (rent)		110	
Cash at bank		435	
Cash in hand		25	
		960	
Less current liabilities :			
Creditors	590		
Accruals (wages)	40		
Corporation tax payable	90		
Dividend payable	120		
		(840)	
			120
			£2 674
Financed by:			
Share capital			2 000
Reserves (540+134)			674
			£2 674

(b) The important relationship is between dividend and profit for the year available for dividend (ie net profit after tax). The payout ratio is 120/254 × 100/1 = 47%, which is more generous than for many companies, but still reasonable. Dividends in excess of net profit after tax may be paid out of reserves. Profits not paid out increase the reserves as 'retained profit'

8.2. Grumbleweed Ltd Manufacturing Account for the year ended 31 December 2000

		£
Opening stock of raw materials		35 000
Raw material purchases		260 000
		295 000
Less closing stocks of raw materials		28 000
Raw materials consumed		267 000
Manufacturing wages		250 000
Prime costs		517 000
Factory expenses		
Rent	45 000	
Power	10 000	
Light and heat	7 500	
Insurance	4 500	
Production director's salary	15 000	
Depreciation of plant machinery	45 000	127 000
Factory cost of production		644 000
Add opening stock of work in progress		63 000
		707 000
Less closing stock of work in progress		47 000
		660 000

Grumbleweed Ltd Trading Account for the year ended 31 December 2000

	£	£	£
Sales			1 300 000
Opening stocks of finished goods		125 000	
Transfers from manufacturing account		660 000	
		785 000	
Less closing stock of finished goods			
		100 000	685 000
Gross profit			615 000
Selling expenses:			
Advertising	95 000		
Carriage outwards	25 000	120 000	
Establishment expenses:			
Directors salaries	65 000		
Rent	9 000		
Light and heat	1 500		
Insurance	900		
Office salaries	83 000		
General administration expenses	30 600	190 000	
Financial expenses:			
Increase in bad debt provision	2 000		
Bank Interest	8 500	10 500	
Depreciation:			
Office equipment	20 500		
Motor vehicles	15 000	35 500	356 000
Net trading profit			259 000

Grumbleweed Ltd Appropriation Account for the year ended 31 December 2000

	£	£	£
Net profit for the year before taxation			259 000
Corporation tax on the years profits			100 000
Net profit after taxation			159 000
Dividends – Ordinary 20% Proposed			40 000
			119 000
Unappropriated profit b/f			121 000
Unappropriated profit c/f			£240 000

Grumbleweed Ltd Balance Sheet as at 31 December 2000

	£ Cost	£ Depreciation	£ WDV
Fixed Assets			
Plant and machinery	300 000	125 000	175 000
Office equipment	205 000	65 000	140 000
Motor vehicles	100 000	55 000	45 000
	605 000	245 000	360 000
Current Assets			
Stocks and raw materials		28 000	
Work in progress		47 000	
Finished goods		100 000	
		175 000	
Debtors (250 000 – 2500)		247 500	
Prepayments		6 500	
		429 000	
Less current liabilities :			
Creditors	178 000		
Accruals	1 000		
Dividends	40 000		
Taxation	100 000		
Bank overdraft	30 000	349 000	80 000
			£440 000
Financed by :			
Share capital – authorised, issued and fully paid:			
400 000 ordinary shares of 50 pence			200 000
Reserves – profit and loss account			240 000
			£440 000

SEMINAR EXERCISES 9

9.1 Alan, Bill and Chris

Dr		Realization Account		Cr
		£		£
Fixed assets		930 390	Liabilities	324 724
Stock		328 422	Car – Bill	6 000
Debtors		181 875	Stock – Bill	30 000
Legal expenses		751	Premises – cash	112 500
Profit on realization:	£		Consideration	1 050 000
Alan	27 262			
Bill	27 262			
Chris	27 262			
		81 786		
		£1 523 224		£1 523 224

Note : The profit is divided equally among the partners. In the absence of an agreement the Partnership Act 1890 applies

Dr	Cash Account		Cr
	£		£
Opening balance	15 624	Legal expenses	751
Sale of property	112 500	Paid to Bill	127 373
	£128 124		£128 124

Dr				Capital and Current Account				Cr
	Alan	Bill	Chris			Alan	Bill	Chris
	£	£	£			£	£	£
Car		6 000		Opening				
Stock		30 000		balance		300 000	300 000	150 000
Cash		127 373		Opening				
14 per cent				balance		41 118	94 260	36 209
debentures		258 149						
Ordinary								
shares	368 380	—	213 471	Realization				
				surplus		27 262	27 262	27 262
	£368 380	£421 522	£213 471			£368 380	£421 522	£213 471

Dr	Alchris Ltd		Cr
	£		£
Consideration	1 050 000	14 per cent debentures	
		Alan	210 000
		Bill	258 149
		Ordinary shares:	
		Alan	368 380
		Chris	213 471
	£1 050 000		£1 050 000

Dr	Loan Account for Alan		Cr
	£		£
14 per cent debentures	210 000	Balance	210 000

9.2   Eric, Fred and Geoff

(a)

Dr	Revaluation Account		Cr
	£		£
Premises	88 000	Premises	118 000
Plant	39 000	Plant	37 000
Stock	63 479	Stock	54 279
Doubtful debts	2 000		
Profit on revaluation : £			
Eric 8 400			
Fred 5 600			
Geoff 2 800			
	16 800		
	£209 279		£209 279

Dr	Goodwill Account		Cr
Goodwill raised – to capital account	£	Goodwill written back to capital account	£
Eric (3)	10 500	Eric (3)	9 000
Fred (2)	7 000	Fred (2)	6 000
Geoff (1)	3 500	Hal (2)	6 000
	£21 000		£21 000

Dr Capital Account **Cr**

	E £	F £	G £	H £		E £	F £	G £	H £
Goodwill	9 000	6 000	–	6 000	Balance b/d	92 500	67 500	25 000	–
Retiring partners account–			28 500		Goodwill	10 500	7 000	3 500	–
					Cash	–	–		79 000
Balance c/f	104 000	68 500	–	73 000	Transfer from				
					current account	10 000			
	113 000	74 500	28 500	79 000		113 000	74 500	28 500	79 000
					Balance b/d	104 000	68 500	–	73 000

Dr Current Account **Cr**

	E £	F £	G £	H £		E £	F £	G £	H £
Balance	–	2 009	–	–	Balance b/d	4 714	–	4 178	–
Retiring Partners Acct.	–	–	6 978	–	Profit on				
Transfer to capital	10 000	–	–	–	revaluation	8 400	5 600	2 800	–
Balance c/f	3 114	3 591	–	–					
	£13 114	£5 600	£6 978	–		£13 114	£5 600	£6 978	–
					Balance b/d	3 114	3 591	–	–

Dr Retiring Partners Account **Cr**

	£		£
Car	2 900	Capital Account	28 500
Cash	29 578	Current Account	6 978
Balance c/f	30 000	Loan Account	27 000
	£62 478		£62 478
		Balance b/d	30 000

Balance Sheet Eric, Fred and Hal 30 June

	£	£		£	£
Capital:			Fixed assets:		
Eric		104 000	Premises		118 000
Fred		68 500	Plant		37 000
Hal		73 000	Vehicles		11 100
			Fixtures		3 000
					169 100
Current accounts :			Current assets:		
Eric	3 114		Stock	54 279	
Fred	3 591		Debtors	31 880	
		6 705	Bank	49 422	
Loan – Geoff		30 000	Cash	560	
Current liabilities					
Creditors		23 036			
					136 141
		£305 241			£305 241

9.3   Garner, Murray and Wilkins

Dr	Realization Account		Cr
	£		£
Land and Buildings	901 640	Vehicle – Murray Current account	14 000
Plant	154 230	Consideration – Scott Plc	1 002 000
Vehicles	24 130		
Vehicle – Murray	12 000	Loss £	
Stock	74 000	Garner 54 000	
Bad debts	8 000	Murray 54 000	
Cash discounts	4 000	Wilkins 54 000	
			162 000
	£1 178 000		£1 178 000

Dr				Current Accounts			Cr
	Garner	Murray	Wilkins		Garner	Murray	Wilkins
	£	£	£		£	£	£
Balance b/d	–	–	6 000	Balance b/d	10 000	16 000	–
Vehicles	–	14 000	–	HP on car	–	6 000	–
Loss on realization	54 000	54 000	54 000	Balance to			
				capital account	44 000	46 000	60 000
	£54 000	£68 000	£60 000		£54 000	£68 000	£60 000

Dr				Capital Accounts			Cr
	Garner	Murray	Wilkins		Garner	Murray	Wilkins
	£	£	£		£	£	£
Ex current account	44 000	46 000	60 000	Balance b/d	140 000	70 000	42 000
Balance c/d	96 000	24 000	–	Balance c/f	–	–	18 000
	140 000	70 000	60 000		140 000	70 000	60 000
Balance b/d	–	–	18000	Balance b/d	96000	24000	–
* Wilkins deficiency	12 000	6 000	–	Wilkins deficiency	–	–	18000
Shares in Scott Plc	84 000	18 000	–				
	£96 000	£24 000	£18 000		£96 000	£240 00	£180 00

Dr	Scott Plc		Cr
	£		£
Consideration Realization A/c	1 002 000	Trade creditors	162 800
		Cash	737 200
		Shares	102 000
	£1 002 000		£1 002 000

Dr		Cash		Cr
	£			£
Debtors	90 000	Balance b/d		607 200
Scott Plc	737 200	Mrs Wilkins loan		200 000
		Special trade creditor		20 000
	£827 200			827 200

* Wilkins deficiency is shared by Garner and Murray in their last agreed capital ratios
(140 000 : 70 000 : 2 : 1)

SEMINAR EXERCISES 10

10.1 Mr Feckless, Statement to Compute the Stock as at 30 November

	£	£
Sales, September, October, November		85 627
Less goods despatched in August		7 346
		78 281
Add goods despatched but not yet invoiced		7 912
		86 193
Less mark up of 25 per cent on sales		21 548
Cost of sales		£64 645*
Opening stock per accounts		53 278
Less error of transposition	(1 800)	
Add pricing error $(400 \times 17 - 1.7)$	6 120	
Less casting error	(81)	4 239
		57 517
Add purchases during the quarter	64 539	
Less received in August	2 643	
	61 896	
Add received but not yet entered	3 129	
	65 025	
Less returns	958	64 067
		121 584
Less cost of sales net of returns, *£[64 645 − (796 × 75%)]		64 048
		57 536
Less scrapped		725
Stock as at 30 November		£56 811

10.2 D. Lerr, Trading and Profit and Loss Account for the Year to 31 December

	£	£
Sales, £(11 600+3 000+1 000)		15 600
Purchases	14 800	
Less closing stock	3 500	11 300
Gross profit		4 300
Provision for doubtful debts (10 per cent of £1 000o/s)	100	
Rent	700	
Petrol and diesel	800	
Expenses	500	
Interest (accrued) (2000 × 0.1)	200	
Lorry depreciation (£1 680 ÷ 6)	280	2 580
Net profit		£1 720

Balance Sheet as at 31 December

	£
Capital at 1 January	10 000
Add net profit	1 720
Less drawings, £(2 080+1 200)	(3 280)
	8 440

Represented by	£	£	£
Fixed assets:			
Lorry at cost			1 680
Less depreciation			280
			1 400
Less loan outstanding on vehicle (1 680 – 400)			1 280
			120
Current assets:			
Stock £(3 000 + 100 + 400)		3 500	
Debtors less provision (1 000 – 100)		900	
Prepayment (rent)		100	
Bank		9 800	
Cash		620	
		14 920	
Less current liabilities :			
Creditors £(4 000 +400)	4 400		
Accruals (interest)	200	4 600	
Working capital			10 320
			10 440
Long term loan			2 000
Net assets			£8 440

Cash 1 000 + 3 000 – 800 – 500 – 2 080 = 620
Bank 11 000 – 400 – 800 – 8 000 + 11 600 – 2 400 – 1 200 = 9 800

10.3 Women in Lumber – Workings | | | £

1. Calculate Credit Sales	–	Cheques banked	25 000
	–	Cheques not yet banked	480
	–	Closing debtors	24 000
			£49 480

2. Calculate Total Sales	–	Sales cash banked	180 000
	–	Sales cash used – wages	31 200
	–	Other cash used	10 325*
	–	Cash not yet banked	432
		Cash sales	221 957
		Credit sales	49 480
		Total sales	**£271 437**

3. Calculate Purchases	–	Cheques to suppliers	170 000
	–	Closing creditors	34 000
	–	Credit purchases	204 000
	–	Cash purchases	4 650
			£208 650

4. Calculate Costs

–	Launch – Bank	8 000	
–	Wages – cash	31 200	
–	Petty cash – cash	1 410	
–	Repairs – cash	975	
–	Printing – cash	1 430	
–	Insurance (1860 – 465)	1 395	Payment in Advance B/s
–	L+H (4000+550)	4 550	Accruals B/s
–	Rates (9000-3000)	6 000	Payment in Advance B/s
–	Motor – bank	14 000	
–	Bonus – bank	2 000	
–	Interest – bank	7 500	
–	Bad debts	2 400	10% of 24 000 Prov B/s
–	Depreciation – lease	1 500	30 000 ÷ 20 B/s
–	– van	3 000	(10 000-1 000) ÷ 3 B/s
–	– F/F	2 500	(200 000 ÷ 8) B/s
		£87 860	

5. Bank balance 205 000 – 214 500 + 480 = O/D 9 020

*1 410 + 975 + 1 430 + 1 860 + 4 650 = 10 325

Women in Lumber Trading and Profit and Loss Account

			£	£
	Sales			271 437
	Less Cost of Sales	Opening stock	–	
		Purchases	208 650	
		Less closing stock	(48 209)	
				(160 441)
	Gross Profit			110 996
	Expenses			
	Launch costs – bank		8 000	
	Wages – cash		31 200	
	Petty cash – cash		1 410	
	Repairs – cash		975	
	Printing – cash		1 430	
Prepayment	Insurance (1 860 – 465)		1 395	
Accrual	Light and Heat (4 000 + 550)		4550	
Prepayment	Rates (9 000 – 3 000)		6000	
	Motor Expenses – bank		14 000	
	Bonus – bank		2 000	
	Interest – bank		7 500	
B/S	Bad Debts provision		2 400	
B/S	Depreciation	– lease	1 500	
B/S		– van	3 000	
B/S		– fixtures	2 500	
				(87 860)
	Net profit			23 136
B/S	Dividend provided			(6 000)
B/S	Retained profit			£17 136

Women in Lumber   Balance Sheet as at 31st December

Fixed Assets	Cost	Depreciation	Net
Lease	30 000	1 500	28 500
Vehicle	20 000	2 500	17 500
Fixtures and fittings	10 000	3 000	7 000
	60 000	7 000	53 000

Current Assets			
Stock		48 209	
Debtors	24 000		
Less provision	(2 400)	21 600	
*Prepayments		3 465	
Cash		432	
		73 706	

Current Liabilities			
Creditors	34 000		
Accruals	550		
Overdraft	9 020		
Dividend	6 000		
		(49 570)	

Working Capital		24 136
Net Assets		£77 136
Share Capital		60 000
Retained Profit		17 136
		£77 136

* Insurance 465 + Rates 3 000

SEMINAR EXERCISES 11

11.1   Reconcile Ltd Cash Book Adjustment

	Receipts £	Payments £
Balance per Cash Book before adjustment	1 888	
Standing Orders – Loan Interest		1 200
–		732
Dividend Received	1 248	
Opening balance c/d in error	9	
Cheque returned written back		167
Cheque drawn entered at a higher figure	27	
Cheque drawn entered as a receipt – Reversed		341
Cheque drawn entered as a receipt		341
Bank Charges		213
Receipts side undercast	400	
Balance after adjustment £578	£3 572	£2 994

Note : Item (b) is to be ignored

Reconciliation to Bank Statement	£
Balance per Bank Statement (516 + 112(c))	628
Add Receipts not yet credited	780
Less Cheques not yet presented	(830)
Balance per Cash Book	£578

11.2   (a)

Fisheries Ltd Sales Ledger Control Account

	£		£
Balance b/d	68 300	Cash	23 750
Sales	19 600	Discount	850
		Goods returned	1 550
		Balance c/f	61 750
	£87 900		£87 900
Balance b/d	61 750	Freds restaurant (Contra)	650
C Lion & Co Ltd sale	2 100	Bad debt written off	1 650
Returned cheque written back	1 900	Credit Note	4 500
	£65 750	Balance c/f	58 950
	£		£65 750
Balance b/d	*£58 950		

425

(b)
Individual Ledger Account

	£		£
R. Herring & Son	1 100 +	cheque returned £1900	3 000
S. Newt Ltd	11 600 +	sales £4900	16 500
C. Lion & Co Ltd	28 350 +	sales £2100 – cash £7450	23 000
Fish Food Ltd	4 900		4 900
The Eating Plaice	1 950		1 950
Freds Restaurant	2 350		2 350
H. Addock	1 800		1 800
Trout farms	7 300		7 300
Codds Ltd	–		(1850)
	£59 350		*£58 950

SEMINAR EXERCISES 12

12.1   Digger Plc   Workings

Sales per T.B. £3 815 900 – £7 000 Investment Income = £3 808 900

	Administration	Distribution	Finance	Cost of Sales
TB	699 269	140 000	7 500	1 985 789
Interest accrued			7 500	
Directors remuneration	353 500	78 000		
Directors pension	120 000			
Directors fees	12 000	4 000		
Overdraft interest	(4 134)		4 134	
Bad debts (38 089 – 23 610)		14 479		
Audit fee	40 000			
Depreciation – buildings	14 000			
– plant				18 500
– vehicles		7 500		
	1 234 635	243 979	19 134	2 004 289

Digger Plc Profit and Loss Account for year ended 31 December 2003

	£	£
Turnover		3 808 900
Cost of sales		2 004 289
Gross profit		1 804 611
Administration expenses	1 234 635	
Distribution costs	243 979	
Investment income	(7 000)	
Financial charges	19 134	1 490 748
Net profit before tax		313 863
Tax		160 000
Net profit after tax		153 863
Dividend		39 000
Retained profit for the year		114 863
Transfer to general reserve		75 000
		39 863
Retained profit b/d		131 203
Retained profit c/f		£171 066

Digger Plc Balance Sheet as at 31st December 2003

	£	£	£
Tangible Fixed Assets			810 000
Investment			82 000
Current assets – stock		291 628	
– debtors		451 442	
		743 070	
Creditors falling due within one year			
Trade creditors	201 122		
Other creditors (16 000 + 7 500)	23 500		
Taxation	160 000		
Dividend	39 000		
Bank overdraft	275 382	699 044	
Net current assets			44 066
Total assets less current liabilities			936 066
Creditors falling due in more than one year – 10% debentures			150 000
Net assets			£786 066
Capital			
Ordinary shares			300 000
General reserve			315 000
Retained profits			171 066
			£786 066

Notes to the accounts

1. Directors Emoluments £567 500 (Pensions £120 000, fees £16 000) Chairman £108 000,
   Highest Paid £164 000)
2. Audit fee £40 000

3. Trade Investment has a current market value of £55 000. It is a 10% investment in voting shares of Fork Ltd
4. 10% Debentures, secured on the premises are repayable in 2010.
5. Dividend is provided at 6.5 pence per share
6. Interest on loans repayable in more than 5 years £15 000
   Interest on loans repayable in less than 5 years £4 314
7. Tangible Fixed Assets

At Cost	Buildings	Plant	Vehicles	Total
Opening balance	–	145 000	64 000	209 000
Purchases	700 000	40 000	–	740 000
Closing balance	700 000	185 000	64 000	949 000
Depreciation				
Opening balance	–	65 000	34 000	99 000
Charge for the year	14 000	18 500	7 500	40 000
Closing balance	14 000	83 500	41 500	139 000
Book value at 31.12.2003	686 000	101 500	22 500	810 000
Depreciation rates	2%	10%	25%	
	Straight Line	Straight Line	Reducing Balance	

SEMINAR EXERCISES 14

14.1   Puzzle Ltd

Net Profit to capital employed = 1 600 : 20 800 = 7.7 per cent. Disappointing return. Investigate whether the profitability of operations or the underuse of capacity is the cause.

Net profit to sales = 1 600 : 16 000 = 10 per cent. Sales to capital employed = 16 000 : 20 800 = 0.77 times. The profit margin on sales is fairly good, but could be improved. Resources do not appear to be working hard enough, since every £1 of assets earns only 77 pence of sales in the year. 0.77 × 10 per cent = 7.7 per cent.

Sales to fixed assets = 16 000 : 8 000 = 2 times. Sales to current assets = 16 000 : 12 800 = 1.25 times. Fixed assets to current assets = 8 000 : 12 800 = 1:1.6. Current assets earn less per £1 than fixed assets, yet current assets have more weight in the asset structure. This may reflect the nature of the business, or could be evidence of over investment in current assets.

Debtor period = $\dfrac{7\ 200}{16\ 000}$ × $\dfrac{365}{1}$ =164 days = five months +

Stock turnover = $\dfrac{4\ 800}{12\ 800}$ × $\dfrac{365}{1}$ =137 days = four months +

Five months credit to customers seems excessive. Credit control could reduce the investment here, so long as it did not harm sales effort. Perhaps stock control could reduce the four month period which, on average, stocks wait in stores before being used. Gross profit to sales = 3 200 : 16 000 = 20 per cent. Expenses to sales = 1 600 : 16 000 = 10 per cent. Half of the gross profit margin is used up by the expenses.

14.2 David and Charles

(a)

	David	Charles
ROCE	7 per cent	12.6 per cent
Net profit to sales	6 per cent	5.5 per cent
Sales to capital employed	1.16 times	2.29 times
Gross profit	16.7 per cent	14.3 per cent
Expenses to sales	10.7 per cent	8.8 per cent
Fixed assets to sales	2.68 times	4.14 times
Current assets to sales	2.06 times	5.12 times
Fixed assets to current assets	1:1.3	1:0.8
Stock turnover	4 times	30 times
Debtors	10 weeks	4 weeks
Current ratio	4.5:1	0.9:1

(b)

Charles has a better return on capital than David, not because his business is more profitable, but because he works his capital harder. He has a lower gross profit margin, but his expenses ratio is lower too, so this compensates for much of the difference. Charles earns more sales per pound on both fixed and current assets, but this difference is most marked for current assets. The two firms have different asset structures. Charles uses less current assets and this is reflected in his much better stock turnover and debtor performance and in the current ratio. The profitable operations of Charles may be halted, since he has negative working capital. Perhaps Charles' high stock turnover indicates dangerously low stocks to service activity.

14.3 St Denys Press

Comparative Ratios		St Denys	Others
ROCE	(43 315 ÷ 850 692)	5%	14%
Gearing	(300 000 ÷ 850 692)	35%	20%
Turnover	(2 880 416 ÷ 850 692)	3.4 times	2 times
Current	(582 870 : 200 385)	2.9:1	1.6:1
Quick Asset	(362 458 : 200 385)	1.8:1	1.1:1
Gross Profit	(254 046 ÷ 2 880 416)	8.8%	14%
Net Profit	(43 315 ÷ 2 880 416)	1.5%	7%
Stock Turnover	(220 412 ÷ 1 804 630 × 365)	44.5 days	30 days
Debtors Collection	(357 620 ÷ 2 880 416 × 365)	45 days	30 days
Creditors Payment	(150 385 ÷ 1 804 630 × 365)	30 days	60 days

Comment

St Denys is less profitable than the average because its gross profit is less than the average. Assets are working harder than in other companies and the Expenses to Sales ratio is about the same (8.8 − 1.5 = 7.3% versus 14 − 7 = 7%)

The current ratio shows a much larger investment in working capital than with other companies and this is substantiated by a longer stock holding period, a longer credit period allowed to debtors and a shorter creditors payment period. The company has very little cash, and control of Stock, Debtors and Creditors should be undertaken to remedy this situation.

Material costs, Labour and Factory overheads should be investigated to improve the gross profit rate. The small investment in fixed assets may mean that St Denys is not working with adequate or modern machinery which may affect production costs.

SEMINAR EXERCISES 15

15.1 **(a)**

BBP Co Ltd. Cash Flow Statement	£ 000s
Trading profit	460
Add back depreciation (218 + 15)	233
Stock increase (600 – 150)	(450)
Debtors increase (700 – 360)	(340)
Creditors increase (650 – 280)	370
Cash flow from operations	£273

Cash Flow Statement

£000s

Cash flow from operations		273
Servicing of finance – interest		(230)
Tax (100 + 20 – 20)		(100)
Capital expenditure Plant purchased	(850)	
Plant sold	582	
Vehicles purchased	(40)	
Vehicles sold (30 – 25)	5	
Premises sold (100 + 80)	180	
Investments sold (600 - 100)	500	377
Acquisitions – joint venture		(1 130)
Dividend (40 + 80 – 80)		(40)
		(850)
Management of liquid resources – deposits reduced		350
Financing – long term loan increased	100	
preference shares repaid	(600)	
ordinary shares (500+100)	600	100
Net cash inflow (OD 320+ cash 80)		£400

(b) (i) Cash Flow from operations is insufficient to cover interest, tax and dividend

(ii) Investment sold, Joint Venture acquired – strategic change of direction

(iii) Preference share repaid replaced by LTL and Ordinary Shares at a premium. Gearing reduced from 25% to 13% but Preference shares at 8% were a cheap form of finance

(iv) Investment in Fixed Assets 303, Stock 440 and Debtors 340 = 1093 suggests expansion partly financed by Creditors 370, Overdraft 320 and long term loans 100 and a reduction of deposits 350 – Not fresh shareholders funds

15.2   Alco Plc   Cash Flow Statement   Year Ending …………

	£000s	£000s
Net cash inflow from operating activities		11 110
Returns on investment and servicing finance		
Interest received	40	
Interest paid	(280)	
Preference dividend paid	(150)	
		(390)
Taxation (3 200 + 5 600 – 5 600)		(3 200)
Capital expenditure and financial investment		
Purchase of fixed assets [17 600 – 5 500 – 25 570]	(13 470)	
Sale of plant	1 000	
Sale of trade investment	10 000	(2 470)
Acquisitions and disposals		
Purchase of an interest in a joint venture		(4 000)
Equity dividends paid (3 300 last year + 2 000 Interim)		(5 300)
Cash outflow before use of liquid resources and financing		(4 250)
Management of liquid resources		
Cash withdrawn from deposit	500	
Purchase of govt securities	(5 000)	(4 500)
Financing		
Share capital issued – preference shares	1 000	
15% debentures repaid	(3 550)	
3 year bank loan	5 000	2 450
Net Cash Outflow (Cash 100× O/D 6 200)		£(6 300)

Reconciliation

	£000s
Operating profit	24 360
Less profit on sale of investment – note 2	(2 000)
Plus loss on sale of plant – note 1	700
Profit from operations	23 060
Addback depreciation	
[(9 500 – 3 800) – 9 750]	4 050
Stock increase (12 000 – 5 000)	(7 000)
Debtors increase (22 100 – 8 900)	(13 200)
Creditors increase (11 000 – 6 800)	4 200
	£11 110

(b)

(i) There has been an expansion during the year suggested by more fixed assets £13 470, more stock £7 000 and more debtors £13 200 = £33 670. This has been financed by creditors £4 200, depreciation £4 050, asset sales £11 000, retained profit £10 370 and overdraft £6 200 = £35 820

(ii) Why has the company purchased government securities for £5 000 when it has an expensive overdraft £6 200, which could have been repaid?

(iii) Gearing has been reduced from 53% to 35%. Preference shares and a 3 year loan have more than covered the debenture repayment but the retained profits have increased.

(iv) Solvency has improved from .71 :1 to .94:1, but this improvement depends on how quickly debtors can be made to pay

(v) Trade investment sold – Joint Venture purchased. Is this a strategic change?

SEMINAR EXERCISES 16

16.1 (a)

	1	2	3	4	5	6
Receipts						
Opening debtors	14 850	14 850	–	–	–	–
Cash :						
Wizzbang	10 000	10 000	10 000	20 000	20 000	20 000
Plugman	2 500	2 500	2 500	2 500	2 500	2 500
Credit:						
Wizzbang	–	–	29 700	29 700	29 700	59 400
Plugman	–	–	7 425	7 425	7 425	7 425
Total Receipts	27 350	27 350	49 625	59 625	59 625	89 325
Payments						
Cost:						
Wizzbang	–	30 000	30 000	30 000	60 000	60 000
Plugman	18 000	9 000	9 000	9 000	9 000	9 000
Machinery		15 000		15 000		
	18 000	54 000	39 000	54 000	69 000	69 000
Surplus/deficit	9 350	(26 650)	10 625	5 625	(9 375)	20 325
Opening balance	(30 000)	(20 650)	(47 300)	(36 675)	(31 050)	(40 425)
Closing	(20 650)	(47 300)	(36 675)	(31 050)	(40 425)	(20 100)

(b) Adjust timing of flows

    (i)   Negotiate late payment for machinery – 1 month delay. For first instalment, month 2, £32 300/month, 3 no change/month 4, no change maximum overdraft now £7 000 less and three months later.

    (ii) Encourage customers to pay sooner; persuade creditors to wait longer.

    (iii) Increase mixture of cash sales to credit sales – discount.

    (iv) Introduce HP – so use HP companies' funds and customer pays the interest.

    (v) Seek cheaper finance – long term loan – overdraft never less than £20 000.

Workings

Plugman sales before the six month period begins are 1 000 × £20 a month, with 75% on credit terms of two months less 1% discount:

        (£20 000 × 0.75) × 0.99 = £14 850 cash received in months 1 and 2, and half that amount in months 3 – 6, when sales volume is reduced.

Wizzbang sales are 500 × £80 with 75% on credit terms of two months less 1% discount:
        (£40 000 × 0.75) × 0.99 = £29 700.

SEMINAR EXERCISES 17

17.1 **(a)**

The financial structure of a business is the range of funding sources from which the total finance to pay for the assets, has been raised. Careworn Construction is a plc, and has raised capital from :-

		£000s
1.	Ordinary Shares	2 000
2.	Retained Profit	2 260
3.	Unsecured Loan Stock (12%)	2 000
4.	Overdraft (20%)	1 000
5.	Other short term creditors	1 200
	Total Capital Employed	£8 460

£4 260 (50%) is contributed by the legal owners of the business, and a further £2 000 is in the form of long term loans. The remaining £2 200 (26%) is short term finance, of which £1 000 of bank overdraft is contributed by a single creditor who can withdraw at will and is therefore in a powerful position to advise the managers.

(b) Significant points are :-

(i) Negative working capital (.91:1) and a dangerously illiquid acid test ratio (.64:1). The significance of this comment depends on how quickly debtors and work in progress can be turned into cash. There is only £10 000 of cash at present.

(ii) Overdependance on outside finance is a sign of weakness. Gearing is 32% (2 000 ÷ 6 260) and the debt to equity ratio is 98% (2 000 + 2 200 : 4 260). The strength of the bank managers position with overdraft underlines the weakness of management. If the property could be revalued upwards, reserves would increase and the gearing and D/E ratios would fall. However the company needs more share capital to replace part of the overdraft.

(iii) Yield (£280 000 ÷ 4 000 000 shares = 7 pence of dividend. 7/140 = 0.05%) Yield is low but the Price/Earnings ratio is respectable.
(Profit is £548 000 – tax £170 000 = £340 000 ÷ 4 000 000 shares = EPS 8.5 pence)
P/E = 140 p ÷ 8.5 p = 16.4 so investors have confidence in Careworn
Are shareholders expecting a take over bid or a profit breakthrough?

(iv) Interest Cover is 988 ÷ 440 = 2.24 times
(548 Profit + 200 Overdraft interest + 240 loan stock interest = 988)
This could be better, especially as the loan stock is not secured

(v) Retained Profit 98 (548 Profit – tax 170 – dividend 280 = 98)
This is not enough to pay for expansion and renewal of Plant. The payout ratio is 74% (280 ÷ 378) of funds available, but this gives a low yield. It seems future prospects rather than present performance is motivating shareholders.

17.2   Solution

(a)

1.   The business is highly geared at $\left(\dfrac{1\ 400}{1\ 400 + 1\ 356}\right)$ at 51%, and

Debt to Equity ratio [2 531 + 1 400 : 1 356] 2.9:1 indicates over reliance on outside finance. High gearing can be dangerous if profits fluctuate. Of the shareholders funds [300/1 356] 22% is revaluation reserve. The business is under capitalised.

2.   The long term loan is only covered 1.43 times by its security, the factory, and is repayable in two years time. It may be difficult to re finance this loan even at an interest rate of [252/1 400] 18%.

3.   Interest is only covered twice by the operating profit. This is not enough for a highly geared business.

4.   The payout ratio is 53% [180/336] leaving only £156 as profit ploughed back into the business. Even after this, retained profit in the BS is only 56, so there must have been accumulated losses of 100 at the beginning of the year.

5.   There is negative working capital .92:1 and the acid test ratio shows .71:1. There is not enough liquid cash in the BS. Survival of this business could depend on the support of the bank and the speed with which debts can be collected.

6.   The business is too dependent on the bank, and should take more trade credit to reduce the overdraft. Suppliers may not wish to give credit to a business which is in such an illiquid solvency position. Debtors are allowed 4 months credit (1 698/5 094 × 365) and this is too long.

7.   The dividend is 18p per share [180/1 000] giving a yield of 5% [18/360]. The P/E is 10.7 [336÷1 000=33.6. 360÷33.6 = 10.7]. A low yield but the high P/E shows that the market believes there is potential for growth.

8.   The business is profitable this year with a ROCE of 40% [1 108/1 400+1 356], but the impact of interest costs from the undercapitalised financial structure reduces this to ROI of 24% [336/1 356]

(b)

250 000 ordinary shares gives a share stake of 20% [250/1250], but this may not be enough to control the business

£1 million injected into Croxton could reduce the gearing, help to repay the long term loan, and repay part of the overdraft. This would considerably reduce the lack of liquidity and reliance on outside finance

How much will profit increase as a result of the injection of £1 million, and what return can the investor expect, especially if profits fluctuate

SEMINAR EXERCISES 18

18.1

(a) Gearing calculated as fixed return capital over FRC + equity interest is (180 + 60 ÷ 180 + 60 + 160) 60 per cent and is high. This gearing may deter other lenders, both long and short term. The debt/equity ratio (180 + 50 : 220) is 1.05:1, and also indicates an overexposed position. Interest cover is weak – net profit before tax and interest covers loan interest (12 per cent on £180 000) only 2.3 times

The working capital situation is strong at 3.8:1 and so is the acid test ratio at 1.8:1

(b) *Suggestions to finance £100 000 of expansion*
   (i) *Share capital.* The price at which shares could be issued depends on how investors see this company. It is not a PLC, so a private placing may be needed to float the shares. The high gearing would discourage equity investors, and the effect of new shares on 'control' will worry existing shareholders.
   (ii) *Preference shares.* Will 8 per cent be enough to persuade investors to risk their money? Cover for loan interest is not good and this increases the risk to preference investors. From the companys point of view, preference shares increase the gearing without being tax efficient.
   (iii) *12.5 per cent long term loan.* Increases gearing and debt equity ratio, but is tax efficient. Real rate of interest would be (12.5% × (1 − 0.31) 8.6 per cent. Cover is poor. Much depends on what security can be offered. The premises are not worth enough to cover the existing LTL, but the balance sheet does not say if that loan is secured. Suggest a leasing operation for extra fixed assets and trade credit to finance stock and debtors.

18.2 (a)

Ratios	A		B	
Return of shareholder funds	765/2 522	= 30.3 per cent	303/1 400	= 21.6 per cent
Gross profit rate	2 400/12 000	= 20 per cent	1 200/6 000	= 20 per cent
Gearing	1 000/3 522	= 28.4 per cent	1 534/2 934	= 52.3 per cent
Debt : equity	4 634:2 522	= 1.8:1	2 450 : 1 400	= 1.75 : 1
FA : L.T. debt	3 000 : 1 000	= 3 : 1	1 500 : 1 534	= 1 : 1
Interest cover	1 650/385	= 4.2	810/287	= 2.8
Plowback	465/765	= 60.8 per cent	203/303	= 67 per cent
Yield	30/250	= 12 per cent	20/250	= 8 per cent
P/E	765/1 000		303/500	
	= 76.5p		= 60.1p	
	250 ÷ 76.5	= 3.3	250 ÷ 60.1	= 4.2

Comments

Both companies make the same gross profit rate but A makes a better return for its shareholders, because of its capital structure. B has high gearing so should give a better return to shareholders by exploiting long term funds, but the debt/equity ratio shows that both companies are equally dependent on outside finance. A uses more interest free trade credit to finance its operations, and uses a smaller proportion of loans to cover fixed assets, so it is, perhaps, more risky. B has less interest cover than A, but retains a larger proportion of profit, causing a lower yield.

(b) Weighted Average Cost of Capital

A	Equity	2 522	56% × 17	=	9.52
	LTL	1 000	22% × 10.35	=	2.27
	O/D	984	22% × 12.42%	=	2.73
		4 506		=	14.52 per cent
B	Equity	1 400	42% × 16	=	6.72
	LTL	1 534	47% × 10.35	=	4.86
	O/D	316	10% × 12.42	=	1.24
		3 250			12.82 per cent

Workings

$$\text{Equity} \quad \frac{D}{P} + G = \qquad \frac{30}{250} + 5 = 17 \text{ for A} \qquad \frac{20}{250} + 8 = 16 \text{ for B}$$

Loans   LTL   = $15 \times (1 - 0.31) = 10.35$ per cent
            O/D   = $18 \times (1 - 0.31) = 12.42$ per cent

B has a lower WACC because of its higher gearing using a greater proportion of cheaper tax-efficient long term loans. Shareholders of B will accept a lower yield because of its greater growth prospects.

(c)

£750 000 is a more significant figure for B than for A, being over half of B's net assets

(i) *Borrowing long term* – depends on gearing now and after the loan, and on the existence of uncharged assets to use as security.

A's gearing would be 1 750/4 272= 41 per cent
B's gearing would be 2 284/3 684= 62 per cent – high!

How would other creditors react to this increase, especially if assets which they see as covering their loan are now charged against this new commitment? A has significant current liabilities.

(ii) *Share Capital* – depends on the markets view of each company, and whether the shares could be issued at a premium. The number of shares issued might upset the control exercised by a dominant shareholder. If access to the market is considered expensive an institutional placing might be the best way to proceed. Convertible unsecured loan stock should be considered as a compromise suggestion.

(iii) *Retained Profit* – this source could make a contribution to the funds required but not at the expense of dividend reduction, otherwise a takeover bid might ensue. Already the market value of B (500 000 £1.00 shares at £2.50), at £1 250 000, is less than the book value of the net assets.

(iv) *Short term sources* – it is wrong in principal to borrow in the short term to tie up funds in a long term project. In any case, A is over exposed by its borrowing from creditors and the bank.

(v) *A combination of sources* – this is the most likely solution for this problem. Interest cover must be considered, but the project should pay for itself from cash flow over its lifetime. Leasing to provide part of the capital investment is a method which could exploit the ability of the project to pay for itself.

SEMINAR EXERCISES 19

19.1 Ginger Ltd

		1 January		31 December	Change
	£	£	£	£	£
Current assets :					
Stock		17 000		70 000	+ 53 000
Debtors		7 000		10 000	+ 3 000
Cash		18 000		20 000	+ 2 000
		42 000		100 000	
Current liabilities :					
Trade creditors	12 000		14 000		(+ 2 000)
Tax	11 000		12 000		(+ 1 000)
Dividends proposed	6 000		8 000		(+ 2 000)
		29 000		34 000	
Working capital		£13 000		£66 000	53 000

Significant increase in stock.

19.2 Unimix

(a) Points to be covered in the report

1. Extra working capital requirements consequent upon expansion – fund more stock and debtors. Adequate fixed assets
2. Must plan to fund extra requirements – overdependence on outside finance is a sign of weakness – 'overtrading'
3. Sources of finance available :
   (a) trade credit;
   (b) Short term bank finance – loan or overdraft
   (c) Factor debtors;
   (d) HP or lease fixed asset requirements – free funds for working capital;
   (e) Increase velocity of circulation of working capital – reduce debtor period, hold lower stocks;
   (f) Increase rate of ploughback – dividend restraint

(b) Income from scheme
    Increased turnover £60 000 pm × 12   =   <u>£720 000</u> pa
    Gross profit earned thereon at 15%   =   <u>£108 000</u>
Cost of Scheme
    Debtors at present (1 months sales)   £300 000
    Debtors in future (£360 000 × 2)   =   <u>£720 000</u>
    Working capital required   <u>£420 000</u>   × say 18% = £75 000
    Increase in bad debts 1% × £300 000 × 12   £36 000
    Up to 2% × £360 000 × 12   <u>£86 400</u>   £50 400
    Increased administration costs   £12 000
                                           <u>£138 000</u>

Scheme Rejected

19.3   (a)   Calculation of Working Capital Required

If opening stock = closing stock, the amount of materials purchased equals the amount used.

                                                                £
Raw Material Stock
            30/365 × £14 400 000   1 183 562
Finished Goods Stock   Materials used   14 400 000
                          Labour cost   5 250 000
       (£30 m × .15)   Overhead   4 500 000
                     Cost of Production   <u>£24 150 000</u>
            20/365 × £24 150 000   1 323 288

Debtors £30 m × 0.8 × 12/52   <u>5 538 461</u>
                                                                  8 045 311

Less Credit from suppliers
            £14 400 000 × 8/52   2 215 384
Working Capital Required   <u>£5 829 927</u>

(b) Debtor and Creditor periods at present

     Debtors   £4 442 307   ÷ £21 000 000 × 52   =   11 weeks – 1 = 10
     Creditors   £1 225 962   ÷ £12 750 000 × 52   =   5 weeks + 1 = 6

     Debtors will be £21 000 000 × 10/52   £4 038 461
     Creditors will be £12 750 000 × 6/52   <u>£1 471 154</u>
     Working Capital will be   2 567 307
     Working Capital was £4 442 307 – £1 225 962   3 216 345
     Working Capital saved   <u>£649 038</u>
     Interest Saved £649038 × 0.12 = £77 885

Index